BABY NAMES NOW

From Classic to Cool—
The Very Last Word on First Names

ST. MARTIN'S GRIFFIN
NEW YORK

BABY NAMES NOW

LINDA ROSENKRANTZ and
PAMELA REDMOND SATRAN

www.stmartins.com

Book design by Michelle McMillian

Library of Congress Cataloging-in-Publication Data

Rosenkrantz, Linda.
    Baby names now : from classic to cool, the very last word on first names / Linda Rosenkrantz and Pamela Redmond Satran.—1st ed.
      p. cm.
    ISBN 0-312-26757-6
    1. Names, Personal—Dictionaries.   I. Satran, Pamela Redmond.
    II. Title.

    CS2377 .R6645 2001
    929.4'4'03—dc 21   2001019579

An earlier edition was published under the title *The Last Word on First Names*.

10   9   8   7

For
Hope Dellon

ACKNOWLEDGMENTS

Thanks to Jane Sandor for her research help, to Michael Shackleford for supplying Social Security statistics, and to all the extremely accommodating people at the various State Departments of Health.

INTRODUCTION

Baby names now are different from baby names then—then being as recently as a few years ago. Even people who aren't in baby-naming mode have noticed the tremendous explosion of new kinds of names, of new attitudes toward names, of naming trends going in many different directions at once, and of the new creativity in baby naming. Now, more than ever, with this profusion of choices, parents are taking their baby-naming responsibility seriously, putting a tremendous amount of thought and effort into finding the perfect names for their children.

And that is why this book moves beyond our previous name books. *Beyond Jennifer & Jason, Beyond Jennifer & Jason, Madison & Montana,* and *The Last Word on First Names* all focused mainly on conventional names in their conventional spellings. But now, with celebrities giving their children names like Alchamy, Arpad and Atticus, Sonnet, Sage, Sailor, Satchel and Seven—and other parents following their lead—and with Destiny, Autumn, Trinity, and Jada having entered the Top 100 list, we decided it was time to move beyond the standard lists ourselves.

The world of names has become so wide these days that no baby-naming book can include every last possibility. With the full complement of surnames, ethnic as well as Anglo, now up for grabs; with the universe of place-names and the dictionary full of words that can become names and the endless combinations of invented names, there is not enough paper in the world or bandwidth on the Web to contain what can only be thought of as the now-infinite choices. But what you will find here are exotic examples

from other cultures, as well as foreign versions and creative spelling variations of classics, an expanded atlas of place-names from Abilene to Zion,
colorful flower, jewel, and other newly admissible nature names, many
more Old and New Testament choices, plus a trunkful of quaint and neglected treasures we've dusted off in the appellation attic.

And, as always, we—unlike any other baby-name authors—are not
afraid to give you our honest opinions of these names, informing you of the
plusses of Paloma, for example, and the minuses of Max. The classic A to Z
format again lets us examine thousands of names in the light of the questions that burn in the minds of every parent in search of the perfect name.
How popular, how trendy is this name and how will it affect my child? What
image does it project and what will that communicate to other people
about our family's style and values, and aspirations for our son or daughter? What's the downside of names I like? What are some great names I
haven't thought of?

To answer these questions, we have drawn on sources as far-ranging as
the Bible and the Internet, on old and new movies and current TV shows,
foreign baby-naming guides and academic journals, popularity lists and
celebrity gossip magazines. There is no rigid formula: We include a name's
origins and literal meaning when they have some relevance in the modern
world, foreign versions if they are interesting, appealing, and U.S. user-
friendly, and variant spellings if they have come into common usage. Once
again we caution you not to be offended if you look up your own name and
find that we've said something less than positive about it. Remember that
we are treating these names as twenty-first-century baby options, and a
name that might be perfectly fine for a parent or grandparent—Pam or
Linda, say, or Gary or Barry—just doesn't have the same appeal for a child
of today.

Also bear in mind that although there is a much more tolerant baby-
naming climate today than there was in the past, kids still tease each other,
and really outlandish spellings can cause embarrassment—not to mention
irritation or even resentment—throughout a child's life. Community context is another consideration. Where you live, what you do, and who you
hope your child will become all play an important part in determining which
name is best. For example, Presley, son of supermodel Cindy Crawford,
might have super play dates with Mingus Lucien, son of supermodel

Helena Christensen, but would those names be accepted in your neighbor-hood?

All these considerations may make choosing the right name from the thousands of possibilities seem like an overwhelmingly daunting prospect. But we hope that this book will help you avoid the pitfalls as you navigate the naming maze, and arrive at your ultimate destination—the special name that you and your child will love forever.

GIRLS

A

AALIYAH, ALIYAH. In both its spellings, with the first making it especially distinctive, this Hebrew name meaning "to descend" is being considered by increasing numbers of parents, some of them undoubtedly inspired by the award-winning, single-named soul-star, Aaliyah. It's pronounced, in case you're wondering, a-LYE-ah.

ABELIA, ABELLA. A distinctive and pretty pair of French names, which relate to the male form Abel, connoting can-do capability. The latter might appeal to parents looking for a novel name in between the popular Isabella and Bella.

ABIAH. This biblical name, which means "Jehovah is my father," has several attractive permutations, including **AVIA, AVIAH,** and **AVIYA.**

ABIGAIL. Long considered a quintessential spinster name, Abigail has successfully shaken off that fusty image to become a more than feasible baby name—in fact, it was among the twenty most popular girls' names across the country last year, reaching fifth place in Montana and placing eighth in Iowa, possibly influenced by the fact that it appeared in three soap operas. In the Old Testament, Abigail—which means "father's joy" in Hebrew—was the wife of King David, renowned for her beauty, wisdom, and prophetic powers. Later, it became a slang term for a lady's trusted maid-confidante, and it also has the distinction of being the name

1

of two of our First Ladies—three if you count the one on TV's *The West Wing*. Nickname **ABBY** has taken on an even more contemporary flair—recent Abby characters have appeared on *Dawson's Creek, ER, Felicity,* and *Dharma & Greg,* and others have been played by Gwyneth Paltrow, Heather Locklear, Jeanne Tripplehorn, Janeane Garofalo, Lori Loughlin, and Demi Moore.

ABILENE. A new place-name up for consideration, Abilene combines the cowgirl spunk of the Texas city with the Midwestern morality of the Kansas town where Dwight D. Eisenhower was raised. An extra bonus is the possible sharing of the popular nickname Abby.

ABRA. This soft, sensitive biblical name, the female form of Abraham, was most widely used in seventeenth-century England, making a later appearance in the John Steinbeck novel and James Dean movie *East of Eden.* But while the name itself has a good deal of creative charm, a girl named Abra could easily tire of it being followed by "Cadabra" and, during those sensitive pubescent years, having her name separated into the words *a bra.*

ABRIELLE, ABRIANNA. The popularity of Abigail has inspired many knock-offs. These are two new creations, blends of Abigail and Gabrielle or Brianna, that result in an ultrafeminine sound and image.

ACACIA, ACANTHA. Two rarely used Greek botanical names that might appeal to parents looking for something unusual but meaningful. The acacia is a shrub of the mimosa family, with clusters of showy yellow or white blossoms, which symbolizes resurrection and immortality (making the name appropriate for an Easter baby), while Acantha derives from the acanthus plant which also presents white or colored flowers and grows in the Mediterranean region.

ADA, ADAH. When pronounced AY-dah, Ada is a Germanic name that was popular in this country a century ago, and, though it literally means "beauty," still feels a bit too great-grandmotherly to be revived. Pronounced AH-dah, it's a Nigerian Ibo name meaning "firstborn girl." Spelled

Adah, it's a completely different, Old Testament name, actually the first female name mentioned in Genesis after Eve. We think the latter two feel more fresh and interesting than AY-dah.

ADANNA. With its winning *anna* ending, this is an appealing name used by the Ibo people of Nigeria. It means "father's daughter."

ADDISON. Maybe it's all those reruns of *Moonlighting*—in which the younger, cuter Bruce Willis played David Addison—but whatever the inspiration, this is definitely a comer in the category of unisex surname names being used for girls, and **ADDY** is a friendly, feminine nickname.

ADELAIDE. Adelaide's quaint image could be updated if it were thought of as one of the potentially popular place-names. The capital city of South Australia was named for the beloved nineteenth-century British "Good Queen Adelaide," the wife of William IV.

ADELE, ADELA, ADELIA. Since Adele is pretty much stuck in fashion limbo, parents wishing to honor an ancestor of that name might want to consider Adela—a final *a* definitely seems to make any girl's name sound more fashionable these days—or the even fresher-sounding Adelia, which gains in contemporary appeal from its similarity to the stylish Amelia.

ADELINE. Adeline is definitely the modern hit of its family of names, with many contemporary parents responding to its old-fashioned "Sweet Adeline" charm, perhaps also seeing it as a less used phonetic cousin of the ultratrendy Madeline. Its more relaxed nickname, **ADDY.** has been publicized by the doll in the American Girl series, and **ADETTE** is a rarely heard French variation. We've also heard **AVELINE,** which seeks to capitalize on the newfound fashion status of Ava.

ADINA, ADENA. In the Bible, this is a male name, but it is now used exclusively (if infrequently) for girls. At one time, the major flaw of the name was the fact that it sounded made up, as if you rearranged Scrabble letters until you hit on a euphonic combination, but now, as so many parents are creating their own names, this could be considered a plus.

3

ADITI. In Indian mythology, the goddess of heaven and the mother of all gods.

ADORA. There was a Princess Adora on the TV series *She-Ra, Princess of Power,* and, like Cherish and Precious, this is a name for parents who want to proclaim their adoration of their own little princesses in no uncertain terms.

ADRIENNE, ADRIANA. Adrienne is a name with a lot of substance and dignity, one that reaches the happy medium between familiarity and popularity. But, as with many other names these days, the version ending in *a* (think of Joanna versus Joanne, Diana versus Diane) is a more stylish and exotic choice and, also spelled **Adrianna,** is rising in popularity, perhaps influenced by the character on *The Sopranos* (where it is pronounced with a hard initial *a*). **ADRIA** is another Italianate female form of the male name Adrian.

AFRICA. As a name, there are two Africas. One is an ancient Irish name often used by medieval royalty—there is even an Irish Saint Africa. The other, more usual, form is a place-name that refers to the continent and is gaining in popularity as a first name along with that other hot continental choice, **ASIA.** Africa, also sometimes spelled **AFRIKA,** stands out from the rest of the place-name crowd, however, because of its special significance for African-Americans and its real history as a personal name.

AFTERNOON. Naming children after days is an African tradition that came here with the slaves and was Anglicized to include such names, found on plantation records, as Afternoon, Christmas, and Monday. After the Civil War, African-Americans left such remnants of their former lives behind, but we can see these ancient name possibilities being revived along with other word names, old and new.

AGATHA. Unlike other Victorian names that have been resurrected, Agatha still summons up visions of mauve silk and filigreed brooches clasped to high lace collars, and is closely tied to the period mysteries of Agatha

Christie. Popular in the Middle Ages, Agatha is the name of the patron saint of firefighters and nurses, which some adventurous parents might want to dust off and restore to prominence in their families.

AGLAIA. One of the Three Graces of Greek mythology, this name originally meant "brightness and splendor" but these days would too often be abbreviated to "ugly."

AGNES. Another of those quintessentially antiquated names that's been relegated to the attic for many years, Agnes, which means "pure," may be so far out that it's almost ready to come back in. It does sound infinitely hipper and more graceful pronounced the French way (an-YEZ), but that would be a bit pretentious for an American child. Believe it or not, for four hundred years, Agnes, then pronounced AN-nis, was one of the three most common English girls' names (along with Elizabeth and Joan), and was even in the Top 50 in this country a century ago. Scottish parents have liked the name so much they devised a backward version: **SENGA.** The Scots also use the nicknames **NESSIE** and **NESSA,** while the Welsh prefer **NESTA.** Other variants include **ANAIS** (see listing), **INA, INEZ, OONA, UNA,** and **YNEZ.**

AIDA. This melodic name is largely associated with the title character in the Verdi opera, an Ethiopian princess enslaved in Egypt, who dies to save her people. Often heard in Hispanic families, it's beginning to be used more frequently by others as well.

AIDAN. This onetime strictly masculine Irish name was brought into the girl's camp by newsperson Faith Daniels, and other namers of girl babies are beginning to consider it a viable possibility. **AIDEEN** is an older-sounding version, one used in Irish mythology.

AILEEN. See **EILEEN.**

AILSA. A Scottish place name, pronounced ALE-sa, gaining in popularity. A good substitute for the parent looking to move beyond the overused Ashley or Alex.

AINSLEE. This version of the Scottish surname **INSLEY,** meaning "meadow," has recently made a landing on this side of the Atlantic. Contemporary parents might also consider the spellings **AINSLEA** or **AINSLEIGH.** Some parents are attempting to get rid of that potentially nasty *ain* sound at the beginning of the name by varying it to **ANSLEIGH** or **ANSLEY.** Ainsley Hayes is an efficient female character on *The West Wing.*

AISHA. Pronounced i-EE-sha, Aisha is one of the more popular African-American girls' names—Stevie Wonder, for one, used it for his daughter. It derives from both the Swahili and Arabic cultures and means "life." Aisha was also the name of the prophet Muhammad's chief wife and, to go from one extreme to the other, the name of the Yellow Ranger in the *Mighty Morphin Power Rangers* series a few years back. Alternate spellings include **AYISHA** and **AYEESHA,** which Mick Jagger and Jerry Hall chose as the third name of their daughter Georgia May.

AISLING. Pronounced AH-shling and meaning "vision" or "dream," this Celtic name, until recently rarely heard here, is very popular among contemporary Irish parents, who also use its phonetic spelling, **ASHLING,** as well as **AISLINN.** Any of these variants might make an interesting, if challenging, choice for Irish-American parents who are attracted to the sound of the now dated Ashley, but want something more original.

AKIBA. This African name has a melodic sound and energetic image.

ALABAMA. This is not a geography-name-come-lately: There have been girls named Alabama dating back well over a century.

ALALA. The sister of Mars in Roman myth, traditionally bestowed upon girls born under Aries and Scorpio, signs ruled by Mars.

ALANA. At one time reserved for daughters of dads named Alan, this name came into more public prominence thanks to the tagalong fame of Alana Hamilton Stewart, ex-wife of both George and Rod. **ALANNA** is one alternate spelling, another is **ALANNAH,** as in singer Alannah Myles. Far more original is the name of another female singer, **ALANIS** Morissette. Also coming to the fore are variants **ALAINA/ALAYNA**.

ALBA. This name, which means "white" in Latin, belongs to a Spanish noble family—the Duchess of Alba posed for the famous Goya portrait, *The Naked Maja*. Unfortunately, it is now associated with an instant hot chocolate product.

ALBERTA. In the days of Queen Victoria, when she campaigned hard for the use of her beloved consort Prince Albert's name in any form, Alberta did come into fairly common use, along with such rarer examples as **ALBERTINE** and **ALBERTINA.** Now, however, despite the song of that name made popular by Eric Clapton, and the fact that it is a place-name, Alberta is almost as unappealing as **ALFREDA.**

ALCHEMY. One of the most extreme of the new "word" names, this is recommended only to the most mystical-minded parents. Rocker Lance Henriksen spelled his daughter's name **ALCHAMY.**

ALETHEA. A lyrical Greek name meaning "truth" that was popular in the seventeenth century and is unrelated to the better known Althea, Alethea could appeal to seekers of a flowery name.

ALEX. In the last decade or so, this name has definitely broken away from its popular longer form to become a top name on its own for girls as well as boys—smart, efficient, slightly boyish and hip. From the late 1980s through the 1990s, it seemed to be the name of every other independent heroine in the movies, played by actresses from Cher to Glenn Close. **ALIX** and **ALYX** are more contemporary-looking spellings.

ALEXA, ALEXIA. Alexa is another shortened member of the Alexi family of names to have seceded to stand on its own, and is rapidly increasing in popularity, being the most feminine of the group. It was chosen for their daughter by Christie Brinkley and Billy Joel, while Rod and Alana Stewart opted for the more exotic Alexia.

ALEXANDRA. Although it is high on popularity lists, and even appears on a soap opera or two, Alexandra has not become one of the crowd, managing, like its twin brother, Alexander, to maintain its sophisticated, even regal aura. Combining a classic pedigree with high fashion appeal, it's a top-of-the-line Ralph Lauren of a name. Tasteful and elegant, it has an impressive pedigree dating back to at least the first century B.C. and is well used to this day by British and other royals. Many celebrities, from Mikhail Baryshnikov to Lorenzo Lamas, have chosen Alexandra as a name for their daughters, while Andy Garcia went for the appealing Italian alternative, **ALESSANDRA.** The Spanish form, **ALEJANDRA,** makes the Hispanic Top 10 list in several states. **ALEXANDRINA** was the real first name of Queen Victoria; other variations include **ALEXANDRINE, ALEXINA** (Scottish), and **ALEXINE,** plus short forms **ALESSA, ALESSIA, SANDRA,** and the more exotic **ZANDRA.**

ALEXANDRIA. Alexandria earns a separate listing because it has declared its independence and has even begun chasing Alexandra up the popularity ladder. It started with parents (such as Keith Richards and Patti Hanson) trying to set their girls apart with an even more imposing name, some perhaps attracted by its geographical and cultural associations, Alexandria being the Egyptian city founded by Alexander the Great that would later become the center of Hellenistic society. More recently, Iman and David Bowie have chosen the name for their daughter.

ALEXIS. At this moment, Alexis, not that long ago considered an obscure Russian boys' name, has continued its remarkable upward vault over the past couple of years to become the sixth most popular girls' name in the country. It has actually reached number 1 in Arizona, Louisiana, and the District of Columbia, being particularly popular with African-American families. So there's no doubt now that its tarnishing association with the over-the-top Alexis Carrington in the early 1980s nighttime soap *Dynasty* has been wiped away by time. Some parents, perhaps influenced by the luxury car marque, have begun to spell it **ALEXUS.**

ALICE. A sweet and pretty classic name that is high on the list for stylish parents in Britain—it reached the number 2 spot there a couple of years ago—Alice has long been ignored in this country in favor of its more modern-sounding offshoots. It persists in being associated with Lewis Carroll's heroine in *Alice's Adventures in Wonderland,* with her long, flowing hair and pastel-colored hairbands, despite its later incarnations in two classic working-class sitcoms and such punk rockers as Alice Cooper and Alice in Chains. We think it's time to brush all these associations aside and reconsider this noble name. Parents with a literary bent might favor it because of the unusually large number of important contemporary writing Alices, including Walker, Munro, Adams, Hoffman, McDermott, and Elliott Dark. Two interesting variations are **ALIZ,** one of the original forms of the name, still used in Hungary, and the Hawaiian **ALEKA,** while **ELKE** is a German pet form, and **AILIS** or **AILISH** is the Gaelic version.

ALICIA. A frillier, more balletic form of Alice, Alicia (the birth name of Jodie Foster), has been moving back into favor, perhaps prompted by the prominence of actress Alicia Silverstone. Hitchcock buffs also may recall that it was the name of Ingrid Bergman's character in the classic *Notorious.* The name has innumerable spelling variations, including **ALISHA** and **ALYSHA** (See also **ALYSSA.**) Taken for its sound alone, Alicia is a beautiful, feminine name, but parents should be aware that its innumerable corruptions have led to its losing much of its character.

ALISON, ALLISON. Spelled both ways in almost equal numbers, this name has been widely used for a long time—teenaged Annette Funicello played one back in 1959, teenaged Mia Farrow was Allison MacKenzie in *Peyton Place* in the mid-1960s, right up to the more recent character on *Melrose Place.* Yet another derivative of Alice that has far surpassed the original in popularity, this medieval diminutive with a Scottish accent is, in fact, still in vogue to the point of overuse. We caution against creating some "unique" spelling, such as **ALYSON, ALLYSON,** or **ALISSAN,** which will only complicate and confuse your daughter's life. A clever new surnamey spin: **ELLISON.**

ALIZA. This sultry, dark-eyed name means "joy" in Hebrew. An alternate, more phonetic spelling is **ALEEZA.**

ALLEGRA. The quintessential ballet dancer's name—a feminization of the musical term *allegro,* which means "cheerful and lively"—Allegra can be a perfect choice for a child who is able to live up to its promise. But be aware that a name with such a powerfully graceful image can prove a burden to a girl who'd rather work out on the basketball court than at the barre. Emmy-winning performance artist John Leguizamo named his daughter Allegra Sky.

ALLY, ALLIE, ALI. Say the name Ally these days, and most people would respond "McBeal," associating it with the quirky attorney played by Calista Flockhart on TV. Because of this, Ally/Allie/Ali has escaped the obsolescence of the other tomboyish nickname names of the sixties, such as Jody, Kerry, and Jamie, and is once more being used on its own. It still might be preferable, however, to keep Ally as a short-form option in case the girl you name Alicia or Allegra should prove to be more of a tree climber than a toe dancer.

ALMA. When Donna Reed took on the part of Alma the bad girl in *From Here to Eternity* eons ago, she was trying to change the image of both Donna Reed and the name Alma. Unfortunately, Donna Reed remained Donna Reed and Alma remained Alma. Solemn and soulful, it is one of those serious names, like Bertha and Esther, that enjoyed a burst of popularity around the turn of the last century, and then gradually faded away into the flowered wallpaper, associated now more with the term *alma mater* than with a woman under forty-five. Always popular among Hispanic parents (it has roots in Hebrew, Latin, Spanish, and Celtic, and means "kind and generous" and "soul"), we can see it making a comeback much in the way that Ella has, appreciated for its simplicity and integrity— and soul.

ALONDRA. A mid-nineties Spanish-language television show of this name may be one factor in its growing popularity—there were more than two thousand little Alondras born in this country last year.

ALPHA. Alpha is the first letter of the Greek alphabet and the brightest star in every constellation. It would make an interesting choice for a first daughter, although it does give off some spectral sci-fi reverberations.

ALTHEA. A poetic, almost ethereal name found in Greek myth and seventeenth-century pastoral poetry, Althea comes from the Greek, meaning "wholesome" or "healer." It has a disparate set of modern associations— 1950s tennis star Althea Gibson was the first black woman to win at Wimbledon, there was a Grateful Dead song named "Althea" and Courtney Love played Larry Flynt's ill-fated real-life love in *The People vs. Larry Flynt.*

ALYSSA. Alyssa is by far the most popular of all the Alice variations, still among the dozen top names across the country, seen as a *Star Trek* character and publicized by the actress Alyssa Milano. Many parents try to individuate it via more singular spellings, such as **ALISSA, ELISSA, ELYSSA, ILISSA,** and **ILYSSA.** Unlike Alison, for which some spellings are more correct than others, the "best" spelling for this name is up to you.

AMA. Also spelled **AMMA,** this simple but rhythmic name comes from a word in several African cultures, with several different meanings: "a female born on Saturday," "happy," and "beloved." **AMARA,** which was the ancient Abyssinian word for "paradise," is a related possibility.

AMABEL. Amabel, which means literally "beautiful lover," is an older name than Annabel and a lot more unusual, and therefore, we think, definitely worthy of consideration. The downside is the frequency of your child having to explain that no, her name is *not* Annabel.

AMANDA. After having been used as the name of the prettiest senior in so many high school movies, Amanda is beginning to slip on the popularity lists, and is losing some of its glossy sheen—maybe it was the bitchiness of the Heather Locklear character on *Melrose Place* that finally did it. It has had a good run, though, being among the romantic-sounding names, along with Samantha, Vanessa et al., that rocketed to stardom in the eighties. Despite its trendiness, Amanda is a certifiable classic—it appears in a play as early as 1694, and was prominent among saints, eighteenth-century literary heroines, and in plays by Noël Coward and Tennessee Williams. If you are looking for a fresher choice, you might consider the almond-flavored French version, **AMANDINE** (used by John Malkovitch for his daughter), or the Italian **AMADEA** (pronounced am-a-DAY-a), particularly if you're a Mozart lover. **ANANDA** Lewis is an MTV personality.

AMARIAH. The name of nine minor biblical characters, this might make a singular substitution for the popular Mariah. **AMARI** is also sometimes used, as is **AMAYA.**

AMARYLLIS. If you're looking for a showier flower name than Lily, in the same botanical family, consider Amaryllis, which is not as outré as it might at first sound. It was used in Greek poetry for pure, pastoral beauties, as well as in the George Bernard Shaw play *Back to Methuselah,* and means "refreshing" or "sparkling."

AMBER. The most popular jewel name of our era, that of the rich, translucent, golden-brown semiprecious stone, has at this point lost most of its luster—Jade is a much cooler (and hotter) gem name at the moment, this despite the glamour of supermodel Amber Valletta and the use of the name for the Julianne Moore character in *Boogie Nights.* The then-shocking novel *Forever Amber* brought the name into prominence over fifty years ago, and we fear that today's Ambers, unlike girls given such timeless classic names as Anna, will bear the date-stamp "born between 1975 and 1995." A twist that might transform the name: use the Italian version, **AMBRA.**

AMELIA. Amelia, once considered as fatally old-fashioned as the character in the novel *Vanity Fair,* is definitely back and on the rise as a less common and more interesting alternative to such high-ranking favorites as Amanda and Emily, even employed for the ultramodern Angelina Jolie character in *The Bone Collector.* Used by Shakespeare, and by Henry Fielding for the idealized heroine of his eponymous 1751 novel, its connection to aviation (and feminist) heroine Amelia Earhart only adds to its formula for success. The Italian-Spanish-Dutch-Slavic version, **AMALIA** (**AMALYA** in Hebrew), although attractive, might require your child to pronounce, spell, and explain the name endlessly throughout her life. Ditto for the French **AMALIE** in relation to Emily.

AMERICA. America is probably one place-name that totes too much patriotic baggage to be used as a first name, although it was given for girls as well as boys as far back as Colonial times. It might be an inventive possibility, however, for the parent in search of a middle name with meaning. The 1960s-flavored **AMERIKA** should not be on the table. **AMERISSA**, while more name than noun, seems to combine the worst of both worlds.

AMETHYST. This clear purple gem, the birthstone for February, has given its name to babies in the past, and now, with Ruby and Diamond making comebacks, Amethyst might too. Trivia note for parents who care: The amethyst is said to prevent intoxication.

AMINA, AMINAH. The name of the mother of the prophet Muhammad, Amina, which means "trustworthy and faithful," is well used among Muslims everywhere, and is especially popular among the Hausa of West Africa, while **AMINATA** is a name commonly used in Senegal.

AMIRA. This lustrous Hebrew name is often used for girls born on the harvest feast of Shavuot.

AMITY. What nicer gift to give your little girl than a name that signifies friendship and harmony? This virtue name also has the asset of being more rhythmic and feminine than the single-syllable Hope, Faith, and Grace, which are all gaining in popularity.

AMY. Sweet and well-loved (exactly as its French meaning signifies), Amy rocketed to popularity in the late nineteenth century along with the other Louisa May Alcott *Little Women* names (Amy was the artistic one), fell from favor, then burst onto the scene again in the 1960s, when parents were turning back to basic names like Jessie, Maggie, and Molly. But now, after all this time, Amy is definitely ready for another respite, even though it has gotten some attention in the movie *Chasing Amy* and TV show *Judging Amy*. **AIMÉE,** the original French version, is sometimes used here, although it verges on the pretentious. Other names—all similar in feel if not related to the original—to consider if you like Amy but you want something more out of the ordinary: the Hebrew **AMARIS; AMICA,** an ancient Roman name still used in Italy; the Latin form **AMATA;** and **AMINTA,** an Italian adaptation of an ancient Macedonian royal name. **AMIAS,** more often a male name, is attractive and spirited when used for girls.

ANAÏS. This unusual, creative name, which means "graceful" in Hebrew and is a French Provençal version of Anne, has been largely associated with the daring Paris-born American novelist and diarist Anaïs Nin, who was, in fact, the inspiration for the naming of the daughter of musician Noel Gallagher. A newer reference is the popular perfume of this name.

ANASTASIA. No longer a forbiddingly regal Russian name, Anastasia has begun to be seen as a viable option, perhaps influenced by the acceptance of its cousins Alexandra and Alexandria. Anastasia's greatest claim to fame is in relation to the "lost" daughter of the last czar of Russia, whose story has been told and retold in books and movies, most recently in a popular animated film. An old Greek name and also that of an ancient saint—the patron saint of weavers—Anastasia was well used in medieval Britain and in Ireland, as well as in Russia. Its meaning relates to resurrection, making it an apt choice for an Easter or spring baby. Stacy is the usual, but way too wispy nickname, **STASIA** or **STACIA,** pronounced with an *ah* sound, is a much more substantial choice.

ANDREA. Each of Andrea's three pronunciations projects a different image. The most prevalent, ANN-dree-a, which has been moderately popular since the 1940s, can pretty much sound like the girl next door, as do the nicknames **ANDI** and **ANDIE** (as in MacDowell, who was born a Rosalie). Pronounced ON-dree-a, as it was on *Beverly Hills 90210,* it becomes a bit more affected, while on-DRAY-a pushes it over the edge into the exotic. Originally the Italian male form of Andrew, Andrea is found in many European cultures for one sex or the other. Variations include the Scottish **ANDRENA** and the arty **ANDRA,** as well as **ANDRÉE,** pronounced ON-dray.

ANDROMEDA. The mythological Andromeda was an Ethiopian princess whose mother bragged about her beauty, incurring the wrath of Poseidon, who sent a sea monster to punish the earth. Andromeda was then offered

14

up as a sacrifice to the monster, but was saved by Perseus, a son of Zeus. Now a famous star—the kind in the sky—Andromeda has distinct possibilities as a baby name.

ANEMONE. For the flower-loving name giver who wants to move beyond Daisy and Rose, this would make a unique, if somewhat challenging choice. In Greek mythology, Anemone was a nymph who was turned into a flower by the wind.

ANGEL. Angel first appeared as a male name in Britain in the seventeenth century, but when the Puritans came along they deemed it, along with the avoided names of such angels as Gabriel and Michael, presumptuous for a mortal child. Angel continued to be used for both men (the hero of Hardy's *Tess of the d'Urbervilles,* for example) and women, although it was still considered too loaded ever to become a favorite in English-speaking countries. With the recent relaxing of such scruples and the reconsideration of previously shunned names, there have been many more sightings of earthly Angels of both sexes, but be aware that a good proportion of them are Latin males. Another modern male Angel is the ex-beau of TV's Buffy the Vampire Slayer, now starring in his own show. Rocker Dave "The Edge" Evans called his daughter Blue Angel.

ANGELA, ANGELINA. Angela has been the most widely used of this family of names through most of the twentieth century. Now, however, despite the strong persona of Angela Bassett and the protracted residency of *Angela's Ashes* on best-seller lists, Angela is the one that, with its nickname **ANGIE,** seems most terminally dated. The image of the Italian diminutive, Angelina, has been empowered by the equally strong persona of actress Angelina Jolie.

ANGELICA, ANJELICA. The lacy and poetic Angelica, partly because of its association with Anjelica Huston, is by far the hippest form of the angelic names—though to other kids it will inevitably call to mind the nasty nursery-schooler on *Rugrats.* Other variations worthy of consideration include the German **ANGELIKA,** the French **ANGELINE,** (which happens to be the

full name of Angie Dickinson) and—although it's a bit over the top—
ANGELIQUE, not surprisingly, a soap-opera character.

ANIKA. Some of the most interesting names span widely divergent cultures, and so it is with this one, which has distinct African and Scandinavian roots. Pronounced ah-NEE-ka, Anika is a modern African-American name as well as an eighteenth-century slave name that derives from the African name **ANNAKIYA,** which means "sweet face" in Hausa. Spelled **ANNIKA,** the name is a melodious Scandinavian diminutive for Anne.

ANN, ANNE. Originally, Ann was the British form of this classic name and Anne the French one, but that distinction was muddied as long as five hundred years ago and now which spelling you use is simply a matter of taste. (The heroine of *Anne of Green Gables* pronounced the Ann spelling "dreadful" and said the *e* made the name more distinguished.) It's kind of academic these days anyway, because not many parents are choosing either Ann or Anne for their daughters. Where once the name was seen as elegant in its simplicity, today it's viewed by many as plain and drab, and no longer has stature even as a middle name, with parents rejecting such harmonious "bridge" names in favor of middle names with more personal meaning. Further out: the dated Spanish diminutive **ANITA** and the French, beach-blanket **ANNETTE.** Possible: the Italian **ANINA,** the Irish **AYN** or **AINE,** the Scottish **ANNELLA.** But **ANNA** is now the only really fashionable version.

ANNA. Until quite recently, Anna was viewed as too unfashionably Old World for use as a baby name, a result of its having been used for generations throughout Europe, from Russia to Italy, Spain to Romania. Now, however, Anna is appreciated for just that very Continental charm, to the point that it is rapidly climbing the national popularity list, rating as high as number 5 in one state—Mississippi—and having been used for the fashionable Julia Roberts movie-star character in *Notting Hill.* Anna is classic and simple, yet has an exotic Anna Karenina–style charm. It's also an excellent choice for parents in search of a name that will bridge two different cultures, say Jewish and Hungarian or Wasp and Italian—Anna is indeed the perfect compromise name. **ANA** is an alternative spelling.

ANNABEL. Annabel has attitude. It's saucy and stylish, a reputation it earned during the Swinging Sixties, when it was the name of London's trendiest disco. Never used that often in this country, it's a tad upscale, has a sense of humor, is melodious and lively with much intrinsic appeal; you expect an Annabel to be engaging even before you meet her. Originally a bastardization of Amabel and common since medieval times in Scotland, it also recalls the romantic Edgar Allan Poe lyric poem, *Annabel Lee*. But be sure to distinguish such variations as **ANABEL, ANABELLA** (the name of Sela Ward's daughter) and the German **ANNELIESE** from 1950s combo names like **ANNAMARIA** and **ANNEMARIE** which now, although still used in some Italian-American families, seem as outmoded as Billie Jo.

ANNIE. Annie is one of the most open and optimistic, the-sun'll-come-out-tomorrow-type names in the book, having been celebrated over the years in song ("Annie Laurie"), comic strip (*Little Orphan Annie*), folklore (Annie Oakley, born Phoebe), and film (*Annie Hall*), It strikes a nice old-fashioned-but-jaunty chord that still appeals to today's parents, but we do suggest that you do your daughter a favor and present her with an alternative as a future option, inscribing a more formal version of the name, such as Ann, Anna, or Annabel, on her birth certificate. Singer **ANI** Di Franco streamlines the spelling.

ANOUK. This nearly singular name—does anyone remember sultry French actress Anouk Aimee?—is newly popular in the Netherlands. There is a supermodel called **ANOUCK. ANOUSHKA** is a diminutive.

ANTHEA. Like Althea, this is a pastorally poetic Greek name used by creatively inclined Brits but totally neglected here. In ancient Greece, the name, which means "flowering" and symbolizes spring, was bestowed as a title on Hera, Queen of Olympus.

ANTONIA. Antonia is stronger than most feminized versions of male names, reflecting the pioneer spirit of Willa Cather's *My Antonia*. It almost disappeared, however, during the period when nickname **TONI** eclipsed it, but is starting to show signs of a comeback in our more formal era. **ANTONIE** is one interesting variation we've heard; otherwise, stick with the original—

the French versions **ANTOINETTE** and **ANTONETTE** and diminutives **TONIA** and **TONYA** all take the name markedly downscale.

ANWEN. An undiscovered Welsh name, more unusual than Bronwen but with the same serene feeling. **ANWYN** is an alternate spelling, though the *wyn* ending is used only for male names in Wales. **ARIANWYN** is an extended Welsh form, meaning "shining silver."

ANYA. Anya is one of those evocative, faintly exotic, pan-European names that occurs in various forms in many countries, and is now beginning to catch on here in the wake of the growing popularity of Anna (especially since the introduction of the Anya character on *Buffy the Vampire Slayer*). Pronounced either ON-ya or AN-ya, Anya is the form found more frequently in Russia, Poland, and other East European countries, while **ANJA** is the spelling usually preferred in Germany, and **AINE** is the Gaelic form prevalent in Ireland.

AOIFE. Although this name is widely popular in the Emerald Isle (currently number 4), the fact that most Americans would not have a clue as to how to pronounce it (EE-fe) precludes is ever being used to any extent in this country, even though it has a lovely meaning—"radiantly beautiful." In Celtic legend, Aoife was a fierce, but very beautiful, warrior.

APHRA. Aphra Behn was the first female professional writer of the English language. She lived in England in the seventeenth century, where her plays were produced and novels were published during her lifetime. She was a spy and early feminist who was honored with burial in Westminster Abbey. An alternate spelling is **AFRA,** but the name is so tied to its inspirational early bearer that we see no reason for variation. Aphra means "ashes" in Hebrew.

APOLLONIA. This name came to the American public's attention a few years ago via Prince's costar in *Purple Rain*, but is still considered far too bigger-than-life to be adopted by many parents—although actor Nicholas Turturro did just that for his daughter. It is associated with the Greek deity Apollo, god of music, poetry, prophecy, and medicine; there was also a Saint Apollonia who was an early Christian preacher in Alexandria, where she had grown up the daughter of a ruler. She is a protector of teeth: does that make the name perfect for the daughter of a dentist? Maybe an extraordinarily adventurous one. **APOLLINE** is the French version.

APRIL. This springtime name is heard more in music ("April in Paris," "I Remember April") and movies (Geena Davis in *Tootsie,* Carrie Fisher in *Hannah and Her Sisters*) than it is in real life. It's been used as a proper name for a century now, but, like June, exists in some seasonless style limbo. The French **AVRIL,** an accepted form in England for the past fifty years, seems affected here.

ARABELLA. A lovely, feminine name, as melodic as the Strauss opera with that title, Arabella has been well used over the centuries by Scottish and British royalty. Rarely heard here but an equal in every way to the mega-amodish Isabella, Arabella rates serious consideration by parents seeking a name with both a respectable pedigree and contemporary appeal.

ARAMINTA. An eighteenth-century British invention that is still used occasionally in England, and so enchanting that we think it's positively ripe for the plucking by parents with a taste for the exotic. The short form is the refreshing **MINTA.** Added attraction: Araminta was the given name of abolitionist heroine Harriet Tubman.

ARCADIA. If Heaven and Eden are being used as first names, why not Arcadia? It projects a pleasant, leafy image of pastoral ancient Greece, yet manages to sound like a real twenty-first-century girl's name as well. And then there's **ACADIA,** the lovely national park in Maine.

ARDEN. A place and surname most familiar from the Forest of Arden in Shakespeare's *As You Like It,* this makes a plausible unisex name.

ARETHA. Aretha, a Greek name meaning "virtuous," has been thought of by most people as a single-owner name since the rise of the Queen of Soul, but some music-loving parents are now starting to share it with their own daughters.

ARIADNE, ARIANNA, ARIANA. The Greek name Ariadne is somewhat more familiar in its *d*-less forms, **ARIANE** (Audrey Hepburn was a glowing Ariane in *Love in the Afternoon*) and the Italian **ARIANNA** (as in Huffington), used by singer Marc Anthony for his daughter, also spelled **ARIANA.** While they are all graceful names with the foreign flair that has become so fashionable now, Ariadne itself seems a bit showy, and allows little margin for error. If a child proves to be less than gorgeous and sylphlike, she could find her own image in hazardous conflict with that of her name. In Greek lore, Ariadne was the daughter of the Cretan King Minos, who later married Dionysius.

ARIANELL. An undiscovered Welsh name with an irresistibly melodic sound.

ARIEL. There are few names quite as delicate and ethereal as Ariel, with its varied spectral connections. Ariel was a water spirit in demonology, an air spirit in medieval fable, and the male spirit in Shakespeare's *The Tempest*. Apart from that, it is an Old Testament place-name, as another name for Jerusalem, and it is frequently used in modern Israel for both boys and girls, not to mention its tie to poet Sylvia Plath's revelatory work of that name. It enjoyed a burst of popularity after the release of Disney's *The Little Mermaid*, featuring an animated Ariel, but this wave has crested and fewer parents are choosing it these days. Ann-Margret presented a much more earthbound image of Ariel in the *Grumpy/Grumpier Old Men* movies. Related options: **ARIELLA, ARIELLE, ARI, ARIE** (chosen by singer Jody Whatley for her daughter) and **ARISSA** (parented by Kelly LeBrock and Steven Seagal).

ARLENE. Arlene has been sequestered in baby-name limbo with her sound-alike sisters Marlene and Darlene for quite some time, and shows no signs of emerging. The French **ARLETTE** sounds a bit fresher, simply because it's never been used much in this country.

ARMANI. Brand names in general do not make the best baby names. So while Lauren and Karan may be okay, we advise you to think twice about such other designer brand names as Armani, Versace—and Hilfiger.

ARTEMIS, ARTEMAS. An interesting choice for the bold name explorer. Artemis was the goddess of the moon and of hunting, one of the twelve major Greek deities and the twin sister of Apollo. The given name sometimes has the Artemas spelling.

ASHANTI. An African tribal and place-name used as a first name for both boys and girls by some African-American parents. Other possibilities are the variants **ASHANTA** and **ASHANTE**. **ASHA** is an attractive Arab and Indian name.

ASHLEY. For several years in the 1990s, Ashley was the most popular name for girls born in this country, vanquishing such stalwarts as Jennifer and Jessica—quite an accomplishment for a name occasionally used for upper-class boys and not even listed in the girl's section of most earlier baby-naming books. The main catalyst seems to have been a single soap-opera character, Ashley Abbott, who debuted on *The Young and the Restless* in 1982. Its soft and pretty, yet ambisexual, image was undoubtedly one factor that attracted droves of parents to Ashley, but the name has definitely peaked and making its descent down the list. Parents still drawn to the name are just as likely to look for a more unusual spelling, such as **ASHLEIGH, ASHLEE, ASHLIE,** or **ASHLEA,** to set their daughters apart from all the others. Another variation is **ASHLYN/ASHLYNN,** which has taken off as a name of its own, as have, to a lesser extent, **ASHTON** and **ASHDEN.**

ASHLING. See **AISLING.**

ASIA. One of the most popular of the trendy place-names, Asia is particularly prevalent among (not surprisingly) Asian-Americans, and also with black parents—it's currently on the Top 20 list for African-American girls born in Texas, for example. **AJA** is an alternate spelling.

ASPEN. Definitely a name to watch, as more and more parents respond to the appealing place and nature images it evokes. Aspen is a chic celebrity ski resort in Colorado, and the aspen is a tree with leaves so delicate they flutter in the gentlest breeze.

ASSISI. One of Mick Jagger's granddaughters (yes, he has grandchildren) bears this name. Assisi is a lovely little city in Tuscany, most famously home of Saint Francis the animal lover.

ASTRA. Astra is a rarely used Greek name which, like the more familiar Stella, means "star" and possesses a celestial aura. The Scandinavian **ASTA,** on the other hand, lost many points when it was attached to a dog in the *Thin Man* series of movies back in the 1930s.

ASTRID. A Scandinavian royal name meaning "divinely beautiful," Astrid has never assimilated into our culture in the way that, say, Ingrid has. Many people associate it with the author of the *Pippi Longstocking* stories, Astrid Lindgren. With the renewed interest in ethnic names, Astrid might be worth consideration by parents with Norse roots, or who even have enjoyed a holiday among the fjords. Variations and nicknames include **ASTRI, ATTI,** and **SASSA; ASSA** and **ASSI** are out for obvious reasons.

ATLANTA. This name of a beautiful and fleet-footed mythical huntress who refused to marry unless she could find a man who could outrace her is heard occasionally among the British nobility and is gaining some small measure of attention here as an ersatz place-name. **ATLANTA,** as in Georgia, will undoubtedly be used more often, simply because it's more familiar. **ATLANTIC** and **ATLANTICA** are other related, though somewhat hippier-sounding, options. **ATALIA** is a rhythmic New Testament name, as is **ATARAH. ATIANA** is the name of Oscar de la Hoya's daughter.

ATHENA. The name of the daughter of Zeus who was the Greek goddess of wisdom, as well as of fertility and arts and crafts, could appeal to enlightened parents who particularly prize intelligence as a quality in their daughters.

AUBURN. A color name—think Gray and Brown—that's one of the few that sounds better for girls than for boys.

AUDREY. The near-deification of the late actress Audrey (born Edda) Hepburn as humanitarian and style icon has shed reflected glory on her otherwise ordinary name which, believe it or not, derived from the Old English Aethelthryth. Audrey had some modest popularity from the 1920s to the fifties, and still reigns as the number 1 name in Quebec right now. Warning: The word *tawdry* comes from the cheap relics that were sold at the feast of Saint Audrey. **AUDRA** is a variant that was occasionally used in the 1960s, and **AUDINE** is a French version. The male name **AUBREY** has recently been co-opted by namers of girls as a newer-sounding variant on Audrey.

AUGUSTA. True to its literal meaning of "venerable," Augusta does seem to be the quintessential great-great-aunt name. Still, it possesses a certain fussy charm and could even be conceived as fashionable when considered as one of the revived Abigail/Amelia/Adeline-type ancestor appellations. In ancient Rome, Augusta was a title conferred on the wives and female relatives of emperors. Augusta might also be considered a place-name: It's the capital of Maine as well as a city in Georgia. Variants include **AUGUST** (used by Garth Brooks for his daughter), which is hip in a more obvious way, as well as **AUGUSTINA** and **AUGUSTIA,** which seem too dusty to bother shining up. **AUGUSTEEN** is an Irish version. Dan Ackroyd and Donna Dixon went even further by using **AUGUSTUS** as one of their daughter Stella's middle names.

AURELIA. This richly evocative name, meaning "golden" in Latin, was one of the most common in the Christian inscriptions of the Roman Empire, but is rarely heard in modern America, even if Maria Shriver and Arnold Schwarzenegger did use it as a middle name for their daughter Christina, in honor of his mother. Still, it, and variants **AURALIA, AURIEL,** and the French **AURÉLIE,** have possibilities for the adventurous parent. **AURON** is a similar-sounding Welsh name, and **AURA** is a less worldly choice.

AURORA. With its mythic, fairy-tale aura, Aurora might be too theatrical and airy a name for real life. In mythology she was the beautiful Roman goddess of the dawn, whose tears turned into the morning dew, and Aurora has also made appearances in the poems of Byron and Elizabeth Barrett Browning, and as the princess in *Sleeping Beauty* and the Shirley MacLaine character in *Terms of Endearment*. With all that, a parent with a flair for the dramatic might want to consider Aurora or its French form, **AURORE,**

keeping the short form **AUREA** and even the nickname Rory in reserve for down-to-earth occasions.

AUTUMN. Crisp and colorful, Autumn is, among all the seasonal possibilities, gaining the most acceptance from parents seeking an unconventional but recognizable name—there were almost four thousand Autumns born in this country last year.

AVA. Among the hip Hollywood parents of today—Heather Locklear and Richie Sambora, Reese Witherspoon and Ryan Phillippe, for example—Ava, a name redolent of the black-and-white glamour of the Hollywood of yesterday, is definitely making a comeback. Simple yet strong, it meets the golden mean of names that are neither too ordinary nor too outré.

AVALON. An island paradise in Celtic myth (where King Arthur was taken after his death) and the capital of an island paradise off southern California, this name makes an attractive addition to the gazetteer of place-names now usable for babies.

AVERY. Avery is one of the surname names that sprang to prominence in the 1980s, when it was given to TV's Murphy Brown's (male) baby, but it wasn't long before it was also being given to girls, as it does possess a distinctively feminine lilt. One of the main female characters in the movie *Jerry Maguire* was named Avery.

AVIS. Meaning "bird" in Latin, this name has rarely been used since the outbreak of the rental-car company rivalries. After all, who wants their daughter to be number two? This question wouldn't arise with the French version **AVEZA**.

AVIVA. A Hebrew name, very popular in Israel, that means "spring," connotes youthfulness and freshness, and is often given to girls born in that season.

AVRIL. See **APRIL**.

AYANNA. This a recently coined name, growing in popularity, whose *anna* syllable makes it sound feminine and familiar.

AYESHA. See **AISHA.**

AZALEA. The name of this brilliant pink springtime blossom translates smoothly into a distinctive girl's name, with more than a touch of the exotic.

AZIZA. Aziza is a familiar name in four different languages: Hebrew, Arabic, Kiswahli, and Somali. A common name in Egypt, it's also one that will allow a child both to fit in and to stand out in American culture. The two *z*s give it a zippy feel, but it's also easy to spell and pronounce.

AZURA. The Persian name for the semiprecious stone lapis lazuli evokes pleasant images of cloudless, clear blue skies. **AZURE** is another option.

B

BAILEY. This jaunty last-name-first name was one of the earliest examples to be used for a female character on television, when *WKRP in Cincinnati* debuted back in 1978. Since that time it has really caught on, probably because of its feminine *ey* ending (distinguishing it from the more masculine and Waspy Porter- and Carter-type surnames), even though the attractive Bailey Salinger on *Party of Five* brought it back for boys again. Bailey has reached as high as number 5 on South Dakota's girls' list, and was chosen for her daughter by Melissa Etheridge. One of those names with a long roster of spelling variations, these include **BAYLEE, BAYLEA,** and **BAYLEIGH.**

BAMBI. For most people, Bambi will forever be identified with the Disney deer. After the release of that movie, parents ignored the fact that the endearing animal was a male, and began using the name for their daughters. Short for the Italian *bambino,* Bambi may be cute, but it sounds far too helpless, too vulnerable, too negligible for a girl of today, much less for a woman of the future.

BARAKA. A Muslim name meaning "blessing," which can be similarly translated in Kiswahili, Baraka is a native African name that has gained some popularity among African-American parents. **BARIKA** is an Arabic name meaning "excelling."

BARBARA. Most Barbaras in the public eye today, such as B. Bush and B. Walters, are of a certain age, and that is definitely the image their name projects—a sad but inevitable fate for a name that was second only to the immovable Mary in 1925, and was still hanging on at number 27 twenty-five years later. An ancient Greek name meaning "foreign woman," Barbara was a medieval saint, the patroness of mathematicians, engineers, architects, carpenters, and firemen, as well as a protector against thunder. As Barbara itself faded, most of its nicknames went with it—**BARB, BABS, BOBBIE**—all but the eternally nubile **BARBIE,** which, despite the doll's many careers, from astronaut to doctor, still remains a euphemism for "bimbo." **BARBRA** Streisand dropped one letter and came up with a version that is uniquely hers. Foreign forms include the French **BABETTE,** the Scandinavian **BARBRO,** and the Russian **VARVARA.**

BATHSHEBA. This name of a famed biblical beauty, the wife of King David and mother of Solomon, was fashionable in medieval Europe and later used by the Puritans. There was also a Thomas Hardy heroine with that name in *Far From the Madding Crowd,* but still (or maybe therefore) it would be a heavy load for a modern girl in this country to carry. Pet names **BASHA** or **BATYA** might be more manageable. The Hebrew **BAT-SHEBA** and **BAT-SHEVA** are other options.

BEATRICE, BEATRIX. Beatrice, which means "one who brings happiness," was locked firmly in the name-storage attic until Prince Andrew and the Duchess of York restored it to the realm of possibility when they bestowed it on their first little princess a few years ago. Popular in the Middle Ages, it was well used in this country around the turn of the last century, reaching the Top 40 in 1900. Beatrice also has a long and splendid literary history, both as Dante's enchanting guide through Paradise, who becomes the symbol of spiritual love, in *The Divine Comedy,* and as the clever and witty heroine of Shakespeare's *Much Ado About Nothing.* Much more recently it was Julia Roberts's character name in *Oceans II* and used by Emma Samms for her daughter. Beatrix is the Italian, French, German, and Scandinavian form, a livelier version which we slightly prefer—and not only for its association with Beatrix (born Helen) Potter, creator of Peter Rabbit and the present queen of The Netherlands. The final *x* adds a playful element to the name's imposing history. Both versions have a legion of variations and nicknames including **BEATRIZ** (Spanish), **BEATHA** (Irish), **BEATA, BEA/BEE, BEAH, BEBE, TRIXIE,** and **TRISS.**

BECHET. Following the current trend for naming children after personal heroes and heroines, Soon-Yi and Woody Allen honored the New Orleans jazz saxophonist, clarinetist, and composer Sidney Bechet when naming their daughter. We think it has a catchy Gallic feel. Their second daughter was named Manzie Tio, after Sidney Bechet's drummer and teacher.

BEDELIA. This name is familiar almost solely through its connection to the wacky series of children's books about Amelia Bedelia, the literal-minded maid. Also spelled **BIDELIA,** it originated as a nickname for girls named Bridget in Ireland, but stands perfectly well on its own.

BELINDA. Belinda, along with cousins Melinda and Linda, has long been sitting on the Not in Current Usage shelf, despite an impressive history. It comes from the Latin, meaning "beautiful snake" (coined at a time when snakes were a sacred symbol of wisdom and immortality) and it still does seem to have a certain lingering serpentine charm. In Babylonian mythology Belinda was the goddess of heaven and earth, and the name later was used for the heroine of Alexander Pope's satirical poem *The Rape of the Lock.*

BELLA, BELLE. The surge in popularity of the names Isabella and Isabelle has carried in its wake a revival of the short forms Bella and Belle. Belle, a favorite of a hundred years ago, which means "beautiful" in French, and led to phrases like "belle of the ball" and "Southern belle," was neglected in the years following its use for a character in *Gone With the Wind,* until it reemerged a few years ago as the name of the spirited and much-admired heroine of Disney's *Beauty and the Beast.* Celebrity parents in particular have found it a stylish, sweet middle name for their daughters Tallulah Belle (Demi Moore and Bruce Willis), Delilah Belle (Lisa Rinna and Harry Hamlin), and Chelsea Belle (Rosie O'Donnell), and other baby namers are following suit. Bella, which still retains a slightly old-world grandmaish residue, is also pretty and gaining in popularity. **BELIA** is a pleasant Spanish variant.

BENJAMINE. An unusual feminization of the biblical Benjamin, used in France but not here. **BENJAMINA** is another possibility, though this is one case where we prefer the ending without the final *a*.

BENTEN. The Japanese goddess of the sea and one of the seven gods of good fortune. Parents attracted to boyish surname names might want to consider this cross-cultural possibility.

BERENICE, BERNICE. Since most Bernices were called **BUNNY** or **BINNIE** or **BERNIE** anyway, the world will hardly notice that this old Greek name has faded into oblivion—despite the fact that it was the name of the wives and daughters of many Macedonian kings.

BERIANA. A Cornish name that comes from a twelfth-century saint.

BERNADETTE. A pleasant, feminine but strong name that was once the exclusive property of Catholics, as a result of the fame of Saint Bernadette of Lourdes, whose experiences of seeing visions of the Virgin Mary beginning when she was fourteen have been portrayed in novels and a 1943 movie. Bernadette Peters is a contemporary bearer, and Minnie Driver's breakthrough film role was as Bernadette "Benny" Hogan in *Circle of Friends*. The related **BERNADINE** was celebrated in an old Pat Boone song, and **BENEDETTA** is an Italian version.

BERTHA. Poor Bertha is considered the ultimate ugly name, bringing to mind a pasty complexion, orthopedic shoes, and mounds of flesh. Its association with Big Bertha, the nickname given to an enormous German gun used during World War I, made the unattractive connection official. Who would believe (or care) that Bertha was the name of a beautiful Teutonic goddess? Much more usable is the French **BERTILLE.**

BERYL. Unlike Pearl and Ruby, this is one early twentieth-century jewel name that never caught on in this country the way it did in England. Its namesake is a gleaming dark green gemstone that is said to bring good luck. Beryl does retain a small measure of dash, however, thanks to adventurer, aviator, and author Beryl Markham. **BERRY** is a more modern-sounding but less substantial substitute.

BESS, BETH. These two short and simple pet names for Elizabeth have long been used on their own. Beth has a softer, more starry-eyed and sensitive image, partly because of its association with the tragic sister in *Little Women*; Bess, although older, manages to sound fresher, despite onetime ties to "Good Queen Bess"—Queen Elizabeth I—and Gershwin's *Porgy and Bess*. Longer form **BESSIE** was permanently buried by its traditional association with cows and horses, though some may appreciate the fact that it was the given name of the greatest of all blues singers, Bessie Smith.

BETHANY. Following the lead it's taken with our British cousins (where it is currently in the Top 15 of girls' names), Bethany has been moving up in this country because of parents who see it as a perfect, less trendy, substitute for the overused Brittany. Bethany is one of the primal place-names, being the village where Jesus stayed at Lazarus's house on his way to Jerusalem before the crucifixion. **BETHA** and **BETHAN** are also found.

BETTY, BETSY, BETTE. Three nicknames for Elizabeth dating from the time when gals were gals. Betty was hugely popular from the Betty Boop twenties through the Betty Grable 1940s and fifties, when it was the all-American girls' name blanketing the country, often in combination with such single-syllable extenders as Jo, Ann, and Lou. Betsy, which goes back to the days of Betsy Ross, was (but no longer is) a perkier, younger-sounding alternative to Betty. The Bette version came in with Bette Davis and has been perpetuated by the Divine Miss M., Bette Midler. Yet another spin is **BETTINA,** used by Danielle Steel in her novel *Loving*. The bottom line on all these names, however, is that most little Elizabeths these days are called Elizabeth.

BEULAH. Beulah—mentioned in the Bible as a name for Israel and sometimes taken as a reference for heaven—was fatally damaged by being stereotyped as a black maid's name, initially in Mae West's famous line, "Beulah, peel me a grape," and then in the early fifties TV series of that name, the first to star an African-American performer. It would take a courageous baby namer, indeed, to attempt to resuscitate this name.

BEVERLY. More visible now as half of the name of a wealthy southern California community than as a girl's name, Beverly (also sometimes used for men in England) was often heard here from the 1920s to the fifties—too recently to allow for a revival.

BIANCA. The Italian version of Blanche, this exotic but not eccentric name was brought to prominence by Nicaragua-born Bianca Jagger, who has managed to remain in the public eye decades after her split with Mick. Biancas of the past have included characters in *Othello, The Taming of the Shrew* and its derivative, *Kiss Me Kate;* more contemporary ones are a character on *All My Children* and the daughter of Jean-Claude Van Damme. **BLANCA** is the Spanish version.

BIJOU. A jewel of a name—just as it means in French—but perhaps too precious for its own good. It was chosen by John Phillips and Genevieve Waite for their daughter, now an actress in her own right. Warning: We have known more than one poodle with this appellation.

BILLIE. As Billy is to William, Billie is to Wilhelmina—a friendly, tomboyish nickname name that far predates the Jamies and Caseys that came along in the late 1960s. It also has a country feel—maybe because of the word '*hillbilly,*' or because it has in the past often been followed by such additives as Jo or Jean. Jazz immortal Billie Holiday was actually born Eleanora. One contemporary celebrity who named her daughter Billie is Carrie Fisher.

BLAIR, BLAINE. Ever since the days of *The Facts of Life,* Blair has been seen as the snobby rich girl. This Scottish surname was indeed one of the first upwardly mobile androgynous names to hit the big time—followed by Whitney, Ashley, Courtney & Co.—and to become almost exclusively female. A compatible chum for Blair would be **BLAINE**—the name of Donald Trump's socialite sister-in-law.

BLAKE. One of several single-syllable ambigender *B* surname names, Blake has a briskly efficient image when used for a girl. It was a (male) *Dynasty* character and a (female) *Guiding Light* soap-opera character, but is still used more frequently for males.

BLANCHE. Because of its fictional associations, Blanche has long evoked the stereotype of the faded Southern belle, à la Blanche DuBois in *A Streetcar Named Desire* and Blanche Devereaux in TV's *Golden Girls*. Originally a nickname for a pale blonde (it means "white" in French), Blanche was commonly used in this country a century ago, and some modern parents are beginning to look at it again as a more plainspoken alternative to Bianca, particularly as a middle name. **BLANCHETTE** is another, more feminine, French version.

BLAZE. Blaze is hot, but more in striptease terms than in popularity.

BLISS. Beyond Joy, there is Bliss, the kind of name that puts extreme pressure on a little girl, particularly one prone to tantrums.

BLOSSOM. With the large bouquet of flower names available, few modern parents are picking this generic floral name that had a showgirl aura back in the Floradora days. Although it came back to life briefly via the television series of that name, we don't foresee it gaining any ground in the near future, considering all the fresher and brighter flower names to choose from.

BLUE. Okay, John Travolta and Kelly Preston didn't give their daughter Ella the middle name Blue, they gave her the middle name **BLEU,** the similarly pronounced French word for *blue*. (What do they call a rare Big Mac in Paris, John?) Whatever language you say it in, Blue seems to be one of the hottest middle names around. But Cher was first, when she named her now-grown son with Greg Allman Elijah Blue.

BLYTHE. "Hail to thee, blithe spirit," said the poet Shelley, and this name does indeed embody a cheerful, carefree spirit. Despite its attractive image, it is rarely used, and has most frequently been associated with Blythe Danner, actress mother of Gwyneth Paltrow.

BOLIVIA. Too many Olivias in your neighborhood? Be the first one on the block to introduce this really original sound-related place-name with South American spirit.

BONNIE. The Scots really do say "bonnie" for pretty, thus the root of this name, from the French *bonne*. *Gone With the Wind* gave it a big push when Scarlett and Rhett used it for their daughter (her full name was Eugenie Victoria, but her pet name came from the fact that she had "eyes as blue as the bonnie blue flag"). The name's last moment in the limelight came in the late sixties with the film *Bonnie and Clyde,* about outlaw Bonnie Parker, and it is still visible via singer Bonnie Raitt, but has been out of the fashion loop for decades, as have the related **BONITA** and **BENITA.**

BRANDY. One of the few girls' (or boys' for that matter) names to celebrate a strong alcoholic beverage, Brandy dates back to the Candy/Mandy/Randi era of names. Now, despite the popularity of actress/singer Brandy (*Moesha*) Norwood, we don't see it making a comeback, because although it might be cute and saucy, it doesn't give your offspring much to aim for. **BRANDI** is even slighter.

BREE. Jane Fonda won an Oscar for playing a complex character with this name in the 1971 film *Klute,* prompting a limited contingent of baby Brees. It was also Helen Hunt's name in *Dr T. and the Women*. You may find appeal in the name's sophisticated yet upbeat image, but we must warn you against the cheesy spelling **BRIE,** even if that is a geographical region of France.

BRENDA. From the 1930s to the fifties, Brenda had a respectable run as a name symbolizing a form of slinky glamour, and summoning up the image of a faded 1940s B-movie star or well-publicized debutante, or the intrepid vintage comic-strip girl reporter Brenda Starr. Then the name was revived to some measure by the infamous Brenda Walsh of *Beverly Hills 90210*, but now that Brenda is gone too, taking her name with her.

BRENNA. A number of parents are finding this other female form of Brendan, which means "dark-haired," a fresher alternative to the outmoded Brenda and the megapopular Brianna. **BRANNA** is a Celtic version.

BRETT. The dashing and seductive Lady Brett Ashley of Hemingway's *The Sun Also Rises* was a captivating enough character to offer naming inspiration. Although some might find it a tad affected, Brett combines a pleasingly brisk androgyny with a distinctive feminine softness. **BRITT** is a similar-sounding but more brittle Scandinavian name. **BRETTA** is also possible.

BRIANA, BRIANNA, BREANNA. One of the epidemically popular names of the 1990s and into the new millennium, Brianna did not even appear in most naming dictionaries before 1985, and if it did it was merely as the feminine form of Brian. But although it does sound like a recent spun-sugar confection, the name actually appeared as far back as the sixteenth century in Edmund Spenser's poem *The Faerie Queen*. Now, in an attempt to individualize the ubiquitous name, parents have propelled all three of the above spellings onto the pop charts (added together they would drive the name into third place on the girls' name popularity list), but have also improvised endlessly on the theme, using variants from **BRYANNAH** to **BRIARRA**. The shortened **BRIA/BREA** version has been embraced by many parents, including the Eddie Murphys, as well. But Brianna's best attributes, a certain energy combined with an exotic feel and melodic quality— can also be found in other, less-used names with more history and meaning, such as Bianca or Bryony, now that Brianna's sleek, striving image has lost a lot of its sheen. Actor Blair Underwood has a daughter named **BRIELLE.**

BRIAR. Romantic, fairy-tale-loving parents have recently discovered Briar, the alternate name of Princess Aurora in *Sleeping Beauty*, often using it in combination with Rose, as in the age-old story.

BRID, BRIDE. Ancient Gaelic names, related to Brigid, these are pronounced breed and BREED-ee.

BRIDGET, BRIGITTE. For years, Bridget was second only to Mary in Ireland, and it became one of the earliest Irish names to emigrate to this country. At first Bridget was the family cook, but by 1950 she, and her foreign variants, had morphed into a sex kitten, à la Bardot. Now she is somewhere in between, her attractive image reflected in someone like the versatile Bridget Fonda, as well as the character in the best-selling diaries of Bridget Jones. More authentic than the shopworn Erins and Colleens, Bridget is the Anglicized form of the name of the ancient Celtic goddess of wisdom, a saint who became the patroness of Ireland, as well as patron saint of poets and healers. Irish variants include **BRIGIT, BRIGID** (the devious character in *The Maltese Falcon*), **BRIDIE** and **BEDELIA.** Scandinavians use **BIRGITTA, BIRGITTE, BRIGITTA, BIRGIT, BRITT, BRITA, BRITTA,** and **BITTAN.** Sinead O'Connor introduced yet another possibility when she named her daughter **BRIGIDINE.**

BRISEN. The name of a female magician in the tales of the Knights of the Round Table, responsible for the romance of Sir Lancelot and Elaine.

BRITTANY. Although Brittany is, of course, a place-name, the recent wild popularity of this name does not seem to be tied directly to the place-name craze. A soap-opera staple for about twenty years, it has more in common with names like Kimberly and Tiffany than with geographical names like Dakota and Sierra. It started as an upscale name, then quickly filtered down to every level of society, finally becoming overused to the point of cliché. Like Ashley, it has spawned a veritable school of variant spellings: **BRITNEY/ BRITTNEY** (especially with the megapopularity of teen idol Britney Spears) has taken on a life of its own, and there are also **BRITNI, BRITENY,** and more others than we care to mention. Other members of the ever-growing land of Brittany: **BRITTON, BRYTON, BRITTYN, BRINLEY,** and **BRYLEIGH.**

34

BRONA. A lovely name with an unfortunate meaning: like Deirdre, it's "sad" in Gaelic.

BRONTE. Admirers of the sisters who authored *Jane Eyre* and *Wuthering Heights* have begun to give their surname to their own daughters. Bronte was initially heard as a first name in the film *Green Card,* for the Andie Mac-Dowell character.

BRONWEN, BRANWEN. Bronwen is one of the best known of the traditional Welsh girls' names, although it's still so seldom heard that it retains an exotic ring. In Welsh mythology the name of the daughter of Llyr, god of the sea, we think this is a real winner. The common alternate spelling, **BRON-WYN,** is culturally incorrect, since Welsh female names end in *wen* and only the males get the *wyn* spelling. Similar in sound but different in meaning—it means "beautiful raven"—is **BRANWEN,** famous in legend as a figure in the romance of Sir Tristram.

BROOKE. Brooke might have been just another surname name, had it not been for Brooke Shields (actually christened Christa), who took it from quietly fashionable to ultratrendy when she was just a mere slip of a girl. At one time considered almost too sophisticated for a baby girl, it has now become popular enough for that not to be a consideration. Brookes have been a soap-opera staple, beginning with the introduction of Brooke Bentley Clinton on *General Hospital* in 1965. A more distinctive choice might be **BRYCE,** the name Ron Howard picked for his oldest daughter.

BROOKLYN. Large numbers of parents have now divorced this name from the harsh realities of the New York City borough, seeing it as the combination of two pleasant syllables. Spice Girl Posh chose the name for her son, as did director Jonathan Demme, but it is much more frequently used for girls.

BRYN. An appealing Welsh name meaning "hill," Bryn is definitely middle-name material. **BRYNNE** is an overly complicated spelling alternative, and **BRYNNA** is a variation.

BRYONY. A nature name—the bryony being a perennial vine with greenish flowers—it comes from the ancient Greek meaning "to grow luxuriantly." Found on the invitation lists for parties in Knightsbridge, Belgravia, and other posh London enclaves (also often attached to boys in Wales), Bryony could make an interesting alternative to the megapopular Brittany.

BUFFY. In the past, Buffy was either a clenched-teeth Seven Sisters school sorority girl with a roommate named Muffy, or a cute little moppet in pigtails, as on the old TV show *Family Affair*. But that was before *Buffy, the Vampire Slayer* hit the large and small screens, giving the name some moxie and muscle. It's still basically a fluffy retro name, however, so save this one for your puppy.

BURGUNDY, BURGANDY. Color names are suddenly hot, from Gray to Teal to Rose to one of the newest hues, Burgundy. And of course, Burgundy is also a place, a province of France, as well as a wine.

C

CADENCE. See **HARMONY.**

CAIRO. Model Beverly Peele picked a winner when she named her daughter Cairo several years ago. The Egyptian capital has an exotic aura and is much less faddish-sounding than such closer place-names as Montana and California, and the final *o* has more energy than the usual *a* ending.

CAITLIN. An Irish and Welsh form of Catherine (later Anglicized to Kathleen), Caitlin was a boom name of the eighties, rocketing from obscurity (Americans first heard it via the wife of doomed poet Dylan Thomas) to the height of popularity in the space of a decade. The original name has been gradually eclipsed, however, by its myriad spelling variations—**KATELYN** and **KAITLYN** both top it on the popularity lists—and there are many others as well, such as **CAITLYN**—in fact there were twenty-nine different spellings of the name in Kansas alone last year. But it's the original form that's the name of the moment for the sexy TV heroine, such as Heather Locklear on *Spin City* and Yasmine Bleeth on *Nash Bridges*. No matter how it's spelled, though, there is nothing particularly novel or creative about the name anymore.

CALEDONIA. When singer Shawn Colvin gave this name to her daughter, she created something both musical and territorial, as Caledonia is the old poetic name for Scotland. It also becomes more user-friendly with the sweet nickname **CALLIE.**

CALICO. It's a fabric, it's a cat, and now it's a baby name.

CALIFORNIA. As probably the premier capital of creative baby naming in the U.S., California would seem to be an inevitable place-name possibility.

CALISTA, CALLISTA. The actress who plays *Ally McBeal* has made this one of the most publicized names of the decade. Before Ms. Flockhart hit the headlines, Calista was an unmined gem, a Greek name that had been used by actor David Carradine for his daughter several years earlier. Now we anticipate that many other parents will pick up on this pretty name which, indeed, means "most beautiful."

CALLA, CALLIE. It began as a nickname, but now Calla is being appreciated on its own for its unique, lilylike beauty. It has appeared on the soap opera *The Guiding Light,* and as a character on the animated *Gummi Bears,* and Mare Winningham chose it for her daughter. **CALLIE** takes it further into nickname territory, and fits in with other current sound-alikes such as Hallie and Allie.

CALLIOPE. Calliope was the ancient Greek muse of eloquence and epic poetry, whose name means "beautiful face." Aside from a long-running role on the soap opera *Days of Our Lives* and various appearances in dramatizations of the Hercules myth, the name is rarely heard in real life—perhaps because it's also the name of a shrill circus steam-whistling musical instrument.

CAMBRIE. A newly created name, used by Rick Schroder for his daughter, Cambrie sounds like a cross between the name of a fabric and the name of a cheese. Although it seems to be catching on across the country, you might want to consider something more traditional, like, say, Camille.

CAMDEN. Camden is another recent invention that seems to be taking off, particularly among younger parents. It has several things going for it—the popular hard *c* opening and a resemblance to the popular Cameron, a unisex feel, and the fact that it's also a geographical name, as both a New Jersey city on the Delaware River and a section of London.

CAMEO. A word name that suggests the sentimentality of Grandma's beautifully carved brooch, combined with an upbeat *o* ending.

CAMERA. When the late Arthur Ashe and his photographer wife gave this name to their daughter, it was at a time when few people considered using significant words as names. Now that has become less unusual, and Camera would make an interesting first or middle name possibility for parents similarly involved with photography.

CAMERON, CAMRYN. Credit or blame Cameron Diaz for almost single-handedly transporting this sophisticated Scottish male surname name into the girls' camp. And credit or blame another actress, Camryn Manheim, star of TV's *The Practice,* for popularizing the phonetic, more feminine spelling of the name to the point where it is now almost equally prevalent.

CAMILLA, CAMILLE. Both these names, the ancient classic and its French version, make excellent choices, accessible but by no means ordinary. Camilla, the frillier of the two, was associated in Roman myth with a swift-footed huntress who, according to Virgil, was so fast that she could run over a cornfield without bending a blade of grass. In England, it is now tied to Lady Camilla Parker-Bowles, close companion of Prince Charles. As for Camille, at one time just the sound of the name could start people coughing, recalling the tragic "Lady of the Camellias" heroine played by Greta Garbo in the vintage film, but that image has certainly faded sufficiently now for the name to be safely and successfully used, as it has been recently in such movies as *Cookie's Fortune,* such TV series as *Chicago Hope,* and such soap operas as *As the World Turns.*

CANAIRE. Though this name is virtually unknown, Canaire was a sixth-century Irish saint who, if legend is correct, was one of the earliest feminists. She demanded admittance to an all-male island monastery and her arguments for equality gained her entry.

CANDACE, CANDICE. Candace, originally the name of a dynasty of Ethiopian queens mentioned in the New Testament, and meaning "brilliantly white," has long been associated with actress Candice Bergen. It is rarely used for babies today, perhaps because of the sticky sweetness of its nickname, **CANDY,** or because any name with "can" in it is just too ripe for teasing. **CANDRA** is a newly hatched variation.

CANDIDA. This ancient name—it was used in the Roman Empire, and also for several saints—became known in the modern world via the George Bernard Shaw play with that title, whose heroine was one of the playwright's most delightful creations. Rarely heard today, Candida (accent on the first syllable) could make a solid yet original choice—although some may find it more familiar as the name of an infection than as one for a child.

CAPRI. This name of the romantic island near the Bay of Naples, which has a lively capricious sound, is ripe for visitation by parents in search of a place-name.

CAPRICIA. When Hillary Clinton was First Lady instead of Senator, she had a social secretary whose first name was the singular Capricia. This was a new one on us, though it is listed—along with **CAPRICE**—by a few name sources. Pronounced either to rhyme with Patricia or as ca-PREE-sha or even ca-PREE-chee-a, Capricia has the feel of an up-and-comer, with its hard *c* initial and its distinctive, feminine sound despite its similarity to the word *capricious*.

CARA. Cara, which means "dear" in Italian, has, despite its affectionate quality, never become widely popular in this country. Its diminutives include **CARINA, CARISSA,** and **CARITA,** all more decorative than but ultimately as insubstantial as the original. **CAERA** or **CEARA** are the Gaelic versions, both pronounced as the original Cara.

CARLA, CARLOTTA. Except on reruns of *Cheers,* Carla, the somewhat severe feminization of the Germanic Carl, has rarely been heard for years, especially not as a baby name. The same can be said of such gussied-up variants as **CARLENE, CARLEEN, CARLINE,** and **CARLINA.** The Italianate form, Carlotta, has considerably more exotic charm and substance, despite being the name given to a thoroughly unpleasant character in Disney's *The Little Mermaid.*

CARLY. Carly has been in the public eye since the emergence of Carly Simon in the late 1960s, but it has taken all this time—and some assistance by several soap-opera appearances—for her name to become as popular as her music. Nowadays, it's nearly as likely to be spelled **CARLEIGH** or **KARLEE,** but we think that you can find a name for your daughter that's a lot more substantial than any of these versions. **CARLIN** is a surname-style variation with a bit more backbone.

CARMEL, CARMELA. Rarely heard in this country—probably because of its similarity to the name of the chewy candy—Carmel is quite commonly used in Ireland, often given in honor of Our Lady of Mount Carmel, the mountain near Haifa famous for its lush vegetation which was, according to legend, often visited by Mary and the infant Christ. Carmel is, in fact, the Hebrew word for "garden." The choice of the attractive Carmela has been pretty much restricted to Italian families, such as TV's Sopranos.

CARMEN. For much of the public, Carmen is associated with the sensuous, tragic heroine of Bizet's opera, based on a novel by Prosper Mérimée. Its meaning, quite appropriately, is "to sing, be lyrical," but it has, thus far, been rarely heard outside the Hispanic culture—although the enticing image of Carmen Electra and the cool beauty of supermodel Carmen Kass may change all that.

CAROL. There must be thousands of new mothers (and even more grandmothers) named Carol, but perhaps only a handful of new babies—we've left this musical favorite of our own parents behind along with diaper pins and car beds, in favor of the more classic Caroline. Ditto its variants **CAROLE, CARROLL,** and **CARYL,** though the German **CAROLA** retains some modern appeal.

CAROLINE, CAROLYN. A traditional favorite revived by taste-conscious contemporary parents (one of whom is Katie Couric) who have been exposed for years to the privileged lives of such celebrities as Caroline Kennedy and Princess Caroline of Monaco, Caroline became one of the quintessential yuppie names of the 1980s. On the other hand, it's not a name that could ever be considered trendy, because of its impressive royal pedigree and composed, capable image, especially stylish when pronounced to rhyme with *wine*. An appealing alternative would be to change it to **CAROLINA**, affording it a more contemporary, Latinate/place-name spin. Carolyn, which was very popular from the 1920s to the sixties, takes the name considerably down-market. An attractive nickname for all of the above, often used in England but distinctive here, is **CARO**.

CARRIE. This Little-House-on-the-Prairie-type pet form of Caroline was a hit in 1875 and again a century later, despite the chilling effect of the Stephen King book and movie of that name, released in 1976. At this point, we'd stay with the original Caroline: Carrie is too reminiscent of the sixties nickname names that seem as dated now as go-go boots.

CARSON, CARTER. Two upscale, androgynous Waspy surnames that sounded a lot fresher a decade ago than they do now, when the trend is more toward ethnic (particularly Irish) family names. The somewhat friendlier Carson has a distinguished connection to writer Carson McCullers (born Lula), while Carter could conjure up visions of Little Liver Pills or children's underwear. Actor Ray Liotta has a daughter named **KARSEN**.

CASEY. Although Casey is a common surname in Ireland, it is rarely used as a girl's name there. In this country, it bounced onto the scene in the late 1960s, boasting the twin appeal of traditional Irish flavor combined with an energetic and what seemed then like a new, modern androgyny. It has several folkloric associations, including the mythologized (but very real) heroic train engineer Casey Jones (born Jonathan Luther Jones—he hailed from a town called Cayce), the poem "Casey at the Bat," and, to a lesser extent, colorful Hall of Famer Casey Stengel. The name has remained viable for both boys and girls, but most modern parents interested in an Irish name are now seeking something more substantive.

CASSANDRA. In the past couple of decades, Cassandra has moved from being an esoteric Greek mythological name—that of a prophetess cursed with the fate of not being believed—to an exotic character name in movies (*Wayne's World*), soap operas (*The Guiding Light*), and other TV shows (*Buffy the Vampire Slayer*), and also to becoming an increasingly popular baby name. It combines the initial *K* sound so popular today with the feminine formality of such other fashionable names as Alexandra and Amanda. One celebrity dad who chose it for his daughter is Charlie Sheen. The nickname **CASS** may still be too tied to the unfortunate Mama, but **CASSIE** is cute and provides a down-to-earth alternative to the name's full and somewhat imposing image.

CASSIA. A Greek name that means "cinnamon" and is an unusual yet straightforward possibility for today. **CINNAMON** can be used too, though we think the obscured version sounds more like a name and less like an opportunity for teasing.

CASSIDY. Kathie Lee Gifford's incessant talking about her boy Cody sent that name, almost single-handedly, soaring up the popularity lists when he was a baby. The same thing, however, did not happen with her daughter, leaving Cassidy as just another cowgirl name.

CATHERINE. Catherine, together with its other standard English forms Katherine, Katharine, and Kathryn, is one of the classic girls' names of the Western world, rarely dropping out of the Top 25. It has been well used throughout history for saints (one of whom, Catherine of Alexandria, is the patron saint of philosophers, students, craftsmen, nurses, and librarians), queens, and commoners alike. Catherine has also been associated with some of the great romantic heroines of literature, including Heathcliff's love in *Wuthering Heights* and the passionate nurse Catherine Barkley in Hemingway's *A Farewell to Arms*. In recent years, American parents have preferred the *K* spelling, partly because they relate more strongly to the nickname Kate than to the 1950s favorite, Cathy. While this name is too classic ever to be considered trendy, it is extremely popular, and parents may want to consider some of its many foreign variations, such as: **CATE-**

RINA (Italian), **CATALINA** (the Spanish/geographic version), **KASIA** (Polish), **KATINKA, KATYA** (Russian), or **KATJA** (German). The Scottish **CATRIONA** and the Irish **CAITRIONA** both seem quite appealing until you realize that they are pronounced just like Katrina. Trivia note: If you're wondering why all these interchangeable Cs and Ks, it's because when the name was introduced into Anglo-Saxon Britain, Catherine was spelled with a C because the letter K did not yet exist in the English alphabet.

CAYENNE. Hot and peppery, this is one of the new spice names, like Cinnamon and Saffron, that parents are appraising in terms of whether they're so far out they might be coming in. Cayenne's usability rises because of its similarity in sound to the popular Cheyenne.

CECILIA. This lacy valentine of a name seems, to some people, one of those quintessential Catholic appellations that sound incomplete without the word "saint" in front of it. And, indeed, Cecilia was the name of a popular saint, designated the patroness of musicians because she supposedly sang directly to God while the musicians played at her wedding (making it a fitting name for opera star Cecilia Bartoli). This feminine form of Cecil, most popular here at the end of the nineteenth century and the beginning of the twentieth, has a delicate feel that just might appeal to parents of the new millennium (designer Vera Wang has a daughter named Cecilia), as could such variants as **CECILE, CECILY,** and **CICELY** (chosen for her daughter by Sandra Bernhard). The latter two might tend to sound to the American ear like the ultimate British upper-crust names, summoning up genteel images of pale pink cashmere, tea in flowered china cups, and dainty cucumber sandwiches. Cecily has been naturalized to the point of becoming a soap-opera character—the zany Cecily Kelly on *All My Children.*

CELESTE. Celeste is a softly pretty and somewhat quaint name with heavenly (celestial) overtones and a bit of a forties feel, recalling actress Celeste Holm or Queen Celeste of Babar's elephant kingdom. But it never became popular enough to have a real date-stamp of a particular period of the past, and so still sounds fairly fresh—especially since it appeared on

Beverly Hills 90210. Both its diminutives, **CELESTINE** and **CELESTINA** also have a certain fey charm, while a few parents have gone right to the root and used the word **CELESTIAL** as a name.

CELIA, CELINE. Underused today, the delicate but energetic Celia is found sprinkled throughout Elizabethan literature—Shakespeare is sometimes credited with introducing it in *As You Like It,* and it was to Celia that poet Ben Jonson penned the immortal line "Drink to me only with thine eyes." French-Canadian singer Celine Dion has focused attention on that version, and **CEIL** is a friendly short form.

CERES. The Roman goddess of agriculture and a name with real revival possibilities. One couple we know varied it to **CERE,** pronounced SEER-ee which has a sleek modern sound.

CERI, CERIAN. These are two popular Welsh names that are pronounced with a hard *c*, like Kerry.

CESSAIR. Pronounced with an initial hard *c*, Cessair was a woman of Irish legend who was so saddened by her husband's death that she soon followed him to the grave—a dismal meaning for an intriguing if somewhat industrial-sounding name.

CHANDA. One of the aspects of Devi, the ultimate Indian goddess.

CHANEL, CHANTEL. Classy things do not necessarily translate into classy baby names, as for example Porsche, Lexus, Diamond—and Chanel. Chanel suits and purses may be elegant and timeless, but the name is not—although its melodiousness, plus its popular *sha* sound, have been appreciated by some parents. Chantel or **CHANTAL,** on the other hand, is an authentic French name related to the word for *song* that could make a distinctive pick.

CHARIS. Pronounced KAR-is, this is the name of one of the Three Graces in Greek mythology. The Welsh **CERYS** sounds the same, and is similarly unfamiliar in this country. If you're attracted to names with the trendy hard *c* sound, as in Caitlin, Kayla, Carly, but want something further off the beaten track, Charis might fill the bill.

CHARITY. Charity is one of the Big Three "abstract virtue" names, along with the more frequently used Hope and Faith, and the one of which the Bible says "but the greatest of these is charity." This group of names in general is sounding decidedly fresher these days (contemporary enough to appear on the soap opera *Passions*), and Charity also has a pleasing *y*-ending rhythmic sound as well as a kindhearted, generous association. However, if the name's image is a bit *too* generous for you (i.e., *Sweet Charity*, Shirley MacLaine's hooker with a heart of gold), you might want to pursue alternative virtues, such as Amity, Felicity, or Verity.

CHARLOTTE. Charlotte has long been an ultrafashionable baby name in England—it started the 1990s at number 1 and is still in fourth place there—but, while it's definitely been rediscovered here, it hasn't yet made its way onto the U.S. popularity charts. Charlotte has a somewhat similar image and pedigree to Caroline—they're both classic names favored by royals (Princess Caroline of Monaco's daughter is named Charlotte) and both carry a soigné, socially conscious air today. Charlotte has had some disparate associations in the past, from novelist Charlotte Brontë to the gallant spider in E. B. White's children's classic *Charlotte's Web*, to the grotesqueries of *Hush Hush Sweet Charlotte*, to the very contemporary character in *Sex and the City*. Celebrity parents who have chosen the name include Sigourney Weaver, Amy Brenneman, and Rickie Lee Jones. Aside from these classic French feminizations of Charles (via the Italian Carlotta), there are some more modern inventions, such as **CHARLENE** and **CHARLAYNE**, which definitely do not share the same patina of class. Actress **CHARLIZE** Theron has introduced yet another variation. Our advice: Stick with the classic Charlotte.

CHARMAINE, CHARMIAN. These two names seem similar but actually have little in common. Charmaine (pronounced with a *sh* sound) was popularized in the 1920s by a theatrical character and hit song, while Charmian (pronounced like the word "charm"), which derives from the Greek word for "joy," was used by Shakespeare for the faithful and kind servant of the Egyptian queen in *Antony and Cleopatra*. Unfortunate association to both names: "Please don't squeeze the Charmin."

CHASTITY. Once considered a one-person celebrity name appropriate only for the daughter of someone as outrageous as Cher, Chastity is now being cautiously considered by the most intrepid of virtue-name-loving parents.

CHAYA. Chaya is a Hebrew name meaning "life, living, alive," and is said to have the power to restore life to the ill. Its similarity to the currently trendy Maya would assure its easy assimilation.

CHELSEA. This name first came into the American consciousness in a major way via the character Jane Fonda played in *On Golden Pond* in 1981, and later of course was frequently in the headlines when Chelsea Clinton (whose name was inspired by the lyric of a Judy Collins song) became First Daughter. Even more recently, Rosie O'Donnell has kept the name current when reporting the activities of her daughter, Chelsea Belle. Of late, however, the name has been falling in favor, no longer sounding as fresh or creative as it once did, even with diverse new spellings like **CHELSEY**.

CHERRY. Although it sounds like one of the new noun names, Cherry has been around since the days of Dickens. But think twice and then twice again before you use it—the poor girl with this name will suffer mightily from embarrassment come puberty and the inevitable barrage of jokes from her male classmates. So, if you value your child's psychological well-being, steer far clear of this name and its variations, **CHERI** and **CHERIE** (Marilyn Monroe's character in *Bus Stop*). Other related names present their own problems—**CHER** is one of the all-time great one-person names (if you don't count her namesake character in *Clueless*), and **CHERYL** and **CHERILYN** are as firmly frozen in the pre-Beatles 1960s as panty girdles. The somewhat more substantial French version is **CERISE**.

CHEYENNE. Along with other cowgirl/boy place names like Sierra and Dakota, Cheyenne has been galloping wildly across the country for over a decade, and is beginning to feel a little tired and saddle sore. And spelling it **CHEYANNE** (or worse, **SHYANNE**) just confuses the issue.

CHINA. Long before the current place-name craze, a pair of the more daring pop singers of the Age of Aquarius picked this name for their daughters, Grace Slick choosing the conventional spelling, Michelle Phillips going further afield with **CHYNNA.** Both versions are a lot less far-out and acceptable today.

CHLOE. Chloe has been the most popular name in England, Wales, Scotland, and the Republic of Ireland for four years running now. In this country, it has been playing hopscotch with Zoe for quite a while, and now seems to be pulling out ahead in the popularity race—there were close to seven thousand babies named Chloe born in the United States last year. Much more dynamic than most of the other old Greek-based romantic literary names of the seventeenth century, Chloe is a pretty springtime name symbolizing new growth, and a current soap opera favorite. It was picked for their daughters by such celebrities as Candice Bergen and Olivia Newton-John, and is the real name of Nobel prize-winning writer Toni Morrison. Since one of us has chosen it for her own child, we can give it a very personal stamp of approval, but be warned: Chloe is no longer as offbeat as some first-time parents might think it is.

CHRISTINA, CHRISTINE. Pristine and crystal clear, these are a pair of centuries-old, multicultural, long-popular names whose roots and offshoots have become too numerous and complex to untangle. The earliest forms of the name are probably **CHRISTIAN** (a female name in medieval times) and **CHRISTINA,** which is still lovely and distinctive today. Christina, originally an abbreviated form, became a royal name in Sweden (Greta Garbo played Queen Christina in one of her classic films) and Spain, and is more fashionable today than the French Christine, which prevailed here from the 1940s to the 1970s, being in the Top 10 in 1970. Christina is now well represented by young actresses Applegate and Ricci and singer Aguilera. Over the past several years, the trendiest forms of the name have been the Scandinavian Kristin and Kirsten, although they have definitely begun to fade. Variant spellings and pet forms of the name, many of them used as names in their own right, abound. **CHRISTIE** became popular via model Christie Brinkley, and **CHRISSY** with the wiggly Suzanne Summers character in *Three's Company*. **CHRISTA** is a German pet form that is occasionally used here, and **KIRSTY/KIRSTIE** is a Scottish diminutive now found as often in Abilene as in Aberdeen. **CHRISTABEL** is an oddball distant relative. Please note: "Creative" spellings of all these names have proliferated, but we feel that the variations are numerous enough without stretching to such debasements as **KRYSTYNE**.

CHRISTMAS. It was used as a slave name, in keeping with African day-naming traditions, and we think it might make a melodic and intriguing choice for a girl or boy today—one that any child is likely to find pleasant and exciting.

CLARA. See **CLARE**.

CIERRA, CEARA. See **SIERRA**.

CINDY. Supermodel/mom Cindy Crawford has been single-handedly keeping this 1960s, *Brady Bunch* nickname name alive for quite a while now, but few parents are choosing it for their new-millennium daughters. It was originally a pet form of Cinderella (yes, that really was a name), Lucinda, and Cynthia.

CINNAMON. See **CASSIA**.

CLARE, CLAIRE, CLARA. Parents looking for a simple, strong, but delicate classic name for their daughters are giving more and more consideration to Claire (the currently preferred spelling). As is often the case, this name first found favor in England, but Americans are beginning to catch up—Albert Brooks's little daughter, for example, is Claire Elizabeth—realizing that Claire is one of those special names that combines familiarity with distinction, clarity with solidity, historical depth with a modern lack of pretension. It's also been heard increasingly as a name for fictional characters, such as Michelle Pfeiffer's in *What Lies Beneath*. Clare, in the original French version (it means "clear, light"), was the medieval saint who was made the patron saint of television in 1958 because of her reputed power to see events at a distance. Clara, a quainter-sounding variation that was popular in this country at the end of the nineteenth century, also seems to be showing signs of a comeback: One celebrity dad who chose it for his daughter is actor Ewan McGregor. The Irish form **CIARA** (pronounced KEER-a), the second most popular name in the Republic of Ireland last year, and the Italian **CHIARA** (kee-AH-ra) (sometimes spelled **CIARA**) are two other attractive options. Two we do not recommend are **CLARICE**, maybe because we can still hear Hannibal Lecter hissing it at Agent Starling, and **CLARABELL**, a clown forever.

CLARISSA. Clarissa, the daintier version of Claire, has a long literary history of its own, having been featured in the novels of Richardson, Dickens, and Virginia Woolf—not to mention the cable TV teenage show, *Clarissa Explains It All.* This is a name definitely worth considering as an alternative to the overused Vanessa and Melissa.

CLARITY. A clever departure from both Claire and Charity, Clarity is a very desirable quality in this confusing world, and it also, unlike some other new word names, sounds like a real name.

CLAUDIA. Like other feminizations that had long been relegated to the attic—Olivia, for instance, and Michaela and Georgia—Claudia has been retrieved, spruced up, and is now ready for a reappraisal. Straightforward but soft, with a hint of ancient Roman splendor, Claudia is in that category of distinctive, classic, yet slightly offbeat names favored by parents unafraid of being a little different. Michelle Pfeiffer chose it for her daughter, Claudia Schiffer gave it an infusion of glamour, and it appeared on the show *Party of Five.* Chic French versions are **CLAUDIE** (pronounced like *cloudy*) and just plain **CLAUDE** (yes, it really is used for girls in France), but both **CLAUDINE** and **CLAUDETTE** seem to date back to the era of wavy Claudette Colbert bangs. A fact to forget: In Wales, Claudia is a name closely related to Gladys.

CLEA. This attractive, underappreciated name, pronounced CLAY-a, was given to a main female character in Lawrence Durrell's *Alexandria Quartet.* Its longer form, **CLEANTHA**, would make an interesting choice as well, as would the Italian version, **CLELIA**.

CLEMENTINE. Forget the song and the size 9 shoes—Clementine is one of the most appealing names around. In England, where people do not automatically say "Oh my darling" when they hear it, Clementine (it was the name of Mrs. Winston Churchill) is particularly fashionable and popular for well-born young ladies. There, they sometimes pronounce it Clementeen—which might sidestep the unfortunate association here. We also like **CLEMENTINA,** again pronounced with the long *e,* the name of one of America's first female publishers, Clementina Rind. **CLEMENCY,** which can be seen as a Puritan virtue name, is interesting too, if justice-system related. **CLEMENTIA,** however, sounds like it might be a gynecological problem.

CLEO, CLIO. Cleo is, of course, short for **CLEOPATRA,** and is pronounced the same as Clio, who was the Greek muse of history. Both are names with modern spirit—Cleo was most recently seen as a doctor on *ER,* Clio was a character in the animated *Hercules*—and share that great *o* ending. Cleopatra, on the other hand, would almost certainly prove a bit much.

CLODAGH. A Clodagh ring is the traditional Irish symbol of friendship, with its interlocking hands. As a name, it's the Gaelic version of Claudia pronounced CLOH-da.

CLOTILDE, CLOTILDA. Clotilde, while perfectly acceptable in France, sounds cloddy and heavy-footed to the American ear. And the German Clotilda makes an even duller thud.

CLOVER. The exception that proves the rule, Clover is one soap-opera (*The Young and the Restless, One Life to Live*) name that did not inspire its fans to pick up on it as a baby-naming inspiration. With the new interest in nature names, though, maybe this perky, plucky, lucky botanical example may finally come into its own.

COCO. Coco, like its cousins Gigi and Fifi, is a French nickname that is sometimes used on its own—as singer Sting did for one of his daughters. This one has a bit more solidity and elegance because of its association with French designer par excellence Coco Chanel, famous for her boxy suits, little black dresses, and numbered perfumes—and whose given name was Gabrielle.

COLETTE. The French novelist Colette, who wrote under her surname (her first name was the equally attractive **SIDONIE**), is a literary and feminist heroine, now receiving lots of biographical attention, and is the inspiration for the name's newfound stylish status. *The Practice*'s Dylan McDermott chose it for his baby girl. Parents may also want to consider using the name's long form, Nicolette.

COLLEEN. Colleen is the Irish word for "girl," and while considered a quintessentially Irish name in countries outside of Ireland, you won't be finding it in Country Cork. Today, along with other *een* names used from the 1920s through the forties (Pegeen, Doreen, Maureen, Eileen, Kathleen), and with other inauthentic Irish names (Erin, Shannon), Colleen sounds passé. A parent in search of an Irish ethnic name would do better to investigate genuine Gaelic choices, such as Maeve or Maire.

COLOMBIA, COLUMBA. We grouped these two names together because of their similarly powerful sound, not their pedigrees. The first is, of course, a South American country and so qualifies as a hotter-than-hot place-name. Columba, on the other hand, was the name of several early saints, many of them male but one female, a Cornish noblewoman who refused to marry a prince.

COMFORT. One of the least-used Puritan virtue names, but easier to live up to than the more demanding Prudence or Chastity, Comfort is just beginning to be considered again by modern parents.

CONCHITA. A diminutive of **CONCEPCIÓN**—they're Spanish names used to honor the Blessed Virgin—this name has been brought before the public eye by actress Maria Conchita Alonso.

CONSTANCE. Used in full, this name has an icy and forbidding image, and so has not infrequently been given to the strong matriarchal figures in television show dynasties. Although it has been around for centuries, being an early Christian name that was adopted by the Puritans as a virtue name (sometimes in the form of **CONSTANT** or **CONSTANCY**), Constance and short form **CONNIE** hold little appeal for modern parents.

CONNOR. For several years, soap operas have been crawling with Connors, one of whom happens to be a female (on *As the World Turns*). Add in the trends toward surname names and fresh Irish choices and we expect to see playgrounds full of little girls named Connor (or **CONOR**) before long.

CONSUELO. This sophisticated Spanish name works well with Anglo surnames, and can often be found in international social columns. Meaning "to console or comfort," it was used by George Sand for the title character of a novel about a beautiful Venetian singer.

CORA. Cora, until recently a middle-aged-waitress-with-sensible-shoes kind of name, is undergoing a rejuvenation, becoming closer to Laura than Dora, as evidenced by the attractive Julianne Moore character in *Cookie's Fortune*. The name was probably invented by James Fenimore Cooper for the heroine of his novel *The Last of the Mohicans,* written in 1826, and has been quietly used ever since. In recent years, **CORETTA** has been associated with the widow of Dr. Martin Luther King. **CORALIE** is another possibility.

CORAL. Coral is one of the late nineteenth-century gem names that, together with Beryl, had much greater popularity in England than it ever has in this country. And it still doesn't have much luster for name-seeking American parents today.

CORDELIA. The name of King Lear's youngest and only loyal daughter is one with character as well as style, and is among the somewhat formal, grown-up-sounding names that are making a comeback as an antidote to all the fly-by-night inventions proliferating today. Cordelia has been promoted by the character on both *Buffy the Vampire Slayer* and its spin-off, *Angel,* played by an actress with the unusual name of **CHARISMA** Carpenter.

CORINNE, CORINNA. Both these names come from an ancient Greek female appellation meaning "daughter." In England, Robert Herrick made good use of Corinna in his famous 1648 poem "Corinna's Going A-Maying," Corinne is the French form, heard somewhat more often in this country, and worthy of consideration—Annette Bening and Warren Beatty chose it as their daughter Ella's middle name, while singers Amy Grant and Vince Gill called their daughter **CORRINA.**

CORNELIA. In ancient Rome, Cornelia was considered the paragon of womanly virtues, and, like Cordelia, it is a handsome name with an excellent pedigree. But it does have the downside of the possible nickname Corny.

COURTNEY. Courtney, like its sisters Morgan and Blair, is a fashionable, once-androgynous name that, a few years ago, seemed to have a thick upper crust. Now, its image, as well as its popularity, has begun a gradual descent, and it's barely hanging on in the Top 50, more associated today with adults like Courtney Love and **COURTENEY** Cox than with newborn infants.

CRESSIDA. Used far more often in Britain than the United States, this Greek name had a long evolution, moving from Briseida to Chryseida to Criseyde, and finally to the Shakespearean version, Cressida. Although the Trojan heroine of that name didn't have the greatest reputation—she was faithless to Troilus—the name today sounds fresh, crisp, and creative.

CRICKET. Cricket is one of the few names to appear on not one but two 1980s soap operas and *not* to have moved into the real world, probably because it's just too cutesy and chirpy.

CRIMSON. Scarlett may be inexorably tied to *Gone With the Wind*, but Crimson has fresh and colorful possibilities for a twenty-first-century child.

CRYSTAL. When the jewel-name fad took hold around 1900, Crystal, formerly a male name used in Scotland and the north of England, was one of its shining examples. After being quietly used for most of the century, it rose in popularity as a member of the *Dynasty* clan—although Mrs. Carrington opted for the nouveau **KRYSTLE** spelling—and reached the Top 10 in some states in the 1980s. It has now dropped precipitously, after being branded as tacky à la Tiffany, and being attached to working-class women on shows like *Roseanne*. Nowadays, its old turn-of-the-century companions like Pearl and Ruby seem a lot classier by comparison.

CYNTHIA. Cynthia, a classical name last popular in this country in the 1950s, seems to be making a bit of a comeback—at least in terms of movie characters if not babies—there have been Cynthias in the films *Magnolia*, *Secrets & Lies, Ed TV,* and *First Wives Club.* An alternate appellation for the Greek moon goddess Artemis, it was also given by plantation owners to slaves in the early nineteenth century. Its nickname, Cindy, endured for several years after the name itself faded. An appealing variation is the Italian **CINZIA** (CHIN-zi-a).

D

DACEY. An Irish name meaning "southern girl" that in this Macy/Lacey/Gracie era has real possibilities. Also, **DACY** or **DACIE**.

DAFFODIL. Although never as popular as Daisy, this bright yellow spring flower name was, believe or not, used to some extent around the turn of the last century. The big and most obvious drawback to its revival: the nickname Daffy.

DAGMAR, DAGNY. Dagmar is a royal Danish name (also used for males in that country) that possessed a sexpot image in the early days of TV. Much more distinctive, we think, is the similar Scandinavian name Dagny.

DAHLIA, DALYA. Dahlia is a flower name that is used occasionally in Britain (especially in P. G. Wodehouse novels) but seems a bit pretentious—its sound reminiscent of the affected dah-ling—for American tastes, although soap-opera fans will be familiar with Dahlia from its appearance on *The Guiding Light.* Its phonetic cousin, **DALYA,** is a Hebrew place and botanical name that might be easier for a modern girl to carry.

DAISY. Fresh and energetic, Daisy is one of the flower names bursting into full bloom again after a century's hibernation. Originally a nickname for Margaret (the flower was the symbol of Santa Margherita), Daisy comes from the phrase "day's eye," representing the sun. The name has had a colorful history, as the innocent Daisy Miller in the Henry James novel, as Daisy Buchanan, the hero's object of desire in *The Great Gatsby,* in the 1890s song "Bicycle Built for Two" ("Daisy, Daisy, give me your answer true . . ."), as the sexy barefoot blondes in *L' il Abner* and *The Dukes of Hazzard,* and, more recently, as the older Daisy in *Driving Miss* . . . as well as Julia Roberts's character in her breakthrough movie, *Mystic Pizza,* and the energetic Daisy on *All My Children*. MTV host Daisy Fuentes is a contemporary bearer, and both Markie Post and Lucy Lawless have chosen it for their daughters.

DAKOTA. As a girl's name, Dakota has been around a lot longer than most of the currently trendy Western place-names — it appears in several oaters of the 1930s and 1940s, and singer Dakota Staton has been cutting jazz records since the 1950s. Inspired by the two states which in turn were named for the Dakota branch of the Great Sioux nation, Dakota was picked up for both their sons and daughters by celebrities several years back, but now such notables have galloped on to less developed lands in search of names for their baby girls, a path other new parents might well follow.

DALE. Dale is one of the original ambisexual names, famous for both females Dale Evans (born Frances) and Dale Arden, sidekick of Flash Gordon, and male Dale Carnegie as far back as the 1930s. In baby naming, this counts as ancient history, which helps give Dale some measure of depth and a pleasing patina. As with so many of the ambisexual names that have survived over the years, Dale has become almost exclusively feminine. An interesting variation: the Dutch spelling, **DAEL.**

DALILA. A Swahili name, pronounced da-LEE-la, very different in feel and meaning from its near-homonym Delilah — this name means "gentle and tender."

DALLAS. Like Dakota, a cowgirl name with some history, Dallas was originally inspired by a locale in Scotland, not Texas, and has been used for both sexes since the nineteenth century. Unfortunately, it now sounds like a generic Sierra-type trendy name of the early 1990s.

DAMARA. This name of an ancient fertility goddess is associated with the month of May and might make a winning, unusual name for a springtime baby.

DAMARIS. In the New Testament, Damaris was a Christian woman known for her charitable work, and the name was a favorite among the Puritans. Long neglected, Damaris might be worthy of resurrection by parents in search of an unusual biblical name that still remains on the safe side of weird.

DAMITA. The middle name of singer Janet Jackson, this name that literally means "little noblewoman" possesses a petite, feminine charm.

DANA. Comedian Dana Carvey to the contrary, this once all-male name is now just about the opposite. Dana or Danu was a Celtic goddess who gave her name to the main group of otherworldly beings in Irish mythology, and in Scandinavian lore was the mother of the gods. The real name of Queen Latifah, this strong, independent name is now most associated with Agent Dana Scully of *The X-Files*.

DANAE. Another name with connections to Greek mythology, Danae was the mother of Perseus, a goddess of music and poetry who refused to requite the love of Apollo and to whom Zeus appeared in a shower of gold. Distinctive yet familiar sounding, it's a novel name worth considering.

DANICA. This Slavic name meaning "morning star" first came to the American public's attention via the young actress who played Winnie on *The Wonder Years,* Danica McKellar. A unique spin on the megapopular Danielle and Daniela. Another idea: **DANIQUE.**

DANIELLE, DANIELA. Danielle, the French feminine form of Daniel, was one of the hottest names of the 1970s and eighties, but has now, although it continues to be used by considerable numbers of parents, just about burned itself out. The Italian **DANIELA,** or **DANIELLA,** is a marginally more stylish option for those wanting to honor an ancestral Daniel or carrying an undying torch for the name, but it, too, has begun to seem shopworn, as has the nickname **DANI.** A fresher choice: the Scandinavian **DANIA.**

DAPHNE. When the creators of *Frasier* sought a recognizably British name for the character of Dad's live-in companion, what they came up with was Daphne, which to many Americans does seem quintessentially English. Its roots are classical—in Greek mythology Daphne was a nymph who was saved from an overamorous Apollo by having the gods transform her into a laurel tree. First used in this country as a slave name, as were many classical names, it does have the unfortunate nickname of **DAFFY.**

DARIA, DARA. These two pretty but somewhat undistinguished names do have a few interesting references in their backgrounds. Daria was a Greek woman who became an early Christian martyr, and Daria Morgendorffer is currently the smart and cynical, bespectacled star of her own animated MTV show. Dara, which means "compassionate" in Hebrew, was a male name in the Bible, and was also the Persian angel of rivers and rain. Both are used as female forms of Darius, Darryl, and Darren.

DARCY, DARBY. Darcy, also spelled **DARCI,** is an Irish surname (originally d'Arcy), now used as a delicate ballerinaish (Darci Kistler is a principal dancer of the New York City Ballet) female first name. Unfortunately, although graceful, it sounds neither Irish nor distinctive enough to pack any real power. Darby is a similar kind of name, used for both sexes (remember *Darby O' Gill and the Little People*?), worn by Julia Roberts in *The Pelican Brief.*

DARYL. Time was when parents wanted to honor a relative named Daryl, they'd feminize it à la Daria or Darla, but since the emergence of actress Daryl Hannah, the recognition has hit—why not opt for the original? Daryl and **DARREN** (and all spelling variations thereof) are now perfectly acceptable for girls. Such feminizations as **DARINA** seem dated by comparison.

DAVINA. This name sounds a lot more exotic and interesting than what it really is: a Scottish female form of David. Used by the British royals, it's not a bad choice if you want to honor an Uncle David, and a far sight better than **DAVIDA** or **DAVETTE.** The spelling **DIVINA** takes the name into a more celestial realm which could prove a burden if your child dares ever be less than divine, though some parents go all the way to **DAVINE** or even **DIVINE.**

DAWN. Dawn is a fairly recently coined name—it was first used in the late nineteenth century, but it didn't become superhot until about 1970, when optimistic parents responded to its suggestion of sunrise and a fresh new day. But it always had a bit of a goody-goody image, and with most modern parents seeking more substantial identities for their daughters, dawn has broken. For anyone still enchanted by Dawn's golden image, Aurora would make both a more classic and brighter choice, or, a little further afield, Zora (Arabic for "dawn") or Roxana (the same meaning in Persian).

DEANNA, DEANDRA. See **DIANA.**

DEBORAH. In the middle decades of the twentieth century, there were so many Debbies, Debbys, and Debras on the block that the beauty and meaning of the original name was all but lost. The fifth most popular girls' name in 1950 and still hanging on at number 13 in 1970, Deborah today doesn't even make the Top 100. But, in addition to having a lovely sound, and feeling fresher, at this point, than the classic but overused Sarah, Rachel, and Rebecca, Deborah has the further modern appeal of a particularly strong Old Testament heritage—Deborah was a poet, judge, and heroic prophet who first predicted that the Israelirtes would win their freedom from the tyrannical Canaanites, then led a successful revolt that helped accomplish it, celebrating the victory in a famous song of triumph. Because of this, parents in search of an Old Testament name with character may be the first to revive Deborah— that's Deborah, not **DEBRA** or that perennial cheerleader, **DEBBIE.** Parents with strong ties to Israel may want to consider the Hebrew version, **DEVORAH.**

DECEMBER, DECEMBRA. Word names, nature names, and what might be called time names are fashionable now, especially those that haven't been used much in the past. December, in other words, is much cooler than April or June.

DECIMA. In the days when huge families were common this name of the Roman goddess of childbirth would be reserved for child number ten. Nowadays it could be used for a girl born in October, the tenth month of the year. But don't settle on it until you think about its similarity to the word *decimate*—which the other kids in school inevitably would.

DEIRDRE. Unfortunately, this strong Celtic name often has the phrase "of the sorrows" appended to it, because of the tragic fate of the character in Irish legend, the most beautiful woman of her time, retold in the works of Yeats and Synge. It also tends to sound a little tired when compared with more recently imported authentic Gaelic names. While spelling and pronunciation variations abound—such as in the name of soap star **DEIDRE** Hall, Deirdre is the most Celtically correct.

DEJA. This name seemed to pop up almost out of nowhere to hop onto African-American popularity lists—it was, for example, the fifteenth most popular name for black girls born in Texas last year. The French word for "already," as in *déjà vu* (already seen), it made one of its first public appearances as the name of the character played by Tyra Banks in the 1995 film *Higher Learning*.

DELANEY. This is one of the hottest Irish-surname names of the moment, projecting buoyant enthusiasm and (because of the *lainie* sound embedded in it) a feminine feel as well. Country singer Martina McBride is the mother of a Delaney.

DELIA. A rich and appealing name with a Southern accent, Delia was an epithet for the Greek moon goddess Artemis, who was born on the small Aegean island of Delos. A favorite of the eighteenth-century pastoral poets—and much more substantial than most of those names, like Phyllis and Chloris—it is sometimes used as a nickname for Cordelia.

DELIGHT. Delight was the mythical daughter of Eros and Psyche, and in this era of word names it's certainly got a positive meaning. But we must warn you it can also sound like the name of a staff member at a professional escort service.

DELILAH. Although it has begun to be used more frequently, Delilah still has to battle with her biblical image as a seductive temptress, so that even a twenty-first-century bearer of the name will have to combat assumptions and jokes sparked by people's perceptions of it. Too bad, because Delilah is one of the most haunting female names in the Bible—sexy, yes, but also melodic and strong and somehow modern. If you love the name so much you find it irresistible, you can just hope that your little Delilah has the fortitude to withstand everyone asking her where Samson is, or hiding the scissors when she comes into the room. It was Whoopi Goldberg's character's name in *When Stella Got Her Groove Back,* and has been featured musically in songs performed by singers as diverse as Tom Jones, Chuck Berry, and Queen. Delilah Belle is the daughter of Lisa Rinna and Harry Hamlin. **LILAH** is an appealing nickname and **DELILA** a variant spelling.

DELLA. Della started out as a nickname for such names as Adela, but has been used on its own for personalities dating as far back as Perry Mason's secretary Della Street and singer-turned-TV-star Della Reese (born Deloreese Early), which is to say its current image is anything but youthful. On the other hand, since Bella has had a big revival, Della just might start to rejuvenate.

DELPHINE. A sleek French name with a couple of nature associations—to the dolphin, and to the delphinium, the bluebell-like flower—as well as to the Greek city of Delphi, this would definitely be a fresher alternative to the over-the-hill Danielle. The Spanish/Italian version is **DELFINA.**

DELTA. Sort of a semiplace-name—the mouth of a river—as well as the fourth letter of the Greek alphabet, the richly evocative Delta has strong ties to the South and has in recent years been associated with actress Delta Burke.

DELYTH. Here's a really unusual and distinctive Welsh choice for parents whose interest has been sparked by comparable names from that culture that have recently come to the fore—such as Gwyneth, Bryn, Bronwen, Branwen et al.

DEMETRIA, DEMI. In Greek mythology, this is the name of an earth-mother goddess of fertility and the harvest. In Hollywood it's the full name of Demi Moore. Demi is at the moment megapopular among the Dutch, standing at number 7 on the most popular girls' name list of Holland. **DEMETRA** is also occasionally used.

DENISE. Denise is one of the French names that became enormously popular in the United States in the 1950s and sixties, reaching number 15 on the pop charts. It is definitely out of the loop now, hardly ever given to babies. **DENI** is the short form chosen for his daughter by Woody Harrelson.

DESDEMONA. Because the beautiful and innocent wife of Othello came to such a tragic end, her name has been avoided for centuries.

DESIRÉE. Other baby namers may disagree, but to us Desirée is one of those over-the-top names that we feel would put undue pressure on a young girl. Its sexiness borders on the salacious, and giving it to a child would only invite a lifetime of unfortunate presumptions. Early Christians, on the contrary, often used it for a longed-for child—the object of their desire—and it was also famous as the name of Napoleon's great pre-Josephine love. The Pilgrims used the English form, **DESIRE,** which is more unusual but no less suggestive. If you find the idea of an ultrafeminine, blatantly attractive-sounding name appealing, consider some other options—from Angelica to Sabrina, even to Dominique—that move beyond sex to a softer sensuality and beauty. Trivia Tidbit: Desirée was Lucille Ball's middle name and the first name of her mother.

DESTINY. Surfacing a few years ago as a character on the *Baywatch* beach, this name was almost immediately picked up on by parents attracted to its karmic aura and rhythmic sound—to the point where it became the third most popular name for African-American girls born in South Carolina, and is now among the Top 25 girls' names nationwide. It has also inspired the use of such offbeat spellings as **DESTINI, DESTINEY,** and **DESTINEE.**

DESTRY. In the old movie classic *Destry Rides Again,* Destry was Jimmy Stewart's last name, but in today's almost-anything-goes naming climate, it was chosen as their daughter's first name by Kate Capshaw and Steven Spielberg, perhaps in tribute to Hollywood history. Unlike many new names imported from other worlds, though, we think this one is a winner.

DEVON. A name with several spellings, at this moment used more frequently for boys (in the more masculine, **DEVIN** version), Devon can also be thought of as one of the loveliest place-names in the atlas, evoking the beautiful county of dramatic seascapes and moors in southwest England. It has been used for a female character on the soap opera *All My Children.*

DEVI. The Hindu mother goddess whose many incarnations include both good and evil, this is a name with a cute sound and a powerful background.

DEXTER. When Diane Keaton named her daughter Dexter Dean, she took not one but two previously male names and carried them into the unisex column, perhaps contributing to the rising feeling that before long there won't be any names left that are completely safe for boys—now that George, Dylan, Elliot, and Spencer and many others have been seized by girls as well. In this particular case, though, there weren't very many boy Dexters on the horizon anyway, so there's no great loss.

DHARMA. Dharma, in the Hindu and Buddhist religions, takes in the basic principles of cosmic existence, a fitting name for the hippyish character on the sitcom *Dharma & Greg,* whose parents were probably big fans of the Jack Kerouac novel *Dharma Bums.*

DIAMOND. Not heard of since the 1890s—and it was quite rare even then—Diamond has recently sparkled back into favor, particularly among African-American families. This most sought after of jewels was the inspiration for parents of more than two thousand little Diamonds born in this country last year, reaching the black Top 10 in both Maryland and South Carolina.

DIANA, DIANE. The name Diana, attached as it was to the Princess of Wales, got more publicity, both good and sad, throughout the 1990s than almost any other girl's name, but its tie to a glamorous figure did not lead to baby name popularity. It is the Latin name for the Roman goddess associated with the moon and virginity, hunting, and the protectress of wild animals, represented in myth as both beautiful and chaste. This lovely classic, which means "divine," undoubtedly was an enormous influence on the trend toward preferring *a*-ending versions of names that might also end with an *e*. Where Diane and Joanne and Christine were once by far the favored forms (Diane was on Top 25 popularity lists from 1940 to 1960), today they're far surpassed by Diana, Joanna, and Christina. Spelling variants of Diana and Diane include **DYAN** (as in Cannon—born Samile), **DIAHANN** (Carroll, born Carol Diahann), **DEANNA** (Durbin—born Edna Mae), and **DEANNE**. Somewhat demeaning nicknames for all of the above: **DI, DEE,** and **DIDI/DEE DEE.**

DIANTHA. A melodious and unusual—but close enough to Diana not to seem weird—Greek name meaning "heavenly flower." In classical mythology, Diantha was the flower of the supreme god, Zeus.

DINAH. As the song says, "Dinah, is there anyone finer?" This is a really attractive, underused Old Testament name, which has probably been shunned because of a onetime slave-name stereotype, having appeared as such in *Uncle Tom's Cabin*. We hope that parents will finally feel free to use this vivid name for their contemporary girls. Besides its biblical roots— Dinah was the beautiful daughter of Leah and Jacob, the heroine of the best-selling novel *The Red Tent*—this name was also a favorite of the Puritans and appeared in novels by Laurence Sterne and George Eliot, as well as having been adopted by two great singers, Dinahs Shore (born Frances) and Washington (born Ruth). The related **DINA** was the name of the guardian angel of wisdom and the law, and is, along with **DENA,** a nickname for such unfortunate fossils as Bernardina.

DIONNE. Dionne, popularized by singer Dionne Warwick, is a Greek mythological name, stemming either from Dionysus, or **DIONE,** Zeus's consort and the mother of Aphrodite. It means "divine queen," and has led to a torrent of variations, including **DEONA, DEONNE, DIONA, DIONDRA, DIONDREA,** and **DEONIA.**

DIVA. The Zappa family boasts a Diva as well as a Dweezil and a Moon Unit. Need we say more?

DIXIE. A saucy showgirl wisecracking waitress kind of name, Dixie can also be considered a place-name, although it won't be found on any map, being a generic term for the whole American South (coming from the ten [*dix*]-dollar bills used in French-speaking New Orleans, which came to be called dixies). A modern incarnation is the Dixie on *All My Children*.

DOLLY. One of the least challenging names on the menu, Dolly has been around as a nickname since the sixteenth century, and one of them (who spelled it **DOLLEY**), Mrs. James Madison, was among our most famous first ladies. More recently, there was a namesake who became successful enough to build her own Dollywood. But we think Dolly is definitely too cutesy for a child born into this postfeminist age. So, it's not hello, Dolly, but goodbye.

DOLORES. A Spanish name related to the Virgin Mary (in Latin countries she is known as Santa Maria de los Dolores—the lady of sorrows), it developed at a time when Maria itself was considered too sacred to use. Although it has now lost much of its power, Dolores was once considered the height of sensuality, the name of the exotic Mexican-born movie star Dolores del Rio, and the mother name of seductive pet forms Lola and Lolita.

DOMINIQUE. The exotic Dominique had a surge of popularity, particularly with African-American parents, following the dramatic entrance of Diahann Carroll's powerhouse character Dominique Devereaux onto the set of *Dynasty* in the mid-eighties, but it has pretty much subsided in the wake of newer names like Deja and Destiny. Other, more stylish forms today include **DOMINICA** and **DOMENICA** and, as actor Andy Garcia used for his daughter, the no-longer-for-boys-only **DOMINIC** or **DOMINICK.** In Germany, **DOMINO** is accepted as a girl's name.

DONNA. Literally meaning "lady" in Italian, Donna was the perfect ladylike name of *The Donna Reed Show*—in the fifties and sixties. And there were plenty of namesakes: Donna was in the Top 10 in 1964. These days, we'd be more apt to associate it with the emancipated clothes of Donna Karan or with Madonna than as a prospective baby name. And speaking of fashion, **DONATELLA,** as in Versace, might make a more stylish update. Trivia tidbit: Disco singer Donna Summer was actually born with the name **LA DONNA.**

DORA. Starting as a pet form of Theodora, Dora emerged as a name on its own in Charles Dickens's *David Copperfield,* in which she was the pretty but impractical first child-wife of the hero. The name also suffered for years from the stigma inherent in the title of the long-running comic strip *Dumb Dora.* Today, Dora continues to lag behind the much more favored Laura and Nora and isn't likely to catch up any time soon. More modern sounding would be **DORIA** or, especially, the unisex **DORIAN.**

DORCAS. A classic name—both the Romans and Puritans favored it and Shakespeare used it as well—that's pretty much out-of-bounds today because of the unfortunate connotations of its two syllables.

DORIS. As heavy-footed as the name sounds to us now, Doris was considered the very paragon of grace when it was part of a group of *s*-ending names (Phyllis, Frances) fashionable in the 1920s, and it got another shot of life when it was attached to the perky Doris Day in the fifties. In classical mythology, Doris is the daughter of Oceanus, god of the sea, who gave birth to fifty beautiful golden-haired sea nymphs. No wonder the name sounds tired.

DOROTHY, DOROTHEA. In the 1930s Dorothy left Kansas and landed in Oz, by the eighties she had become a Golden Girl, living in Miami with roommates Blanche and Rose. The name did have a good run, though—it was the sixth most popular girl-baby name in America in 1900, third in 1925, and still in the Top 25 in 1940. From the Greek, meaning "gift of God," it has been used in Britain since the fifteenth century, and was so common that nickname Dolly led to the word *doll*. Today, it is the more flowing, romantic,

Victorian-sounding Dorothea—and its inverse, Theodora—that are being embraced. Dorothea has had a long literary tradition, including as the idealistic heroine of George Eliot's *Middlemarch,* Dorothea Brooke. The Hebrew version, **DORIT,** is popular in Israel. The revival of Dorothea is sure to breathe life into some old nicknames, such as **THEA, DORRIE, DORY,** and **DORO.** Forms of the name nearly certain to remain on the shelf: **DOT** and **DOTTY, DOREEN,** and especially **DODIE** and **DODO.**

DREE. This unique one-syllable name was added to the mix by Mariel Hemingway when she bestowed it on her daughter. For the rest of us, it could make a distinctive middle name.

DREW. This elegant, formerly male surname, a member of the Paige/Brooke/Blair sorority, was brought into the female camp by Drew Barrymore, who came to mass public recognition at the age of seven when she played Gertie in *E.T.* in 1982. Barrymore comes by the name legitimately—it's a surname that has been in her famous acting family for generations. And now it's been accepted enough to be a character on the daytime drama *The Guiding Light.*

DRUSILLA, DRUCILLA. This quaint and dainty New Testament and Roman clan name that was last widely used by the Puritans has been popping up on the TV screen lately, from characters on shows *Buffy the Vampire Slayer* and *The Young and the Restless.* The nickname **DRU** makes it sound more modern, being a homonym for the contemporary Drew. There was a Cornish saint **DRUSA.**

DUANA. Okay, her daddy's name is Duane and you've just got to name her Duana. That kind of thing went out with names like Roberta and Geraldine, but then again, Duana—pronounced but we hope never spelled DWAYN-a—is almost more attractive than its male progenitor.

DUFFY, DUFFIN. Irish surname names that pack a good bit of attitude and could prove attractive for a girl who had the spunk to live up to their promise.

DULCIE, DULCY. Though it sounds as if it might have been invented a few decades ago, Dulcie was actually a common female name at the time of the Roman Empire, as were more ornate versions, **DULCIA** and **DULCITA**. Dulcy was later found in the ante-bellum American South, particularly among African-Americans, and we think it is probably too lightweight to merit a revival.

DUSTIN, DYLAN. These are two names that are part of the trend toward appropriating boys' names for girls, rather than gussying them up with feminine frills. Both have been used by celebrities for their daughters, particularly Dylan, which was also chosen to be one of the new Charlie's Angels (Drew Barrymore), but our feeling is that these names are trying so hard to be cool that they really aren't.

E

EARTHA. An almost single-ownership property because of its long association with Eartha Kitt, this name with its obvious meaning dates back to the nineteenth century and thus sounds somewhat dated and dry when compared with some of the other, fresher, nature names parents have begun to use.

EAVEN. Pronounced EE-vahn, this is a popular—in Ireland anyway—Anglicization of the original Gaelic Aoibheann, which means "beautiful." Problems: In this country it would probably be mispronounced to rhyme with "heaven," and, correctly pronounced, it would be confused with Yvonne.

EASTER. This unusual, rarely heard holiday name, used for the character played by Jasmine Guy in the miniseries *Queen*, would make a novel choice for a springtime baby. The word/name originated when the seventh-century Anglo-Saxon scholar Bede took the name of a goddess whose feast was celebrated at the vernal equinox and applied it to the festival of the resurrection.

EBBA. This soft yet strong Scandinavian and German name—widely used in those countries—was the name of a seventh-century saint and is one that could be readily assimilated.

EBONY. Beginning in the 1970s, African-American parents were attracted to this name, that of a rare type of rich black wood, as well as of a popular magazine, as a symbol of racial pride. The name peaked in the late 1980s and early nineties, now having dropped off Top 10 lists, as parents consider more far-out species such as Mahogany.

ECHO. Although there was an old tune about Little Sir Echo, this would be a much more fitting name for a girl, especially since it was a female name in Greek mythology—a nymph whose unrequited love for Narcissus caused her to fade away until all that was left was the sound of her voice. Obviously, a name with a lot of reverberations.

EDDA. A name with an unstylish feel in our time, in a class with relatives like Hedda and Nedda, it comes from the Old Norse meaning "poetry," and is found in several cultures, including Scandinavian and Polish. It's also the name that was dropped by young Belgian-born Audrey Hepburn when she became an actress.

EDEN. A semiplace-name with obvious intimations of Paradise, Eden is one of several such locale names drawn from the Bible (such as Bethany and Sharon) by the Puritans in the seventeenth century and, in modern times and genres, has been a character on the soap opera *Santa Barbara*. The two long *es* make it sound especially serene.

EDITH. The name of two American First Ladies, Mrs. Theodore Roosevelt and Mrs. Woodrow Wilson, as well as that of the wife of William the Conqueror, Edith is one of the oldest surviving Anglo-Saxon names. Its image got a bit skewed via its association with the warm but ditzy Edith Bunker character, still seen in reruns of *All in the Family*, but at the same time has been somewhat rehabilitated with the revival of interest in the novels of Edith Wharton, and we can foresee some parents beginning to view it again as an attractive, if conservative, choice. **EDITA** is the Spanish version.

EDNA. Edna is one of those names that, until what seemed like a few minutes ago, felt so terminally dowdy that no one could imagine a parent choosing it for an innocent modern baby girl. But with the great upswing in names honoring family members, Edna—along with dozens of other similar choices ranging from Adeline to Ella to Zelda—might be pulled along in the slipstream. This would certainly follow the hundred-year rule, that names often come back into style after a century. Edna, which means "delicacy, tenderness," is a biblical name, and was enormously popular in this country in the late nineteenth century. It also relates to Eden, a name option for those who want to honor Great-aunt Edna but prefer something more contemporary sounding. Two literary bearers of the name are Edna St. Vincent Millay and Edna O'Brien, and to some—particularly in England and Australia—the name is identified with Dame Edna Everage, the outrageously campy character created by Barry Humphries.

EDWIGE. Although it sounds as though it would be related to the Edward/Edwin/Edwina family, this sophisticated, upswept-hairdo French name, pronounced ed-WEEGHE, is actually a cognate of the German Hedwig. But we like it anyway.

EDWINA. Edwina becomes a much more attractive name when pronounced like Edwin, rather than Edween. It then takes on a mauve-tinted Victorian charm, summoning up lacy shawls fastened with carved cameos. It had quite a different image in the cult Coen brothers' favorite, *Raising Arizona,* in which Holly Hunter played a police officer named Edwina who was usually called Ed. **EDUARDA** is a Latin cousin.

EGYPT. Ever since Little Egypt practically invented the striptease with the belly dance she did at the 1893 Chicago World's Columbian Exposition, this name has had a suggestive aura. Modern parents, even those who were fans of the soap-opera character on *Loving,* would probably prefer to use Cairo, the country's capital.

EILEEN. An Irish form of Helen that was among the Top 10 of 1925 and still remained stylish in the fifties, Eileen's star has fallen far, as has its twin, **AILEEN.** Eileen does seem, from this viewpoint, like a slim name at a time when modern parents quite reasonably want more texture, depth, and substance for their daughters.

EITHNE. This Gaelic name of a goddess, many legendary queens and nine saints is very popular among Irish parents and just beginning to be considered by adventurous American parents with Irish roots. Pronounced ETH-neh, it has been Anglicized as **ETHNA, ENA, ETNA,** and even Annie and is the given name of the haunting singer **ENYA. EMER** (pronounced like the word *ever*) and **ETAIN** (pronounced E-den) are two other Gaelic choices that are well used in the Emerald Isle, but might prove problematic for an ordinary American child.

ELAINE, ELENA, ELANA. Elaine has had quite a history, going from appearing as one of the shining heroines of the Arthurian legends, the princess who fell in love with Sir Lancelot and became the mother of Sir Galahad, to being the name of the most famous of New York's celebrity restaurants, to being the archetypal New York neurotic in *Seinfeld*. None of this has worked to shine up the image of this dated name, which had its most recent heyday in the World War II period. Nowadays, more stylish spins are **ELENA,** the Spanish form that's pronounced e-LAIN-a, the Italian **ELIANA,** the Hebrew **ELANA, ILANA,** and **ELIANA,** and the Irish **ELAN** (pronounced EE-lan). A common nickname for Elaine is **LAINIE,** now sometimes used on its own.

ELARA. In Greek myth, she gave birth to a giant fathered by Zeus. If you like Elana or Elena but fear they're too widely used in your neck of the woods, you might consider this distinctive alternative.

ELEANOR, ELLIE. Even though Eleanor was one of the first conservative, no-nonsense girls' names to be dusted off by the new generation of stylish parents—including Katie Couric (who used the streamlined **ELINOR** spelling) and Diane Lane—many people will still be surprised to hear that this solid classic is fashionable again. But its straightforward feminine image combined with its royal medieval origins (Eleanor of Aquitaine introduced the name to England in the twelfth century) is striking just the right note for parents in search of a girl's name that combines substance and style. Some may find further appeal in the Eleanor Roosevelt connection, others in Jane Austen's heroine **ELINOR** Dashwood, the sensible element of *Sense and Sensibility*. **NELL** is a nice old nickname for Eleanor (as in Nell Gwyn and Dickens's Little Nell); other appealing short forms that have become favorites on their own: **ELLIE** (heating up at the moment and very much an independent name in England, where it's in the Top 25), Ella, and Nora (see separate listings). The Italianate **ELEANORA** and **ELEONORA** make the name more feminine, thanks to their final *a*.

ELECTRA. Perhaps one reason this name isn't heard more frequently is the violence attached to it in Greek myth, which was modernized in the Eugene O'Neill play *Mourning Becomes Electra*. On the bright side, the name does mean "one who shines brilliantly." (as in electricity), and not everyone is up on their Greek mythology. In recent times, it was the name of the Julianne Moore character in the movie *Assassins,* and Isabella Rossellini chose the gentler Italian version, **ELETTRA,** for her daughter.

ELIOT. This is a boy's name that seems to be knocking at the girls' room door. Perhaps it's because of the feminine *ellie* first two syllables, perhaps it's because it's rarely used for male children these days, perhaps it's because singer Sting has already broken the barrier and used it for his daughter, perhaps it's the connection to writer George Eliot or the poet T. S.—or all of the above—but we will not be surprised to see more and more girls answering to the name.

ELISE. This French diminutive of Elisabeth, also spelled **ELYSE** (as it was for the mom on *Family Ties*), seems to be making a minicomeback. Calista Flockhart played an Elise on *The Guiding Light* in her pre-Ally days, and it was also the name of Goldie Hawn's character in *The First Wives Club*. **ELIESSE** is the middle name choice of Kim Basinger and Alec Baldwin for their daughter Ireland.

ELISSA. See **ALYSSA.**

ELIZA. One of the most independent of Elizabeth's short forms, Eliza was a highborn favorite of the eighteenth century, used by poets for the first Queen Elizabeth, that had slid way downscale by the era of *Pygmalion/My*

Fair Lady's Eliza Doolittle and has never quite recovered its upper-class image. It's a lot livelier than the original Elizabeth, though, and parents who would like to honor an Elizabethan ancestor, but want something with a bit more edge would do well to consider Eliza. **LIZA** is the less substantial short form; variation **ELISA** was used by Magic Johnson for his daughter.

ELIZABETH, ELISABETH. Elizabeth is a name that lies outside the boundaries of style, being, in many ways, the girls' name with the most of everything: the richest history, the broadest appeal, the greatest variety of offshoots and nicknames. Elizabeth entered the twenty-first century attached to the world's premier queen (and richest woman) as well as to its most enduring female movie star; Elizabeth is both an Old Testament figure and a Christian saint, and is currently among the dozen most popular names in America—which for some people is the one strike against it. But although more people are calling their Elizabeths by their full name than they have for centuries, there are literally dozens of nickname and variation choices for parents who would prefer to take that road. Elisabeth, for one, is the accepted version in many European cultures, that middle *s* serving to soften the name and set it apart. Eliza is an excellent option for parents who love Elizabeth but want a name that's less widespread. Other, more nouveau variations, however, from Elisa to Elise to Elissa to Alyssa, do not carry the same pedigree, nor do **LIZETTE, LIZBETH,** or **BETTINA.** Some exotic foreign variations to consider: the Hebrew **ELISHEBA,** the Italian **ELISABETTA.** Of the nicknames, **LIZZIE** and **LIZ,** having been prime yuppie names in the eighties, are now nearing baby-name retirement age, **BETTY, BETTE, BETSY,** and even **LISA** and **LIZA** are all dated, albeit to different eras, while **BESSIE** and **ELSIE** are stuck down on the farm. **BESS** and **LIBBY** are two more fashionable possibilities. The most trendy twist on Elizabeth is **ISABEL** or **ISABELLA,** the Spanish/Portuguese form.

ELKE. See **ALICE.**

ELLA. Ella is one of the fastest-rising names among the cognoscenti and the glitterati, those who are ready to move beyond Emily and Emma, finding it just right for today's little girls: serious yet soft, spirited but traditionally grounded. A British royal name, Ella rose to the Top 30 in England and Wales last year. Although sometimes used as a short form for Eleanor, Ella has been recorded for centuries as a name unto itself. High-profile parents who have chosen it for their daughters include Kelly Preston and John Travolta, Annette Bening and Warren Beatty, and Gary Sinise, and some parents today may want to use it to honor jazz great Ella Fitzgerald.

ELLEN, ELLE. Like Lisa and Sharon and Karen, Ellen is one of those names that belong to lots of today's moms but very few babies. An Old English form of Helen, the sensitive but clear-eyed Ellen has swung in and out of style for centuries, often alternating with the parent name. In Edith Wharton's *The Age of Innocence,* set at the end of the nineteenth century, one character wonders why another has not changed her "ugly" given name of Ellen to something prettier, like Elaine—a statement no one would make today, even though Ellen is not most parents' first choice. Some feasible foreign variations are **ELENA,** the well-used Italian and Spanish form, and **ELENI,** the Greek one. Model **ELLE** McPherson took a French pronoun and turned it into a usable name.

ELLERY. Probably the only Ellery known to most people didn't even exist— Ellery Queen was a made-up pseudonym for two mystery writers posing as a fictional male detective. Its resemblance to names like Hillary, however, make it a good bet to become an agreeable girl's name. **ELERI** is a name from Welsh legend whose equally intriguing variant is **TELERI.**

ELLISON. Many of the newly invented names gaining in popularity take several overall trends as well as fashionable names and roll them into one. Ellison combines Ellie and Elissa and Emerson and Allison, mixing a soft sound with a surname feel.

ELODIE. Pronounced to rhyme with Melody but sounding a lot more sophisticated, this is an attractive French name all but unknown in this country. Recommended for parents with exotic tastes and a very straightforward last name.

ELOISE. Eloise will forever be the imperious little six-year-old who roams the Plaza Hotel; the name also recalls Heloise of Household Hints fame. These are not the worst associations in the world for a name, but not the best either. **ELOISA** is an Italian alternative, adding some vintage charm.

ELSA, ELZA. Elsa is yet another name related to Elizabeth, this one a German derivative of Elisabeth. But although Elsa was the operatic bride in *Lohengrin* and the first to walk down the aisle to Wagner's famous wedding march, the name is too leonine and terminally Teutonic to have much of a shot at revival. The *z* in the Hebrew Elza gives that version a bit more zip.

ELSBETH, ELSPETH. Two easily confused names, Elsbeth and Elspeth have quite different roots. Elspeth is a Scottish pet form of Elizabeth that was used by Sir Walter Scott for several of his female characters, while Elsbeth has German roots. Since neither is often heard on these shores, they could make interesting, exotic choices. Indiana-born, South Africa-raised actress **EMBETH** Davidtz added another distantly related name to the pot when she traded in her given name of Gretta.

ELSIE. Elsie is a second-generation Scottish nickname for Elizabeth (via Elspeth), that was very popular in this country at the end of the nineteenth century, the heroine of many novels and poems. But then along came Elsie, the Borden cow, and that was the end of that.

ELVIRA. Before there was the campy, vampirish television Elvira, Mistress of the Dark, a few years back, the name had quite a different image, first as the long-suffering wife of Don Juan (what fun that must have been!), then as the romantic heroine of the movie *Elvira Madigan,* not to mention appearances in several operas, the ghost in Noël Coward's *Blithe Spirit,* and as Michelle Pfeiffer's breakthrough role in *Scarface.* In spite of this colorful background, however, Elvira, and cousins **ELMIRA** and **ELVINA,** all sound too old-ladyish for today's baby.

EMANUELLE. The French Emanuelle has a much sexier image than it deserves, thanks to the erotic heroine of the sensational film of several years back. Other, more respectable feminine forms of Emanuel are **EMANUELA** and **MANUELA**.

EMBER, EMBRY. Cooling an Amber? Then consider new name Ember, although it might prove a confusing choice. Embry, while less familiar, could be more user-friendly.

EMELINE, EMMELINE. Emeline is a very old name with a history distinct from both Emma and Emily. Introduced to Britain by the Normans in the eleventh century, it has spawned many variants over the years, including **EMMALINE, EMELYN,** and **EMALEEN,** which reflect the name's varied pronunciations—the last syllable spoken as *een, in,* or, most correctly, to rhyme with the word *line.* New Age guru Marianne Williamson used it as the middle name of her daughter India, and way back in 1980 it was the name of young Brooke Shield's innocent character in *The Blue Lagoon.*

EMERALD. The name of the precious deep green stone, which has been worn and treasured as far back as in ancient Egypt, comes from the Persian word for "green" and is supposed to open one's heart to wisdom and to love; it could make for an interesting, near unique name for a girl. And, if the name feels too weighty for a little girl, there's always that attractive nickname **EMMY** until she grows into it.

EMERSON. When actress Teri Hatcher chose this somewhat stern and masculine surname name for her daughter, she softened it with the middle name Rose, a combination we've seen several other parents adopt. Once again, it's a name that can be further relaxed with the nickname Emmy.

EMILY. Why is Emily now the number 1 girls' name across the country? Simple—it's because everyone loves Emily. Kids love it, mothers and fathers love it, teachers love it. It has dignity, daintiness, and drive, as well as a legacy of having been borne by such distinguished writers as Emily Brontë and Emily Dickinson, not to mention the Miss Manners of her day, Emily Post. Now, unfortunately, having reached such widespread use that it is heard almost every day in almost every playground and preschool,

Emily has nowhere to go but down, just as it did a century ago when it rose to popularity in the 1870s and then declined steeply after 1900. Because of this, parents are seeking alternatives, having already made Emma supertrendy as well. Now they are looking further afield for substitutes, to Amelia, the Italian **EMILIA,** the French form **EMILIE,** to Emeline and Ella. An undiscovered Gaelic version is **EIMILE,** which is pronounced—yes, Emily.

EMMA. As Emily's popularity has soared off the charts, many parents have turned to Emma as a less well used alternative, only to find its own star zooming skyward—it's already entered the national Top 20, and ranked as high as number 4 in the state of Maine. A very old royal name well used throughout the centuries, Emma has substance as well as style and a dulcet sound. Notable Emmas of the past—the Jane Austen heroine, for instance, or Flaubert's Madame Bovary or Lady Hamilton or socialist leader Emma Goldman or even Avenger Emma Peel—may have inspired some parents to turn from Emily to Emma, but if you want a name that sets your child far apart from the crowd, we're afraid you'll just have to keep looking. And varying it to **EMME,** the name of the popular plus-size model, is not going quite far enough.

ENID. Though we haven't seen a record of every name on every birth certificate filed in the United States, we'd be surprised if there was even a single baby girl born this year named Enid. And yet, hard as it is to believe, this Celtic goddess name was once thought of as a lovely and romantic appellation, for in Arthurian legend, the beautiful Enid was the personification of feminine nobility, and the greatest compliment you could pay a woman was to call her "a second Enid." Tastes do change.

EOS. The Greek goddess of the dawn, though it's easy to see why Aurora's name is more popular. Another similar Greek goddess name: **IO.**

ERICA. For thirty years, this name has been associated with the notorious soap-opera character Erica Kane Martin Brent Cudahy Courtlandt Montgomery Courtlandt Marrick Marrick played by Susan Lucci on *All My Chil-*

dren, endowing this female version of Eric with a power it might otherwise not have had. Used in Scandinavia since the early eighteenth century, where it is usually spelled **ERIKA**, it was in the Top 50 girls' list in this country in the 1970s and eighties. Nickname **RICKI**, however, is stuck back in the black-and-white era of *I Love Lucy*.

ERIN. Erin (originally **EIREANN**), the poetical name for Ireland, along with cousins like Shannon and Tara, were the successors to such earlier Irish-American favorites as Kathleen and Maureen, but now they, too, have moved aside to make room for the new wave of more authentic Irish names: girls' names like Maeve, Siobhan, and Grania, and androgynous surname choices such as Delaney and Kennedy. The real-life character and Julia Roberts's Oscar-nominated portrayal of Erin Brockovich did bring this name back into the spotlight, but not as a baby name. Parents in search of an Irish name should also be aware that Erin is not used as a name in Ireland at all.

ERNESTINE. If it hadn't already been dead—which is pretty much was— Lily Tomlin killed off Ernestine as a baby-name possibility when she created her eccentric, snorting telephone-operator character for the old television show, *Laugh-In*.

ESMÉ. The unique appeal of this distinctive name is as singular and enduring as that of the classic J. D. Salinger story "For Esmé, With Love and Squalor." Related to the French Aimée, which means "beloved," and to the concept of esteem, it was originally a male name exported from France to Scotland via a member of the royal family. Anthony Edwards, Meshach Taylor, and Samantha Morton have all chosen this winner for their daughters.

ESMERALDA. Esmeralda comes from the Spanish word for *emerald,* and as such was one of the jewel names that started being used in the 1880s. Victor Hugo gave his heroine in *The Hunchback of Notre Dame* the nickname La Esmeralda because she wore an amulet with an imitation emerald in it. The name is rarely used outside of Spanish-speaking families.

ESSENCE. A number of parents have started to use this word as a name, despite the fact that it's not to be found in any baby-naming books but this one. Some may be attracted to its meaning, the intrinsic, fundamental nature of a person or object, while other parents may relate it to the magazine for African-American women.

ESTELLE, ESTELLA. Estelle is a canasta-playing, muumuu-wearing matron of a certain age, definitely not a modern baby. Estella, on the other hand, which was introduced by Dickens in *Great Expectations,* and which means "star," has a lot more energy and charm, as well as an engaging short form, Stella.

ESTHER. One of the major female figures in the Old Testament, Esther, originally named **HADASSAH,** was the captured Jewish wife of the king of Persia (the name means "star" in Persian), who risked her life to save her exiled people from the plots of Haman to annihilate them. It is the story that Jews celebrate on the holiday of Purim, and thus Esther is a name that has traditionally been given to girls born around that time. In the Top 10 at the turn of the last century, it, along with Hester and Lester, has not been used much since the 1920s, but with parents now seeking more unusual, older biblical names with strong meanings and histories, Esther might conceivably be in for a revival. Judy Garland played two Esthers—in *Meet Me in St. Louis* and *A Star Is Born,* and Esther Greenwood is the autobiographical character's name in Sylvia Plath's *The Bell Jar.*

ETAIN. A beautiful woman in Irish mythology who married a high king, a lovely legacy for any child who gets this name.

ETHEL. Ethel sounds almost as dated these days as the old Anglo-Saxon names that hatched it—Ethelinda, Ethelreda, Ethelburga et al. Hard to believe that in the early years of the twentieth century, when Ethel Barrymore was the belle of Broadway, her first name was wildly popular. In the interim there have been the booming Ethel Merman, the prolific Ethel Kennedy, and Lucy's cohort, Ethel Mertz, the sound of whose name may have killed off Ethel forever.

EUDORA. Names beginning with the letters *Eu*—the "you" sound—were fashionable around the turn of the twentieth century, but for the most part now seem terminally dated. Eudora, however, which means "a good gift," and was in Greek mythology one of five goddesses who controlled the tides, is one of the more euphonious of the group. It also has something special to recommend it in namesake Southern writer Eudora Welty.

EUGENIA, EUGENIE. When Prince Andrew and Sarah, Duchess of York, christened their second daughter Eugenie in 1990, they rescued the name from the fate of being relegated to fashion limbo along with most of the other *Eu*-starting names, restoring a patina of royal sheen it hadn't had since the time of Napoleon III's glamorous empress. Both versions are rare enough in this country to make for truly distinctive choices.

EULALA, EULALIA. Saying these names aloud is almost like singing a song, they are that rhythmic and melodic. They come from the Greek, meaning "sweetly spoken," and have a definite Southern cadence. Oscar-winning actress Marcia Gay Harden named her baby girl Eulalia Grace. The short form **EULA** is sometimes used, but **LALIA** or **LALLY** would make more appealing and modern-sounding nicknames.

EUNICE. Eunice, the New Testament mother of Timothy, is most recognizable now as the name of one of the Kennedy sisters, the mother of Maria Shriver, who used it as the middle name for her and Arnold Schwarzenegger's oldest daughter. Eunice's image was not helped by its association with Carol Burnett's unlovable character on *Mama's Family*. The original Greek pronunciation was with three syllables: you-NICE-ee.

EUSTACIA. Another Greek name, this one meaning "fruitful," Eustacia is more noteworthy now as the name from which the (now dated) nickname Stacy derived than as the passionate Eustacia Vye in Thomas Hardy's *The Return of the Native*.

EVAN. This once strictly male name—the very common (in Wales anyway) Welsh form of John—has long seen sporadic use for girls and does have a pleasantly soft, androgynous sound.

EVANGELINE. Evangeline combines an exotic femininity with an offbeat quality that conjures up a poetic image of a young beauty with flowing, waist-length hair. The name, which means "bearer of good news" in Latin, was introduced to the English-speaking world by Longfellow in his eponymous 1847 poem, and can also be found in *Uncle Tom's Cabin* (it was Little Eva's full name) as well as in two novels by Evelyn Waugh. Evangeline would be a delightful name for a fashionable little girl, who can either conform to its image or successfully play against it. John Goodman used it as the middle name for his daughter Molly.

EVE, EVA. Not for nothing does a name manage to survive from the beginning of time. Eve's appeal is its simple elegance, its synthesis of sensuality and innocence. The name was popular even before the Reformation (when Old Testament names were rarely used) because of a belief that girls named Eve would have long lives. The form Eva was heard less often until the 1852 publication of *Uncle Tom's Cabin,* the best-selling novel of the nineteenth century, whose tragic figure, called Little Eva, made a huge impression on the Victorian reading public. Nowadays, neither version is particularly prevalent, although both Susan Sarandon and Harry Anderson have picked up on Eva, and Bono on Eve, for their daughters. Eve may have had some bad moments in the films *All About Eve* and *Three Faces of Eve,* but we still think this form is particularly appealing, as either a first or middle name. Beware, however, of **EVITA**, as in Perón, dominatrix of Argentina.

EVELYN. A name so soft it has simply faded away, Evelyn was in the Top 50 in this country from 1900 to 1925. A form of the Irish **EIBHIN,** it moved from **AVELINE** to **EVELINE** to Evelyn, and its most famous bearer was a male writer, Evelyn (with a long *e*) Waugh. Another similar-sounding old Irish name is **EVLIN (EIBLEANN),** which means "radiance" and originally was the name of a sun goddess. Variations **EVELINA** and **EVELENA** add a more rhythmic, feminissima appeal.

EVER, EMER. The Irish Emer is pronounced as "ever"—a good sound, somehow, for a name. And you can stop pretending it's a name and just spell it Ever, as does the young actress Ever Carradine of the theatrical family.

EXPERIENCE. The Puritans often used word names, usually ones that connoted such virtues as prudence and patience, but this more unusual choice was spotted on a woman's headstone in an old New England graveyard. We may not want to name our children Adulterina, Dust, or Helpless, other genuine Puritan choices, but we might consider the following from that culture and time: **ACCEPTANCE, ASSURANCE, CONSIDER, EARTH, LIVELY, PLEASANT, TEMPERANCE,** or maybe even **SAVAGE.**

F

FABIA, FABIOLA. Although we very occasionally hear the male name Fabian (remember the 1960s teenage singing idol?), there is scarcely any use in this country of the several pleasant foreign-accented female versions. For example, the Italian **FABIOLA** was the name of a fourth-century Roman saint who established one of the first hospices. Fabia is another Italian variation, and **FABIENNE** is the translation with French flair.

FAITH. Faith is no longer the quiet, subdued, proper name it once was, as evidenced by the fact that over the past few years, the following leading actresses have embodied characters named Faith: Michelle Pfeiffer, Marisa Tomei, Helena Bonham Carter, Cybill Shepherd, Diane Keaton, and Juliette Lewis, and there have also been Faiths on two soap operas, and on *Felicity* and *Buffy the Vampire Slayer,* as well being represented by the singer Faith Hill. Several of the Puritan virtue names have quite suddenly come back into fashion, and Grace, Hope, and Faith are definitely in the vanguard. Choosing the latter expresses a certain confidence that you'll be a good parent and your child will turn out well—if you don't have that kind of faith, better opt for Hope. One caveat: Parents we know of a girl named Faith say people often ask if the name symbolizes their religious zeal, so if you're less than zealous, think twice.

FALLON. This was one of several forward-looking boyish last-name names to have been spawned by *Dynasty* (a hotbed of creative character naming), back in the late eighties. Despite its somewhat tacky origins, we find this English version of the original Irish O'Fallamhaen, to be an attractive Gaelic surname choice, much better suited to a girl than a boy.

FANNY. Ever since this word/name started to be applied to a part of the human anatomy in the nineteenth century, it has been problematic as a baby name. A pity, because it is just the kind of old-fashioned nickname name, like Josie and Winnie, that parents are beginning to find appealing again. So, as quaint and charming a name as Fanny may be, and as colorful as its literary heritage is (appearing in such novels as *Fanny Hill, Little Dorrit, Dombey and Son, Sense and Sensibility, Mansfield Park,* and even Erica Jong's *Fanny*), we would have serious qualms about any modern Fanny's early years at school—and even more about her later years at school.

FARRAH. For a few seconds there in the late seventies, Farrah Fawcett's name was as frequently copied as her hairdo. Both are now equally passé. The name does have some legitimacy though—it means "happiness" in Arabic.

FATIMA. An Arabic name, Fatima was Muhammad's favorite daughter and one of the four perfect women in the world. The name's problem if used in an English-speaking culture: possible nicknames referring to fat.

FAWN, FAUNA. As retrograde as Bambi, Fawn had its moment of infamy via Oliver North's loyal secretary-shredder, Fawn Hall, a few years back. And, like other such names as Tawny and Taffy, it does not, in our opinion, give a girl enough to live up to. The similar-sounding Fauna, besides being the Latin blanket term for the animal kingdom, was the name of one of the three fairies—Flora, Fauna, and Merryweather—who protected Disney's Sleeping Beauty.

FAY, FAYE. Beginning as a shortened form of Faith, but also related to an archaic French word for *fairy,* Fay was used on its own starting in the 1890s. Although it now sounds more dated than Faith, some celebrities have begun to use it as their daughters' middle name, and it was the name of Liv Tyler's character (spelled the Faye Dunaway way) in *That Thing You Do.*

FEDORA, FEODORA. These two Slavic spins on the name Theodora are occasionally heard among the British Mayfair and Belgravia set, but almost never in this country. Fedora has the problem of possible confusion with a kind of hat; Feodora (the first syllable is pronounced *fay*) would make a more appealing choice for the intrepid name giver, especially with its dynamic nickname, **FEO.**

FELICITY. The hit television show has done a lot to soften and modernize the once somewhat buttoned-up and forbidding image of Felicity. In addition, particularly among six- to thirteen-year-old girls and their parents, it's gained considerable attention as the name of the red-haired Colonial doll in the American Girl series, not to mention the fact that it was also the name of Heather Graham's bodacious character in *Austin Powers: The Spy Who Shagged Me,* and has appeared on at least three soap operas. In the distant past, the more usual form of the name was **FELICE** or **FELICIA**— Felicity has surpassed those versions in popularity only in the past hundred years. There was also a saint **FELICITA,** a nice spin on the name. All are versions of Felix, have been around since Roman times, and connote good luck and happiness; in fact, the Roman **FELICITAS** was the goddess of good fortune. Other girls' names that mean luck: **FAUSTINA, FORTUNA,** and **FORTUNE.**

FENELLA. See **FIONNUALA.**

FERN. Fern is a name with a terminally barefoot, backwoodsy, feel. Among the botanicals, it's never really moved from the front parlor into the nursery. Its most appealing reference is to the young human heroine of E. B. White's classic story of a pig and a spider, *Charlotte's Web.*

FIFI. Actually a pet name for Josephine, Fifi would be best left for your French poodle.

FINN. The greatest, most enduringly popular hero of Irish mythology was called Finn MacCool, and his name is, indeed, one of the coolest ever. It was used for the female protagonist of the novel *How to Make an American Quilt,* played in the film by Winona Ryder, which established the fact that it's as hip for a girl as for a boy.

FIONA. Since the opening of *Brigadoon* in 1954, Fiona has been the best known of a group of related Gaelic names, which is ironic because it's the only one without genuine traditional roots—it was invented in the late nineteenth century as a feminine pseudonym for a Scottish male writer. Today, Fiona is well used in England, Scotland, Australia, and even Ireland, and is found here occasionally, as in the case of singer Fiona Apple. It is also Julia Roberts's middle name. If you want to really call attention to your child, you could use the Welsh spelling, **FFIONA.**

FIONNUALA. Pronounced finn-OO-la, this lovely Irish name might prove too much of a challenge to the American child in its authentic spelling. There are several options to get around this, such as using its nickname, **NUALA** (NOO-la), or one of the more phonetic versions, **FINULA, FINOLA, FINELLA,** or **FENELLA,** the last two of which are Scottish. **NOLA, NELLA,** and **NELL** are all possible nickname names.

FLANNERY. Long before the vogue for using Irish surnames for girls was in full swing, writer Flannery O'Connor gave this name some credence and visibility. It also has a warm (flannelly) feel and the currently popular, rhythmic, three-syllable *ee*-sound ending. Short form **FLANN** is sometimes used on its own—it has been the name of well-known Irish poets, scholars, saints, queens, and kings—as well as a custard dessert. **FLANNA** is one of the many Irish names that means "red-haired."

FLAVIA. This ancient Roman clan name, heard again in the seventeenth-century poetry of John Donne, means "golden yellow," indicating that its original bearer was probably a blonde. Virtually unused in this country, Flavia might appeal to parents seeking a unique but historic name.

FLEUR. The French Fleur, which emigrated into the English-speaking world when John Galsworthy bestowed it on one of the Forsytes in his celebrated saga, sounds a bit precious and snobby in this country, although it is megapopular in Europe—it's in the Top 20 in Holland, home of the tulip and other fleurs. As for the literal translation, **FLOWER,** just bear in mind that it was the name of the little skunk in *Bambi*. Better to pick a single bloom from the bouquet, such as Violet or Lily or Daisy.

FLORA. Flora is one of the gently old-fashioned names that, along with other more specific botanical favorites, is due for a comeback. The Roman goddess of flowers, gardens, and spring, who enjoyed perpetual youth, Flora was the name of a saint and has long been a favorite in Scotland, especially in the MacDonald clan, because of the young heroine of that name who helped Bonnie Prince Charlie make his escape to France. **FLORIA** is a long-dormant variation with possibilities, as are the Italian **FIORELLA** and **FIORA.**

FLORENCE. Florence is a quintessential place-name (Florence Nightingale was named for the Italian city of her birth), and could get some new life from the current boom in geographical names. Even if you haven't heard it on your block yet, take it from us—it's already a very stylish name in London. Florence began life as a male name and was used for both sexes in the Middle Ages. Two nicknames à la the Bobbsey Twins: **FLORRIE** and **FLOSSIE. FLO** got a touch of verve from the late great Olympian Florence Joiner, but no parent today would take it seriously as a modern nickname. Some European versions: **FLORENCIA, FLORENZA,** and **FLORENZ.**

FLORIDA. Florida was one of the first place-names to be heard on television, in the character of Florida Evans on *Good Times,* the compassionate African-American mother who had formerly worked as a maid for Maude. The state was given its name by explorer Juan Ponce de León, who was impressed by its profusion of flora. Still, this name does not have the cachet of some of the more Southwestern and international examples.

FLYNN. Flynn, like Flann and Finn, is an Irish surname beginning to be used for girls as well as boys. It is associated with the color red and could make an appropriate first or middle name for a little redhead.

FRANCES. This was a name that was perceived as far too faded until a few years ago when it began to be chosen by such superhip parents as Courtney Love and Sean Penn as first (Love) and middle (Penn) names for their daughters, Love and the late Kurt Cobain having been inspired by the doomed 1940s star Frances Farmer. With that kind of promotion, Frances has leaped the heights of high fashion in a single bound. This spelling has become standard for girls, although until the seventeenth century, both men and women shared the Francis version, now reserved for males. Pretty in its full form, Frances (the real name of both Dinah Shore and Dale Evans) becomes more down-to-earth with nicknames **FRAN** and **FRANNY, FRANCIE** and **FRANKIE** (the last used as his daughter's full first name by rocker Nikki Sixx), and even earthier with Fanny (see above). Some attractive foreign versions include **FRANÇOISE, FRANCE** (place-name plus!), **FRANCA,** and **FANIA. FRANCINE,** however, is both dated and déclassé.

FRANCESCA. The increasingly popular Francesca, which is the Latin version of Frances, is a lot more feminine and light than the English classic. It made an appearance in Dante's *Inferno,* and then, centuries later, in the best-selling novel *The Bridges of Madison County,* whose Italian-born heroine was played in the movie by Meryl Streep. Clint Eastwood, director Martin Scorsese, and actor Erik Estrada all have daughters named Francesca.

FREDERICA. Frederica is an interesting possibility for the parent not intimidated by such a formal, old-time appellation. It's got some vintage charm and verve lurking within its stuffiness. The name emerged in eighteenth-century Prussia when supporters of King Frederick the Great began to name their daughters in his honor, and is currently represented by opera star Frederica von Stade. **FREDDIE** or **FREDDI** are perhaps a tad too Ricki/Ronni for today's parent, but a perversely cute nickname would be the boyish **FRED.**

FREESIA. A really exotic flower name for the parent who wants to move beyond Rose and Daisy. The flower itself is a member of the iris family and has particularly fragrant blossoms—and the syllable *free* adds a nicely liberated element to the name.

FRIEDA, FREDA, FRAYDA. The Germanic Frieda holds little appeal for the modern baby namer, though many admire painter and potential namesake **FRIDA** Kahlo. Freda, pronounced as Fred with an *a,* is sometimes heard in England, but among an older generation. Frayda is a Yiddish name meaning "joy."

FREYA. Freya was the Norse goddess of love, beauty, and fertility, considered the most beautiful of the goddesses, but unfortunately her name, which sounds similar to *fryer,* as in chicken, is not very sonorous to the modern American ear. The Swedish version is spelled **FREJA.**

G

GABRIELLE, GABRIELLA. As Danielle has begun its slide down the popularity charts, Gabrielle has jumped in to take its place, in a quieter, less trendy-feeling way than Isabelle. Gabrielle is one of the quintessentially graceful and worldly French names—it was the given name of designer "Coco" Chanel—and is totally accessible to parents here. Its Italian sister Gabriella, also spelled with one *l* (as on the soap opera *Port Charles* and softened and enlivened by the *a* ending, is borne by the Argentinian tennis star Gabriela Sabatini and is rivaling its French sister in popularity. Short form **GABY** presents a different, chattier, image; the version you would hear in Israel is **GAVRIELLA,** often abridged to **GAVI.**

GAIA, GAEA. When actress Emma Thompson named her daughter Gaia (after jokingly referring to her as jane.com while she searched for a name), she stated in an interview that she was attracted by its ecological element. And, indeed, in Greek mythology, Gaia was the earth goddess, the universal mother, one of the most important divinities. It's pronounced GUY-a and sometimes spelled Gaea.

GAIL. Now that Abigail had made a major comeback in its full form, with Abby as its designated nickname, Gail, which sounded really spiffy fifty years ago, is off the radar screen. Ditto for alternate spellings **GALE, GAEL,** and **GAYLE.**

GALATEA. If you want a name you're absolutely sure will be your child's alone, instead of doing something like spelling Blake as Blaque, why not consider a name like this that has some history but is still completely ignored? Pronounced gal-a-TAY-a, it was, in Greek mythology, the name of an ivory statue of a beautiful maiden that Aphrodite brought to life to answer the prayers of the sculptor Pygmalion, who had fallen in love with his own creation. The *gala* part means "milk" or "ivory," which probably referred to the color of the material used.

GARNET. A neglected gem name with a strong, almost masculine sound that makes it feel right for today. A good choice for a redhead or a child born in January, which has garnet as its birthstone.

GAY. Gay, along with kindred names such as Joy and Merry, not only puts unreasonable pressure on a child to appear happy at all times, but has the added burden of the slang meaning of the word. Less problematic alternatives would be **GALEN,** a onetime character on *All My Children,* or **GALIA,** a Hebrew name, also spelled **GALYA,** that is well used in Israel and seems eminently adaptable to American life.

GELSEY. Thanks to ballet superstar Gelsey Kirkland, this name has taken on a lithe and graceful image. Parents who are finding too many little Kelseys or Chelseas in their neighborhood might want to consider this instead. The *G,* by the way, is soft, as in *gelatin.*

GEMMA. This jewel of a name has had great acceptance in England, especially favored by the upper echelons of society in that class-conscious country, but in the United States it's hardly heard at all, except occasionally in Italian-American families. Stemming from a medieval Italian nickname for a precious jewel, it was used by Dante, and was borne by a nineteenth-century saint. Spelled either Gemma or **JEMMA,** we think it could make a classy and stylish choice.

GENESEE. Genesee is an Iroquois word meaning "beautiful valley," which gave its name to a river running from Pennsylvania across western New York. Its soft, flowing sound could translate into a winning girls' name, as opposed to the more artificial-sounding Tennessee, for example.

GENESIS. This name, which of course means "beginning" or "origin" and is the first book in the Old Testament, has begun to be used in significant numbers (there were more than 1,600 baby girls given it last year), particularly in African-American and Latino families. It is currently the number 2 girls' name in Puerto Rico.

GENEVA. Unlike the somewhat cold and formal Swiss city it represents, Geneva is a lively and appealing place-name with an historical foundation. It's begun to surface more frequently on this continent—it was even heard on a couple of sitcoms in the nineties. Trivia tidbit: Geneva was First Lady Mamie Eisenhower's middle name. **GENEVRA** and **GINEVRA** are Italian variations.

GENEVIEVE. A name that might be of Celtic, Germanic, or French origin, Genevieve also leads a double life in its pronunciation—it may be either GEN-uh-veev or JHON-vee-ev. This is a perfect choice for anyone who wants to retain the *gen/jen* sound but is tired of Jennifer, Jenny, and Jenna; it's both dainty and substantial, with the faint whiff of dried roses clinging to it. Saint Genevieve is the patron of Paris, credited with saving her city from Attila the Hun through her rational thinking, courage, and prayer. **GEN-OVEVA** is the melodic Spanish version, **GINETTE** and **GINETTA** French pet forms.

GENOA. One of the newest geographical sites on the board, this one has the advantage of sounding like a real name because of its *jen* opening and feminine *a* ending. Since Genoa is a seaport in northern Italy—the home-town of Christopher Columbus—you could go all the way by using the authentic Italian **GENOVA.**

GEORGIA. Georgia is a name so rich, so lush, so luscious, we wonder how anyone could fail to fall in love with it. After a few decades of languishing, this peach of a name has now begun to scale the heights of fashion (it's the eleventh most popular name on the British list), having been selected by such luminaries as Mick Jagger and Jerry Hall and Harry Connick Jr., and having had major roles on such TV shows as *Ally McBeal* and *As the World Turns*. Other attributes: being attached to one of America's most renowned female artists, Georgia O'Keeffe, being one of the original place-names, and being among the once-quaint feminizations—like Josephine, Char-lotte, and Claudia—that have begun to sound fresh and fashionable again.

But most of all, it's a beautiful name, redolent with sweet-scented Southern charm. On the other hand, beware **GEORGETTE,** at one time associated with the vacant wife of Ted Baxter on the old Mary Tyler Moore comedy—it's several degrees downscale. **GEORGE** itself has begun to be used as a female middle name by such celebs as Greta Scacci and Vincent D'Onofrio, and Kate Capshew and Steven Spielberg.

GEORGINA, GEORGIANA. While Georgia is being heard more and more frequently in this country, its more sophisticated cousins, Georgina and Georgiana, have yet to cross the Atlantic in large numbers. Both the Scottish Georgina (which still bears echoes of *Upstairs, Downstairs*) and the even more patrician Georgiana (Georgiana, Duchess of Devonshire was a famed beauty and ancestor of Princess Diana and the name was also favored by Dickens and Jane Austen) have been ultrapopular in England for the past few decades, and earn our enthusiastic stamp of approval.

GERALDINE. Geraldine is one feminized male name that does not seem ready for a revival. Why? Maybe it's because Gerald itself, as well as the ambisexual nickname. **GERRY/JERRY,** all feel terminally dated, while other male stalwart—Joseph and Charles and Julian—are coming back into fashion in tandem with their female forms. It was invented in the time of Henry VIII by a noble poet who fell in love with a Lady Elizabeth Fitzgerald and, taking off from her surname, referred to her as the "Fair Geraldine." It had its fifteen minutes of fame in this country in the early seventies as Flip Wilson's sassy female alter ego, and more seriously, as the name of the first woman to be a major party vice presidential candidate, Geraldine Ferraro.

GERMAINE. In the early days of feminism, this name was chain-linked to one of its prime theoreticians, Germaine Greer, but now that feminism has softened, so has its ties to this name. A French name, it might nevertheless be dismissed by some because of its apparent connection to the word "German."

GERTRUDE. Gertrude is a very old name that was at the pinnacle of fashion from the 1860s to around 1900 but feels as heavy as lead today. It's tempting to dismiss Gertrude as a name on its way through the door marked OUT FOREVER, except that its long and honorable pedigree—as a goddess in Norse mythology, as a saint's name (the gentle and mystical Saint Gertrude the Great), and in its use by Shakespeare for Hamlets's (not exactly exemplary) mother—earns it a place on the permanent roster. And who knows? Our own parents considered names like Abigail and Sophie and Sam and Jake too dowdy and old-fashioned ever to be used again, and look at them now. And we must admit, the nickname **GERTIE** did sound kind of cute when worn by the young and innocent Drew Barrymore in *E. T.* **GERDA**, an unrelated Norse name that is nevertheless sometimes used as a short form of Gertrude, takes its sole charm from the young heroine of Hans Christian Andersen's "The Snow Queen." Another shortened form of Gertrude is the now dated **TRUDY.**

GIGI. Gigi, like Mimi and Bebe and Coco and Fifi, has a lot of high-kicking Gallic spunk but very little substance. In the eponymous novel by Colette, later made into an exuberant film, it is explained that Gigi is short for **GILBERTE.**

GILA. Gila and its many variants all have meanings that convey joy in Hebrew. Only problem: Other kids might connect it to the monster. Alternatives include **GEELA, GILANA, GILAT, GILIA, GILADA,** and **GILL.**

GILDA. Gilda, although related to the words *gold* and *gilded,* has definitely tarnished. It once shimmered with the seductive image of Rita Hayworth in the torrid film *Gilda,* then was associated with the beloved *Saturday Night Live* star Gilda Radner. In opera it lives on as the name of the daughter of Rigoletto.

GILLIAN. In medieval England, the name Gillian was so common that it was used as a generic name for a girl, just as Jack was for a boy, hence the nursery rhyme Jack and J(G)ill, and the expression "Every Jack had his Jill." It remained in common usage in Great Britain, but until recently had not crossed the Atlantic in significant numbers except in its short form. Now, however, with the popularity of Gillian (*The X Files*) Anderson and such starbabies as the daughters of Patty Hearst and Vanessa Williams (who used the alternate, more phonetic **JILLIAN** spelling), that definitely seems to be changing, with Gillian becoming an attractive and accessible option. Variations include **GILIANA, GILLIE,** and **JILLY**—and **GILLIA,** the name of a James Joyce character.

GINA. Originally an abbreviation for such names as Georgina and Regina, Gina has been used on its own since the 1920s. The sexy Italian actress Gina (born Luigina) Lollobrigida popularized the name in this country in the 1950s, and Oscar-winner **GEENA** Davis updated it with a new spelling. But as a nickname name, Gina has never quite grown up and seems, somehow, like only part of a name. The unrelated Hebrew name Gina, while identical in spelling and pronunciation, means "garden" and would be a good name for bridging cultures and ethnic backgrounds.

GIOVANNA. Giovanna is, like Leonardo and Lorenzo, one of the Italian names that fashionable American parents, and not just those with Italian backgrounds, have started to choose for their daughters. The Italian equivalent of Jane, it was used by Vanna White for her daughter, perhaps because of the tie to her own name.

GISELLE. This French form of the German **GISELA** (hard *G*) has a fluid, graceful aspect both through its association with the ballet (pronounced jiz-ELLE) and similarity to the word *"gazelle."*

GLADYS. Hard as it is to believe, Gladys was the Brianna of 1900, emerging from nowhere to take the naming world by storm, becoming a favorite among parents—and writers of romantic novels—for several decades. A Welsh form of Claudia, Gladys was seen, in its heyday, as exotic and romantic. Today, it's so far out we wonder if even a single child has been given the name in the past decade.

GLENDA, GLYNIS. Glenda and Glynis, as well as **GLENYS** and **GLENNA,** all derive from the same Welsh root and seem rooted, themselves, in the 1930s and forties. A few British actresses, including Glenda Jackson and South African–born Glynis Johns, have transported their names across the

Atlantic, though American children will undoubtedly be more familiar with the similar but different Good Witch **GLINDA** from *The Wizard of Oz*. As a group, all these names seem outmoded for the modern American baby, though **GLENN,** the related male name, has some feminine force via actress Glenn Close.

GLORIA. Playwright George Bernard Shaw was the first to use this form of the ancient Latin name **GLORIANA** in his play *You Never Can Tell*. From the time of Shaw's invention in 1898 through the first half of the twentieth century (it was number 6 in 1928), Gloria was seen as a modish, almost exotic name. Now, however, it feels dated and lackluster, except maybe if you're watching a Gloria Estefan video. **GLORY** is one of those high-pressure names that seems overly challenging.

GODIVA. This name evokes two distinct images: the legendary female who rode through town naked on a white horse and the luxury brand of chocolate—neither of which we imagine you'd want attached to your little girl.

GOLDA, GOLDIE. Despite the fact that these names reflect the glow of one of the world's most precious metals, they don't hold much luster for the modern name seeker. Used primarily in Jewish families, Golda is associated with American-raised onetime Israeli Premier Golda Meir (born Goldie), and Goldie with actress Hawn.

GRACE. *Grace Under Fire, Will & Grace,* daughter Grace on *Once and Again*—Grace has recently become one of the hottest names on TV, on the big screen (Ashley Judd, Heather Locklear, Jennifer Lopez, Julia Roberts, and Liv Tyler have all played Graces in recent films), and also in the nursery. Wynonna Judd and Lou Diamond Phillips have little Graces, while Faith Hill and Danny DeVito and Rhea Perlman call their daughters **GRACIE.** Why Grace? Because it's one of the simplest, purest, and most luminous of names, recalling the cool elegance of Grace Kelly. It existed as **GRACIA** in the Middle Ages but was not in common use until the Puritans adopted it, along with other Christian-attribute names, in the sixteenth century. Embraced for its virtuous image by Americans of the Victorian era, it was the eleventh most popular name in this country in 1875 and now, well over a century later, is beginning to make its way up the popularity lists again—it's currently number 19—both as a first and middle name. **GRACIELA** is the Spanish and **GRAZIA** and **GRAZIELLA** are the attractive Italian versions.

GRANIA. Grania, the phonetic version of the Irish **GRAINNE,** could hold some appeal for parents searching for an authentic Gaelic first name rather than one of the trendier surnames. In addition to being the appellation of an ancient grain goddess, it was also borne by two mythic Irish figures. In a famous medieval love story, Grainne was betrothed to the legendary chieftain Finn MacCool—until she ran off with his irresistible nephew Diarmaid instead. Then there was the sixteenth-century pirate queen of the Western Isles Grainne Ni Mhaille, who bravely fought against the forces of Queen Elizabeth I. Her name (known to the English as Grace O'Malley) passed into poetry as a symbol of Ireland.

GREER. Actress Greer Garson put this name before the public on movie-theater marquees in the 1940s. It was the family name of her Irish mother, and is, in fact, the contraction of the Scottish surname Gregor. Today, it still has some vitality because of the popularity of androgynous surname names for girls, and certainly is a good middle-name prospect.

GRETA, GRETCHEN. These German pet forms of Margaret, along with **GRETEL,** have been used sparingly by American parents for some time, parents who want a somewhat, but not too, ethnic name for their daughters. Of the three, Gretchen (currently enjoying a dash of modern glamour via actress Gretchen Mol), is the most Americanized, while Greta, having finally loosened its strong tie to Garbo, is enjoying a bit of a revival, having been chosen for their daughters by Phoebe Cates and Kevin Kline, and by Rachel Ticotin and David Caruso. Gretel still seems to be out strewing crumbs in the forest with brother Hansel.

GUADALUPE. Always well used in Spanish-speaking countries, as is its short form **LUPE,** which means "wolf," this is a name that could, like Soledad and Consuelo, jump the fence into more multiethnic territory. Guadalupe is the patron saint of Mexico.

GUINEVERE. Since, for so many years, this name has been eclipsed by its modern Cornish form, Jennifer, few parents in recent history—except perhaps for some rabid Round Table buffs—have considered the original Guinevere. But with parents becoming more adventurous in their choices, some might want to consider this evocative name of King Arthur's beautiful—but unfaithful—queen. It shares the attractive short form **GWYN** with Gwyneth.

GWENDOLEN. Decades ago, Gwendolen, an ancient Welsh name, retired in favor of its more modern-sounding short form, **GWEN,** but now, as is the case all across the naming board, the nickname has faded and the more distinguished original is being reappraised. Gwendolen means "white circle," probably alluding to an ancient moon goddess, and appears in both Welsh and English legend: One **GUENDOLEN** was a fairy with whom King Arthur fell in love and another was the wife of the wizard Merlin. Later the name appeared as a main character in Oscar Wilde's *The Importance of Being Earnest,* and in 1950, **GWENDOLYN** (currently the most common spelling) Brooks became the first African-American woman to win a Pulitzer prize for poetry.

GWYNETH. In a sense Gwyneth has almost become a one-person name over the past few years, but only in the way that if you talk about a movie starring Gwyneth we'll all know who you mean, not in the prohibitive there's-only-one Oprah sense. Also used as **GWENYTH** and **GWENETH** and abbreviated to **GWYNNE,** this mellifluous appellation means "blessed" or "happy" and is definitely becoming more and more appreciated by American parents. Its media appearances have included a stint on the soap *Loving,* and it's the name of one of Richard Thomas's triplets. A cute Welsh nickname for any of the Gwen-starting names is **GWENNO.**

GYPSY. Even though it has a certain exotic charm, Gypsy also connotes a nomadic existence, and perhaps even distant memories of the refined stripper Gypsy Rose Lee, neither of which make for appealing destinies for a daughter. You might consider **ROMANY** instead, which has a similar meaning but in a less obvious, off-putting way.

H

HADASSAH. When the wife of Senator Joseph Lieberman was introduced to the American public, many people had never heard her first name before. Although this Hebrew form of Esther, which means "myrtle," an ancient symbol of love, is well used in Israel, it has for the most part been shunned by non-Orthodox parents here, no doubt because its strong association with the Zionist women's philanthropic organization gives it a hyperreligious feel—something like, if you're a Catholic, naming your daughter Mary Immaculata. Too bad, because removed from that context, it's a pleasant, if weighty, name with a significant history. Like Esther, it is traditionally given to girls born around the holiday of Purim.

HADLEY. Hadley may not be heard much in real life, but it is often used for characters on film—it's been played recently by actors as diverse as Melanie Griffths, Annie Potts, and Jane Seymour. The name of one of Ernest Hemingway's wives, Hadley came into being as an English surname meaning "heathery fields." So, if you feel that Heather is dated, you might be inspired to consider this equally soft but more modern-sounding name.

HAILEY. See **HAYLEY.**

HALCYON. Pronounced HAL-see-on, this highly unusual name conjures up images of utter tranquility and happiness because of the phrase "halcyon days" or maybe because of the tranquilizer Halcion. It is related to the Greek Halcyone, a mythic bird said to have a calming effect on the seas during winter storms. And if Halcyon gets too heavy to carry throughout childhood, there is always the friendly nickname Hallie to be held in reserve.

HALEY. See **HAYLEY.**

HALLIE, HALLY, HALLEY. Hallie, not to be confused with Haley or Holly (although it often is), is one of those comfy, cozy, nicknamish names that are coming into style perhaps in opposition to the sternly serious Hopes and Helens. Actress **HALLE** Berry introduced a new spelling option.

HANNAH. In its quiet, unassuming way, the sweet biblical Hannah has scaled the heights of baby names, now the second most popular girls' name in America, as well as being number 1 in at least ten states (mostly in the South). The ascent started soon after the release of Woody Allen's 1986 film *Hannah and Her Sisters,* as parents warmed to its many sources of appeal. Hannah is a classic, with Old Testament roots (in the Bible, Hannah was the mother of Samuel) and a stylish background in Georgian England and the pioneer West. Its charm may be perceived as traditional or homey, aristocratic or down-to-earth. As Hannah, **HANNA,** or **HANA** (the latter used for the Juliette Binoche character in *The English Patient*), it relates to many different cultures, from Hebrew to Arabic, European to Asian. It has appealed to a number of celebrity parents, including Jessica Lange and Sam Shepard, Mel Gibson, Tom Selleck, Elizabeth Perkins, Helen Slater, and the model Vendela, and is currently on several soaps and sitcoms, often as a baby or child character. So, with all this, although Hannah is a wonderful name, you should be aware of its silent-epidemic status before you choose it.

HARLEY. Harley might be just one of your run-of-the-mill unisex surname names, if it weren't for the motorcycle connection which gives it some extra voltage. The name of a character on *The Guiding Light,* it can be considered as an alternative to the overly popular Carly or Haley.

HARMONY. Harmony is a hippie name of the 1960s that has come back to haunt us every week as a character on *Buffy the Vampire Slayer.* If Melody and Lyric are on your shortlist, you might want to add Harmony as well. **CADENCE** is another, less obvious, possibility.

HARPER. Harper Lee, author of the classic *To Kill a Mockingbird,* brought this family name into the public consciousness as a female first name. Used for a character on *ER,* it has an offbeat, boyish, Southern charm.

HARRIET. See **HENRIETTA.**

HASSIBA, HABIBA. A Muslim name popular in North Africa and the name of the runner Hassiba Boulmerka, who won Algeria's first Olympic gold medal. It sounds similar to another popular North African girl's name, **HABIBA,** which means "beloved."

HATTIE. Hattie is one of the next wave of relaxed grandma names supplanting Molly, Annie, Becky et al., and joining the spunkier Mamie, Millie, and Mitzi. A nickname for Harriet, it was last used at the end of the nineteenth century. Also spelled **HATTY.**

HAVANA. Politics aside, this is one of the most rhythmic and exotic of place-names. The question is, can politics be put aside?

HAVEN. Haven denotes a safe spot, a place of comfort and protection, which is what you will provide for your child. The shifting of this common noun into a proper name is a fairly recent innovation, and would be an adventurous choice for the parent who doesn't want to go quite as far as Heaven.

HAYLEY, HALEY, HAILEY. This name can be traced back directly to Hayley Mills, whose mother's middle name became her first. But, strangely enough, the boom name did not take off à la Halley's comet at the time of the young Disney actress's greatest popularity, in the very early sixties, the time of *Parent Trap* and *Pollyanna*. It wasn't until her young admirers grew up and had children of their own in the 1980s that the name reached mass popularity. With all three spellings taken together (especially Haley and Hailey), the name is still firmly planted in the Top 10. Other, more fanciful, spellings also abound, from **HAYLEIGH** to **HAILEE.** However, although we like the original Hayley as much as the next baby boomer, and still can appreciate its breezy, androgynous but not pretentious charm, we find Haley to be a name that's too thoroughly of the moment: It could become a Shirley of tomorrow.

HAZEL. Hazel has a double image. It has a pleasantly hazy, brownish-green-eyed feel, which is combined with—or contradicted by—an opinionated, middle-aged *Hazel* the maid cartoon. One of the botanical names—coming from the hazelnut tree—that were all the rage at the turn of the twentieth century, Hazel had a short run and then fairly quickly fell out of favor and has hardly been heard of since. But though it seems so musty as to be nearly moribund, it could conceivably be restored to favor by the kind of parents who are considering such names as Mabel and Sadie, and who also like the fact that there was a time when a wand of hazel symbolized protection and authority.

HEATHER. Whereas Hazel has been hidden beneath thick, overgrown bushes, Heather lies trampled underfoot, the victim of too much traffic. The name's chronic popularity (it was number 5 in the early seventies) was celebrated in the 1989 movie *Heathers,* in which every girl in its snotty high-school clique was named Heather, while rebel Winona Ryder was a Veronica. Heather is an undeniably pretty name—all those Scottish-moor implications—but, even though Heather Locklear continues to reign on TV, it's beginning to feel as dusty as a bouquet of dried flowers.

HEAVEN. Not too long ago, names like Genesis, Trinity, Angel—and Heaven—were considered beyond the pale for baby-name use in the secular world, but of late there seems to be a minitrend developing of choosing just such names—there were over 700 little Heavens born last year and 1,600 Genesises. The decision to use such names would depend entirely on your own views in terms of appropriateness and projected peer pressure.

HEDDA, HEDY. As far back as most of us can remember, Hedda's been the basis of cruel-joke names like Hedda Hare (yes, there are parents who really do that), as well as a card-carrying member of a category of slightly bohemian, urban names such as Nedda, Andra, and Petra. For better or for worse, it does have two strong associations: the heroine of the Ibsen play *Hedda Gabler* and the madly hatted Hollywood gossip Hedda Hopper (born with one of those aforementioned cruel names: Elda Furry). Hedy, although linked to one of the most exquisite creatures ever to appear on the screen, Hedy Lamarr, has never appealed much to Americans, but not as little as her full German name, **HEDWIG.**

HEIDI. Despite decades of American Heidis of every size, shape, coloring, and age—including an upscale Beverly Hills madam—the name somehow seems permanently tethered to that little girl on the Alpine mountaintop whose story was first published in 1881. It's actually a Swiss nickname for the unmanageable German name **ADELHEIDE** which sounds like something used by morticians.

HELEN. Helen has been a name that has connoted female beauty since ancient times when, in classical mythology, Helen, ravishing daughter of Zeus and Leda and wife of the king of Sparta, ignited a ten-year war because the Trojan prince Paris just had to have her. She had, as Christopher Marlowe later wrote, "the face that launched a thousand ships." The name's popularity in England was due to the fourth-century Saint Helen(a), mother of Constantine the Great, and soon took on a variety of forms, moving from Elena to Elaine to Ellen. Over more recent centuries, it's gone in and out of favor both in the United States and Britain, often alternating with Ellen. Helen was last popular here in the first half of the twentieth century (it was number 8 in 1930), then faded. Now, however, we see signs of a possible comeback, with such attractive actresses as Lara Flynn Boyle and Sarah Michelle Gellar being cast as Helens in recent productions—a sure indication that its image is being shined up. Beware, however, **HELENE** and **HELAINE,** which still seem dated. Eastern European variants include **JELENA, JELINKA, GALINA,** and **ILONA,** while **LENA,** originally a pet form, is now used in its own right, as are other offshoots Elaine, Ellen, Leonora, Eleanor, Nell, Nellie, Eileen, and Elena.

HELENA. Helena is a more delicate and dainty version of Helen, a favorite of Shakespeare, who used it in *All's Well That Ends Well* and *A Midsummer Night's Dream*. The porcelain-skinned British star Helena Bonham Carter has done much for the name's image and it was the name of Catherine Zeta-Jones character in *Traffic,* all helping to make it the preferred choice for those who find Helen a bit bland.

HELOISE. This rather pretentious-sounding French version of Eloise was borne by the beloved of the twelfth-century French philosopher Pierre Abelard—considered to be one of the most learned women of the Middle Ages—and, more recently, by a prolific purveyor of household hints.

HENRIETTA, HARRIET. This is one of the few instances where we are of two minds. The member of our team who has spent more time recently in London sees these names as they're seen over there—as charmingly offbeat and sophisticated—while the other of us still sees them as fusty old maiden aunts in black galoshes and clear plastic rain bonnets. The bottom line: These names are unlikely to inspire neutrality in *anyone*. If you choose one of them for your child, be prepared for years of double takes or downright disapproval. The two are paired because Harriet emerged as a short version of Henrietta, which is a feminization of Harry's proper form, Henry. Henrietta has the advantage—if you see it that way—of being a name with a well-padded royal pedigree, while Harriet is more literary (Harriet Beecher Stowe and the perennial kids' favorite *Harriet the Spy*) and historic (Harriet Tubman, the former slave who led hundreds to freedom on the Underground Railroad), later becoming half of that fifties/sixties happy-family icon, *Ozzie and Harriet*. **HENRIETTE** is the usual French form of Henrietta, **ENRICA** the pretty Spanish version. There are loads of name-softening offshoots and nicknames, including **HETTY, ETTA, HENNY, HANK, HARRIOT, HARRIETTA, HATTY,** and **HATSY.**

HERMIONE. The *erm* sound, as in Herman and Irma, and, now that we think of it, *germ* and *vermin,* is not one that particularly appeals to the twenty-first-century American ear. And so we doubt if Hermione (pronounced her-MY-oh-nee), the Greek name of the mythic daughter of Helen of Troy and King Menelaeus and used by Shakespeare in *The Winter's Tale,* will catch on in this country anytime soon. On the other hand, the name's appearance as a lively young character in the Harry Potter books could suddenly vanquish all those doubts.

HESTER. An undeniably disagreeable-sounding name, almost at the level of **HEPZIBAH,** this variant of Esther is associated with the persecuted heroine of Hawthorne's *The Scarlet Letter.*

HILARY, HILLARY. Hilary is on hold. It's so closely identified with the former first lady and present Democratic senator from New York that it's difficult for most parents to get past that and think of it as a baby name. Which is a shame, because it's got so much going for it. Originally a boy's name (though there was a famous female Saint Hilaria in the fifth century), Hilary's assets include the rhythmic three-syllable structure so popular at present, the fact that it is strong but light, proper yet jaunty, and has an irresistible meaning, deriving from the same root as *hilarious.* So we're sure that, even if it takes a generation, Hilary/Hillary will be back.

HILDEGARDE, HILDA. Hildegarde is one of those unfortunate names that have become synonymous with a heavy, plodding, caricatured Teutonic stodginess—it did take a detour in the 1940s when it was tied to an over-dressed (never without long white gloves) chanteuse, but that association is all but forgotten. While Hilda (the name of one of the Valkyrie of Teutonic legend) and **HILDY** may pick up the pace, we doubt if you'd really want to hang any of these iron ID tags on your modern American child.

HIMALAYA. A place-name that suggests the highest heights and carries a hippyish aura.

HOLLAND. Holland is one of the coolest of the new geographical names unadorned and elegant, evocative of fields of multicolored tulips and fine Rembrandt portraits, and one that venturesome parents are beginning to use. Holland Taylor is the actress who won an Emmy for her work on *The Practice.*

HOLLY. Holly enjoyed a surge of popularity in the sixties—largely inspired by the madcap Holly Golightly in Truman Capote's *Breakfast at Tiffany's,* played on screen by Audrey Hepburn. More popular in England, where it's in the top 30, than here, Holly has always been favored for girls born around Christmas, because of the evergreen hung on doors during that holiday season for good luck. In Galsworthy's *Forsyte Saga,* there was a pair of siblings named Jolly and Holly. Parents wishing to put an androgynous modern spin on Holly could consider transforming it into the surname **HOLLIS.** Rocker Dave (U2) Evans spelled his daughter's name **HOLLIE.**

HONOR. This virtue name, heard less often than Hope or Grace, might be a little harder for a child to carry, simply because it is not immediately recognized as a name. But it is so strong and true it may be worth the effort. In ancient Rome, the name was originally **HONORIA,** though that form and the equally interesting Norman version **HONORA** have all but died out except in Ireland, where they are still fairly common. The Irish have also turned the name into **ANNORA,** soon shortened to Nora; **ONORA** is another possibility. While all these variations have merit, we like the undiluted English version—Honor—the best.

HOPE. If a name as virtuous as Hope can be considered hot, then hot it is. It all started with the saintly Hope Steadman on *thirtysomething* a few years back, and now there are Hopes on several soaps and as characters on both the big and small screen. But Hope—which was used by the Puritans for both boys and girls, sometimes in such elaborated forms as Hope-on-High and Hopeful—is too high-minded (if we don't have hope, what have we?) and pure to be corrupted, and is such a lovely classic name that it deserves all the attention it is getting.

HORTENSE. No!

HUNTER. Hunter had a trendy image almost before it was popular enough to deserve it, one of the ambisexual, formerly male surname names that emerged in the 1990s, like Taylor and Carson, and were quickly snatched up by soap operas and their ilk. In fact, the Taylor character on *The Bold and the Beautiful* was played by high-profile actress/model Hunter Tylo, who did a lot to publicize the name for girls. More recently, it became the name of the trendy-teen best friend of the perfectly named Meadow on *The Sopranos.*

HYACINTH. Not as likable as Lily or as gentle as Jasmine, Hyacinth still might hold some appeal for the parent seeking a truly exotic flower name. In Greek mythology Hyacinthus was a Spartan youth accidentally killed by Apollo, from whose blood sprang a beautiful and fragrant flower, and it is also the name of several early saints. To the ancients, Hyacinth was, in addition to being a bluebell-like blossom, the name of a blue stone. There was an early nineties British sitcom in which Hyacinth was the imperious, social-climbing sister in a family where all the sisters were named for flowers.

I

IANTHE. An unusual, romantic, almost ethereal Greek name chosen by the poet Shelley for his daughter. In Greek myth, Ianthe was the daughter of Oceanus, supreme ruler of the seas. **IANTHA** is a similar Greek name meaning "purple flower."

IDA. A century ago, Ida was considered "sweet as apple cider," and was number 10 on the hit parade of girls' names. Its popularity then was prompted by the Gilbert and Sullivan operetta *Princess Ida* (which was based on a Tennyson poem), and perhaps vaguer associations with Mount Ida, where Zeus was supposed to have been raised in Crete, but neither of those facts means enough today to give this great-grandma name any chance of reviving—even if Swedish-born action star Dolph Lundgren did use it for his baby daughter. The Italian **IDALIA** sounds somewhat more modern.

ILANA, ILLEANA, ILONA. Ilana (also spelled **ELANA**) is an Israeli name that means "oak tree," and is therefore sometimes chosen for little girls born on the holiday of Tu b'Shavat, the New Year of the Trees. Mariah Carey played a character named Ilana in *The Bachelor*. The more melodious Illeana (or **ILEANA** or **ILIANA**) is, like Ilona, a Hungarian form of Helen, and means "bright one." Illeana Douglas is one of the queens of independent film.

ILSA. Ilsa is remembered as the radiant but tragic heroine of *Casablanca*, portrayed by Ingrid Bergman. On quite another note, there is the cult film *Ilsa, She-Wolf of the S.S.* Spelled **ILSE,** the name is now having a resurgence of popularity in Holland, currently on its Top 20 list.

IMAN. A Somali and Muslim name that means "faith," Iman is one of the best-known African names in this country because of the famous Somali-born model and wife of David Bowie. The similar-sounding African **IMANA** is the name of the supreme god of the Batitsi of Rwanda and Burundi. **IMANI,** which means "believer" in Arabic, is popular throughout the Muslim world and was chosen for her daughter by Jasmine Guy.

IMARA. This Kiswahili word meaning "firm" could make a hauntingly evocative first name. As an ethnic name for an American child, it strikes the perfect balance of the exotic and the familiar.

IMELDA. If you can put aside thoughts of Mrs. Marcos, the shoe-collecting ex–First Lady of the Philippines, this can be seen as a soft-sounding Spanish saint's name, used more often by the British than Americans. The problem: Even if you can put it aside, can everyone else?

IMOGEN. This name, which originated as a Shakespearean misspelling of the Celtic **INNOGEN,** is one of the intriguing group of names that are highly fashionable in Britain but rarely used here. That may be because, spelled **IMOGENE,** and pronounced Im-o-JEAN, we still associate it with the daffy comedian Imogene Coca on early TV. More correctly the name is pronounced IM-o-jen, and is a choice that's as pretty and classy as it is distinctive. It was used by Shakespeare for a charming and impetuous character in one of his last plays, *Cymbeline;* was the name of one of our most noted female photographers, Imogen Cunningham; and was chosen for his daughter by Andrew Lloyd Webber.

INDIA, INDIANA. India has decades more history as a name than most of the place-names that are all the rage today. The British aristocracy used it during the years of the Raj, and some Americans adopted it after the character India Wilkes in *Gone With the Wind,* which was a catalyst for almost every name it contained. As a name, India is both exotic and euphonious, fashionable but with much more depth than the blow-away **INDIANA**s and Montanas newer to the map. It's been chosen for their daughters by such diverse celebrities as actors Catherine Oxenberg and Philip Michael Thomas, Heather Thomas and spiritual guru Marianne Williamson. India Edwards was a one-time Secretary of the U.S. Treasury.

INDIGO. Color names have joined place, flower, and jewel names in the pool of newly discovered and rediscovered name possibilities. Indigo, a deep blue-violet dye made from plants native to India, can be used for either girls or boys, along with other blue tones, such as Teal and Azure.

INDRA. Indra is the name of the chief god of the early Hindu religion, also the god of the sky, rain, and thunder, while **INDRE,** pronounced the same way, is a river in France. Occasionally heard as a name for girls in England, Indra might be worth considering if you have a strong taste for the unorthodox ethnic. **INDIRA** Gandhi was prime minister of India for eleven years.

INEZ. This Spanish form of Agnes has a touch of the exotic but has also been fully integrated into the American name pool. Inez was the mother of Don Juan in the poem by Byron and means "pure." Other spellings are **INES, YNES,** and **YNEZ;** a Russian version is **INESSA.**

INGRID. Ingrid Bergman's appeal throughout her long career was strong enough to lend universal charisma to this classic Scandinavian name, and parents with Nordic roots may want to consider it. It's a usable feminine form of the name of the god Ing—ruler of fertility and crops, peace and prosperity. But other versions—**INGA, INGER, INGEBORG**—remain permanently tied to the Old Country.

IOLA, IOLE. Iole was the name of a princess with whom the god Hercules fell in love in Greek mythology. Iola was a disagreeable character on *Mama's Family*. No question which of the two has more potential.

IOLANTHE. Known to Americans primarily as the name of an 1882 Gilbert and Sullivan operetta, Iolanthe is a Greek name meaning "violet flower." We'd recommend choosing the more manageable Violet instead.

IONA, IONE. Another pair of similar but different names, both of which are being used with increasing stylishness in England. Iona is a tiny Scottish island in the Hebrides, while Ione (pronounced aye-OWN), a Greek flower name for violet, has gained attention via actress Ione Sky, daughter of the "Mellow Yellow" pop star, Donovan.

IRA. Ira for a girl? you well may ask. Yes, we think Ira is eminently suited to a gender switch, sharing, as it does, tonal similarities with such feminine names as Tyra, Myra, Elmira, and Elvira. Annette Bening and Warren Beatty have broken the ice by using this Old Testament name, previously associated with one of the Gershwins, as a middle name for their daughter Isabel. Possible problem: Association with the savings account.

IRELAND. Kim Basinger and Alec Baldwin added a new element to the naming atlas when they called their daughter Ireland Eliesse, stating at the time that geographical names were a family tradition. It certainly sounds a lot more contemporary than Erin or Shannon.

IRENE. There is a tendency for Irene to be lumped in with the jumble of *een/ene* names so popular from the 1920s through the fifties (Maureen, Arlene et al.), but Irene has a more classical pedigree. One of the most popular names of the Roman Empire and the name of an ancient saint, this originally Greek name (then spelled **EIRENE**), representing a daughter of Zeus who was the Greek goddess of peace, has spawned variations throughout the cultures of Europe, where it usually has a three-syllable pronunciation. A lot of its British usage derived from the character of Irene (again with three syllables) in Galsworthy's *The Forsyte Saga,* while Americans identified it with the sparkling Irene Dunne of Hollywood's Golden Age. But although it was found among the Top 50 then, parents started singing "Goodnight, Irene" decades ago. Eastern European versions such as **IRINA** (one of Chekhov's *Three Sisters*), **JERENI,** and **IRENA** sound a bit fresher.

IRIS. Around the turn of the last century, Iris was lucky enough to be caught in the updraft caused by two simultaneous fads—those for flower names and for classical names ending in *s.* But although many of the flower names are returning, Iris has long been wilted (except in flower-happy Holland, where it's in the Top 10). And it has such a colorful history too. In Greek mythology, Iris was the goddess of the rainbow, a messenger for Zeus and Hera who rode the rainbow as a multicolored bridge from heaven to earth, which makes it a logical name for both the brightly hued flower and the colored part of the eye. In ancient times the iris was considered a symbol of power and majesty, the three petal segments representing faith, wisdom, and valor. Perhaps glamour couple Jude Law and

Sadie Frost, who named their daughter Iris, will help restore the name to fashion.

IRMA. There was an old show called *My Friend Irma,* but unfortunately, most of Irma's friends by now have senior-citizen passes and have retired along with the name, which was originally short for such doozies as Ermengarde and Ermentrude.

IRNAN. One of three magical sisters in Irish mythology who had the power to change shape. Unfortunately, it does not have a very euphonious or feminine sound.

ISABEL, ISABELLE, ISABELLA. For several years now, all you've had to do was eavesdrop at a playgroup in SoHo or Santa Monica and you'd be sure to hear at least one version of this hot-and-getting-hotter-every-minute name. A venerable Spanish and Portuguese variation of Elizabeth (it went from Elizabeth to Ilsabeth to Isabeau to Isabelle), Isabella is known to every schoolchild as the Queen of Castile and Aragon who helped finance Christopher Columbus's expedition to the New World. And since then it has had an incredibly rich history as a royal name, and a literary one (in Shakespeare's *Measure for Measure* and *Henry V.* and novels by Jane Austen and Henry James). More recently it's appeared in soap operas and movies (it was Julia Roberts's character's name in *Stepmom,* for one). All three forms are great favorites of the celeb set: Annette Bening and Warren Beatty have an Isabel, Tom Cruise and Nicole Kidman, Kirk Cameron, Lori Loughlin, Jane Leeves, Lorenzo Lamas, Andrew Lloyd-Webber, and Lou Diamond Phillips all have Isabellas, and Geraldo Rivera and Jeff Bridges are fathers of Isabelles. But despite all this burgeoning popularity, we still can't restrain ourselves from recommending it, because it's simply one of the most enduringly beautiful names we know. It's got some terrific nicknames and foreign variations too: **IZZY, IBBY, ISA, ELLA, BELLA,** and **BELLE;** the Gaelic **ISHBEL** and the Scottish **ISOBEL;** the Old French **ISABEAU** (the name of Michelle Pfeiffer's character in *Ladyhawke*); and **IZABELLA,** the Slavic version used by Hunter Tylo for her daughter and the subject of an old Jimi Hendrix song.

ISADORA. This is a name that we can see parents reevaluating, especially as the once dominant image of Isadora Duncan, the arty early modern dancer who was done in by her long flowing scarf, is finally fading. With that linkage aside, the name has quite a lot going for it, namely a pleasant sound and its relation to Isis, the mythological goddess of fertility and birth. According to ancient Egyptian texts, Isis was a black woman, which could offer further appeal to African-American parents. Isadora Wing is the heroine of Erica Jong's *Fear of Flying*. **ISIDORA** and **IDORA** are variants.

ISAK. When the Danish author Baroness Karen Blixen chose Isak (Dinesen) as her pen name, she, like other female writers such as George Eliot, deliberately chose a male pseudonym. We think this could make a distinctive choice for admirers of such works as *Out of Africa* and *Seven Gothic Tales*.

ISIS. Isis was the supreme Egyptian goddess who ruled over the moon and fertility. Her name (pronounced ICE-iss) crosses over the line into too exotic and arcane territory, and too icy as well.

ISOLDE. Isolde is an artistic, even esoteric, name à la Ariadne and Eurydice, that is recommended only for the child born into a permissive and creative community. Isolde was a beautiful Irish princess of medieval legend, and the tragic lover of Tristam in Arthurian romance, later immortalized in the Wagnerian opera *Tristan und Isolde*. Other versions are **ISOLDA, ISEULT, YSOLDE,** and **YSEULT.**

ITA, ITE. Modern forms of the ancient Irish Ide, pronounced EE-da, and not very substantial.

ITALIA. While the Anglicized **ITALY** might prove a bit obvious and harsh as a girl's name, the native version is a soft and pretty possibility. It was used by rapper LL Cool J for his daughter. **ITALINA** has also been heard.

IVANA. Ivana was just another rarely used Slavic-sounding name until the Czech-born ex-Mrs. Trump infused it with her own brand of over-the-top personality and glamour. The name was caricatured in *Austin Powers: The Spy Who Shagged Me,* with the character Ivana Humpalot, indicating all kinds of possible playground cruelties. The Donald and the Ivana named their daughter **IVANKA,** an affectionate name for a mini-Ivana.

IVORY. Soon after the Paul McCartney–Stevie Wonder recording of the song "Ebony and Ivory" became a huge hit in 1982, both those words became equally huge hits with African-American parents seeking distinctive names for their daughters. Ivory has other meaningful associations—its relation to the Ivory Coast, the precious African material—but above all it's a fashionable name with a smooth surface and cool sheen.

IVY. Many parents are beginning to appreciate the assets of this offbeat, kinetic, energetic name and are choosing to ignore its possible playground debits: the phrases "clinging ivy" and "poison ivy." The ancient Greeks saw the virtue in the clinging quality of the vine; they presented a wreath of ivy to newlyweds as a symbol of fidelity. Uma Thurman played a villainous Ivy in *Batman and Robin,* Drew Barrymore was the title character in *Poison Ivy,* and actress Sheryl Lee Ralph formed a hyphenated version for her daughter, Ivy-Victoria, while the Eddie Murphys made it the middle name of their daughter Zola.

J

JACINTA. This Spanish word for Hyacinth is a lot softer and sweeter than the English version. **JACINDA** is a variation, **JACEY** a possible nickname.

JACOBINA. Now that Jacob is the number 1 boys' name across the land, we wonder if there's a chance for a comeback of this feminine version. Since it's somewhat clunkier than Gabriella, Georgina, or even Josephine, we think the odds are against it, although we can conceive of a little girl nicknamed **JAKE.**

JACQUELINE. Even though this is a centuries-old French name, to most Americans it represents the Kennedy era, the years of a cultural Camelot.

The name was imported into England by a French sister-in-law of Henry V (known as Dame Jack) and had reached the Top 50 in this country by the 1920s. By now, the name has lost most of its glamorous image, and even its Gallic gloss, so that parents looking for a fresher French image might consider such *noms* as Amalie, Elodie, or Fabienne. This is one of those names with more spellings than you can shake a pillbox hat at, from **JACQUELYN** to **JACLYN** to **JACALIN** to **JACQUELEAN,** but each of them diminishes the toney image of the name even further. **JACQUETTA** is another feminization of the French Jacques.

JADA. Although this name, the Spanish form of Jade, has been associated with the actress Jada Pinkett Smith recently, it has long been used in Spanish-speaking countries. Pronounced as Jade with an *a* ending, it has swiftly risen to popularity among African-American parents, and is now in the black Top 10 in such states as Texas; in all, there were more than 3,700 Jadas born last year. **JADIA** is a variation.

JADE. The hard green gemstone may be cool to the touch, but as a name Jade is definitely hot. The most modern of all the jewel names, it projects a contemporary polish lacking in all the others. Although it had been long used in Western depictions of Asian female characters—Katherine Hepburn played a Jade in the movie version of *Dragon Seed* in the 1940s—its glamorous image was updated and enhanced by the fact that it was chosen by Mick and Bianca Jagger in 1971 for their daughter, who now has a trend-setting daughter of her own, named Assisi, and more recently by Darryl Strawberry. At this point Jade has appeared on at least four different soap operas, is in Britain's Top 25, and is gaining in popularity in this country as well, especially as a strong, slightly exotic middle name. A plus: The jade stone is said to transmit wisdom, clarity, justice, courage, and modesty— not a bad combination of attributes.

JAEL. Pronounced Yah-el, this attractive Old Testament name is also a geographical name for a place in north Israel. **YAEL** is the more phonetic version.

JAFFA. This Hebrew name, pronounced YA-fa, comes from the Hebrew word for "beautiful." It's also the name of the city founded by the Phoenicians, taken by the Israelites, and now the part of Tel Aviv that gave its name to the juicy oranges imported into this country.

JALEESA, JALISA. In both its spellings, this name has enjoyed popularity among African-American families for more than a decade. Like several others—Kadeem, Jasmine, Whitley—it was given a substantial boost by the names of cast and characters on the TV show *A Different World,* which premiered in 1988.

JALILA. The two *l*s in this Arabic name give it a particularly strong rhythmic quality. It means "greatness" or "glory."

JAMAICA. Among the most appealing and colorful of names found in the atlas, Jamaica almost sings out the rhythms of the West Indies. Antiguan-born writer Jamaica Kincaid dropped her birth name of Elaine when she took on her nom de plume.

JAMESINA. For decades, Jamie has been the most favored female form of James, but with that kind of androgynous nickname name sounding terminally dated, parents of today might want to consider this more traditional, yet fresher sounding form, especially since other old-style feminizations, such as Edwina and Theodora, have shown signs of making comebacks.

JAMIE. Jamie is one of the prototypical ambisexual nickname names that seemed like the epitome of cool in the sixties, especially after decades of Jeans, Joans, Joannes, and Janets. The Scottish diminutive for James, Jamie is one of the few names that managed to become popular for girls while remaining well used for boys. **JAIME** is a common alternative (and the one used, for some reason, as the name of *The Bionic Woman*), though every Spanish student knows that that's correctly pronounced HY-mee and is the spelling of the Spanish version of James. On more recent TV, Jamie was visible as the lead character in *Mad About You*—whose husband often called her **JAMES**—the newest-sounding possibility in this family of names.

JAMILA. Jamila derives from the Arabic word meaning "beautiful and elegant" and is part of a group of related names with soft, appealing sounds that are now popular with African-American parents. Sometimes spelled **JAMILLA.**

JAMISON, JAMESON. Another way to go when wanting to name a girl after a friend or family member named James, these are a lot more substantial than the passé Jamie. Jim Belushi may have been naming his daughter after himself when he called her Jamison, the same name chosen by Chynna Phillips and Billy Baldwin with the Jameson spelling.

JANE. No, we don't consider Jane too plain. In fact, for a venerable and short one-syllable name, we think it packs a surprising amount of punch, as compared to others like Jean and Joan. A very old name, Jane has been around since Tudor times: Just as in our day Jessica replaced Jennifer, so did Jane come in to replace Joan. In this country it has moved in and out of fashion, at one time being so common that it became a generic slang term for a girl, with G. I. Jane being the female equivalent of G. I. Joe, and Jane Doe the counterpart of John Doe, then spent a considerable period being half of such double names as Mary Jane, Betty Jane, and Janie Lou. Now, after rarely being heard from for several decades, it seems poised for a comeback; especially with the newsstand visibility of the eponymous magazine for young women. Jane has that unpretentious brand of honesty so prized these days—think of other stylish names like Grace, Jack, Rose— plus a strong grounding in history. Consider, too, all those great Janes of the past: Eyre, Austen, Grey. Even **JAYNE** Mansfield (born Vera) contributed something to popular culture when she came up with a new spelling of the name. **JANAE** is another feminine form of John, and **SINEAD** (pronounced shin-AID) is the Irish translation.

JANNA, JANA. Pronounced either as Jan with an *a* added or YAN-a, the European way, this is a name with many cross-cultural ties, popular in the Slavic countries and also found in Holland, Scandinavia, and Ireland. The *jan* part of the name links it to the first month of the year. In Roman mythology, Jana was the wife of Janus.

JANET. Janet started as a pet form of Jane, but has long been used independently. Five hundred years ago Janet was a royal favorite in Scotland, where it remains a popular name. Here, however, Janet has been on a downhill slide since the 1960s, and we see no signs of a turnaround, its general image at present matched more to Janet Reno's than to Janet Jackson's. Also in fashion limbo are most variations: **JAN, JANICE, JANIS,** and **JANINE.** If you are interested in translating Janet into your own ethnic heritage, you could consider **SHEENA** (Scottish), **SINEAD** (Irish), or **JANICA** (Czech). **JANELLE** and **JANEL** are sometimes heard forms, but are likewise far from stylish.

JASMINE. The aromatic Jasmine, evocative of the delicate and fragrant bloom, was first used here as a girls' name around 1900, during the blossoming of floral-name fashion, then was rarely spotted again until a few years ago, when two almost concurrent forces combined to bring it back. The first was the emergence of TV and movie actress Jasmine Guy, the second was the explosion of Disney's Princess Jasmine onto the screen in the movie *Aladdin*. While names popularized by film characters—animated ones, especially—are usually flimsy and faddish, Jasmine is one of the rare exceptions. The French version of the Arabic **YASMIN,** it's a lush and exotic beauty that has risen to the general Top 30 list, and is number 1 in the ratings of popular African-American girl's names in several states. Jasmine has appeared on a couple of soap operas and was the name of Vivica A. Fox's character in *Independence Day*. Michael Jordan and Martin Lawrence both have daughters named Jasmine, while basketball great Julius Irving chose the alternate spelling **JAZMIN.**

JAY, JAYE. This is one of the boys' names newly appropriated for girls, used either on its own, as a nickname for any *J* name, or as a distinctive middle name.

JEAN. Like sisters Janet and Joan, Jean has been falling from grace for almost half a century now: There are many grandmas and even mothers carrying the name, but few babies. Not that lots of men haven't dreamed of **JEANNIE**—first there was the Stephen Foster song of that name, then the TV series, and somewhere in between there was the ultimate symbol of Hollywood glamour, Jean (born Harlean) Harlow. Originally a feminine of

John, Jean was popular in Scotland long before it found favor in the world at large. The French form is **JEANNE;** variations **JEANETTE, JEANNETTE, JEANINE, JEANIE,** and the unisex **GENE** have all followed Jean down the ladder and out of the picture.

JEMIMA. Jemima is a name we'd love to liberate. Chained in this country to the stereotypical smiling Aunt of pancake and syrup fame, in England Jemima is among the most chic of aristocratic favorites, bestowed on fashionable young ladies who are brought up to read Beatrix Potter's *Jemima Puddleduck* and later go on to marry men named St. John or Sebastian. It's time we, too, focused on Jemima's classic roots. In the old Testament, Jemima was one of the three daughters of Job, a trio so strong and beautiful that Job treated them as sons in his will. It also means "dove" in Arabic. **JEM, JEMMY,** and **JEMMA** can be used as nicknames.

JEMMA. See **GEMMA, JEMIMA.**

JENNA. Jenna began to take off after the 1983 introduction of the character Jenna Wade (played by Priscilla Presley) on the hit series *Dallas*. Since then it has been steadily used, in some places rivaling Jennifer in popularity, but now, unfortunately, has begun to sound as anemic as most of the other *Jen*-starting names.

JENNIFER. When we called our first name book *Beyond Jennifer & Jason,* it was because Jennifer had already become, in the late 1980s, the embodiment of a name that was so overly trendy that there are now on-line support groups for grown-up Jennifers who have suffered the pangs and pains of bearing the most overused name of their era. It was an overnight success in the early seventies, partly because of the heroine of *Love Story,* and it's still easy to see why Jennifer was able to hold on as the most popular girls' name for so long: It was one of the first names with the sentimentally feminine Victorian flavor that would dominate the 1980s, and it came with a ready-made ideal nickname for everyday use. Jennifer was replaced by the similar-sounding Jessica, but at this point most parents are tired of both, eschewing them in favor of fresher alternatives. Among the most unusual are the Celtic saint's name **JENIFRY,** the Romanian **JENICA,** and the surnames **JENSEN** (the first name of a soap star), and **JENNISON.** The most intrepid of parents could also consider the name's Welsh original, **GUINEVERE.**

JENNY. At the height of the Jennifer craze, many parents were cutting straight to the nickname and using Jenny as the name on the birth certificate. Like Molly and Maggie, Jenny is both a long-popular nickname and an established independent name. Long before Jennifer became the *nom de l' âge,* Jenny was a fashionable nickname for Jane, Janet, and Jean, and, spelled **JENNIE,** was in the Top 20 names of 1875. But now that Jennifer has faded, Jenny has diminished in use as well.

JERSEY. An established feminine place-name that carries a lot more weight when you attach it to the British island than to the state where Tony Soprano rules.

JESSICA. When Jennifer began to slip down the popularity lists, Jessica jumped in to take its place. At first this seems like a logical substitution: They both begin with the letter *J,* have three syllables and an old-fashioned flavor. In reality, though, Jessica is a much more classic name than Jennifer and also one that's long been associated with Judaism, first in the Old Testament and later as the name of Shylock's daughter in *The Merchant of Venice.* Still, in the mid to late eighties, lots of parents of all ethnic backgrounds flocked to the name Jessica, and it is still in the Top 10 nationally, retaining first place in the state of California. But parents searching for a fresher alternative might consider the short form **JESSA,** or one of the attractive British trio **JESSAMINE, JESSAMYN,** and **JESSAMY.**

JESSIE. Jessie is not found as much as an independent name as Jenny is, probably because Jesse is such a well-used boys' name. Primarily a nickname for Jessica—although in Scotland it's a diminutive of Janet, and has also been used for names ranging from Josephine to Jocelyn—Jessie has a friendly and unpretentious, pioneer feel.

JETTA. Despite the fact that this is a legitimate name, we are in general against the use of car-model names for humans. **JETTE,** pronounced with two syllables, is quite popular in Denmark and Germany.

JEWEL. When Alaska-raised singer Jewel dropped her last name (Kilcher), she focused high-intensity attention on her first, whose lights had been hidden for decades. Jewel is, just as Flora is for botanicals, the generic gemstone name, its usage having begun in the 1930s, and it could be interpreted as a symbol of how precious you consider your baby daughter to be. The French version is **BIJOU.**

JEZEBEL. Like Désirée, this name gets an R rating: not suitable for children.

JILL. Probably because of its nursery-rhyme associations, Jill has the air of a perpetual, rosy-cheeked child. In fact, Jill is one of the oldest names on the roster, a medieval variation on the Roman Julia—the latter going through a mass revival right now. Knowing Jill's history bestows on it a patina of depth and character, even elegance in its simplicity; otherwise it would feel like a cute but shallow mid-twentieth-century invention.

JILLIAN. See **GILLIAN.**

JOAN. Joan has become a middle-aged name, not surprising since it hasn't been used much since the 1940s. Its first English bearer was Henry II's daughter, **JHONE,** but the modern spelling was soon established, which is why Saint Jeanne d'Arc was translated as Joan, making her the most illustrious bearer of the name. By Shakespeare's time, Joan had become so overused that it was ripe for replacement by the newly coined Jane, the reverse of what happened in twentieth-century America. There were lots of **JOANIE**s still around in the *Happy Days* fifties and sixties, but we can't imagine anyone giving the name to a baby of today. Singer **JONI** (born Roberta) Mitchell made the nickname into a name when she came into the spotlight, and there are several foreign versions with a lot more personality than Joan: **GIOVANNA, SIOBHAN, IONE,** and **JUANA.** We have also seen the phonetic spelling, **JONE.**

JOANNA, JOANNE, JOHANNA. As in the case of Julia and Julie, Joanna is an example of a name that is quite fashionable, in an unobtrusive way, but unfashionable in its fifties version, Joanne, which took over from Joan and managed to reach fifteenth place on the popularity polls of the day. Joanna is found in the New Testament as one of Jesus's early followers, **JO** is its sprightly nickname, **JOJO** even sprightlier. **JOHANNA,** we feel, may be a bit affected with its Old Country *h*. Other *jo* names that sprang to life in the 1940s: **JOLENE, JOELLE, JOBETH,** none of which has any contemporary flair.

JOBINA. Few people would consider calling their sons Job, the name of the most severely tested figure in the Old Testament, but the female version does not carry quite the same negative weight—in fact its derivation is far from obvious. **JOBY** is its perky and unusual nickname.

JOCASTA. A mythological name fashionably used among high-class Brits but mostly ignored here. Jocasta was the mother of Oedipus whom he (oops!) married. Any parent in search of a *J* name that's neither overused nor terminally dated should consider this one.

JOCELYN. Jocelyn never really caught on in this country the way its cousin Joyce (both were originally boys' names) did—a shame, we think, because we find it a much prettier, softer name. The parents of the first female United States Surgeon General managed to combine both names to arrive at **JOYCELYN** Elders. Jocelyn was chosen by director Ron Howard as the name for his daughter, twin sister of Paige. **JOSELYN** and **JOCELIN** are alternate spellings.

JODY. Jody, like Jamie, is one of the cute bouncy nickname so popular in the sixties and seventies, though these names haven't made a comeback the way bell-bottoms and beanbag chairs have. Alternate spellings include **JODEE, JODEY, JODI,** and **JODIE,** à la Foster, though the star's strong, intelligent persona has not bolstered that of her name.

JOEY/JOELY. The image of these two similar names has been updated recently by their relationship to two hot young actresses, Joely Richardson, sister of Natasha and daughter of Vanessa Redgrave, and starlet Joey Lauren Adams. Joey is also the name of the attractive tomboy played by Katie Holmes on television's *Dawson's Creek*. **JOLIE,** as in Angelina, means "pretty" in French and has its emphasis on the second syllable. **JOELLE,** which rhymes with Noëlle, is a Joel equivalent with a more dated feel.

JONI. Mainly for hard-core fans of folksinger Mitchell, alternate spellings of this aberration of Joanie include more extreme **JONEE** and **JONY.**

JONNA. The direct feminine version of John, alternatives include **JOHNNA, JOHNA, JONA,** and all spellings of **JOHNNY.** Used mainly to honor a dad or grandpa, the name is one that has never really taken flight on its own, and no matter how you vary it, still feels like a boy's name with an *a* tacked on the end.

JORDAN. The original female Jordan may have been the character Jordan Baker in F. Scott Fitzgerald's 1925 *The Great Gatsby,* but it wasn't until sixty years later that its popularity would take off for both boys and girls. One of the leading androgynous names that have become so fashionable, Jordan was the twenty-eighth most frequently used boy's name of the 1990s and the fifty-second most popular for girls. Bono, Beau Bridges, John Elway, and Leeza Gibbons all have daughters named Jordan. **JORDYN** and **JORDEN** are alternate spellings; other variations are **JORDANA/JORDANNA/JORDANAH.**

JOSEPHINE. Some may find the name Josephine, which harks back to the days of flying machines and Stanley Steamers, too clunky and dated to hold any modern appeal. But while the name is not, admittedly, conventionally pretty, it has tons of class and character and a gently offbeat quality that can count for style. Actress Linda Hamilton and *Titanic* director James Cameron have a daughter named Josephine, as does designer Vera Wang. And there are many wonderful and provocative Josephines in the past to look to: Joséphine Bonaparte (born Marie Josèphe); Jo, the driving force of *Little Women,* and singer-dancer Josephine Baker (born Freda), to name a few. The name has more than its share of vivacious nicknames: **JOSIE,** the best of the lot, was chosen by actress Brooke Adams for her daughter; others include **JO, JOJO, POSEY, FEENY,** and **FIFI. JOSETTE,** a French form, is both less interesting and more down-market than the original, even in France. Other possibilities are **JOSEFINA** or **JOSEPHA/JOSEFA.**

JOURNEY. A word name making its first appearance on the Top 1000 list. A good choice for a traveling child, or one on a spiritual journey.

JOY. Joy is a high-pressure name, like Bliss and Glory and Merry, and we personally are not in favor of placing this kind of personality-control intimidation on a child. Hope would be a safer bet. Also, if the Pokémon craze continues, your poor little Joy will inevitably be called Nurse Joy by her school pals.

JOYCE. A seminal grade-school experience is learning that poet Joyce Kilmer was a boy. The fact is that until the fourteenth century, all Joyces were male. Today, of course, there are no boys being named Joyce—and not many girls either.

JUANA/JUANITA. Among the most familiar of the Spanish female names, these have nevertheless not become fully assimilated into the American culture.

JUDITH. Judith seems to have become the stock name for uptight (paging Judge Judy!) mother characters. The era is right: Judith was the fourth most popular name in 1940, though most Judiths born at that time were called **JUDY** and would rather have died than been called by their more stuffy proper name. Today, Judith, like Ruth and Helen, may have shaken off just enough of its dust to appeal to adventurous parents looking for a traditional-yet-quirky name for their daughters. Judith of Bethulia—the name is Hebrew and related to Judah—was the singularly beautiful wife of Esau who delivered her people from the invading Assyrians. William Shakespeare chose it for one of his daughters. **JUDIT, JUDITA, JUDITHE,** and **JUDYTH** are variations.

JULIA. Julia is one of those rare names that seems to have everything. It feels modern, yet it's got ancient roots: an imperial Roman name given to females in the house of a Julius, as in Caesar, it means "bearded" or "downy." It's the name of several early saints as well as that of some of the most alluring actresses today: Julias Roberts, Ormond, and Louis-Dreyfus; Julianne (born Julie Anne) Moore, Julianna Margulies, and Julie Delpy.

Increasingly fashionable, Julia was the nationwide number 30 at the turn of the millennium. Yet the name has enough classic backbone to withstand spikes (and dips) in popularity. The variations, both foreign and spelling, of the name are legion, and include: **JULIANA/JULIANNA, JULIANNE** in all its possibilities, **JULIENNE, JULINA, JULINE, JULISSA, JULITA,** and **JULYA. JULIE,** the short form of the name also sometimes spelled **JULI,** was in wide favor in the 1960s and seventies but is no longer as fashionable as the name's long forms.

JULIET. Think of Juliet as Julia's more exotic cousin. With the same pedigree and style power as Julia, Juliet seems finally to have shaken off her association to Romeo. The French spelling, **JULIETTE,** is used by actresses Juliette Binoche and Juliette Lewis. Another version: **JULIETTA.**

JUNE. June, a month name, is stuck as the name of Beaver Cleaver's super-mom. Some more lively relatives: **JUNO** and **JUNIPER.** In Roman mythology, Juno was the wife of Jove and the queen of the heavens, and is familiar because of the Sean O'Casey play *Juno and the Paycock.* **JUNIPER,** a fresh-feeling nature name, was the proper name of the female character in the film *Benny and Joon.*

JUSTICE. One of the ultrafashionable word names, Justice was at most recent count used about equally for boys and girls, with roughly five hundred children of each gender given that name last year. This was the name of the title character played by Janet Jackson in the movie *Poetic Justice.*

JUSTINE. *Family Ties* has been off the air for decades, but many people still relate this name to Justine Bateman, who played oldest daughter Mallory. A French name popularized in the late 1950s by the first of Lawrence Durrell's *Alexandria Quartet,* the novel *Justine,* it's the feminine of the Latin Justin and can be varied as **JUSTINA.**

K

KAI. A Hawaiian boys' name used for the young hero of the fairy tale "The Snow Queen," Kai sounds more feminine than masculine in this age of androgyny. A female twist is **KAIA,** the name of one of the women featured on MTV's *Real World Hawaii.*

KALILA. Arabic for "sweetheart," this lilting name can also be spelled **KALEELA** or **KALILLA.**

KALINDI. This lovely name is Ancient Hindi for a sacred river. A similar-sounding Indo-Pakistani name is **KALINDA,** which means "the sun" and is also the name of a range of mythical mountains. Neither is to be confused with **KALI,** a name which may appeal to the Western ear but is the appellation of the destructive goddess of Hindu mythology.

KAREN. Karen, a sweet, good-girl Danish import, was so popular during the baby boom—number 10 in 1950 and all the way up to third place in 1960—that it's locked firmly into fashion limbo today. Adding an *a* to the end spruces it up, as in **KARENNA,** the name of Al and Tipper Gore's accomplished oldest daughter, and **KARINA,** an alternate spelling of Corrina, a name much favored in recent years by an unlikely mix of Hispanic-American parents and Bob Dylan fans. Fresher sounding still is **KARENZA,** which is a Karenization of the romantic Cornish name **KERENSA** or **KERENZA**—the best of the lot. **KEREN**—short for the jawbreaker **KERENHAPPUCH,** one of the three daughters of the Old Testament Job—provides another twist, though many people would consider it either an invented name or a mispronunciation of Karen. **KARYN** is an alternate spelling, but **KARIN** is actually the Swedish diminutive of Katarina.

KARISSA. One of the many new names that draw on the *issa* rage. The traditional Clarissa is a lot more solid.

KATE. Like one of its most famous bearers, Katharine Hepburn, the name Kate is an aristocratic, gutsy, independent, smart, energetic beauty, the kind earlier epitomized by the heroine of *The Taming of the Shrew/Kiss Me Kate.* Very popular over the past few decades, Kate nonetheless has enough character to resist the vicissitudes of naming trends. Its perennial fashion standing has been enhanced by the many attractive and famous young women who bear the name: Kate Winslet, Kate Hudson, **CATE**

Blanchett, Kate Moss, and **KATIE** Holmes. Standing alone, Katie is number 68 on the 1990s Greatest Hits list and Kate is number 299, but the name is also commonly used as a nickname for the top-ranked Katelyn et al., as well as Katherine and Kathleen. The bottom line: Be warned that as distinguished as her name is, your little Kate is likely to have plenty of company.

KATHERINE, KATHARINE, KATHRYN. The classic Katherine and Catherine have been playing popularity leapfrog for centuries. In America these days, it's the *K* version that seems more modern, more forceful, and more stylish, outnumbering the *C*s by more than three to one, while in England the *C* form is gaining ground. And though the pronunciation is identical, Catherine feels somehow softer and is the spelling used for such saintly characters as Catherine Earnshaw in *Wuthering Heights,* while Katherine with a *K* is the spirited heroine of Shakespeare's *Taming of the Shrew.* Maria Shriver and Arnold Schwarzenegger have a Katharine, the Hepburn spelling and the one that relates most closely to the name's Greek roots: the word *katharos* means "pure." The Kathryn spelling was popularized by actress Kathryn (born Zelma) Grayson in the 1940s—not fashionable, but still the second most widely used. **KATHY/CATHY** is the shared but outdated nickname for both spellings. **KATHARINA** is an exotic twist: Eighties rock singer Falco, of "Rock Me Amadeus" fame, has a daughter named Katharina-Bianca. The Russian form **KATYA** was used by actress Hunter Tylo for her daughter.

KATHLEEN. There are at least ten baby girls named Kaitlyn and variations thereof for every one called Kathleen these days. But in a sense the two are really the same name, Kathleen being the Anglicized phonetic spelling of the Irish Gaelic Caitlin and the most usual form of the name in Ireland itself. Caitlin, Kaitlyn et al. have been so overused at this point that Kathleen, popular here in the fifties, is beginning to sound fresh again. **CATHLEEN** is a spelling variation. Warren Beatty and Annette Bening have a **KATHLYN,** named for his mother. **KATLYN**—also spelled **KATLYNN, KATLIN,** or **KATLYNNE**—is yet another variation.

KATRINA. With its distinctly exotic feel, Katrina is the generic form of many European variations of Katherine, from the Gaelic **CATRIONA** (pronounced just like Katrina) to the German **KATARINA** (like ice-skating champion Witt) to the Italian **CATERINA**. Popular all over Europe as well as among African-Americans, the name can also be spelled **CATRINA**, changed to **KATRINE**, or shortened to **TRINA** or **KAT**. A more decorative, but perhaps too tinkly, version is **KATINKA**.

KAY. Kay seems rooted in the 1930s: It's a name that wears bias-cut satin evening gowns and goes to nightclubs where everybody smokes. Kay's been out of style for so long that it may be due for a comeback, and parents in search of a fresh, more cosmopolitan alternative to Kate might look here. **KAYE** is another spelling.

KAYA. A Native American name that means, literally, "my older little sister," suggesting wisdom. A rhyming relation of the trendy Maya.

KAYLA. The name Kayla was virtually nonexistent two decades ago, but now it's solidly in the Top 20. How did it zoom from nowhere to megastardom? A featured role in the soap opera *Days of Our Lives* starting in 1982 gave Kayla its big break. And it's close enough to cousins Kate, Katelyn, Hayley, and Kaylee to bask in their reflected glow. Today, with approximately 140,000 Kaylas born in the United States in the 1990s alone, the name suffers from overexposure. If you love the name, a more unusual and frankly prettier twist is **KELILA** or **KELILAH**, the Hebrew name meaning "laurel crown" from which both Kayla and its Yiddish sister **KAILA** are said to derive.

KAYLEE. Kaylee is one of those names whose true popularity is hidden by its many spellings and variations. According to recent Social Security figures, Kaylee in its myriad forms—taken in order of popularity, these include **KAYLEE, CALLIE, KAILEY, KAYLEIGH, KALI, KAYLIE, KALEIGH, KAILEE,** and **KAYLI,** not to mention the spelling possibilities that didn't make the Top 1000—ranks higher than Jennifer at number 21. Some sources say the name derives from the Hebrew Kelila; another possibility is that it's a euphonic invention in the Bailey/Hayley/Kayla vein.

KAYLIN. A hybrid of Kaylee and Katelin, this name along with its many spelling possibilities—the most popular, after the top-ranked Kaylin, are **KAYLYN, KAELYN,** and **KAYLYNN**—feels like the quintessential turn-of-the-millennium invention.

KEELY. It's not really an Irish first name, but it feels like one. First brought to notice in the U.S. by jazz singer and Louis Prima spouse **KEELEY** Smith, the name's better known bearer these days is much-photographed Pierce Brosnan wife Keely Shaye Smith.

KEENAN, KEAN. Irish names that derive from **CIAN,** a mythological warrior hero, and can be used for girls as well as boys. **KEYNE,** also pronounced as *keen,* was a female Cornish saint who could turn snakes into stones. **KEEGAN** was used for her daughter by telecaster Maureen O'Boyle.

KEISHA, KEZIAH. Keisha is a long-popular African-American name that derives from the biblical Keziah, one of the daughters of Job, which was often used for slaves. **KIZZY** was the version used on TV's *Roots. KESHIA, KEZIA,* and **KETZIA** are a few of the many other spelling possibilities.

KELLY. Kelly used to be the quintessential bouncy-blonde teenager name, but now most of the Kellys seem to have grown up, à la actresses Preston, Lynch, and Rutherford. While Kelly may have helped launched the trend for androgynous Irish names, it now takes a back seat in the fashion standings to such newcomers as Kelsey, Kennedy, and Cassidy. One attempt to compete is **KELLEN.** Fresher alternatives include less familiar Irish surnames including **KILLIAN, CALLAHAN, CLANCY, CONNELLY, QUINLAN,** and **KIRBY.**

KELSEY. Kelsey made its debut as a name back in the 1980s on *L.A. Law,* when attorney Ann Kelsey, played by Jill Eikenberry, adopted a baby girl and gave it her maiden name as a first, launching a style as well as a name. Kelsey has dropped a little in the popularity standings, ranking at number 33 for girls in the most recent poll. And while it has little masculine power, there were a handful of baby boys given the name, most thanks to actor Kelsey Grammer of television's popular *Frasier.*

KENDALL. One of the legion of androgynous *K* names, this surname taken from an English place-name denoting a valley of the river Kent has been a boys' name for a hundred and fifty years. In the most recent year counted, however, there were about 1,600 girl babies named Kendall to 600 boys. Sarah Michelle Gellar played a soap opera Kendall before she became Buffy the Vampire Slayer.

KENDRA. A favorite of African-American parents, Kendra got its start as a feminization of Kenneth. Twin star Tia Mowry played a character named Kendra in a recent film.

KENNEDY. Kennedy represents the confluence of several big baby-naming trends: androgynous names, surname names, *K* names, Irish names, hero names. MTV veejay Kennedy helped popularize the name, now at number 141 in the national charts for girls. Girls with this name outnumber boys eight to one.

KENYA. A popular place-name, especially among African-American parents in search of a name with cultural significance. In Hebrew, Kenya means "animal horn." Nastassja Kinski and Quincy Jones have a daughter named Kenya Julia Miami.

KERANI. A lovely Indo-Pakistani name that means "sacred bells." **KERA** is a diminutive that can stand alone.

KERRY. Kerry was one of the coolest names of the sixties and seventies (though often confused with Carrie) and today it still manages to hang on to a measure of its energy and appeal. The name of one of the most beautiful and lush counties in Ireland, Kerry may get a breath of new life now as a place-name. But if you use one of the cutesy variant spellings—**KERI** (as in appealing *Felicity* actress Russell), **KERRI, KERRIE,** etc.—you risk undermining whatever character the name has. **KERR** and **KERRIGAN** are related surname possibilities that feel newer and more unusual.

KESI. A cute Swahili name whose literal meaning is, unfortunately, "she who was born when her father was in trouble."

KETURAH. Keturah may have replaced Sarah as Abraham's second wife in the Old Testament, but her name certainly won't ever replace Sarah's in popularity. This is good news for anyone looking for a truly unusual and interesting biblical girl's name. The bad news is that most people would consider it an eccentric choice.

KIANA. A melodious synthetic name (also spelled **QUIANA** or **CHIANA**) that has become increasingly popular purely by virtue of its sound.

KIARA. Kiara, popularized by Simba's daughter in *The Lion King II,* may be a form of the Italian **CHIARA,** which means "clear," or it might be a feminine form of **KIARAN,** a seventh-century century Irish saint. No matter how you parse it, Kiara is an up-and-coming name, in the Top 100 by the most recent count, eclipsing its near relative Kira.

KIMBERLY. Kimberly was the Madison of its day, but the sun set on this name a couple of decades ago. It was inspired by the South African diamond town **KIMBERLEY,** an alternate spelling along with the unfortunate **KIMBERLEE.** The shortened form **KIM,** its use for girls inspired by a character in *Showboat,* had its run of popularity earlier, epitomized by Kim (born Marilyn) Novak in the 1950s. Although Kim (born **KIMILA**) Basinger, *Sex in the City* star Kim Cattrall, and rap diva L'il Kim are holding up the name's glamorous image, Kim has lost much of its allure for parents of newborn babies. Alternative **KIMBA** seemed like an interesting possibility for about as long as Judge Kimba Wood was under consideration for Attorney General. **KIMBER** is yet another possibility.

KIMI. A Japanese name meaning "sovereign." **KIMIKO** and **KIMIYO** derive from it.

KINSEY. Kinsey Millhone, the attractive wise-cracking heroine of the alphabet murder mysteries, is single-handedly responsible for the use of this name. Author Sue Grafton has a real-life granddaughter named Kinsey after the character. **KENZIE,** which also can be linked to the megapopular McKenzie, is a related name.

KIRBY. An ambisexual name that more often falls in the boys' camp—it's Anglo-Saxon for "church village"—but that's increasingly used for girls. While there were only about one thousand boys given the name in the entire decade of the 1990s, and not enough girls to register in the Top 1,000 names, it has the right stuff to become more popular.

KIRSTEN, KRISTEN, KRISTEN. One problem with naming a daughter Kirstin is that no one will ever remember whether her name is the Norwegian/Danish form of Christine **KIRSTEN** (as in actress Dunst), the Swedish **KERSTIN** or **KRISTIN** (as in *The English Patient's* Scott Thomas), or maybe even the hybrid **KRISTEN**—ironically, the most popular version. Not to mention **KIERSTEN, KIRSTYN, KRISTYN,** the Scottish **KIRSTIE** (as in Alley), the nicknames **KRISTY, KRISTI,** or **KRISTY,** or any of the scores of variations of **KRISTINE** or **KRISTINA.** Life will be, in other words, confusing. Pity, too, because Kirsten, Kristin, and cousins are some of the prettiest, most delicate, and crystalline-sounding names around: surely the source of their broad and continued popularity. Parents choosing one of these names may be shocked to find how popular they've been. Undercounted because of their myriad variations, Kirsten/Kristen et al. are in fact among the Top 20 names of the last decade. If you still can't resist this name's charms, you might try to find a more distinctive variation: **KRISTA, KRISTIANA, KIRSTA, KRYSIA.** See Christine for other ideas.

KISMET. Along with Destiny and Chance, one of the more popular of the new word names. Its meaning is clear: This child had to be.

KITTY. This name, with its spit curls and deep décolletage, is as outdated as that image of exaggerated femininity. Yet short form **KIT** has been used in recent years for several strong-willed movie heroines, and may prove a strong alternative for Kate.

KULYA. An unusual Native American name that's got possibilities, although many may not find its sound appealing.

KYLIE, KYLA. Kylie is an Australian name with Aboriginal roots—it means "boomerang"—that was brought to the Western world by pop star Kylie Minogue. It's been steadily gaining in popularity over the last decade, along with offshoots **KYLEE, KYLEIGH,** and **KILEY. KYLA** is not as related as it sounds, and is actually a feminine form of the popular boys' name **KYLE,** which can also be used for girls and may be the most attractive of any of the versions.

KYRA. Kyra and her cousins **KIRA** and **KIERA** should be more popular than they are. They're the kind of names people think of as trendy, but if you choose one for your child it's unlikely she'll meet many playmates with the same name. Related to the ancient Irish boys' name **KIERAN,** which means "dark," the feminine versions have been popularized by actress Kyra Sedgwick. Parents who amuse themselves by spelling names in strange ways can have a lot of fun with this one.

L

LACEY. Lacey is one of the few names that combines a surname feeling—as in *Cagney & Lacey,* an early feminist buddy show—with real femininity: for some parents, an ideal and hard-to-find mix. Actress Lacey Chabert was younger sister Claudia in TV's *Party of Five.*

LAILA. See **LEILA.**

LAKEISHA. A long-time favorite among African-American families, Lakeisha stems from Keziah, the name of one of the daughters of Job that was widely used among slaves, and the prefix *La,* which came to prominence in old New Orleans. The illegitimate children of French fathers and black mothers were often given the surname of *La* plus their father's first name—LaJean, for example—which gave rise to the widespread use of the suffix in African-American names.

LANA. Bombshell Lana Turner made this one of the sultriest names of the 1940s and fifties, but it doesn't retain much power to attract today, although it still can be found on soap operas. A stronger and more solid choice for a twenty-first-century girl would be **LANE,** an ambisexual name still more popular for boys but often used for spunky little girl TV and movie characters. **LAINE** and **LAYNE** could be alternate spellings.

LANGLEY. There are countless last-names-that-could-go-first like Langley. What puts this one on the map, besides the Pentagon, is that Mariel Hemingway used it for one of her daughters.

LARA. The name Lara was beginning to vanish along with *Dr. Zhivago*'s theme when the ultimate sexpot video-game heroine, Lara Croft, came along. Fathers of the future will be proposing this name as an appealing one for their daughters-to-be, perhaps without really remembering what inspired them.

LARISSA. The Russians spun off Lara from this more traditionally grounded name, from the Greek meaning "playful" or "jolly." In classical mythology, Larissa was the nymph who was loved by Mercury. Today, this is a very pretty yet underused choice that might provide an alternative for parents who like such feminine names as Melissa and Vanessa but are seeking something fresher. **LARISA** is another option.

LARK. Fashionable again thanks to the trend toward word/nature names, Lark has been around since the 1950s—think of it as a wanna-be Robin— but has never been widely used. **LARKIN** is a yuppier alternative. Other soft and pretty bird names flying into the picture: **DOVE, SPARROW,** and **WREN.**

LASHAUNA. A popular African-American name, with the widely used French New Orleans *La* prefix. Variations include **LASHAWNA, LASHONA,** and **LESHAUNA.**

LATIFAH. Actress and singer Queen Latifah (born Dana) popularized this North African Muslim name—it can also be **LATIFA** or **LATEEFA**—that means "gentle" or "pleasant."

LATOYA. Thanks to Ms. Jackson, this is one of the most popular of the names beginning with the syllable *La.* But while the *La* names used to dominate the African-American popularity lists, they are now crowded out by such new favorites as Jada and Destiny.

LAURA. One of the most fashionable of the classic names, Laura projects a quietly haunting feminine image. It's solidly in the Top 100 but not nearly as widespread as compatriots Emily or Elizabeth, so it retains a good measure of distinction. The name has given birth to many other forms over the years, but we say forget them all. **LAURETTA/LORETTA** is too old-fashioned and back-country, **LAURIE/LORI** is a nickname name stuck back in the sixties. And why make any changes to an eternally lovely name that needs no embellishment, enhancement, abbreviation, or transformation? The only possible exceptions: **LAUREL,** a pretty botanical name, and **LAURENCE,** the original male form used for girls in France.

LAUREN. More popular than Laura and also more trendy, Lauren has managed to stay in the Top 25 for girls since the early eighties. According to a Harvard sociologist's study, it's among the names preferred most by mothers with high educations. And now singer **LAURYN** Hill gives it a new shot of style, picking up where Ralph Lauren, model Lauren (born Mary Laurence) Hutton, and Lauren (born Betty) Bacall left off. **LOREN,** the usual male spelling of the name, is sometimes used for girls as well. **LORENA** is a variation sometimes used for babies, though some parents might remember knife-wielding wife Lorena Bobbitt, who made her husband less of a man.

LAVERNE. A name better left where it is, embroidered on an old poodle skirt or cast in stone, like the talking gargoyle named Laverne in Disney's *The Hunchback of Notre Dame.*

LAVINIA. A prim and proper Victorian-sounding name, Lavinia dates back to ancient times, when it was the name of the wife of the Trojan hero Aeneas, who was considered the mother of the Roman people. More recently, moviegoers heard it in the adaptation of Shakespeare's *Titus Andronicus* with Jessica Lange. Parents who favor lavender-tinged names along the lines of Amelia and Maude may like Lavinia.

LAYLA. See **LEILA.**

LEAF. A nature name that feels more sixties than twenty-first century.

LEANDRA. The female of Leander, which means "lion man."

LEATRICE. It's not quite Beatrice, and it's not really Letitia, but Leatrice has a gently old-fashioned charm of its own.

LEAH. Recently this gentle biblical name—in the Old Testament, Leah was the sister of Rachel, first wife of Jacob, and considered one of the four matriarchs of Judaism—has gained a real following, especially among Jewish families looking for a traditional name not quite as well used as Rachel or Rebecca. Some foreign versions that share the same sweetness: the French **LEA** and the Italian **LIA**.

LEE. Lee sounds as if it had been created for middle-naming purposes, but since parents now favor names with real meaning in all positions, it is losing ground even there. The embroidered spelling **LEIGH** gives it a little more Rachael Leigh Cook–type substance, but with so many more interesting ambigender names available as options these days, we wouldn't expect to find Lee very high on anyone's list. **LEELEE** Sobieski is a wonderful actress who is nevertheless unlikely to inspire many namesakes.

LEILA. There is a whole lush garden full of similarly pronounced, differently spelled exotic names clustered around Leila, which includes **LAILA, LAYLA, LELA, LEILAH,** and **LELIA.** Leila itself is a Persian name meaning "dark-haired," which was popularized by the poet Lord Byron in the nineteenth century when he used it for a Muslim child in a poem with a rich Eastern setting. In contemporary times, Layla is better known as the gender-bending title character of an Eric Clapton song. TV weatherman Al Roker and newswoman Deborah Roberts's daughter is Leila Ruth, and Greta Scacci and Vincent D'Onofrio also have a little Leila while Tanya Tucker's daughter is Layla. Lelia is a Latin name used in Roman times and pronounced LEH-lee-a.

LEILANI. Leilani is a lovely Hawaiian name meaning "heavenly flower." **LEILAN** is a South Pacific variation with possibilities. And we all know the princess **LEIA.**

LENA. A pet form of Helen that became a name in its own right, Lena is famous as coupled with Horne and, more recently, Olin. But Lena still feels like only half a name.

LEONORA, LENORE, LEONA. This group of names started life as European offspring of Eleonora, and have pretty much fallen out of fashion, except for Leonora, whose melliflous sound makes it a revival possibility. It also has the distinction of being the name of three major opera characters, including the heroine of Beethoven's *Fidelio.* Lenore is a "modernization" that no longer feels very modern, and Leona did not gain from its association with the Queen of the Helmsley hotels.

LESLIE, LESLEY. A Scottish place-name and surname that was once androgynous but now is almost exclusively female. Last stylish in the 1960s, Leslie still has a pleasant, heathery feel but has lost out in the popularity stakes to Lindsay and Lucy. **LESLY** shows up in the Top 1,000.

LETITIA. A prim-and-proper-sounding name whose staid image has been unbuttoned recently by Victoria's Secret supermodel Letitia Casta. The older form of the name, **LETTICE,** had all but died out when it was revived by the popular play *Lettice and Lovage.* But since it has never gained a foothold in this country, we're afraid it would provoke a veritable salad of teasing for any American child who bore it. **LETTY** and **LETTIE** are sweet, gold-locket pet forms. Rapper Ice-T spelled his daughter's name Letesha, one of many variations.

LEXI, LEXIE. A pixieish offshoot of the Alex family, from Alexis to Alexandra. Use it as a nickname by all means, but we urge one of the more formal names for the birth certificate. Leeza Gibbons has a daughter Lexi.

LIANA, LEANNE. Liana is a French name for a flowering tropical vine. Leanne and all its variations—which seem, and often are, more like creative spellings of Lee Ann—relate to it.

LIBBY. This is one of the Elizabeth nicknames that has been neglected for years in favor of Beth and Betsy, **LIZ** and **LIZZIE.** These days, it sounds more modern than the rest.

LIBERTY. A word name that harkens back to the hippie days.

LIESL. The German diminutive for Elizabeth—it's pronounced LEE-zel—sometimes heard here, especially in *The Sound of Music* revivals—more grown-up and distinctive than Heidi.

LILA. Pronounced with a long *i,* Lila has been a soap-opera mainstay, as in the long-running character of *General Hospital* matriarch Lila Quatermaine. Sexy and forceful, Lila can also be spelled **LYLA,** and either version can end with an *h.*

LILAC. Tired of Rose? Bored with Lily? Then Lilac, one of the underused botanicals, may appeal to you.

LILIA. Some sources call this a derivation of the Latin name Lelia, others say it's a Lily offshoot. Whatever its origins, it's a lovely name with a distinctive sound.

LILITH. This name has been more shunned than neglected over the years because of the negative associations it bore from Semitic mythology, which portrayed Lilith as Adam's rejected wife (pre-Eve) who, for refusing to obey her husband, was turned into an evil, ugly demon that haunted the wilderness on stormy nights, and was especially threatening to little children. Dr. Lilith Sternin was Dr. Frasier Crane's icy wife on *Cheers:* Their divorce sent him to Seattle and his own TV show. More recently, several top female singers have joined forces annually for the "Lilith Fair" tour.

LILY. One of the delicate century-old flower names making a comeback, Lily has both a cool elegance (it is the symbol of purity) and a slightly off-beat charm. The name seems to be a favorite of celebrity parents, often combined with a middle name: starbabies include a Lily-Rose Melody (Johnny Depp and Vanessa Paradis), a **LILI** Jordan (Lou Diamond Phillips), a **LILLIE** Price (Kirstie Alley), Lily Anne (Chris O'Donnell), Lily Max (Meredith Vieira), and Lily Goddard (Adam Ant). Older Lilys include the daughters of Kevin Costner, Phil Collins, Eric Idle, Dianne Wiest, Jill Clayburgh and David Rabe, Mary Steenburgen and Malcolm McDowell, and Amy Madigan and Ed Harris. It is also the name of Sela Ward's character in *Once and Again*. Despite its popularity in Hollywood, Lily has managed to avoid becoming too widely used, coming in at number 155 in the most recent popularity poll. But parents on either coast or living in style-conscious cities might find an unusually high concentration of Lilys in their neighborhood.

LILIAN. Lily came first, the Italians turned it into **LILIANA,** then the British clipped it to **LILIAN,** which the Americans, when it was popular around 1900, preferred to spell it **LILLIAN.** These days, it's less stylish than the original, though the Italian version and the Gaelic **LILIAS** have possibilities.

LINDA. Linda will live forever in nomenclature history as the name that toppled Mary from its four-hundred-year reign as number 1. Queen of the mountain in 1950, Linda has fallen even further from grace than Mary today. Linda originated as the short form of older German-based names Belinda and Melinda (both mean "serpent"), and also ties in with the Spanish word for "pretty." LBJ's daughter **LYNDA** popularized this variant spelling during the name's last days in the sun.

LINDSAY. Bionic Woman Lindsay Wagner helped legitimize this unusual male name as a fitting one for girls; in the early eighties, riding in tandem with Courtney, it approached the Top 10. But while Lindsay deserves recognition as a style pioneer in the now-booming category of ambisexual-last-names-first, its own currency has faded. **LINDSEY** is a variation.

LINNEA. A Scandinavian name that derives from renowned botanist Carl Linnaeus, signifying (according to different sources) "linden tree" or "mountain flower." Some pronounce it Lin-NAY, others Lin-NAY-uh.

LISA, LIZA. The King's naming his daughter Lisa Marie Presley and the hit song "Mona Lisa" conspired to catapult Lisa from one of many nicknames for Elizabeth to the fourth most popular girls' name in 1970. In 1980 it was still number 12, but its star has now dimmed. **LIZA,** as in Minnelli, was never quite as popular and so feels fresher. **LEEZA** Gibbons added a new spelling to the mix. **LISSA** is usually short for Melissa, but could be a diminutive of Elizabeth or another name and might also stand, though not very sturdily, on its own.

LISETTE, LIZETTE. Originally a diminutive of Elizabeth, these names more often appear on their own these days than as nicknames. **LIZBETH** is another such variation, and **LISANNE** or **LIZANNE** are similar possibilities.

LISSA. This might be short for Melissa, but in its own right it has another, more substantial association: It's the name of a supreme mother goddess in African mythology.

LIV. A Norse name introduced to this country by Ingmar Bergman's star Liv Ullman and now popularized by gorgeous young actress and Aerosmith daughter Liv Tyler.

LIVIA. It sounds like it must be a chopped-off version of Olivia, but the distinctively attractive Livia has been an independent name since the days of the ancient Romans, when it belonged to the wife of the Emperor Augustus. Makes sense when you consider it was also the name of the mother of the Mafia don on *The Sopranos,* played by the late Nancy Marchand.

LOIS. Lois may live on as the name of the eternal fiancée of Superman, but ever since it peaked in 1925, it has sounded more and more like the sweet, gray-haired woman down the street whom everyone in the neighborhood entrusts with their spare keys. Quite fittingly, Lois means "good" in Greek, and was the name of the grandmother of Timothy in the New Testament.

LOLA. Unlike names such as Désirée and Salome, Lola manages to be sexy without going over the top, even though in the past it has been associated with such femmes fatales as the nineteenth-century courtesan Lola Montez (who was actually Irish and born Marie Dolores), the Marlene Dietrich character in *The Blue Angel* and Jean Harlow's in *Bombshell,* the sexpot in *Damn Yankees,* "Whatever Lola Wants, Lola Gets," and, in pet name form, the notorious **LOLITA.** Despite all that, this onetime diminutive of Dolores remains a charming, offbeat name with a good deal of style for those who defy convention: It's the nickname of Madonna's daughter Lourdes and was also chosen by such tastemakers as the Eurythmics' Annie Lennox and artist Julian Schnabel.

LORELEI. Lorelei will be probably forever stuck with its siren image—it was, after all, the name of the beautiful Rhine River seductress whose haunting voice led sailors to hazardous rocks that would cause them to be shipwrecked. Lorelei Lee was the not-so-dumb-blonde siren portrayed on screen by Marilyn Monroe. More recently, Lorelei is the name of a mother and daughter—nicknamed **RORY**—on TV's *Gilmore Girls.*

LORNA. One of those names, like Pamela, Vanessa, and Wendy, that was tailored by a novelist to fit the personality of a particular character, in this case the forlorn Lorna Doone. Judy Garland chose the name for her younger daughter, but not that many other mothers have favored it.

LORRAINE. Sweet Lorraine: This French place-name has moved in and out of fashion in the few hundred years it's been used as a girls' first name, somewhat influenced by the alternate name of Joan of Arc—Saint Joan of Lorraine. It was quite popular in this country from the 1920s to the forties, and very rarely used since. But if it's as firmly fixed in fashion limbo as most people think, how come Jack Nicholson used it for his daughter? The alternate spelling **LARAINE** was popularized by forties star Laraine Day.

LOTTIE. A nostalgic great-grandma name—once short for Charlotte—that conjures up petit-point pillows and lace doilies. It's one of a whole sorority of such names, including Nellie, Letty, Josie, Hattie, Milly, and Tillie, that some modern parents are beginning to reassess. Really.

LOUISA, LOUISE. In most cases, feminine names are more fashionable with an *a* ending (Diana, Susanna, Julia), but in this instance (as with Isabel/Isabella), both Louise and Louisa are making their way back. Louise is seen as a competent, no-nonsense, efficient name, whereas Louisa (chosen by Meryl Streep for one of her three daughters) is a bit more feminine and quaint. Very popular in the eighteenth century, Louisa was finally toppled at the end of the nineteenth by the French form Louise, which rose to and remained in the Top 35 girls' names in America during the whole first quarter of the twentieth century. One of Louisa's attractive namesakes is author Louisa May Alcott; Louise was the character played by Susan Sarandon in the feminist road movie *Thelma and Louise*. The appealing Spanish form is **LUISA;** a place-name variation is **LOUISIANA.** Nicknames include the impudent **LULU** (what Paul Simon and Edie Brickel named their daughter), the hard-driving **LOU,** and **OUISA.**

LOURDES. Pronounced with two syllables and taken from the name of the French town where Saint Bernadette had a vision of the Virgin Mary in 1858, Madonna catapulted this name from obscurity to the spotlight when she used it for her daughter.

LOVE. A highly romantic word name and the middle name used as her first by young actress Jennifer Love Hewitt. But Love could be a hard burden for a child to carry.

LUCILLE. Unlike Lucy, Lucille did get permanently saddled with the Lucille Ball linkage, so that its image has tangerine-colored hair, exaggeratedly round eyes, and a tendency to dress in clown outfits and stage daffy and desperate efforts to perform with her husband's band. Variation **LUCILLA** may have a shot at escape.

LUCY. Lucy is both saucy and solid, making it an attractive choice on several levels. The English form of the equally appealing Roman **LUCIA,** which derives from the Latin word *lux*, meaning "light," Lucy/Lucia was at one time given to girls born at dawn. An early saint's name later used for characters by Fielding and Dickens, Lucy has managed to survive associations with the bossy little girl in *Peanuts,* with the possible psychedelic implications of "Lucy in the Sky with Diamonds," and with *I Love Lucy* (see Lucille, above). Current Lucys Lawless and Liu have imparted a new strength to the name. Actress Mimi Rogers has a Lucy, and Danny DeVito and Rhea Perlman used the French spelling for their little **LUCIE.** From the same Latin source comes **LUCINDA,** an engaging seventeenth- and eighteenth-century variant first used in *Don Quixote* that might appeal to the modern parent looking for an out-of-the-ordinary, old-fashioned name. **LUCIA** (pronounced either LOO-sha or loo-CHEE-a and chosen by Giovanni Ribisi for his daughter), **LUCIANA,** and **LUCIENNE** are further foreign possibilities.

LUNA. Familiar to nature lovers as the name of the redwood Julia Butterfly Hill lived in for two years and to soap opera watchers via the character of Luna Moody on *One Life to Live,* this moonstruck name would make a daring, evocative choice. But "Loony" is an unfortunate nickname possibility.

LUZ. A Spanish name that means "light"; an exotic relative of Lucy.

LYDIA. A very early place name, Lydia was an area of Asia Minor whose inhabitants are credited with the invention of coinage and great musical talent. Although mentioned as a first name in the New Testament (Lydia was the first European convert of Saint Paul), it did not really emerge as such until the seventeenth century, gaining notoriety through the character Lydia Languish in Sheridan's 1775 play, *The Rivals,* and the youngest of the Bennett girls in *Pride and Prejudice.* Today, Lydia is quietly fashionable with an offbeat sort of appeal. Heiress and ex-fugitive Patty Hearst used it for one of her daughters, as did actor Bill Paxton.

LYNN. Lynn came to life in the 1940s as a spin-off from the wildly popular Linda, and enjoyed some independent notoriety as one of the most common of mid-century middle names—along with Ann, Marie, and Lee. With the fad for that kind of follow-the-dots middle name now long over, Lynn is left with nowhere to go. **LYNNE** is a dressed-up spelling. **LYNETTE,** which enjoyed some low-level long-ago popularity as a Lynn/Linda adjunct, is actually an unrelated variation on a Welsh name, **LINET,** who was a female magician who rescued warriors.

LYRIC. A musical name with Greek roots that is used for several hundred babies a year and is sure to gain wider acceptance with the advent of word names.

M

MABEL. A few years ago, when British comic actress Tracey Ullman used this name for her little girl, it seemed like the most outrageously campy choice imaginable. But now—is it just us?—we can really recognize its cheeky charm, that of a whole group of old-fashioned British-barmaid, wisecracking-waitress names. Mabel originated as a shortened version of Amabel, which is French for "lovable," losing the initial *A* somewhere along the way and becoming a Victorian favorite, especially popular in this country from around 1870 to 1900. **MAB** was the queen of the fairies in Shakespeare's *A Midsummer Night' s Dream*.

MACY. Singer Macy Gray wasn't the first to sport this cute and upbeat surname name, but she'll certainly help popularize it. A modern-sounding replacement for such tired old favorites as Stacy and Tracy.

MACKENZIE, MCKENZIE. So far, this is one of the "Mac" names most often used for girls, already in the Top 25 in some states, following the lead of actress Mackenzie (born Laura Mackenzie) Phillips. **McKENNA** is another popular option, and **McCAILEY** (with its many variations—think Makaylee) is growing fast. Other possibilities might be **MACALLISTER** and **MACKIN-LEY**—or any name you can resurrect from your family tree.

MADELINE, MADELEINE. This lovely French name with a soft and delicate image has become wildly fashionable again. It's one of those names whose true popularity is masked by its many spellings—Madeline beats out the others, two to one, with the nonclassic **MADELYN** in second place. **MADA-LYN** also appears. Taken together, all the versions place Madeline squarely in today's Top 50. The Gallic version of the rarely used **MAGDALENE,** Madeline has been found frequently in literature, from the poems of Keats and Tennyson to the charming children's books of Ludwig Bemelmans. Actors David Duchovny and Tea Leoni named their daughter **MADELAINE** West.

MADALENA is an exotic variation, and **MADDY** (or **MADDIE**) is a popular nickname.

MADISON. It's ambigender, it's a place-name, and it's presidential. So how could Madison fail to be wildly trendy? Madison, which got its big break as the name of Daryl Hannah's mermaid character in *Splash* (who named herself after New York's Madison Avenue), was number 3 nationwide at last count. This is also one of those names that seems to inspire a legion of spelling variations: Among the Top 1,000 names last year were **MADDISON, MADISYN,** and **MADYSON.** Many Madisons become Maddys.

MADONNA. To state the obvious, Madonna Louise Ciccone took her reverent Christian name and turned its image inside out. This Italian title for the Virgin Mary, literally meaning "my lady," has been used as a given name only fairly recently, especially among Americans of Italian descent. Madonna herself has said, "I feel I was given a special name for a reason. In a way, maybe I wanted to live up to my name."

MAEVE. Short but strong, this name of a legendary queen of Connacht would make a distinctive choice, particularly for a child with Irish roots. It's already been attached to the Kennedy family tree via a young granddaughter of Robert and Ethel. **MAVE** is also used, and the (very difficult) Gaelic spelling is **MADHBH.**

MAGGIE. Long emancipated from its mother name of Margaret, Maggie has a strong and vigorous, tousled, fun-loving air. It was popular at the turn of the century, was revived in the freewheeling sixties and is still a favorite— though growing somewhat tired, à la Annie and Lizzie—choice. Through the years, it has been well used by writers—there was Maggie Tulliver, the heroine of George Eliot's *The Mill on the Floss,* Stephen Crane's unfortunate *Maggie: A Girl of the Streets,* Maggie the Cat in Tennessee Williams's *Cat on a Hot Tin Roof,* portrayed in the movies by Elizabeth Taylor—and has also been immortalized in songs like "When You and I Were Young, Maggie" and Rod Stewart's "Maggie May." Country singers Faith Hill and Tim McGraw have a little Maggie.

MAGNOLIA. An over-the-top flower name, as showy as the large pink or white heavily perfumed blossom itself, recommended for the adventurous name giver only. Magnolia has gone down in musical theater history via the heroine of *Show Boat,* adapted from the Edna Ferber novel.

MAHALA, MAHALIA. The former is an almost unknown but pleasant-sounding Hebrew name meaning "tenderness" and also a Native American name for "woman." Mahalia is firmly connected to perhaps the greatest of all gospel singers, Mahalia Jackson.

MAIA. See **MAYA.**

MAIDA. An Old English name as outmoded now as the use of the word *maid* for a young woman.

MAISIE. This spirited yet sentimental Scottish pet form of Margaret and Marjorie is a vintage gem, popular in the 1920s and 1930s, ready to be recycled. **MAIZIE** is another spelling, seen in a series of children's books.

MAKAYLA, MIKAYLA, MICHAELA. This name was traditionally Michaela, the female of Michael, but the popularity of Kayla has given it a new twist so that now there are six times as many girl babies given the name with the "new" spellings as with the original. Makayla et al. is also one of those names that, because of all its spelling variations, is much more popular than a parent perusing the list of top names would be led to believe. Its most widespread single spelling shows up only at number 67—invisible on most lists—but if you add all the versions together, the name is firmly in the Top 20. The popularity of *Dr. Quinn, Medicine Woman,* whose name is Michaela, and of Michael itself have added to the name's favor. The Steven Spielbergs have a daughter named Mikaela George, Deborah Norville has a Mikaela, and LeVar Burton has a Michaela. Spelling variations, in order of occurrence, include **MIKAELA, McKAYLA, MICAELA, MIKALA,** and **MAKALA**—and there are undoubtedly many more where those came from. **MAYKAYLEE** is a variation we're starting to hear.

MALLORY. This onetime strictly masculine surname name suddenly became a strong girl's choice in the early eighties, no doubt influenced by the character played by Justine Bateman on the popular sitcom *Family Ties*. It blended in well with the other three-syllable names in fashion at the time, like Brittany and Kimberly, while retaining a firmer, less fluffy image.

MALU. This charming Hawaiian name meaning "peace" was chosen by ex-Talking Head David Byrne for his daughter, Malu Valentine.

MALVA, MALVINA, MELVA, MELVINA. Malvina was coined by an eighteenth-century poet named James Macpherson and became quite popular in Scandinavia. But neither it nor any of its offshoots sound much more appealing today than their male counterpart, Melvin.

MAMIE. Yet another short form of Mary and Margaret (there are dozens), Mamie had a short pageboy and curled-under bangs all through the Eisenhower years, but now, like Maisie, could be ready for a new life. Meryl Streep's daughter Mary Willa is called Mamie, a good example of how the name can be stylishly put to service as a short form for a more formal name—Mary or Margaret or Miriam—used to honor an ancestor. The abbreviated form **MAME** has a dotty, antic feel because of the best-selling *Auntie Mame*, which led to a successful play, movie, and musical.

MANDY and **MINDY.** These nickname names of the sixties just don't cut it in today's more sophisticated times.

MANON. A French name that originated as a diminutive of Marie and has the exotic yet straightforward feel that might make it a viable new import.

MANZIE. Woody Allen named his second adopted daughter with Soon-Yi Previn Manzie after jazz musician Manzie Johnson. The little girl's middle name is **TIO,** after another jazz musician, Lorenzo Tio. The names have a lot of style but probably are not destined for widespread acclaim—undoubtedly just the way Allen prefers it.

MARA. Exotic and evocative, Mara is a biblical name that means "bitter": In the Book of Ruth, Naomi, devastated after the deaths of her husband and two sons, says, "Call me not Naomi, call me Mara." Multicultural, Mara is also a Kiswahili word meaning "a time" and could be conceived as an African geographical name, being a river flowing through Kenya and Tanzania. The spelling **MARAH** is used for a character on *The Guiding Light*.

MARCELLA, MARCELLINE. Marcella, while not heard much here in nearly a hundred years, is still popular in Europe (as is its masculine version, Marcel), which lends it a certain continental charm. Marcella is depicted as the world's most beautiful woman in *Don Quixote*.

MARCIA, MARSHA. A name in which both spellings are used almost equally, this short form of Marcella had a brief run of popularity in the 1940s and fifties. By the sixties, **MARCY** was more popular, but all forms are now in fashion limbo.

MARGARET. After several decades in storage, buttoned securely within its starchy image, Margaret is being aired out by parents attracted to the name's strong sound and classic status. Margaret is also an important family name for many people, having ranked in the Top 10 through the first half of the 1900s. Following the lead of other Stylish Conservatives such as Elizabeth and Katherine, Margaret even has its own trendy Lizzie/Kate equivalent nickname: Maggie. But long-dormant Margaret short forms Maisie or Daisy seem fresher, and in keeping with the overall trend many parents simply stick with the full version. An extremely well used name since medieval times and still considered the "Scottish national name," Margaret derives both from the Greek meaning "pearl" and the Persian meaning "child of light." In Persian mythology, oysters would rise to the water's surface at night to worship the moon and catch a single drop of congealed dew in their shells, which the moonbeam would then transform into a pearl. In various eras and cultures, Margaret has been one of the most Christian and royal of female names—attached to the patron saint of women in childbirth and to various queens and princesses in England, Scandinavia, Austria, and the Netherlands, and in modern times to the first female prime minister of Great Britain, Margaret Thatcher. In the 1950s, it was seen as the quintessential mom name, as in *Father Knows Best*. Many of its offspring in addition to Maggie have become independently used names, including **MADGE, MEG, MARJORIE, MEGAN, MOLLY, PEGGY,** and **RITA.** Foreign versions also found in this country are **MARGO** and **MARGUERITE** (French), **MARGARITA** (Spanish), and **GRETCHEN** and **GRETA** (German). **MAIREAD,** pronounced ma-RAYD, is the lovely Irish version.

MARGO, MARGOT. This French pet form of Marguerite has a lot of elements going for it: Its unusual (especially for a girls' name) *o* ending makes it more dynamic and dramatic than Margaret, though it still shares in the original's classic feel. Movie buffs will remember Bette Davis's archetypal role as Margo Channing in *All About Eve,* while balletomanes will associate the name with the great English dancer Margot Fonteyn. But the **MARGAUX** spelling, as in the Bordeaux wine and the late, ill-fated Hemingway, is too pretentious even for the soaps.

MARIA. The most common girls' name in all Spanish-speaking countries and the favorite form of Mary from Italy to Austria to Eastern Europe, Maria has also been a quietly but consistently used name in upper-class Anglo families. Maria Shriver, daughter of a Kennedy mother and a high-Wasp father, is a prime example of this arcane but intriguing practice. Parents bold (or maybe sophisticated) enough to appreciate Maria's graces will see it as a timeless choice perfect for a child of tomorrow's global village. In Europe, Maria is often combined with another name—witness **MARIA-OLYMPIA,** the name of a daughter of Prince Pavlos of Greece and Marie-Chantal Miller. For further information on all that's right about the name Maria, listen to the classic song from the musical *West Side Story*.

MARIAH. Mariah Carey did what Madonna couldn't: single-handedly popularized what had been an arcane name. This nineteenth-century variation of Maria is now number 76 on the name hit parade, and climbing. **MORIAH** and **MARYA** are other spellings, but the original, for once, predominates.

MARIAN, MARION. Yet another offshoot of Marie, this one a medieval French version, Marian had a respectable run of popularity in this country. It was in the Top 10 in 1900, was still in the Top 20 in the twenties, and is one of the very serious great-aunt names that are up for reconsideration today. Robin Hood's Maid Marian provides a timeless romantic image for the name. Gabriel Byrne and Ellen Barkin have a daughter named Romy Marion. The extended edition of the name, **MARIANNE,** is so endemic in France that it has become the personification of the Republic, analagous to our Uncle Sam. A less sophisticated version is **MARY ANN,** but **MARIANNA,** with that all-important final *a,* may be the most obviously stylish version of all.

MARIE. Marie, the French form of Mary, tends to sound more dated than either Mary or Maria at this point, although at one time it rivaled both, actually reaching the number 2 spot in America at the end of the 1920s. The most visible contemporary bearer of the name, Marie Osmond, was born Olive. **MARIEL,** as in Hemingway, is the Dutch and French diminutive and certainly more inspirational for modern parents. Other versions are **MARIELA, MARIELLE, MARIETTE,** and **MARIETTA.**

MARIGOLD. Occasionally used in England, especially in the novels of authors like Barbara Pym, Marigold would definitely be seen as a wildly exotic flower name in the United States, but it does have a sunny, golden feel to it.

MARILYN. We've all known many Marilyns, contemporaries of the Barbaras and Lindas and Carols born at the peak of their names' popularity, from the 1920s to the fifties. Yet strangely enough, although Marilyn Monroe (born Norma Jean and renamed in tribute to earlier star Marilyn Miller) was the ultimate sex symbol of her generation, no stardust adhered to the name. Now, in particular, Marilyn has virtually none of the freshness or sparkle that would inspire a parent to use it for a millennial child.

MARINA. This pretty sea-born name was used to dramatic effect by Shakespeare in his play *Pericles* for the virtuous princess who says she is "Call'd Marina, for I was born at sea." In France, a very fashionable alternative is **MARINE.**

MARIS, MARISA, MARISSA. Maris is a name that was hardly heard of until it didn't appear as the unseen sister-in-law in *Frasier.* Unusual and appealing, it comes from the phrase "Stella Maris," which means "star of the sea," one of many epithets for the Virgin Mary. Much more familiar is Marisa/Marissa, which never reached the saturation point of its cousin Melissa, and is therefore still a feasible choice. It has been publicized in recent years by Academy Award–winning actress Marisa Tomei. **MARISOL** is the dramatic Latina version.

MARJORIE, MARGERY. Popular among the medieval royals, Marjorie is a Scottish and Margery an English vernacular form of Margaret, both of which were seen as more lively versions of the old standard a hundred years ago. In the 1950s and sixties, **MARGIE** was seen as a prime pert-teenager name in such TV shows and movies as *My Little Margie*. One name expert proposes that all these names faded with the advent of the word "margarine."

MARLENE, MARLENA, MARLA. Marlene, originally pronounced as we now pronounce Marlena, was not heard of in this country until the importation of German screen star Marlene Dietrich, who had compressed the beginning and ending syllables of her original first names, Maria Magdalene, into the more glamorous new version. Americans were quick to change the pronunciation to Marleen, consonant with other names popular at the time like Arlene and Maxine. Marlene is rarely used for babies today, but some related names have taken its place: **MARLA** has made headlines first as Maples, then as Trump; **MARLO** seems to have been invented by Marlo Thomas, who was born Margaret, and **MARLEY/MARLEE** calls to mind reggae great Bob and deaf actress Matlin.

MARNIE. This outdated nickname name of the sixties was up in lights via the 1964 Hitchcock thriller of that title, but now seems indistinguishable from Mandy, Mindy, and the rest.

MARTHA. The name borne by our first First Lady still has a prim and proper DAR image, academic and efficient. That quiet traditional tasteful gestalt is exactly what makes Martha appealing to some parents today: Martha's the dark waxed wood floor, the muted Oriental rug of names. The New Testament Martha, sister of Lazarus and Mary of Bethany, was a solicitous housekeeper who looked after the material welfare of Jesus when he was a guest in their home. For this reason Martha has since been identified with domestic labor and hospitality and is the patron saint of housewives, waiters, and cooks (à la Martha Stewart, who shares the name with her mother). Giving the name a more contemporary spirit are MTV veejay Martha Quinn and actress Martha Plimpton. Livelier foreign forms that have been used in this country are **MARTA, MARTHE, MARTINE,** and **MARTINA,** the latter associated with tennis champs Navratilova and Hingis.

MARY. Someone said recently that if you want to give your daughter a really unusual name nowadays, pick Mary. A true irony for the name that for centuries had been by far the most popular and enduring female Christian name in the English-speaking world (as were Maria and Marie in the Spanish and French)—at least until 1950. That was when Mary was finally dethroned by such trendy upstarts as Linda and Karen. The Greek and New Testament form of the Hebrew Miriam—via the Latin Maria—in earliest times Mary was considered too sacred to be used by ordinary mortals. It finally began to be employed in England in the twelfth century, and by the sixteenth had blanketed the female population, to the point where dozens of pet forms had to be contrived for the simple purpose of distinguishing one Mary in the family from the others. There was a hiatus due to the odious religious persecutions of Mary Tudor ("Bloody Mary"), but then the name was back, bigger than ever, classless and ubiquitous. In this country, Mary has always been a scrubbed-faced good-girl name (to the tune of "Oh what a pal was Mary"), even in the 1940s and fifties when an infusion of energy was attempted with any number of middle name add-ons—from **MARY LOU** and **MARY JO** to **MARY JANE** and **MARY BETH.** Mary was unstoppably pure, as reflected still in those 1960s and seventies icons of propriety and wholesomeness, Mary Poppins and Mary Tyler Moore. Numerous future celebrities in fact dropped their birth names of Mary for something that seemed more glitzy, among them Bo Derek, Debbie Reynolds, Sissy Spacek, Lauren Hutton, Meryl Streep, and Lily Tomlin, while others have returned to it for their daughters in an effort, perhaps, to reclaim its moral imperative, including Paul McCartney and Meryl Streep. Today, Mary remains fashionable only among upmarket Southerners and Catholics, who use Mary as a silent first name to impart traditionalism and saintliness to an offbeat middle name like Walker or Courtney. Virtually every culture in the Western world has a variant of Mary. Among the prettiest are **MAIR** (Welsh), **MAIRE** or **MARE** (Gaelic), **MARO** (Armenian), **MAREN** (Norway), and **MAJA** and **MARJA** (Sweden). Mary nicknames, most of which have long been well used in their own right, include Molly, Mitzi, Mamie, Minnie, Polly, and May.

MATILDA, MATHILDA. A sweet, slightly fussy, onetime German name that now has an Australian accent (thanks largely to the song "Waltzing Matilda" and an old movie about a boxing kangaroo), Matilda seems to be making a bit of a comeback. Not surprising that Australian actor Bryan Brown and wife Rachel Ward would choose it for their daughter, but American Elizabeth Perkins did so as well. Usable nickname offshoots include **TILDA** and **TILLIE** or, for those looking to steer back toward the mainstream, **MATTY**. Matilda was introduced to England by William the Conqueror's wife and then his granddaughter, who was known as Maud. The French spelling **MATHILDE** (it's a fashionable choice there) seems to turn it into another, more sophisticated name.

MAUD, MAUDE. Maud or Maude is a lacy, mauve-colored name that was popular a hundred years ago, partly influenced by the Tennyson poem that included the oft-quoted line "Come into the garden, Maud." In the 1970s, the vociferous and opinionated TV character Maude Finlay put a very different spin on the name, but now that seems like an aberration, and the name has settled back to the Victorian version. It seems particularly ripe for use as a softening middle name, as Glenn Close employed it for her daughter, Annie Maude.

MAURA, MAUREEN, MOIRA. Of all these Gaelic forms of Mary popular in Ireland and Scotland, Maura is probably the most fashionable form today, easier to fathom (and pronounce) than the more authentic Moira. The diminutive Maureen was almost as popular in the 1950s and sixties among the Irish in Boston as among their relatives still over in Bray, but is not used very much anymore.

MAUVE. Another new color name adding life to the naming landscape, Mauve is particularly soft and antique-sounding, bearing associations with the gently old-fashioned Maude and Maeve.

MAVIS. There are plenty of flower names, but not too many bird names. Mavis, a British World War II period name with friends like **BERYL** and **AVRIL,** is another word for the song thrush. One lovely Mavis we know cut her name to make it more fashionable, and is now **MAVE.**

MAXINE. A Frenchified feminization of Max that popped up in the 1930s and now seems condemned to permanent limbo, despite the fashion status of its male counterpart.

MAY, MAE. Definitely sounding fresh and springlike again after more than a century in mothballs, May started as one of the innumerable pet forms of Mary and Margaret, as well as a vernal month name along with April and June. Actors Madeleine Stowe and Brian Benben named their daughter May Theodora. May is well suited to use as a middle name—Mick Jagger and Jerry Hall called their daughter Georgia May. The Mae spelling, long associated with voluptuous Mae West, is more sexy than sentimental.

MAYA, MAIA. In whichever version (both are pronounced MY-ah) these names appeal to parents seeking an exotic, perhaps even mystical, image for their daughter. Maya resonates with the primitive power of the Mayan Indians of Mexico, and is also a Hindu term for God's creative power—perhaps the inspiration for Uma Thurman, who has a Hindu name herself and called her daughter with Ethan Hawke Maya Ray. As for the most famous bearer of the name, acclaimed poet and playwright Maya Angelou, she was born Marguerite, and, the story goes, was given her new name by a younger brother referring to her as "maya sister." Maia is a light, ethereal name with similarly mystical overtones. In Greek legend, she was the fair-haired daughter of Atlas who mothered Zeus's favorite illegitimate son, Hermes. To the Romans, Maia was the incarnation of the earth mother and the goddess of spring, after which they named the month of May. **MYA** is the less-used phonetic version. **MAYRA** is a variation that has been appearing of late, while TV hosts Julie and Rob Moran spelled their daughter's name **MAIYA**.

McKENNA. Piggy-backing on the success of such new favorites as Mackenzie and Makayla, there were nearly three thousand girls named McKenna and **MAKENNA** in the year most recently tallied. Its similarity to those other, even more popular names makes McKenna feel more familiar (and so overused) than it might. Actor Gary Sinise has a daughter named **McCANNA**.

MEADOW. One of the best ironic names in the history of drama, Meadow is the spoiled suburban daughter of the Mafia boss in the acclaimed TV show *The Sopranos*. The name alone makes one imagine fledgling parents Tony and Carmela Soprano as gentle and idealistic—qualities they've largely left behind over their years of raising young Meadow.

MEGAN. Along with Jennifer, one of the most popular Welsh names to come to these shores in recent years, Megan caught on like wildfire in the early eighties with parents who liked its "Irish" sound and spirit. And although it has been so widely used—it's still, when you add up all the spellings, in the Top 10—Megan retains some degree of spunk. The short form **MEG** is more closely tied to the original Margaret, and carries with it the charm of all the *Little Women* characters. Keeping it in the contemporary spotlight is actress Meg Ryan. For some reason parents are often tempted to vary Megan with "creative" spellings—after Megan, the most popular variations are, in order, **MEGHAN, MEAGAN, MEAGHAN,** and **MAEGAN**—but we warn against deviating so much that people aren't sure whether the name is pronounced MEE-gan or MAYG-han or what, exactly. The best, clearest, easiest-to-understand spelling is the original one and still the five-to-one favorite: Megan.

MELANIE. Melanie is one of several names that got their initial impetus from a fictional character, in this case Melanie Hamilton Wilkes in *Gone With the Wind,* played by Olivia de Havilland. The spread of this Greek name (meaning "dark") has been slow but sure, and it's still a viable possibility.

Vanessa Williams has a daughter named Melanie, and two of the Spice Girls, Scary and Sporty, are named Melanie, called **MEL**. An elaborate version is **MELANTHA**. Trivia tidbit: Melanie Griffith was named after the character her mother, Tippi Hedren, played in Alfred Hitchcock's *The Birds*.

MELBA. This name can be traced back to the influence of Australian opera star Nellie Melba, whose stage name was taken from that of her native Melbourne. Now relegated to style limbo along with **MELVA, BELVA** et al., the only contemporary noteworthy example is singer Melba Moore, who, in fact, was born Beatrice.

MELIA. This charming name is sometimes used as a pet form of Amelia and Cornelia, but is also, in classical mythology, the nymph daughter of Oceanus, the Titan god of the outer seas.

MELINA. A Greek name that, like all the *mel* names, means "honey" or "bee," Melina makes a distinctive alternative to Melissa.

MELINDA. In the seventeenth and eighteenth centuries there was a poetic fad for names with the *inda* sound, and Melinda was one of those created at that time. Some name experts relate it to the German root *lindi,* which means "snake." But although it doesn't sound as dated as Linda itself, or as tired as Melissa, Melinda is still not a favorite among modern baby namers.

MELISSA. The fact that the two leading child actresses on the big-time seventies series *Little House on the Prairie* were both named Melissa gives some indication of how popular that name was, and would remain, for the next two decades, chosen by parents for its beribboned and beruffled femininity. Today, though, the name has dropped out of the Top 50. From the Greek for *bee,* suggesting the sweetness of honey, the mythical Melissa was nursemaid to the infant god Zeus. It was used as a given name by the early Greeks, as well as for fairies by Italian Renaissance poets.

MELODY. A lilting but lightweight name favored by parents who might more adventurously choose **HARMONY** or **LYRIC**.

MELORA. An invented name with the popular *mel* (*bee* or *honey*) prefix. An interesting alternative to the timeworn Melissa.

MENA. A new name that feels prettier than it might thanks to the young *American Beauty* actress who introduced it, Mena Suvari. The actress got her name from her Egyptian godmother, who was named after Cairo's House of Mena hotel. This can also be a short form of Philomena.

MERCEDES. This is one of the few names attached to luxury living (as opposed to, say, Tiffany or Sterling) that we can wholeheartedly recommend, it being a legitimate Spanish appellation stemming from one of the epithets given to the Virgin Mary—Our Lady of the Mercies. Val Kilmer and Joanne Whalley-Kilmer have a daughter named Mercedes. The car, by the way, was named after the eleven-year-old daughter of the Daimler company's French distributor in 1901.

MERCY. This Puritan virtue name, quite popular with the early settlers of this country, can make an interesting and meaningful alternative to Faith, Hope, or Charity. **MERRY** is a cheerful shortened form that lacks substance. In the Dickens novel *Martin Chuzzlewit,* the two sisters named Mercy and Charity are known as Merry and Cherry.

MEREDITH. Still commonly used as a male name in Wales (it means "magnificent chief or protector" in Celtic), this is a gentle-sounding, soft-hued name that has easily segued onto the female roll call in this country and would make a good fitting-in-but-standing-out option. TV personality Meredith Viera is a current representative. A new, related sighting on the namescape is **MERIDIAN,** first name of the psychologist Dr. Chase, played by Nicole Kidman in the third Batman movie.

MERLE, MERYL, MERRILL. These are three sleek, smooth, understated names. Merle is a French bird name (for *blackbird*). The contemporary use of Meryl is almost completely due to the fame of Meryl Streep, born Mary Louise, and its homophone Merrill has the possible advantage of being androgynous.

MIA. When Mia Farrow—actually born Maria—became an instant superstar at the age of nineteen via the TV nightime soap *Peyton Place* in 1964, her name was an obscure Scandinavian pet form of Maria. It spread rapidly through the 1960s and seventies, especially liked by American families of Asian descent: It's one of the few Western names (**ALISA** and **HANA** are others) that have Asian-language counterparts. Sometimes used in modern Israel as a derivative of Michaela, Mia is still liked by parents, such as Kate Winslet, who used it for her daughter, but is no longer on the cutting edge of style.

MICA, MIKA. These names are linked only by sound. Mica, pronounced with a long *i* and sometimes spelled **MICAH,** is a Hebrew relative of Michael. **MIKA,** pronounced and sometimes spelled **MEEKA,** is a name that appears in several Asian variations and relates to the number 3.

MICHAELA. See **MAKAYLA.**

MICHAEL, MICHAL. While Makayla and Michelle get all the attention, Michael itself has been used as a girl's name for years—there was a writer (married to John Barrymore) who called herself Michael Strange in the 1920s, Michael Learned played the mother of the Walton clan, and Michael Michelle is one of the female stars of *ER*. Now, in the current climate, when females are appropriating rather than feminizing men's names, we expect to see more girls named Michael. Michal is the independent biblical name of the youngest daughter of King Saul and the wife of King David.

MICHELLE, MICHELE. It was the Beatles song that did it, of that we have no doubt. The tender sound, the loving half-French lyrics "ma belle." The name had certainly been heard before 1966, in fact it was already number 20 in 1960, but we're sure that the soft, sentimental ballad was the key factor in propelling it up to the Top 5. And although it is still widely used, it is definitely, after an unusually long run, on its way out of favor, although Michelle Pfeiffer and Sarah Michelle Gellar still keep it in the public eye.

MILDRED. When scientists do research on the effects of an unpopular name, we're afraid that Mildred is one of the first examples they cite, often in tandem with Bertha and Gertrude. A medieval name (a holdover from the era of **ETHELRED** and **ETHELREDA**), it was revived by the Victorians and quite popular here in the first couple of decades of the twentieth century. The bottom line: This is not a name that will make your daughter's path in life any smoother.

MILLICENT. Sort of a combination of the mild and the innocent, Millicent is sweet and feminissima (quite a contrast to its literal German meaning of "strong worker"), and if that is the kind of name you are seeking, it would make a much more distinctive choice than Melissa or Michelle. The name came from Germany to France in the form of **MELISANDE**, which was borne by a daughter of Charlemagne. This mellifluous version is associated with the romance of Pelleas and Melisande, later made into an opera by Debussy. There is also a charming fairy-tale princess named Melisande, who was cursed at birth with baldness by an evil fairy but later battled the opposite problem: too much hair. The upbeat nickname **MILLY/MILLIE** serves both Mildred and Millicent, and is sometimes used on its own. Christian singer Amy Grant, for instance, has a daughter named Millie. Ukrainian-born actress **MILLA** Jovovich has introduced a pretty Slavic spin on the name.

MIMI. Another nickname name—both for Miriam and Maria—Mimi is the heroine of Puccini's opera *La Bohème,* whose real name, she reveals to us in song, is neither of the above, but Lucia. There's also a Mimi in the *La Bohème* knockoff *Rent.* Cute, perhaps, but without much backbone as a complete grown-up name.

MINERVA. Many of the ancient mythological names, from Greek and Latin myths as well as Eastern ones, sound fascinating again. Minerva, in Roman myth, was the goddess of wisdom and invention, the arts and martial strength—an admirable role model for a modern girl. An even more interesting name is the Cornish **MINIVER,** which comes from a saint who threw a rock at the devil.

MINA, MINNA, MINNIE. Mina (rhymes with Tina) and Minna are a pair of rarely used short forms of Wilhelmina, the former made familiar as the name of the unfortunate love of Count Dracula, the latter also meaning "mother" in some West African languages. Minnie, another Wilhelmina offshoot, as well as being short for several names, has been the beneficiary of an image overhaul thanks to glamorous actress Minnie Driver—although Minnie Mouse still competes for attention. Some parents see Minnie as a cute, slightly dizzy nickname name—akin to Tillie and Maisie—with an unpretentious charm.

MIRA. Thanks to Oscar-winning actress Sorvino, everybody knows that this once-obscure Myra variation is pronounced like "mirror." **MEARA** is an Irish version.

MIRABEL, MIRABELLE. There's a definite resurgence of *bel* names, including Belle itself, Isabel, and this more unusual, elegant example, which comes from the Latin meaning "marvelous" and is also the name of a delicate French plum. The Italian **MIRABELLA** is, now that the fashion magazine of that name has died, another attractive option.

MIRACLE. Like Destiny and Precious, one of the increasingly used new word names.

MIRANDA. A shimmeringly lovely name with nothing but attractive associations, Miranda was invented by Shakespeare for the beautiful and admirable young heroine of his play, *The Tempest*. Be warned, though, that this name is now far from unique—more and more parents are becoming aware of its attributes. Many are using it as an alternate for the overused Amanda, with the result that Miranda is feeling a lot more familiar itself.

MIRIAM. Though this name plays a prominent role in the Old Testament, its sphere has remained more limited than that of other biblical names like Sarah and Rebecca. The oldest known form of Mary—the Old Testament version of the Hebrew **MARYAM** or **MARIAM**—it appears in Exodus as the elder sister of Moses and Aaron, a prophetess who led the triumphal song and dance after the crossing of the Red Sea and deliverance of the Israelites from the Egyptians. It is a name to consider if you are looking for a pleasant-sounding, not overly used biblical name. In modern Israel, the form **MIRA/MIRRA** has become quite popular.

MISTY. To be used in descriptions of picturesque landscapes rather than as a proper name.

MITZI. This spunky German pet form of Maria might appeal to someone who is drawn to the whole genre of period chorus girl names that proliferated in 1930s musicals. The entertainer Mitzi Gaynor was originally named Francesca—a pair of opposites if we ever saw one.

MOLLY. A name with a lot of strength and spirit, Molly, the long-independent English pet form of Mary, has a distinctly Irish feel as well, arising from such Gaelic associations as "Sweet Molly Malone" and the martyred Pennsylvania coal-mining reformers known as the Molly Maguires. Old-fashioned without being sentimental, **MOLLIE** is one spelling variation that appears in the Top 1,000, and **MALI** is the Welsh spelling.

MONA. This Gaelic name doesn't have the most optimistic sound in the world, and it is one we would be surprised to find chosen for a contemporary baby girl.

MONET. This soft and pretty artist's name has begun to attract the attention of families with creative leanings, recalling as it does the lush impressionist paintings of gardens and lily ponds. You also might consider **GIVERNY,** the place where Monet painted his famous water lilies. It's pronounced jhee-vair-nee, but your child will have to spend her lifetime explaining that.

MONICA. Poor Monica. Its association with Ms. Lewinsky has turned this classic saint's name into a notorious no-no, for the time being, anyway. The French version, **MONIQUE,** has been in the Top 40 names used by African-American parents for the past several years.

MONTANA. One of the new posse of androgynous cowgirl/place-names, Montana has ridden right into the heart of trendiness along with Sierra and Cheyenne. Judd Hirsch and Woody Harrelson both have daughters named Montana. It's one of those names that, unfortunately, is so five minutes ago.

MOR, MORAG. Mor was a goddess from whose loins sprang the royals of Munster in Ireland, and Morag is its Scottish form. But to the American ear, Mor sounds a tad slight while Morag is a bit haggish.

MORGAN. A lean, silvery, and sophisticated ambigender name that began as a traditional Welsh male one, girl Morgans now outnumber boys ten to one. There are ancient precedents: In Arthurian legend, Morgan Le Fay was the not very nice stepsister of King Arthur who did, nevertheless, serve as the leader of the queens who carried him away to cure his wounds. Today, the name is number 25 on the popularity list and is beginning to feel somewhat overexposed. Actor Morgan Freeman has a daughter named **MORGANA**; Roman Polanski's child is **MORGANE**.

MORWYN, MORWENNA. Morwyn is Welsh for maiden; it and Morwenna are being revived in that country and would make more interesting Morgan alternatives here.

MURIEL. This onetime poetic name of Celtic origin, the name of the angel who governs the month of June, is now showing signs of age, relegated to playing grandmas on TV sitcoms.

MURPHY. One of the boldest, brightest, and breeziest of the Irish surname names, thanks to the character played so convincingly by Candice Bergen on *Murphy Brown*.

MURRAY, MURRY. If Sydney is one of the hottest girls' names going, why not Murray? Why not **GEORGE, LYLE, MAX, ROY**, or even **SEYMOUR**? Why not indeed. Just as Sydney sounds cute and sweet when applied to a little girl, and brisk and sexy when used for a grown-up woman (and still buried under a cloud of cigar smoke when used for a male of any age), so, too, do Murray and the rest of the boys. Or should we say, former boys.

MYFANWY. An ancient name that at one time was almost a joke for a parochial Welsh female, with renewed national pride this is becoming increasingly chic in Wales and may be ripe for export. Pronunciation: mi-FAWN-wy, it appears in Dylan Thomas's *Under Milkwood*.

MYRA, MYRNA. They come from different places, but their tarnished images have a lot in common. Myra was invented in the seventeenth century by a poet called Fulke Grenville as a short form of Miranda, and it quickly caught on with other poets and romantic novelists. Myrna, on the other hand, is a traditional Irish name related to the strong-scented myrrh, used in preparing perfumes and incense, and was found in significant numbers among secretarial staffs of the 1920s and thirties. Its most well-known bearer was the sparkling portrayer of Nora Charles, Myrna Loy.

MYRTLE. This name is so far out of style that we can conceive of some intrepid, lionhearted parents taking on the challenge of resurrecting it. Myrtle is also the name of a shrub with shiny green leaves and sweet-smelling white blossoms used to make perfume, a plant that in Greek myth was sacred to Venus, and therefore a symbol of love.

N

NAAMA, NAAMIT, NAAVA. The meanings of these three related Hebrew names encompass many of the traditional female attributes: beauty, grace, pleasantness, charm, tenderness, and kindness.

NADIA. This exotic Russian and Slavic name—which means "hope"—took on added energy and charm when it became attached to the Romanian Olympic gymnast Nadia Comaneci in 1976. Its French offshoot, **NADINE,** hit Paris in the early years of the twentieth century when the success of the Ballet Russe set off a fad for all things Russian.

NALA. Disney's *The Lion King II* popularized the name Kiara, the daughter of Simba, but Kiara's mother's name—Nala—has lagged behind, although Keenen Ivory Wayans used it for one of his daughters. It's derived from **NALO,** a West-African name meaning "much loved."

NANA, NANNA. An Old World nickname name, Nana was also an ancient goddess of flowers. But these days it's best left for the sheepdog/nanny in *Peter Pan* or as a substitute name for Grandma.

NANCY. Even though it's no longer in style, Nancy still has a pleasantly light and airy feel. Originally a pet form of Ann and Hannah, it peaked about 1940, when it was the seventh most popular girls' name in America. Around that time it was closely linked with girl detective Nancy Drew and with Frank Sinatra, who crooned the haunting song "Nancy With the Laughing Face" for his newborn daughter—now, like the name, middle-aged.

NANETTE. This harks back to the time when anything French sounded chic, and there was a rage for such names as Annette, Claudette, Jeanette, Georgette, Paulette, Suzette—and Nanette. But if you're considering it for a twenty-first-century baby, I'm afraid we'd have to say "No, no, Nanette."

NAOMI. Unlike other Old Testament female names such as Sarah, Rachel, and Rebecca, Naomi has never been widely used in this country except in Jewish families, and even there it has not had sweeping popularity. Which is too bad, we think, because it has such a soft, melodic sound, and an all-encompassing positive meaning in Hebrew—"delightful," "charming," and "gentle." Its biblical referent is the wise mother-in-law of Ruth, and because of this it is a symbolic name given to girls born on Shavuot when the Bible story of Ruth is read in the synagogue. Naomi moves out of the temple and into secular life with singer Naomi Judd and model Naomi Campbell. **NOEMI** is the mellifluous Italian variation of the name.

NATALIE. This French form of a Russian name has become completely Americanized, and a new generation of parents is reviving it along with former canasta partners like Sophie, Belle, and Molly. Since its literal meaning is "birthday of the Lord," it is sometimes given to girls born on Christmas Day. The most famous Natalie these days are Natalie Cole and young star Natalie Portman. In London, where the name has been more consistently fashionable, the forms **NATALIA, NATALYA,** and **NATANIA** (the female of Nathan) are occasionally used. **NATHALIE** is the French spelling. Cameron Diaz was Natalie in *Charlie's Angels.*

NATASHA. While European iconoclasts like Vanessa Redgrave and Klaus Kinski used this name for their daughters in pre-perestroika days—spawning actresses Natasha Richardson and **NASTASSJA** Kinski—it wasn't until the end of the Cold War that the name achieved widespread acceptability here. Today, Natasha, which is in Britain's Top 40, makes an exotic and appealing choice. Variant spellings include **NATASSIA, NASTASSIA, NATASHIA,** and **NATASSJA,** and the prevailing short form is **TASHA.** Tori Amos came up with her own version for her daughter—Natashya.

NEAL, NEIL. Instead of using one of the obscure feminizations of Neil (**NEILA, NEALA**), we say why not appropriate the boy's name itself? It's one of those names, like Sydney and Seth, that immediately sound zippier as the result of a gender change. Neila (pronounced neh-ee-la) is also the name of the closing service on Yom Kippur, and can be a symbolic choice for girls born on that day. In the same family is **NELIA,** an attractive diminutive of Cornelia sometimes used on its own.

NEITH. The Egyptian goddess of home and femininity—and also the goddess of war.

NELL. A name with a good deal of sweet, old-fashioned charm is Nell, which is officially a nickname for Helen, Ellen, or Eleanor but is most fashionably today a name used in its own right. Nell was the pet name FDR called his wife Eleanor (along with Babs); the famous Little Nell in Dickens's *Old Curiosity Shop* was Elinor; and the infamous mistress of Charles II, Nell Gwynne, was born Eleanor as well. **NELLIE** (or **NELLY**) also recalls the Gay Nineties and bicycles built for two.

NERISSA. An offbeat possible substitute for overused names such as Melissa and Vanessa, Nerissa, whose meaning relates to sea sprites, was the name of Portia's witty confidante in Shakespeare's *Merchant of Venice.* The equally attractive **NERYS** is a Welsh name that means "lady."

NESSA. Like its cousin **TESSA**, Nessa is a nickname—most often for Vanessa—that can stand on its own. There is a Nessa in Irish mythology whose name means "not gentle."

NETTIE. This is a real knitting and crocheting grandma name that might work for a contemporary little girl in search of relief from a more formal name—maybe inherited from her own grandma—like Henrietta or Annette.

NEVADA. Named for the snowcapped mountains of that state, Nevada is a fresh possibility for parents interested in place names—with the usual caveat that today's undiscovered place-name could well be tomorrow's trampled tourist attraction. Another option is **NEVA,** which derives from the Spanish word for "snow" and has an evocatively exotic aura.

NEVE. See **NIAMH.**

NEWLYN. An Anglicization of the Celtic **NAVLIN,** meaning "healing water"—a good choice for a parent with a spiritual bent, although there could be some pronunciation confusion.

NIA. A more modern-sounding alternative to the somewhat dated Mia, Nia has become a favorite among African-American parents for whom the name has special meaning as one of the days of the holiday Kwanza, and is also a heroine of Welsh legend. Nia Peeples and Nia Long are both up-and-coming actresses.

NIAMH. One of the ancient Gaelic names restored to favor in modern Ireland, Niamh is sometimes spelled **NIAV** to more closely reflect its pronunciation, neev. The name **NEVE,** as in actress Campbell and pronounced to rhyme with bev, is a relative. In Irish mythology, Niamh was the Princess of the Land of Promise.

NICOLE. Nicole was one of the most popular girl's names of the 1970s (it reached number 4 in 1980), with parents responding to its French flair. Those who have known a few too many Nicoles might want to consider

NICOLA (pronounced like Nicholas without the *s*). This elegant Italian form of Nicholas (it's used for males in Italy) has long been standard issue for English girls, but for some reason has rarely made it across the Atlantic. Both names, by the way, come from the Greek Nike, which means victory as well as sneakers. Another, more feminine possibility beginning to come into play in **NICOLETTE**, which was the name of an enchanting princess in the medieval French romance *Aucassin et Nicolette,* as well as being associated with the contemporary actress Nicolette Sheridan. **NICOLETTA** may also be used; **NICO** is a much more modern nickname for any of the above than the overused **NICKI** or **NIKKI**.

NINA. This is a name that's about as cross-cultural as you can get. In Spanish, it is the word for "young girl." In Assyro-Babylonian mythology, Nina was the goddess of the oceans; to the Incas, the goddess of fire. And in Russia it's a common name used as a pet form of **ANTONINA, JANINA,** and everything else ending in *nina.* Today, Nina is a stylish possibility that has not approached overuse.

NIXIE. If you think Dixie, Trixie, and Pixie are outlandish, consider Nixie. This is the name of a mermaidlike water sprite in German folklore, half woman, half fish, who could be glimpsed only by lovers in the light of the full moon.

NOA, NOAH. A biblical name (no, not *that* Noah—Noa was the daughter of Zelophehad) popular in Israel. Country singer Billy Ray Cyrus gave his daughter the ark-builder's spelling when he named her Noah Lindsey.

NOELLE, NOEL. The French word for *Christmas* has been given to children of both sexes born on that holiday ever since the Middle Ages. These days, the male spelling might be considered preferable for girls as well, and its usage certainly doesn't have to be limited to any particular time of year. **NOELIA** has also been heard.

NOLA. A name with a haunting, sensual quality, it belonged to the woman everyone wanted, and vice versa, in Spike Lee's groundbreaking 1986 film *She's Gotta Have It.* In the same family are **NONA,** a Welsh name that in the

Victorian era was sometimes given to the ninth child in a family, and **NOVA,** which in astronomy means a star that suddenly increases in brightness, then returns to its normal state (and which might work better for a TV science show than for a child).

NORA. This lovely old Irish name, originally a nickname for Honora, is being rediscovered after a hibernation of close to a century. Soft and refined, it calls up images of women in velvet and fur collars ice-skating in Central Park at the turn of the century—although it was certainly borne by any number of humble washerwomen as well. The most famous Nora in drama is the heroine of Ibsen's *A Doll's House,* who was finally able to slam the door and start a life of her own. Nick and Nora Charles were the sophisticated martini-sipping couple created by Dashiell Hammett and featured in *The Thin Man* series of movies, and Nora Ephron is the witty writer and director of *You've Got Mail.* **NORAH** is acceptable, but pointless. The diminutive form **NOREEN** is much more of the Mickey Mouse Club era and is rarely used today.

NORMA. At this point, Norma is a real mom name—pleasant, but not too clued in about what's really going on in today's world. Invented by the librettist of Bellini's opera *Norma,* its fame was spread by two early real movie Normas (Talmadge and Shearer). And then of course there was Norma Jean, the chrysalis that metamorphosed into Marilyn Monroe.

NORRIS. An English surname that had been used only for males until Mrs. Norman Mailer, Norris Church (born Barbara), came on the scene.

O

OBA. The evocative Nigerian name of an ancient river goddess, this is one African choice unfamiliar here but definitely worthy of attention.

OBEDIENCE. It may have been well used among Puritan families, but if you are interested in a virtue name, we suggest you stick with Hope, Faith, or Honor and not test your child's character by giving her a name like Obedience or Chastity.

O'BRIEN et al. The Mackenzies and McKennas have been around for several years now, opening the door to other Irish descendant names. The *O'* group are prime subjects for exploration, traditional yet almost startlingly unusual as first names, especially for girls. Other possibilities include (but are by no means limited to) **O'DONNELL, O'DONOVAN, O'KEEFE, O'HARA, O'NEILL,** and **O'SHEA.**

OCEANA. The feminine form of Oceanus, the god of the sea, this might be considered a place-name with the advantage of actually sounding like a name.

OCTAVIA. A Latin name meaning "eighth"—which was at one time given to the eighth child born into a family—Octavia was very common in Roman times (it belonged to the daughter of Claudius and pre-Cleopatra wife of Marc Antony), and is interesting for its combination of classical and musical overtones.

ODELIA, ODELE. Odelia is a pretty Hebrew name that would make a truly distinctive choice. Odele has Greek roots and a melodic meaning, and is sometimes heard in the South.

ODESSA. An exotic, original, and attractive place-name. The Russian port city was given the name by Catherine the Great, inspired by Homer's *Odyssey*.

ODETTA, ODETTE, ODILE. One of the first single-name celebrities was fifties folksinger Odetta, who carried the name into the limelight. Odette and Odile, on the other hand, are two French names that appear in the ballet *Swan Lake*; Odette, a lighter, more upbeat name, is the good swan, while Odile, a more sinuous, sensuous one, represents the side of evil.

OKSANA. This Russian name was virtually unknown in the West before the extraordinary young Ukrainian orphan figure skater Oksana Baiul won the gold medal at the 1994 Winter Olympics.

OLA. This simple but distinctive name has an unusual diversity of origins—

both Norse (in Scandinavia it's a boys' name) and Polish as well as being a Nigerian name meaning "wealth."

OLGA. Whatever exotic oomph this Russian name may have had in the past is pretty much faded by now, so at this point it sounds rather drab and dull. Olga was one of Chekhov's *Three Sisters,* the name of the saint who was instrumental in spreading Christianity in Russia, and the name of one of the USSR's most famous and popular gymnasts, Olga Korbut.

OLIVE. Right now it's greatly overshadowed by the far trendier Olivia, but Olive has a more subtle, evocatively shaded appeal all its own—especially if we ignore the fact that its most famous bearer is the elastic-limbed Olive Oyl, Popeye's steady. One of the first botanical names to be applied to people, it has nothing but positive associations: The olive branch has been the symbol of peace since ancient times and an olive wreath celebrates honor and success. Trivia note: Olive is the real first name of Marie Osmond.

OLIVIA. Olivia, a name with an ideal balance of strength and femininity, is now in the Top 20 and widely used in England as well (number 8). It was popularized by Shakespeare in *Twelfth Night* as the name of the pampered, wealthy countess. Denzel Washington chose it for his twin daughter, as did Beverly d'Angelo and Al Pacino, and Lori Loughlin has an Olivia Jade. **LIVIA** is a shortened form as well as an independent name used on its own—particularly in Italy. The nickname **LIVVY** is what Mark Twain always called his wife Olivia.

OLWEN. This name is as common in Wales as the more familiar Bronwen, although it's extremely rare here. In Welsh legend, the beautiful giant's daughter Olwen (which literally means "white footprint") had the magical power of causing white clovers to spring up wherever she walked.

OLYMPIA. Because of its relation to Mount Olympus, home of the Greek gods and to the Olympic Games, this name has an athletic, goddesslike aspect. It was brought into the spotlight in recent years by Oscar-winning actress Olympia Dukakis and by Maine senator Olympia Snowe.

OONA, OONAGH. Any name beginning with double *o*s (and this is the only one we know of) has, almost by definition, a lot of oomph. The Anglicized form of the Gaelic name Una, which means "unity," Oona was made famous in this country by the woman who was both daughter of playwright Eugene O'Neill and wife of the immortal Charlie Chaplin.

OPAL. Opal has lost its luster, a pity, we think, because of the shimmering opalescence this name can reflect on its bearer. There is a long-running character named Opal on the soap opera *All My Children*.

OPHELIA. Poor Ophelia. Ever since the beautiful young maiden went mad and drowned herself in *Hamlet*, the name has carried an unfortunate stigma. It actually means "help" in Greek, and if you can put Shakespeare aside, is a lovely sounding name.

ORA, ORAH, ORALIA, ORALIE, ORIANA, ORIEL, ORLA. All these names relate to the light of dawn and are therefore bathed in a golden glow. Oriana has been used a great deal in Spanish and English poetry; in fact, two queens, Elizabeth I and Anne, were both referred to as Oriana by poets. Oriel is considered the angel of destiny. Possible problems with it: Many adults would think it was a mispronunciation of Ariel, and kids might be tempted to make Oreo-cookie jokes. Orla, Celtic for *golden lady*, is used quite commonly in Ireland.

ORLY. If you can forget that this is the name of a busy French airport, it has an appealing and lively sound.

ORNA, ORIN. Old Irish saints' names that both mean "dark-haired." **ORINTHIA** is a not too pleasant character in George Bernard Shaw's play *The Apple Cart*.

ORPAH. The Orpah Winfrey Show? No, we didn't misspell the biblical name (Orpah was an in-law of Naomi and Ruth); **OPRAH**'s namers did. As a result, Oprah's the name that has become famous and, if you name your child Orpah, everyone will think you're the one who's wrong. The bottom line, however, is that neither name is really a viable choice. The talk show megahostess herself once said, on her own show, "People call me Ophrie, Okrie, Ackrie, Little Grand Ole Oprah . . . Okra the vegetable . . . but after a while you just sort of get used to people not respecting you."

OTTALIE, OTTILIE, OTTOLINE. All three of these French and German feminizations of Otto are a lot more appealing than the original. And the whole trio is used much more among the English elite than they are in this country.

OUIDA. This is one of the only names we know of that arose out of baby talk—it was a mispronunciation of the name Louise, as is the even rarer **OUISA,** used in John Guare's play *Six Degrees of Separation.* (The famous French novelist known only as Ouida was born Marie Louise.) Ouida's image is anything but babylike, however; it has an exotic and mysterious air.

P

PACE. An ambigender word name/surname with an upbeat feel and a rosy future, Pace might make a more distinctive substitute for Grace, Page, or Payton.

PACIFICA. Related to peace, this name might also appeal to the parent for whom the Pacific Ocean holds special meaning.

PAGE, PAIGE. A sleek and sophisticated name that is growing in popularity, especially with the spelling Paige, which was number 69 in the most recent Top 100. It was chosen by director Ron Howard as the name of his twin daughter and also by comedian Sinbad for his child.

PALLAS. This rarefied Greek name—in classical mythology, the title Pallas Athene was given to Athena, goddess of wisdom, industry, and the arts—might just attract literary-minded parents; it did best-selling writer-couple Louise Erdrich and the late Michael Dorris, who named another daughter Persia. Possible problem: People might hear it as Palace.

PALMA. This appealing Latin name is both geographical (the romantic Spanish island city of Palma de Majorca) and botanical: It derives from the palm frond, a symbol of happiness, success, and victory, and has some-times been given to girls born on Palm Sunday.

PALOMA. Thanks to the high-profile daughter of Pablo Picasso, this Span-ish name has taken on a vibrant, ruby-lipped image and is definitely being short-listed by certain trendy types—Emilio Estevez, for one, chose it for his daughter. Picasso herself gives it a lot of credit. As she once said, "I think my name Paloma, which means 'dove,' is the most beautiful gift I was ever given. . . . It's very striking and memorable, and that's good for business."

PAMELA. PAM was a prom queen in the sixties—and a little bit pampered at that—who was never, ever called by her full name. Which is a pity, because Pamela (originally pronounced Pamee-la) is so mellifluous, and so rich in literary tradition. It was first used by Elizabethan poet Sir Philip Sid-ney in his sixteenth-century pastoral epic *Arcadia,* but it was Samuel Richardson's enormously popular novel *Pamela, or Virtue Rewarded* two centuries later that really promoted it. Although it reached the Top 10 in 1970, Pamela is rarely used now—there were only 741 born in the most recent year counted in the U.S.—even if Pamela Lee Anderson turned its image around.

PANDORA. In England, this name is sometimes taken up by the more eccentric gentry (for horsey girls with brothers named Peregrine); in Amer-ica it's all but unheard of, except for the mythological Pandora's box. In case you've forgotten, in classical lore, Pandora was the first woman on earth, sent to bring about the downfall of man, which she did when curios-ity caused her to lift the lid of the box that released all the evils of the world.

PANSY. This was one of the flower names (its much weightier derivation is the French *pensée,* meaning "thought") that came into fashion in the nine-teenth century, found in novels such as Henry James's *Portrait of a Lady.* It was also the original name for the heroine of *Gone With the Wind*—odd, since its image is opposite to that of the feisty Scarlett. Its widespread employment as a derogatory slang term for gays from the 1920s on pretty much canceled whatever limited currency it had.

PARIS. As place-names go, this is one of the most romantic possibilities. Also, more obscurely, a character in Greek mythology whose love affair with Helen sparked the Trojan War—but he was a boy. Michael Jackson played with gender identity when he named his daughter Paris Michael Katherine.

PARKER, PAXTON, PAYTON, PEYTON, PORTER. These are all surnames that initially became male first names and now are used for girls as well. Indie actress Parker Posey has particularly publicized her name, though Payton/Peyton are higher in the popularity standings—taken together, there were 2,700 girls given that name in the most recent year counted, more than were named Chelsea! Peyton with the *e* spelling also has the distinction of having the exact same standing for both girls and boys: number 238. Now that's a truly ambigender name. **PAISLEY** is a new and decorative addition.

PARVATI. A Hindu goddess who is considered the daughter of the Himalayas. It means "of the mountain" and is a popular name in India.

PATIENCE. Not a bad virtue as virtues go, but not a particularly easy name to grow up with either, assuming your child's strong points will not include sitting quietly waiting for something to happen. It was another story in the seventeenth century, when it was quite the fashion to name girls after the Seven Christian Virtues. Patience was also the eponymous heroine of a Gilbert and Sullivan comic operetta.

PATRICIA. Patricia still sounds patrician, though the many nicknames it spawned definitely don't. It began not in Ireland, as you might think, but evolved in Scotland, going on to become mega popular in Britain after the christening of Queen Victoria's granddaughter, known to one and all as Princess Pat. Patricias—though rarely called that except in the classroom or at choir practice—ran rampant from the 1940s (it was the fourth most popular girl's name in 1948), through the sixties (it was still number 9 when the First Lady was Pat—born Thelma—Nixon), but it was the short forms that took on lives of their own. There was **PATSY,** used mostly for Irish girls (and sometimes for Irish and Italian boys as well), which was the sassiest, spunkiest name for the jump-roping, freckle-faced, pigtailed girls of the 1920s and thirties, and which then faded fast. Patsy was replaced by **PATTI/PATTY,** the pervasive, peppy baby-sitter name of the next generation, epitomized by Patty Duke, who pleaded in the title of her autobiography to *Call Me Anna* (her real name). In another ten years or so, Patti was dropped in favor of more upwardly mobile nicknames **TRICIA, TRISHA, TRISH, TISHA,** and **TISH.** The one form that hasn't been picked up here, but which is widely used in England on its own is the fresher-sounding **PATIA.** The French form, **PATRICE,** which is a male name in France, is occasionally heard here.

PAULA, PAOLA, PAULINE, PAULINA, PAULETTE. Paula still seems stuck back in the era of poodle skirts and bobby sox, but its Latinate version Paola is finding an increasing number of followers. The other feminizations of Paul are enjoying an unlikely new day in the fashion sun, thanks to some celebrity associations. Both Monaco's Princess Stephanie and country music's Wynonna Judd have named their recently born daughters Pauline. Czech supermodel/actress Paulina (the Italian spelling is **PAOLINA**) Porizkova added gloss to her name. And Paulette, first stylish during the French fad of the 1920s and thirties, also sounds almost fresh again. A new addition to the list is **PAULE,** brought into the mix by writer Paule Marshall, whose roots are in the West Indies.

PAX. The goddess of peace, a hopeful message to bestow upon a child as well as a very cool—some might think even too cool—name.

PAZ and **PAZIA** (pronounced pah-ZEE-uh). These are two exotic Hebrew names that mean "sparkling" or "golden." In Spanish, of course, *paz* means "peace."

PEACHES. This is one of those litmus-test-type names that define the limits of just how far you are willing to go in your search for a name that is hip, outrageous, never-to-be-mainstream. Irish musician and organizer of Live

Aid Bob Geldof pushed the envelope on this one, naming one daughter Peaches, the younger sister of—who else?—Fifi Trixiebelle.

PEARL. Pearl, like Ruby, is a name that's beginning to be polished up for use for a new generation of fashionable children, after nearly a century of storage in the back of the jewel case. Pearl was the name of the infamous illegitimate child in *The Scarlet Letter*, the alter ego name of Janis Joplin, and notorious rocker Meat Loaf also has a daughter named Pearl. Parents not quite brave enough to choose Pearl as a first name might want to consider it as a fresh-sounding middle name alternative to the becoming-overused Rose. **PERLA** is an occasionally used variant.

PEGGY. Peggy still carries with it the wholesome, pug-nosed, happy-go-lucky image it had from the 1920s and into the 1950s Peggy-Sue-got-married era: perky and pure, the perfect date for the prom. It originated as a pet name for Margaret. But can you remember the last time you heard it applied to an infant? **PEGEEN** is the dated Irish diminutive.

PELE. A Hawaiian volcano goddess who could be both good and evil—like some babies. Also, one of the most famous (male) soccer stars.

PENELOPE, PENNY. Penelope has a kind of starchy feel, perhaps because it has for so long been associated with the faithful, long-suffering wife of Odysseus in Homer's *Odyssey*. New parents will probably run into it if they consult the works of British child-rearing maven Penelope Leach, and it's been given a transfusion of energy by Spanish-born actress Penélope Cruz. Penny, on the other hand, is, like Patsy and Peggy, the kind of zesty moniker the young Judy Garland would don for her let's-put-on-a-show movies of the 1930s and forties. It has scarcely been heard from since, except on the screen where it says "directed by Penny Marshall."

PENINA, PENINAH. A Hebrew jewel name—it means, according to which translation you believe, "coral," "pearl," or "ruby."

PEONY, POPPY, POSY, PRIMROSE. A bouquet of seldom seen, sweet-smelling, Victorian-valentine flower names you might find worth considering. The peony is thought to have healing powers, the poppy's brilliant red flowers have narcotic properties, Posy is also used as a pet name for Josephine, and Primrose is still found in quaint British novels. All four are stylishly used for little girls in England, where gardening is a national pastime; of the four, Poppy is probably the most popular.

PEPITA, PEPPER. These are two names with so much energy—or should we say pep?—they almost bounce off the page. Pepita is the diminutive of **JOSEFINA,** just as **PEPE** is the nickname for the male Giuseppe.

PERDITA. To anyone who ever took a Latin language, this name will, unfortunately, sound lost. It was invented by Shakespeare for an abandoned baby princess in *The Winter's Tale,* but those of us in touch with our childhoods are more likely to recall it as one of the canine characters in Disney's *One Hundred and One Dalmatians.*

PERRY. Perry is a relaxed male name that has begun to be used for girls over the past few years—a fresher alternative to shopworn favorites such as Kerry and Sherry. Spelled **PERI,** as *Frasier* actress Gilpin does, it is a Hebrew name meaning "fruit."

PERSIA. This place-name, used in the pre-Iran days, still retains the brilliant coloration of an ancient Persian miniature, which must have appealed to writers Louise Erdrich and the late Michael Dorris, who chose it for their daughter. **PERSIS** is a related name, signifying a Christian woman of Roman descent in the Old Testament.

PETA, PETRA. Two modern English feminine forms of Peter. Peta gets a sexy edge from *La Femme Nikita* actress Peta Wilson. **PETULA,** which means "saucy" or "impudent" in Latin, surfaced here briefly in the swinging London days of singer Petula ("Downtown") Clark, as did **PETULIA** in the memorable 1968 film of that name starring Julie Christie. Peta is also the acronym for the radical animal rights group, People for the Ethical Treatment of Animals.

PHILIPPA, PHILIPPINE. There is a whole group of boys' names adapted for girls that are used in England far more than here (e.g., Jacoba, Josepha, Georgina, Robina), and Philippa is one of the prime—and most accessible—examples, as common as crumpets in Cornwall, as rare as reindeer meat in Miami. Philippa, like Philip, is from the Greek, meaning "lover of horses," and has been fashionable in England since the fourteenth century when King Edward married Philippa of Hainault. Philippine is a French variation; Saint Philippine was a missionary nun in the early nineteenth century whose specialty was coping with life's disappointments.

PIPPA. One of Philippa's nicknames (others are **FLIPPA, FLIP, PIP,** and **PIPPI,** as in Longstocking) is sometimes used on its own: the effervescent Pippa, made famous in Browning's poem "Pippa Passes."

PHILOMENA. An earthy Greek name, used now in various Latin countries, that belonged to a mythological Athenian princess who was transformed by the gods into a nightingale to save her from the advances of a lecherous king. But the story's much lovelier than the name.

PHOEBE. A captivating name looked upon with great affection by anyone who's ever read *Catcher in the Rye,* as it's borne by Holden Caulfield's sympathetic younger sister. It has also figured prominently on the TV shows *Friends* and *Charmed.* A mythological, biblical, and Shakespearean name, Phoebe means "the pure, shining one" and is one of the titles given by the ancient Greeks to the goddess of the moon. Phoebe is in Britain's Top 40, and we think it shows signs of rising here too. Shakespeare spelled it **PHEBE** in *As You Like It.*

PHOENIX. Scary Spice Girl Melanie Brown chose this evocative name for her daughter. The mythological phoenix was the bird that regenerated itself and symbolizes rebirth. It's also a city in Arizona.

PHYLLIS. It may have a stolid, middle-aged image now, but at one time Phyllis was the very essence of lyrical grace. The name of a mythical Greek princess who pined away for love until she was transformed into an almond tree, it was used by classical poets to represent the idealized country maiden. Phyllis was in the Top 30 in 1925, but has been sinking ever since. On the other hand, **PHYLIS** Wheatley, the poet who was brought over as a slave from Africa in 1761, is a major African-American writer and a worthy name inspiration. One of Phyllis's variants, **PHILLIDA**, is a *Masterpiece Theater* kind of name. And **PHYLICIA**, as in actress Phylicia Rashad, which looks like a variation of Phyllis, is really just an elaborate spelling of Felicia.

PIA. A soft name in the Mia-Nia family, Pia is heard in several languages: in Italian, where it means "pious," and in Swahili and Hindi, where it means "loved one." In the case of telecaster Pia Lindstrom, it came from the combination of her parents' initials, Peter Aaron + Ingrid (Bergman, the movie star).

PIALA. The name of a saint martyred in Cornwall, this makes an unusual choice with traditional roots.

PILAR. The fact that this Spanish name does not end in the conventional letter *a* imparts to it a special sense of strength and elegance, in keeping with its meaning of "pillar of the church." The name of a memorably heroic character in Hemingway's *For Whom the Bell Tolls,* Pilar seems eternally stylish and would make a worthy choice.

PIPER. A light, musical name that's adorable for a child but that may possibly prove a bit wispy should your baby grow up to be a tax attorney. Actress Gillian Anderson chose it for her daughter.

PO, POE. A new name on the block, Po/Poe has several positive elements going for it, in addition to its short, catchy sound. Literary: the link to Edgar Allan Poe. Geographical: the northern Italian river Po. Celebrity: up-and-coming single-named singer Poe (real last name Danielewski), said to be named for an Edgar Allan Poe character she dressed up as one Halloween. Not so positive element: Po is the red Teletubby.

POLLY. Polly projects the innocence of an earlier time, which may explain why it hasn't been revived as enthusiastically as Molly. We think the *P* gives it a peppier sound, combining the home-style virtues of an old-fashioned name with the bounce of a barmaid. Polly and Molly are both off-shoots of Mary. **POLLYANNA** went down in literary history as the eternal optimist.

POPPY. See **PEONY.**

PORTIA. This is the perfect role-model name for feminist-oriented parents, since, as far back as Shakespeare's time, Portia was portrayed as a brilliant, independent-minded lawyer (albeit disguised as a man) in *The Merchant of Venice.* Some parents have corrupted the spelling of the name to **PORSHA,** and even (perhaps this is wishful thinking) **PORSCHE.** *Ally McBeal's* Portia de Rossi started life as Amanda/Mandy.

POSY. See **PEONY.**

PRECIOUS. A popular word name that may be too saccharine for consideration but will certainly make your child feel loved.

PRESLEY. Where Elvis has until recently seemed as taboo a name in America as, well, Madonna, Presley is becoming more acceptable, for girls—singer Tanya Tucker named her daughter Presley Tanita—as well as boys—supermodel Cindy Crawford's little son is named Presley too.

PRIMROSE. See **PEONY.**

PRINCESS. Another word name growing in popularity. Singer Michael Jackson named his son Prince—same idea. Caveat: These have long been canine favorites.

PRISCILLA. Its very construction tends to make this name sound prissy, but thinking of Priscilla Presley could give it a completely different spin. The Brits sometimes get around this by accenting the second part of the name, **CILLA,** as a nickname or even on its own. Priscilla is a New Testament name (the apostle Paul stayed with her while spreading the gospel in Corinth).

PRIYA. A popular Sanskrit name meaning "beloved" or "beautiful" and pronounced PREE-ya.

PRUDENCE. Like Hope and Faith, this is one of the Puritan abstract virtue names that is still viable today, possessing a quiet charm and sensitivity. The name might present difficulties, however, during the adolescent years, when young Prudence would be continually asked whether she is a prude. The related **PRUNELLA,** which means "little plum" and is used in England, could have an even tougher time here because of the disagreeable connotations of prunes.

Q

QUEENIE. If you like cheeky chorus girl barmaid names like Fifi and Trixie, here's another one of that ilk. Originally a nickname for girls christened Regina (the Latin word for *queen*) and for those named Victoria during the long reign of that regent, it is, we must warn you, like most of this breed, much more often used for dogs.

QUINN. This was one of the first post-Ryan Irish surnames to become accepted for both boy and girl babies, and still has a lot of style and strength. It means "intelligent" in Gaelic, and also harks back to the Old English word *cuen,* which means "queen."

QUINELLA, QUINETTA, QUINTA, QUINTANA, QUINTESSA, QUINTILLA, QUINTINA, QUINTONA are all related to the number 5. At one time they were given to the fifth child in the family, but they can also be given to one born on the fifth day of the month or in May, the fifth month of the year. Joan Didion and John Gregory Dunne's now-grown-up daughter is named Quintana Roo, after the Mexican province.

R

RACHEL, RACHAEL. It is probably the delicacy and softness of the name—it does mean "little lamb" in Hebrew—that has made Rachel one of the most consistently popular biblical girl's names since the late 1960s, when parents started to turn back to basic sources like the Bible. At a much earlier time Rachel was considered characteristically Jewish—it wasn't used as a Christian name until after the Reformation—but the fact that it is now the thirteenth most common name given to baby girls in America demonstrates that it has been widely embraced by all ethnic groups. In the Old Testament, Rachel was the beautiful and cherished wife of Jacob, and mother of Joseph and Benjamin. Among the variants are the seventeenth-century **RACHAEL,** the twentieth-century **RACHELLE,** and the Spanish **RAQUEL,** Raquel Welch being half Bolivian.

RAE, RAY. A diminutive of Rachel, these days Rae/Ray is most often used as a middle name. Uma Thurman and Ethan Hawke's daughter is Maya Ray, and Christie Brinkley and Billy Joel's now-teenager's name is Alexa Ray, to honor jazz great Ray Charles.

RAINE. This unusual name popped into the headlines when it was attached to Countess Spencer, stepmother of Princess Diana and daughter of romance novelist Barbara Cartland. Richard Pryor has an actress daughter named **RAIN,** and there is also a Joaquin Phoenix actress sister with that rather gloomy word/nature name. When Will Smith and Jada Pinkett used it as the third name of their daughter Willow Camille, they gave it the queenly spelling of **REIGN.** Andie MacDowell's daughter is **RAINIE.** For **RAINA,** see Regina.

RAISA. The name Raisa entered the American consciousness in the person of Mme Gorbachev, the imperial wife of the former head of the former USSR. A possibility for parents of Eastern European descent (or interests) who want to move beyond the more familiar Natalias, Natashas, and Nadias.

RAMONA. Ramona, which fits into the desirable category of being neither too trendy nor too eccentric, came into prominence in the 1880s via the beautiful half Native American heroine of the best-selling romance novel *Ramona,* by Helen Hunt Jackson. Kids will associate it with the clever character of Ramona Quigley in the series of books by Beverly Cleary.

RANDI, RANDY. Like Mandy and Candy, in the late 1960s and early seventies Randi was out to show the world just how laid-back a name could be. Point proven, there are few Randis still hanging around, though it might still be a misguided nickname for the infinitely more fashionable and lovely Miranda.

RAPHAELA, RAFAELA. This euphonious and exotic name, with its dark-eyed, long-flowing-haired image, is, like Gabriella, Isabella, and other such Latinate names, beginning to be drawn more into the mainstream. **RAF-FAELLA** is another spelling possibility.

RASHIDA, RASHEEDA. An evocative and alluring name meaning "righteous" in Turkish; less familiar than its male counterpart Rashid.

RAVEN. A recent trend among African-American parents has been to seek out name words that celebrate the beauty of blackness, in particular Ebony and Raven. Raven has rated as high as number 7 for black girl babies in some states, such as Texas, and there were about 1,500 girls with that name born in the most recent year counted.

RAZIAH. A Hebrew name meaning "secret," variants include **RAZIA, RAZIELA,** and **RAZILI.**

REBECCA. A name that has represented beauty in both the Bible and secular literature, Rebecca is as popular now as it was in the days of the Pilgrims, still firmly in the Top 50. In the Old Testament, the bearer of the name, the wife of Isaac and mother of Jacob and Esau, was renowned for her loveliness, as was the Rebecca in Sir Walter Scott's *Ivanhoe.* Then there was the haunted Rebecca in the Daphne du Maurier novel of that name, and the **BECKY**s Sharp and Thatcher in *Vanity Fair* and *Tom Sawyer.* While Becky is still the most common nickname, many modern Rebeccas are becoming known as **BECCA.** Another variation is **REBA,** which has garnered a country-and-western flavor, thanks to megastar Reba McIntire. **REBEKAH** is the spelling used in the authorized version of the Bible; **REBEKKA** is the Greek spelling. Trivia note: When the Native American Princess Pocahontas was baptized, she took the name Rebecca.

REESE. This might be just another one of the thousands of androgynous surname-name possibilities if it weren't for the popularity of the spunky actress Reese, born Laura Jean Reese, Witherspoon. It relates to the Welsh male name Rhys, which means "hero." A similar possibility is **REEVE,** the name of one of the daughters of the aviator Charles Lindbergh and his writer wife Anne.

REGAN. This vibrant last-name-first Irish name, while a strong, straightforward choice, does have a few unsavory literary connotations you might want to keep in mind: Regan was the nastiest of King Lear's nasty daughters and the Regan character played by Linda Blair in the classic horror film *The Exorcist* got pretty nasty herself. **REAGAN,** as in the ex-president, is a popular spelling.

REGINA. This queenly name—Queen Victoria like other British queens had Regina appended to her name—has a certain regal elegance. **RAINA,** the Slavic form of the name, was introduced to the English-speaking world by George Bernard Shaw in his play *Arms and the Man* in 1894. Spelled **RAYNA,** it's the name of one of boxer Mike Tyson's daughters. **REYNA** and **RIONA** are other queenly possibilities.

REMEMBER. There was a male Remember on the *Mayflower,* but we vote for the revival of this old Puritan word name as a choice for girls. Related choices: **PROMISE** and **TRUE.**

RENA, RENATA, REANNA. Three names that evolved from the Hebrew word meaning "joyful song." Renata, the most fashionable version of the three, is used in Germany, Czechoslovakia, and Poland, as well as Italy. Writer Renata Adler has made the name semifamous among the literati. Reanna, with its three-syllable pronunciation, is growing in popularity.

RENEE. Renee, like other French names, is no longer at the height of fashion, though actresses Zellweger and Rene Russo keep it sounding attractive and Rachel Hunter and Rod Steward did choose it for their daughter. **RENE,** traditionally the male spelling, is sometimes used for girls, and **RENNY** is an occasional nickname or variation.

REYNOLD. Used for girls in Scotland in the sixteenth century, we think this makes a bonnie not to mention bold choice worthy of revival.

RHEA. The ancient Greeks believed Rhea to be the mother of the gods Zeus, Poseidon, Hera, Hestia, Hades, and Demeter, and the goddess who personified the earth; to the Romans she was the mother of Romulus and Remus, legendary founders of Rome. In more modern times, the name is associated with actress Rhea Perlman, who played waitress Carla on *Cheers*. The similarly pronounced **RIA** is the short form of Maria, and sometimes used on its own.

RHIANNON. If your family has Welsh roots, you might want to consider this lovely name—it's pronounced REE-a-non—which is best known here as the title of one of the most famous Fleetwood Mac songs. In Celtic folklore, it is linked to the moon. **RHIAN** is a short form.

RHODA. The 1970s TV character Rhoda Morgenstern on *The Mary Tyler Moore Show,* played by Valerie Harper and still appearing regularly on Nick at Nite, put a pretty powerful Bronx accent on this name that actually means "rose" in Greek. It was widely used from the 1930s to the fifties.

RHONDA. Rhonda is, talk about surprising origins, a place name of southern Wales. Warning: If you're considering this name for your child, you should know that its original meaning is "noisy one."

RHONWEN. A Welsh name meaning "slender" and "fair," this lovely choice is still a rarity on our shores.

RICARDA. Richard is one of the few traditional male names with no really viable female equivalent, but if you must, Ricarda is a whole sight better than **RICHARDETTE.**

RICKI, RIKKI. This is one of the earliest of the relaxed, unisex names that were so faddish a few decades back, immortalized in the Steely Dan song, "Rikki Don't Lose That Number." The song and the name are both now restricted to classic rock stations and daytime talk shows like Ricki Lake's.

RILEY, REILLY. This is a lively Irish name that projects a particularly upbeat, cheerful feel. One of the truly androgynous names of this era—there are only slightly more boys than girls given it today—Riley is the preferred spelling, eight to one. Like its rhyming cousin Kylie, however, Riley seems to inspire adventurous spellings, including **RYLEE, RYLIE,** and **RYLEIGH.** Smothers brother Tom has a young daughter named Riley Rose, actress Roma Downey has a Reilly Marie, and comedian/screenwriter Howie "Babaloo" Mandel has a daughter named Riley Paige.

RIPLEY. Perhaps inspired by the powerful Lt. Ripley played by Sigourney Weaver in the *Alien* movies, Thandie Newton chose this androgenous surname for her daughter.

RITA. This was a hot name in the 1940s, the heyday of sexy Rita Hayworth (whose full name was Margarita), but is rarely given to babies today. The domain of the saint named Rita covers some pretty contemporary concerns—she is the patron of those in matrimonial difficulties and other desperate situations, as well as of parenthood. Rita is also a Hindu name.

RIVA. This creative name means both "maiden" in Hebrew and "shore" in French. The related **RIVKA** (the Hebrew form of Rebecca) belonged to the wife of Isaac and mother of Jacob and Esau in the Old Testament.

ROBERTA. Roberta is, of course, the male name Robert feminized in the simplest way—with the addition of a final *a*. The title of a Jerome Kern operetta, it harks back to the day when Roberta sat around discussing the newest Sinclair Lewis novel with her friends Lois and Lorraine.

ROBIN. Robin—originally a male nickname for Robert—sounded bright and chirpy when it began to be used for girls in the 1950s and sixties, but by now the name has definitely lost much of its lilt. One Robin still on the scene is the ex-Mrs. Michael Tyson, Robin Givens; another is Howard Stern's sidekick, Robin Quivers. **ROBYN** is a gussied-up spelling. **ROBINA** is occasionally heard, especially in Scotland.

ROCHELLE. Although the meaning of this French name relates to rock, its image is much more feminine, fragile, and shell-like. And while its popularity peaked in the middle of the twentieth century, it still retains a fragrant sweetness and sounds a bit fresher than some of the more current French favorites, like Michelle. Its nickname, Shelley, took on a life of its own, due largely to Shelley (born Shirley) Winters.

ROMA. An old-fashioned place-name—the Italian name for its capital city—Roma has been in use since the 1880s, although it never achieved the popularity of that other Italian city, Florence. Irish actress Roma Downey, of *Touched by an Angel,* got the name from her two grandmothers, Rose and Mary. **ROMY,** which is actually an official short form of Rosemary made famous by actress Romy Schneider, was the unusual name choice of Ellen Barkin and Gabriel Byrne for their young daughter and of Rob Reiner for his. Going even further afield, the related **ROMOLA** was created by George Eliot for her novel, and **ROMAINE** is also occasionally heard, for people as well as salads. With the spelling **ROMANE,** it's a newly popular name in France. **ROMILLY** is the middle name of Emma Thompson's daughter, Gaia.

RORY. Buoyant and brimming with Irish spirit, Rory has a delightful red-headed, freckle-faced, slightly tomboyish image. But let's not be coy: One of us has a daughter named Rory, so we're only too familiar with the real-life ups and downs of the name. On the positive side, a female Rory (or even a male one, on this side of the ocean) always feels special because of her name. The negatives: confusion over one's gender, a serious issue when you're four, plus having to spell your name so people don't think it's Laurie, Marie, or Gloria. Robert Kennedy's youngest daughter, born after he was assassinated, is named Rory. In the British Isles, Rory is a fashionable (and purely male) name, made famous by twelfth-century Irish high king Rory O'Connor. Also, **RORI.**

ROSALIND. Rosalind started out as a lyrical, bucolic name, probably coined by Edmund Spenser for a shepherdess in one of his pastoral poems. It was further popularized by Shakespeare when he applied it to one of his most charming heroines, in *As You Like It.* And today? Rosalind is a name that can go either way, feeling a bit dated but perhaps so far out it's in if used for a hip young child. **ROSALEEN** is the Gaelic version.

ROSAMOND, ROSAMUND. This quintessentially English name is rarely heard on these shores, a situation we think should be rectified. "Fair Rosamond" was a legendary twelfth-century beauty, the mistress of Henry II, who built a house in which to sequester her in the middle of a maze, but his jealous wife, Eleanor of Aquitaine, managed to find and poison her. **ROSEMOND** is the middle name of Elizabeth Taylor.

ROSE. After five centuries of being associated with the fragrant flower, Rose has suddenly become an overnight success—as a middle name. Parents (such as Michelle Pfeiffer, who named her daughter Claudia Rose; Johnny Depp, with his Lily-Rose, and Sylvester Stallone, with Sistine Rose and Sophia Rose) across the country are finding this the perfect connective between first and last names, with much more color and charm than old standbys like Lynn, Sue, and Ann. It has been well used in other languages too—**RAIZEL** in Yiddish, **ROSA** in Spanish and Italian, **ROISIN** (pronounced roh-SHEEN and used by Sinead O'Connor), and is found in countless combination and pet forms, including **ROSALIA, ROSALIE, ROSALBA, ROSANNA, ROSELLE, ROSELLEN, ROSETTA, ROSITA,** and **ROSEANNE. ROSIE,** à la O'Donnell and Perez, is the cute nickname name that can stand on its own. Actress Rene Russo has a daughter named Rose.

ROSEMARY, ROSEMARIE. This particular amalgamation of two classic names projects a sweet, solid, somewhat old-fashioned sensibility, suggesting the aromatic fragrance of the herb. Both names retain popularity in Irish and Italian families. Romy is the German pet form.

ROWENA. A fabled storybook name, Rowena is most identified with the noble heroine of *Ivanhoe*, who marries the eponymous hero. The name comes from the Welsh Rhonwen.

ROXANE, ROXANNE, ROXANA. Roxane has a touch of the exotic, perhaps because of its Eastern origins. It belonged to the Persian wife of Alexander the Great and, even more familiarly, to the beautiful and virtuous heroine of *Cyrano de Bergerac,* to whom Cyrano says, "Your name is like a golden bell." It was chosen for their daughters by actors Ken Olin and Patricia Wettig and also by *Home Improvement* actress Patricia Richardson. **ROXY** (also spelled **ROXIE**) is its far more audacious offshoot.

RUBY. Of the glistening array of jewel names (Pearl, Opal, Crystal et al.) that became popular at the end of the nineteenth century, Ruby was and still is the most colorful. After a hundred-year hibernation, it is once more being used by such state-of-the-art parents as Suzanne Vega, Matthew Modine, and Rod Stewart and Kelly Emberg.

RUE. Unusual and rather mysterious, Rue comes from the Old German meaning "fame" (while also being the French for *street*) and is redolent of the aromatic plant of that name.

RUMER. A lot of people said, "Huh?" when star couple Demi Moore and Bruce Willis bestowed this name, pronounced like rumor, on their first daughter. But when Demi and Bruce explained that it was inspired by English author Rumer (born Margaret) Godden, the name didn't sound quite so weird. Now we can ask them about Scout LaRue and Tallulah Belle.

RUTH. Ruth has an air of gentleness, calm, and compassion, qualities that apply to the biblical Ruth, the loyal and devoted daughter-in-law of Naomi who left her own people to stay with the older woman, speaking the famous lines, "Whither thou goest, I will go." Although it was the second most popular girls' name in the country in 1900, and still right up there at number 5 in 1925, Ruth is rarely heard from now. But parents tiring of Rachel and Rebecca might just want to give it a second thought.

RYAN. This ultrapopular boys' name, taken from the Irish surname, is beginning to be appropriated by girls. Sure, there are still fifty times (literally) more boys than girls named Ryan, but the female Ryans born each year now number in the hundreds and growing. Such high-profile baby-girl Ryans as the daughters of D. L. Hughley and Holly Robinson-Peete and Rodney Peete help popularize the practice. **RYANN** and **RIAN** are other spellings.

SABA, SABAH. This unusual, exotic name has a dual heritage: In the Bible it is an alternative form of Sheba, and in Arabic it means "morning." It is a Muslim name that is quite popular in North Africa.

SABINA, SABINE. An interestingly sleek, but neglected name, perhaps due to the fame of the story and the painting *The Rape of the Sabine Women*. The Sabines were an ancient Italian race raided by the Romans, who were said to have carried off the Sabine women. But when the Sabines sought revenge, it was the women who succeeded in effecting peace between the two peoples. In more modern times, *Griffin & Sabine* were romantic pen pals. **SAVINA** is an old Italian variation.

SABRA. A strong but sensitive name that is now used as a term for a native-born Israeli.

SABRINA. A name with a great deal of bewitching, bright-eyed charm and one that might be considered as a more distinctive alternative to the ultra-popular Samantha. Sabrina was a legendary Celtic goddess and, in more modern times, the heroine of a successful play and movie, with first Audrey Hepburn, then Julia Ormond playing the title character. Sabrina is also, of course, television's Teenage Witch played by Melissa Joan Hart.

SADIE. This name (which originated as a pet form of Sarah) is one of those that can be seen as a litmus test defining where you stand in girl naming. For many people, Sadie is hopelessly out, either old-fashionedly grand-motheresque or low class beyond consideration, except perhaps for a pet. But for a certain forward-thinking, hip segment of the population, particu-larly the British gentry, Sadie is seen as quite the opposite—the coolest of the cool, epitomized by the lovely actress Sadie Frost, married in real life to heartthrob Jude Law. Actress Joan Allen and actor Michael Ontkean both have daughters named Sadie. The related **SADE** (pronounced shar-DAY) was brought to public attention by the Nigerian singer of that name (who was actually born Helen), and **SADIO**, which means "pure," is used in the French-speaking countries of West Africa.

SAFAN. An unusual and ancient name borne by an early Irish saint known for her generosity and hospitality. An interesting choice for the parent who wants an authentic Irish name that is truly out of the ordinary.

SAFFRON. Shades of the 1960s and seventies, Woodstock, the Maharishi, orange-scented incense, and sounds of the sitar; a pretty name for the retro rebel. Rocker Simon LeBon has a daughter named Saffron.

SAGE. A distinctively fragrant name that, of course, also connotes wisdom. Bear it in mind, too, if you're seeking a short but strong middle name. **SAIGE** is a Paige-like variation. And if you like spice, you might also have a taste for **CORIANDER,** occasionally used as a name in England. Sage Ariel is the name of Lance Henriksen's daughter.

SAILOR. Supermodel Christie Brinkley made this a name possibility after she chose it for her third child.

SALLY. Suddenly Sally is bouncing back, after several decades of lying low. A name with a cheerful, fresh-faced, good-girl-next-door image, Sally was originally a nickname for Sarah. It was popular in the eighteenth century and then again from the 1920s to the 1960s.

SALMA, SELMA. Sexy stars Salma Hayek and Selma Blair have double-handedly put the zip back in these once tired names. A Scandinavian relative of Anselm's, Selma was last popular in the 1920s and 1930s.

SALOME. One of the sexiest names in the book, Salome is a lot for a young girl to live up to, and should be approached with caution. In the Bible, Salome danced for King Herod and pleased him so much that he offered her anything she wanted. What she requested and received was the head of John the Baptist, thus tainting the name with an unsavory association. In Hebrew, though, the name is related to *shalom,* meaning "peace." TV actress Alex Kingston named her daughter Salome Violetta.

SAMANTHA. This name began its phenomenal rise in popularity in the sixties as the name of the nose-twitching heroine of TV's *Bewitched* and shows no signs of diminishing—it is still hanging in at number 7 on the national hit parade and has hit the top spot over the past decade in some states. Part of Samantha's popularity owes thanks to the stylishness of her brother **SAM,** a nickname which is the prime appeal for many parents. It is also, by the way, among the Top 10 names given to female dogs in both L.A. and New York.

SAMARA, SAMARIA. A name of Hebrew origin meaning "under God's rule," which is gaining a measure of popularity as a Samantha/Sam alternative. Rapper LL Cool J named his daughter Samaria, and actress Kathy Najimy named hers **SAMIA,** which, like **SAMYA,** is from the Arabic word for *elevated* or *sublime.* **SAMIRA** is another variation.

SANDRA, SAUNDRA, SONDRA. These triplet names were born in the 1930s and were among the most popular girls' names in the class of 1950, but are virtually unused for babies today. Originally offshoots of Alexandra, which is now the favored form.

SANNE, SANNA. One of the most popular names in the Netherlands and Scandinavia, this interesting choice, pronounced SAH-na, is unheard of here. It originated as a short form of Susanne/Susanna.

SAOIRSE. Irish for *freedom,* this name, pronounced SEER-sha, is growing in popularity in Ireland and has even popped up in other European countries, perhaps destined to travel here as a successor to Siobhan and Sinead. It has been used by one of the Kennedy cousins.

SAPPHIRE. Never as popular as such other jewel names as Pearl or Ruby, Sapphire (the birthstone for September) has nevertheless seen some use. The related **SAPPHIRA** is a Hebrew name meaning "gem."

SARAH, SARA. Firmly in America's Top 5—and approaching number 1 when you count both spellings—Sarah has been the premier biblical girls' name here for two decades, offering rich Old Testament associations for those parents wishing to mine their religious roots and a sweet yet strong, patrician yet straightforward image to those in search of more secular name appeal. The big question: Are there too many Sarahs? While thousands of babies of all ethnic backgrounds throughout the country are given the name—the spelling ratio is nearly four with the final *h* to every one without—Sarah has weathered trendiness perhaps better than any other contemporary female example. It's like one of the classic boys' names—Daniel, for instance, or David—in its ability to retain its widespread popularity without ever feeling dated. Long popular in England as well as here, in the Old Testament, Sarah was the wife of Abraham and mother of Isaac—who actually changed her name from **SARAI** at the age of ninety. Probably its most famous bearer, the great actress Sarah Bernhardt, was born Rosine. Two more contemporary actresses are Sarah Jessica Parker and Sarah Michelle Gellar. Among the international variations on the theme are **ZAHARIA** (Greek), **SARI** (Hungarian), **SARKA** (Russian), **SAHAR** (Israeli) **SORCHA**) (Irish, pronounced SOR-ha), and **SARITA** (Spanish and Italian).

SASHA, SACHA. This name started life as a Russian male nickname (for Alexander), but is now used as widely in this country for girls as for boys, projecting an arty and active image. Producer Steven Spielberg and mate Kate Capshaw have produced a Sasha of their own as has Vanessa Williams. The Jerry Seinfelds spell their daughter's name **SASCHA.** Another interesting possibility is the Dutch **SASKIA,** made famous by the wife and frequent model of Rembrandt and more recently by rising young actress Saskia Reeves.

SASSANDRA. An African place-name, being a river on the Ivory Coast. She'd be sure to go through life as **SASSY.**

SATCHEL. This name of oldtime baseball player Satchel Paige seemed unusual enough when Woody Allen revived it for his son (mom Mia Farrow later changed the boy's name to Seamus), but feels downright eccentric when used for a girl, as director Spike Lee did for his daughter Satchel Lewis.

SAVANNAH. A name redolent of magnolias and other sweet smells of the Old South, Savannah is becoming one of the hottest of the hot place-names, as well as one of the most appealing. In its original spelling, Savannah is in the Top 40: myriad other options from **SAVANNA** to **SAVANA, SEVANAH,** and so on boost it even higher. Songwriting author Jimmy Buffet is one parent who chose it for his daughter.

SCARLETT. The blockbuster book and movie, *Gone With The Wind,* had a tremendous effect on American baby-naming: Just think of the characters Melanie, Rhett, Ashley, Brent, and Bonnie—and even the plantation setting, Tara. Somewhat left behind until recently, probably because the character was so strong and forceful that the name was forever linked to her, was that of the heroine (few people remember that she was actually christened Katie Scarlett—her grandmother's maiden name—O'Hara). Now, finally, this seductively Southern name is being looked at on its own; Jerry Hall and Mick Jagger used it as a middle name for their daughter Elizabeth.

SCHUYLER. See **SKYLAR.**

SCOUT. It was the nickname name of the young heroine of *To Kill a Mockingbird,* but what really brought this name back before the public eye was its use by Bruce Willis and Demi Moore for their second daughter. Actor Tom Berenger chose it for his little girl too.

SELA, SELAH. This biblical name was all but extinct when it received two big boosts in popularity, one from actress Sela Ward and the other when singer Lauryn Hill chose the Selah version for her newborn daughter.

SELENA, SELINA. Smooth, shiny, and sensual, Selena is an attractive, underused name. In Greek mythology, **SELENE** was the beautiful goddess of the moon. Every night, as she crossed the skies in her chariot drawn by two white horses, her golden crown would light up the darkness. Admirers of the murdered Tejano singer Selena have helped make the name more popular.

SENECA. This name of a Roman philosopher, dramatist, and statesman, and of a Native American tribe, is occasionally used for both girls and boys.

SEPTIMA. If you have six children, this name is a possibility for your seventh.

SERAPHINA, SERAFINA. Although this name may be related to the word for *seraphim,* the highest form of angels in the celestial sphere, its image is closer to its meaning in Hebrew—"passionate one."

SERENA. As calm and tranquil as its meaning implies, this is a name found more often on the rosters of elite English schools than in the playgrounds of this country, a situation we find ripe for change. **SARINA** is a Sara-related spelling sometimes used. **SERENITY** takes the idea in a less conventional, more straightforward direction.

SESAME. It seems as if every euphonic-sounding word is up for grabs as a first name. This one certainly has a soft and pretty sound, but you might do better to stick with Poppy.

SETH. Although rarely used for girls, the soft, gentle sound of this name makes it a perfect candidate for crossing over to the female camp. **SETHE** was the mother character in Toni Morrison's *Beloved.*

SHANA, SHAYNA. Even many non-Jews know the phrase "shayna maidel" means "pretty girl" in Yiddish, so a child with this creative name will have pleasant expectations set for her. The journalist Shana Alexander brought the name to the attention of the public. The Eddie Murphys named their third daughter **SHAYNE** Audra. Shayne is also the name of the young daughter of Lorenzo Lamas.

SHANIA. Country singer Shania Twain is responsible for the growing popularity of this name, pronounced shan-EYE-a and meaning "I'm on my way" in Ojibwa dialect. **SHANIYA** is another spelling. The less familiar **SHANI** is a Hebrew name meaning "scarlet."

SHANNON. Could a name sound more Irish? Well, Irish it is, but in the Emerald Isle it's a surname and the name of a river, not a name for a colleen. Along with other cheery Gaelic-inflected names like Erin and Kelly it peaked in popularity in the 1970s and is infrequently given to babies today. Former Beverly Hills bad girl **SHANNEN** Doherty publicized another spelling of the name.

SHARIFA. A Swahili name, found in East Africa, that means "distinguished" and lives up to that image. **SHAREEFAH** is another spelling.

SHARON. An Old Testament place-name (the fertile Plain of Sharon), Sharon was the sixth most popular name for girl babies born in 1940, number 9 in 1950 and was still in the Top 25 in 1960. It had pretty much settled into a mom image until the advent of Sharon Stone, who gave the name a sexier image. In Britain, many Americans are surprised to learn, Sharon is seen as the ultimate working-class girls' name.

SHASTA. A place-name—it's a majestic mountain in northern California, much revered by healers and spiritualists—that might have appeal for those who love unusual Western names.

SHAWN. The usual girls' spelling of the Irish boys' name, Shawn has passed its day in the sun, though **SEAN** has some androgynous punch via actress Sean Young. **SHAUNA** is a further corruption of the original, and **SHANE** was used for both boys and girls in the years following the release of the haunting western of that name in 1953.

SHEA. A soft and pretty-sounding last-name name that can work beautifully for a little girl of today. Writer John Grisham used the name for his daughter. **SHAY** is the phonetic spelling; **SHAYLEE** and **SHAYLA** have also been heard.

SHEBA. This exotic biblical place-name for the region in Arabia now known as Yemen is occasionally given to babies, but more often and more appropriately to puppies and kittens.

SHEENA. The Gaelic form of Jane (it's spelled **SINE** in Ireland and Scotland), this is an animated, easily assimilated ethnic name introduced to the American public by singer Sheena Easton. **SIAN,** the Welsh form of Jane, looks pretty on paper, but most Americans would have no idea that it is pronounced shan. Sian is the name of the young daughter of U2's Dave "The Edge" Evans.

SHEILA. This is an Irish name (an offshoot of Celia or Cecilia) that peaked in popularity in this country in the 1930s—although it was still clinging to the edge of the Top 40 list of 1960. Aficionados of Australian movies will be aware that *sheila* is the generic term Down Under for a girl. Modern parents would probably be more likely to select Shelby, Shania, or Celia over Sheila.

SHELBY. One of the androgynous surname names that retains a distinctly female lilt, Shelby has dropped out of the Top 25, which it reached from near nowhere in the mid-1990s, and now is even out of the Top 50, so not a name with much staying power.

SHELLEY. When Shirley Schrift adopted the stage name of Shelley Winters (supposedly inspired by the poet Shelley), a naming trend was born. Previously a male nickname for the now nerdish Sheldon, it became a faddish 1950s female name, in tune with the Sharons, Sharis, and Sherrys coming into style at the same time. It is now very much a parental-generation name.

SHERALYN, SHERILYN. Some of the Mary Lous and Betty Anns of yore grew up to hatch little combo-named kids of their own, and this (recently brought into the spotlight by actress Sherilyn Fenn) was one of their options. Millennial parents for the most part prefer to keep first and middle names separate and distinct.

SHERI, SHERRY. It's a phonetic version of the French **CHÉRI,** an alcoholic beverage, and a peppy cheerleader name of the 1960s and 1970s, sure to evoke the strains of the Four Seasons song of that name (in which it was stretched to three syllables). What it isn't is a likely choice for a modern baby. The similar **SHERYL** began life as a variant spelling of Cheryl. The more contemporary sounding **SHERIDAN** appears in the daytime drama *Passions.*

SHIFRA. A popular name in Israel, Shifra was the biblical midwife who disobeyed the pharaoh's order to kill all the newborn Jewish boys.

SHILOH. One of the new names in the Western fashion, used by actor Tom Berenger for one of his daughters. Shiloh was the site of a major Civil War battle.

SHIRA. A Hebrew name meaning "song," well used in Israel and ripe for adoption here.

SHIRLEY. Shirley Temple almost single-handedly lifted the gloom of the Great Depression, and in tribute (and perhaps wishing for a similarly bright-eyed, curly-headed, dimpled darling of their own), thousands of parents of that generation gave their little girls her name. In an earlier time used primarily for boys, the tide turned with the publication of Charlotte Brontë's novel *Shirley* in 1849, the story of a character whose parents had selected the name for a male child, then decided to use it anyway when he turned out to be a she. Virtually never used for babies today.

SHOSHANA. In Hebrew this is a popular flower name, meaning "lily." A graceful choice, if a bit difficult to pronounce. The English translation is Susannah.

SHULA, SHULAMIT, and **SULAMITH** are all variations on *shalom,* the Hebrew word for "peace," and are often found in Israel.

SIBYL, SYBIL. The ancient Greeks used this as a generic word to represent prophetesses—women who relayed the messages of the gods. It now has a rather dowdy, unfashionable image, despite the blond gloss of the uniquely spelled **CYBILL** Shepherd.

SIDONIA, SIDONY, SIDONIE. These names, which are virtually unknown in America, are most widely used in England and France. Although they might be considered eccentric, all three have a rhythmic (accent on the second syllable), novelistic appeal.

SIENA. A soft and delicate place name, conjuring up the warm reddish-brown tones of the Tuscan town. **SIENNA** is a frequent spelling variation.

SIERRA. This ambigender place-name, which brings to mind snowy peaks and pure air, has made great strides in popularity in the past few years, now climbing official most-popular lists. **CIERRA** is an alternate, if inauthentic, spelling.

SIGOURNEY. A single-celeb name via Sigourney Weaver, who had been born as the more ordinary Susan. At the age of fourteen she rechristened herself after a minor character in *The Great Gatsby*. **SIGNE** and **SIGNY** are two more manageable Scandinavian names, Signy appearing in Norse mythology as the twin sister of Sigmund.

SIGRID. This Scandinavian name that came into the American consciousness around the same time as Ingrid is rarely used in this country outside Norwegian families.

SILVER. It may not sound that way at first hearing, but Silver is a legitimate girls' name and not a flower-child fabrication of the seventies. A gleaming, glistening possibility for parents seeking a creative choice. The similar-sounding (especially if you have a New York accent) **SILVA** is a rarely used saint's name.

SIMONE. This name reverberates with Gallic sophistication (think of Simone Signoret, Simone de Beauvoir), yet its simple spelling and pronunciation make it a perfectly acceptable (and imaginative) possibility for use here. **SIMONA** is the equally appealing Italian version.

SINEAD. Irish for Janet and pronounced shi-NADE, this name may be difficult to separate from the somewhat aggressive demeanor of its one well-known bearer in this country, singer Sinead O'Connor. But if you can do that, it makes a striking choice for a child with strong Irish roots.

SIOBHAN. An Irish form of Joan (pronounced sha-vaun) this name is more familiar here today in its phonetically spelled versions, which range from

SHEVAUN to **SHEVONNE** to **SHAVON** ad infinitum. We admit the original spelling is bafflingly foreign to most Americans; still, using it preserves the ethnic integrity of this, one of the most lovely of the Gaelic girls' names. **SHONA** is another Gaelic form of Joan.

SISTINE. Sylvester Stallone and Jennifer Flavin engaged in some imaginative baby-naming when they came up with this new-to-us conception for their daughter. The Sistine Chapel is the private chapel of the popes in the Vatican, famous for Michelangelo's magnificent ceiling and wall paintings.

SIVE. A name from Irish mythology: Sive (it rhymes with "alive") was transformed into a deer, back to a woman, then back to a deer, marrying superhero Finn MacCool and bearing his son along the way. **SEVE** and **SEVA** are Breton variations.

SKYLAR. Once exclusively male, this Dutch name—it was originally **SCHUYLER,** the spelling both Michael J. Fox and Sissy Spacek used for their daughters—has crossed over to the other gender, with about three girls now being given the name for every two boys. Skylar is the preferred spelling for girls, two to one, while **SKYLER** is the favored one for boys by the same margin. Country singer Clay Walker substituted another vowel to call his daughter **SKYLOR. SKYLA** is sometimes used, and an abbreviated version is **SKYE** or **SKY.**

SLOAN, SLOANE. A gray-flannel-suit, androgynous-executive name, which seems to predict either corporate CEOship or, failing that, considerable charity-ball committee activity.

SOLANGE. A soignée French name meaning "rare jewel" that has never made it here but just might have a chance now.

SOLEIL. It means "sun" in French, and actress Soleil Moon Frye made it something of a possibility here. **SOLANA** is a related Spanish option.

SONIA, SONYA, SONJA. In all three spellings, a wintry, ice-skating name dressed in heavy red velvet and white ermine muffs. Bred in cold climates (it means "wisdom" in Old Norse and is a Russian diminutive of **SOFIA**), Sonia, Sonya, Sonja is/are both exotic and grandmotherly warm.

SONNET. Could there be a more poetic name? Actor Forest Whitaker chose it for his daughter.

SONORA. Yet another of the Western place names that start with the letter *S*, Sonora is a more unusual and melodic choice than Sierra or Cheyenne (aka Shyanne). **SONOMA,** like the wine-growing county in California, is another sometimes-heard choice.

SOPHIA and **SOPHIE.** Both these names have become ultratrendy in the last few years, completely shedding their once-dowdy granny images for more elegant ones. In the popularity standings, Sophia leads Sophie more than three to one—taken together, the names are firmly in the Top 50, while in England Sophia is number 7—though we suspect many little Sophias are called Sophie. Gary Sinise, Luke Perry, and Rebecca De Mornay have daughters Sophie, and Sylvester Stallone has Sophia Rose. Another spelling is **SOFIA,** as in young director Coppolla. When Bette Midler chose it for her daughter, she explained, "We think Sophie sounds like an impoverished Austrian princess who is forced to marry a coarse member of the bourgeoisie." We agree.

SORAYA. A Persian name borne by the last shah of Iran's second wife, with a pleasingly exotic sound.

SORCHA. Virtually unknown in this country, Sorcha is an Old Irish name that has become very popular in contemporary Ireland. It means "shining bright," and is pronounced SOR-ra.

SORREL. A botanical name—it's a rare wild herb—with a Western feel.

SPENCER. Yes, Spencer for a girl. One of those "Doesn't-this-sound-as-good-or-better-for-the-opposite-sex?" names that suddenly seem completely conceivable. Ask Jaclyn Smith, who named her daughter Spencer Margaret a few years ago.

SPRING and **SUMMER.** These are two distinctive, evocative names, conjuring up images of sunshine, warm breezes, and new green growth. One of the nature-named Phoenix siblings is Summer, as is the daughter of rapper Dr. Dre. And if you can't decide between the two, you can always consider **SEASON,** as in actress Season Hubley.

STACY, STACEY. Originally a boys' name (as in Stacey Keach), it became a key cheerleader in the nickname game of the late 1960s and early seventies (reaching number 18 in 1970). A more contemporary-sounding substitute might be **STACIA** or, back to the original, Anastasia or Eustacia.

STELLA. A name that manages to be both celestial and earthy at the same time, primarily because *(a)* it means "star" in Latin, and *(b)* many of us can still hear Brando bellowing the name in *A Streetcar Named Desire.* The name was coined by Sir Philip Sidney in 1590, and was recently used by John Ritter, Elizabeth Shue, and by Melanie Griffith and Antonio Banderas for their daughters.

STEPHANIE. Stephanie is a name that has remarkable staying power, perhaps more than any other feminine form of a male name (the French **STEPHANE**); it doesn't sound dated even though it has been popular (still remaining in the Top 50) for twenty-five years. It is feminine without being frilly and parents seem to like its short forms—**STEFFI** and **STEPH**—never resorting to the French nickname, **FANNY.** Royal bad girl Princess Stephanie of Monaco certainly lends the name some class; **STEFANIE** is how actress Powers (born Stefania) spells the name, and the somewhat flat-footed **STEPHANY** also appears on some birth announcements. **STEPHANA** is another option.

STORM. A tempestuous name that might prove too much for a quiet, retiring girl to live up to. Rocker Nikki Sixx has a daughter named Storm.

STORY. The perfect word name for a writer, Story suggests both a future and a past for its bearer, and has an uptempo Cory/Rory/Tori sound besides. The singers known as Ginuwine and Sole recently called their baby girl Story.

SUMMER. See **SPRING.**

SURYA. An Indian goddess of the sun, this makes an exotic yet simple choice with a vibrant meaning.

SUSAN, SUSANNAH. Susannah (also spelled **SUSANNA** or in its Hispanic version **SUSANA**) is by far the most stylish version of this classic name today, with Susan reserved for moms born during the name's heyday, 1948 to 1964, when it was consistently among the Top 5. It derives from the Hebrew Shoshana, meaning "lily," and its diminutives are found in any number of popular songs ("Sweet Sue," "If You Knew Susie," "Wake Up Little Susie," to name a few). In the New Testament, Susannah was the heroine of the story of Daniel and the Elders. The French versions **SUZANNE** and **SUZETTE** attained a certain measure of popularity, slipstreaming behind Susan, Suzanne coming back briefly into prominence as the name of the high-profile Delta Burke character on TV's *Designing Women*. We've heard the interesting **SANNA** or **ZANNA** as a nickname for the versions that end in an *a* sound. More original than **SUSIE** or **SUZY,** in any case, is the old and charming **SUKIE** or **SUKY.**

SUSHILA. A Hindu Indian name with a lovely sound and exotic appeal for the parent in search of a choice that's unusual yet is backed by tradition.

SYDNEY. When given to a girl, Sydney takes the somewhat nerdy image it has as a boys' name and turns it inside out: The female Sydney is polished, poised, creative, elegant, and intelligent, qualities more and more parents have begun to recognize. Sydney is now in the Top 25—and climbing, if its many variations, including **SYDNI** and **SYDNEE,** are any evidence.

SYLVIA. Many of us have had an Aunt or Great Aunt Sylvia and so might be quick to relegate this name to purgatory, but if we could shake away the dust and listen to the pure sound of Sylvia, we might rediscover its musical, sylvan qualities. Sylvia Plath was the Tragic Heroine of modern poetry. **SILVIA** was the mother of the twins Remus and Romulus, who founded Rome. **SILVIE/SYLVIE** is the livelier French version.

T

TABITHA. Ever since 1965 when the cute little girl with supernatural powers was introduced on the long-running TV series *Bewitched,* the name Tabitha has had a slightly off-center, occult charm. While never as popular as the name of her mom, Samantha, there are still more than a thousand baby girls named Tabitha each year. One of Beatrix Potter's storybook characters is a cat called Tabitha Twitchet, and indeed nickname **TABBY** is decidedly feline. Tabitha appears in the New Testament in the form of a charitable woman who was restored to life by Saint Peter.

TAFFY. A name that also means a kind of candy can hardly help but project sweetness, sexiness, and not much substance. Taffy is in fact the female form of David in Wales, where it is also used as a male nickname.

TALIA. A Hebrew name that means "the gentle dew from heaven." In the mythology of one ancient sect, Talia was one of ten angels who attended the sun on its daily course. A prominent bearer of the name is Talia Shire, doomed to go down in cinema history as the mousy girlfriend ("Yo, Adrienne!") in *Rocky.* **TALLY** is the name of the daughter of rap artist LL Cool J, while **TALI** is the variation singer Annie Lennox chose for her daughter.

TALLULAH. For years this name was taboo because of its iron-clad link with the acid-tongued actress of the 1930s and forties, Tallulah Bankhead. Now, since most prospective parents have hardly heard of the lady, it's time for a reappraisal of this resonant, rhythmic Choctaw Indian name—which means "leaping water." In the vanguard as always, Demi Moore and Bruce Willis chose it for their third daughter. When spelled **TALLULA,** as rocker Simon LeBon did for his daughter, it is also a traditional Irish name that was borne by two early saints.

TAMAR. A strong, rich, out-of-the-ordinary Hebrew name borne by several Old Testament women, including a daughter of King David. Its literal meaning is "date palm," which suggests beauty and grace. In the Jewish culture it is sometimes given to girls born on the holiday of Sukkoth, because palm branches were used in constructing the roof of the Sukkah. The Russian form of the name is **TAMARA,** the final vowel adding a more sensual, Slavic tone; it belonged to a famous twelfth-century Georgian queen.**TAMORA** is the version Shakespeare used in *Titus Andronicus,* and **TAMA** is also heard, as in the name of the art-scene novelist Tama Janowitz.

TAMIA, TAMMY. Singer Tamia (no last name) has inspired a number of followers. Her name is now in the Top 500, while the relatively more established Tammy—as in Wynette, Grimes, and Faye Bakker—does not even make the Top 1,000 count. Ironically, music also prompted the rise of Tammy nearly half a century ago. It was the name of a theme song and movie starring Debbie Reynolds as a wholesome backwoods gal, an image the name has never shaken and that probably was the ultimate cause of its demise.

TAMIKA. A popular and euphonic newly created African-American name. Also spelled **TAMEEKA.**

TAMSIN. An offbeat name that originated as a contraction of Thomasina. Often heard in Britain, it is just waiting to be discovered on this side of the Atlantic. The same might be said of **TANSY,** the name of a yellow wildflower and herb, found in a number of English novels.

TANAQUIL. Tanaquil LeClercq was one of the twentieth century's loveliest ballerinas and maestro George Balanchine's fifth wife, whose career was cut short by polio. Her graceful and appealing name dates back to ancient Roman times. Tanaquil was an aristocratic Etruscan renowned for her prophetic powers who urged her husband to go to Rome, where he eventually became ruler. This name should be on the shortlist of any parent in search of a highly unusual choice with a long pedigree and a lot of style.

TANESHA, TANISHA. A name derived from a West African name for girls born on Monday.

TANIS. An unusual girls' name used in Sinclair Lewis's 1923 novel *Babbitt* and not often since then. But it has the right feel for consideration by today's parents.

TANYA, TANIA. A Russian name that has been fully integrated into the American name pool, retaining just a touch of its slavic flavor. It started life as a pet form of **TATIANA,** which is beginning to be used in this country as well—by Caroline Kennedy Schlossberg for one of her daughters, for instance—and which has a more delicate, feminine appeal to the contemporary ear. **TITANIA** was the name of the fairy queen in Shakespeare's *A Midsummer Night's Dream.* But **TONYA,** which may be spelled differently but sounds and feels the same, has sullied the name's image because of the hijinks of notorious skater Harding.

TARA. It seems that every name associated with *Gone With the Wind,* including this name of the O'Hara plantation, has shared in some of the book's and movie's popularity. The additional advantage of an Irish accent (a geographical name there as well: Tara is the ancient capital of the Irish kings, also the wife of one of them), plus a prominent soap opera character, Tara Martin in *All My Children,* combined to propel this windswept name into the Top 50 in the early 1980s. **TARYN,** an offshoot created in the Sharon-Karen period, has been used by both singer Michael Bolton and baseball player Ken Griffey Jr. for their daughters.

TATUM. Like Shaquille, a distinctive name that may be prime for wider use, especially if your last name is as congenial as O'Neal. **TATOM** is the middle name of Harry Connick, Jr's daughter Georgia.

TAWNY. See **TAFFY,** then add to its definition a golden tan.

TAYLOR. Firmly in the Top 10, Taylor is one of the most popular androgynous surname names for girls. A soap opera favorite, it is used more than five times as often for girls as for boys, and was chosen by singer Garth Brooks and *Baywatch* star David Hasselhoff for their daughters. Spelling variation **TAYLER** is used by several hundred parents a year.

TEAL. A really offbeat color name, this could make an interesting middle-name choice.

TEMPEST. This stormy-sounding name was brought to public attention by the young actress Tempestt Bledsoe (the double *t* is her unique variation) on *The Cosby Show*.

TERESA, THERESA, THERESE. A Greek classic, made famous by the sixteenth-century Spanish Saint Teresa of Ávila, a strong, witty, and intelligent Carmelite nun who combined the active life of establishing and running seventeen convents with mystical contemplation and writing. In more contemporary times, Mother Teresa added to the image of selfless hard work fused with compassion. Thérèse, pronounced, Tay-REHZ, the French form. American parents—particularly Catholics—favored this name from the 1920s to the early seventies. **TERRY** (or **TERI** or **TERRI** or **TERRIE**) was the usual nickname, though **TESS** or **TESSA** are more contemporary short forms.

TERRA. A video game import Terra is the mysterious main character in *Final Fantasy VI*. She has green hair and a name that brings the now-outmoded Terry and Tara into the modern age.

TERTIA (pronounced TER-sha). An unconventional possibility for the third child in a family.

TESSA, TESS. Originally nicknames for Teresa, these choices have become far more fashionable than the original over the past few years. Tessa is now the more popular choice, used nearly three times as often as Tess. **TESSIE** can be an even less formal version of either.

THALASSA, THALIA, and **THEONE.** Three rarely used Greek names worthy of consideration. Thalia is one of the Three Graces in Greek mythology, and also the Muse of Comedy (she's the one holding the smiling mask).

THEA. A name that paints an artistic picture; sensitive and serene. Thea makes a hip choice on its own or short for Theodora/Dorothea.

THELMA. Invented by a late nineteenth-century writer named Marie Corelli for the Norwegian heroine of one of her novels, this name is now as dated as the book, although it did gain some latter-day notoriety through the movie *Thelma and Louise*. Trivia Trifle: Thelma was Pat Nixon's given first name.

THEODORA. We predict that this long-neglected, softly evocative yet serious name is in for a revival (as is its syllable reversal, Dorothea). It was borne by the beautiful ninth wife of the Emperor Justinian, who became the power behind his throne, and, more recently, selected by the daddy of cool, Rolling Stone Keith Richards. Variations include **THEODOSIA, FEODORA,** and **TEODORA,** the Italian, Spanish, Portuguese, Swedish, and Polish forms.

THEONE. See **THALASSA.**

THIRZA. A Hebrew Old Testament name meaning "pleasantness," perhaps rarely used because of its association with *thirst*.

THOMASA, THOMASIN, THOMASINA. These three female derivatives of Thomas are not used very often in these days when women would prefer to appropriate men's names rather than sweeten them with feminine endings.

TIA. Mia is more popular, but Tia is moving up the ranks, thanks in part to *Sister Sister* actress Tia Mowry. (Her twin Tamara's name is only slightly less well used.) **NIA, PIA, BRIA,** and **LIA** are other sprightly Mia alternatives.

TIANA, TIARA, TIERRA. Newly coined Tia relatives, these names are, strangely enough, all running neck and neck in the popularity race. Tiana is slightly ahead, and also gains points from its frequently used spelling variation **TIANNA.** There's something about the *tee* sound that's feminine and attractive, though while Tierra means "earth," none of these names really carries a lot of substance. Jimmy Smits switched the vowels around and called his daughter **TAINA.**

TIERNEY. An Irish surname that means "lordly," this seems particularly well suited for a girl.

TIFFANY. This was the quintessential name of the Booming Eighties, the nominal personification of prosperity, luxury, and extravagance, of breakfast at Tiffany's and dinner at an expensive restaurant every night. It was worn by gorgeous women in James Bond movies, soap operas, and *Charlie's Angels*. But when the economy plummeted at the end of the decade, it dragged the image of the name down with it, so that while Tiffany still may be lingering at the lower edges of the popularity lists, it's definitely lost its silvery sheen. (Apparently unaware that the eighties were over, Marla Maples and Donald Trump named their daughter Tiffany. Trump was quoted as saying he chose the name to commemorate his purchase of the air rights above the famed jeweler Tiffany and Co., which cleared the way for his Trump Tower on Fifth Avenue.) At one time in history Tiffany, which is Greek for "manifestation of God," was reserved for girls born on the Epiphany (January 6 or Twelfth Night).

TILLIE, TILLY. This name hasn't been used in so long that it's beginning to sound cute again. Writer Tillie Olsen is a feminist favorite.

TINA. Tina, the pet form of such names as Christina and Martina, had its moment in the early 1970s, but these days it's more likely to be replaced by the more elegant originals. Tina's image is petite, quiet, and ladylike— unless you think about Tina Turner (born Anna Mae).

TISA. The Swahili word for the number 9, Tisa was at one time used primarily for ninth-born children. In this era of the shrunken nuclear family, though, it's a possible choice for even a first child.

TOBY. One of the earlier unisex names, Toby, when used for a girl, retains its tomboyish quality. It originated as a nickname for the male name Tobias.

TONI. In the 1940s, this nickname began to supersede its progenitor, Antonia. Now, although Nobel and Pulitzer prize-winning novelist Toni (born Chloe) Morrison has heaped honors on the name, modern parents would probably be better advised to reassess the pioneer strength of the original.

TORA, TORIL, TORILL, TOREZ. Scandinavian female names related to the god of thunder Tor or Thor, these have melodic sounds and a fresh flavor that might seem just right here.

TORI. *Beverly Hills 90210* actress Tori Spelling and singer Tori Amos helped re-publicize this seventies name. A nickname for Victoria, which is in the Top 20, it can also stand on its own—more than 1,200 girls were named simply Tori in the most recent year counted.

TOVA, TOVAH. A lively, modern Hebrew name meaning "good" or "pleasing."

TRACY, TRACEY. After taking a typical place-name-to-last-name-to-male-first-name route, Tracy's ascent as a girl's name was due almost solely to the vibrant character Tracy Lord, portrayed first by Katharine Hepburn in *The Philadelphia Story* (1940) and later by Grace Kelly in the musical version, *High Society* (1956). This association gave the name a classy aura, though in Britain, it's considered a quintessentially lower-class name. Fashionable in the late 1960s, these days it's more likely to be replaced by Grace or Gracie.

TRINA. Often short for Katrina, this name can also stand on its own.

TRINITY. Every once in a while, there's a name that explodes from obscurity to widespread popularity. Trinity, spurred by the powerful female character in the cult movie favorite *The Matrix,* is one such name. It didn't even register in the Top 1,000 names of the 1980s. In 1998, it was number 555. By 1999, it had risen to number 216, and then in 2000 it hit the Top 100 at number 74. Trinity is one of the new breed of word names—Destiny and Genesis are other notable examples—that have a spiritual meaning and a euphonic sound. Just be aware that it's very quickly become less than unique.

TRIXIE. A sassy, spunky name for the bold parent who doesn't connect it solely with Mrs. Ed Norton on *The Honeymooners.* Damon Wayans and the late Jerry Garcia both picked it for their daughters. The more formal name, if only for the birth certificate and future resume: Beatrix.

TRUDY. Innocent, sincere, and bright-eyed, Trudy is nevertheless almost as outdated as Gertrude, the name it's short for.

TRUE, TRUTH. Two inspirational-word names that would work especially well as middle names. Forest Whitaker has a daughter named True Isabella Summer, and Sojourner Truth was a slave turned abolitionist and women's rights advocate.

TUESDAY. Days of the week, unlike months of the year, are rarely used as names in this country, but when actress Susan Kerr changed her name to Tuesday Weld, she brought it into the realm of possibility.

TWILA, TWYLA. A Middle English name whose meaning has to do with weaving, this is a creative name largely associated with choreographer Twyla Tharp. It also has a pleasant association with the word twilight.

TYLER and **TYSON.** A pair of handsome male surname names that have begun to be appropriated by females. Tyler, high on the boys' popularity charts, retains a definite masculine edge. Trivia item that gives it a female twist: It's Ashley Judd's middle name. And Tyson is still linked to the hyper-macho boxer Mike, though Singer Nenah Cherry chose it for her daughter.

TYNE. Compact and creative, this name was introduced to the public by actress Tyne Daly.

TYRA. Supermodel and actress Tyra Banks has made this a new possibility for parents. It could be a Kyra alternative or the feminization of Tyrone.

U

UMA. This throaty, exotic name is one of the more than one thousand appellations for the Hindu goddess Sakti—a fact that surely inspired the father of Uma Thurman, a Columbia University professor of Eastern religion. Thurman's middle name, **KARUNA,** is equally exotic. In Hebrew, Uma means "nation," and is therefore often used for girls born on Israeli Independence Day.

UNA. An ancient Irish name, Una can also be spelled Oona (as in the case of the daughter of Eugene O'Neill and wife of Charlie Chaplin) or the even more authentic **OONAGH.** The poet Edmund Spenser used Una for *The Faerie Queene,* daughter of a legendary king and the quintessence of truth and beauty. Another Irish form of the name is Juno.

UNITY. Such Puritan virtue names as Unity, Verity, and Prudence could be due for a comeback, embodying as they do qualities we would all like to impart to our children. The only well-known bearer of the name was British author Unity Mitford.

URSULA. Today's kids will probably associate this name with the exaggerated actions of the campy, corpulent octopus sea-witch in Disney's *The Little Mermaid,* while yesterday's adults will recall the sex goddess Ursula Andress. In any case, its slightly Germanic feel makes it a poor bet for popularity.

UTA. Pronounced OO-ta, this is yet another rarely used three-letter *U* name. This one originated as the diminutive of another rarely used (but more interesting) name: Ottalie.

V

VALDA, VANDA, and **VARDA.** Three names with different roots but a similar, occultish aura. Valda is from the German, meaning "the heroine of a battle," Vanda is a variant of Wanda, and Varda, which means "rose" in Hebrew, is widely used in Israel. **VONDA** Shepard is the *Ally McBeal* songstress.

VALENTINA. An interesting possibility for parents seeking a viable alternative to the more common Victoria and Vanessa. Meaning "strong, healthy one" in Latin, Valentina also has an artistic, slightly exotic image, one that must have appealed to actress Lolita Davidovich, who chose it for her daughter.

VALERIE, VALERIA. Steadily popular since the 1940s, Valerie never made any Top 20 lists, and still doesn't sound particularly dated. Its image is strong (maybe because of the association with "valor"), with the slight suggestion of a French accent. Exotic and more modern-sounding sister Valeria is rising fast through the popularity charts, now at number 195 to Valerie's 163.

VALETTA. Supermodel Amber Valetta inspired not just the popularity of her first name but her last as well, which some parents find a substitute for the overexposed Valerie and/or Vanessa.

VANESSA. A pretty, ultrafeminine name, Vanessa hit its peak in the late eighties, along with other frilly three-syllable names like Melissa and Tiffany, and has retained its freshness longer than the others. It was invented by Jonathan Swift for a young woman named Esther Vanhomrigh, who was in love with him—he combined the first syllable of her last name with the pet name Essa. Vanessa has spawned two viable nicknames: **NESSA** and **VANNA,** though the latter is perhaps too closely associated with *Wheel of Fortune*'s White.

VELMA. Velma shares the spinsterish quality of Thelma and Selma.

VERNA. Another *V* name that, despite its springlike etymology, is not particularly pleasing to the modern ear.

VELVET. How could a name possibly be softer or more luxuriant? It is primarily associated with the character played by twelve-year-old Elizabeth Taylor in *National Velvet:* Velvet Brown was an intrepid young woman willing to masquerade as a boy in order to race her horse in a dangerous steeplechase. With the new ascendance of word names, Velvet might just be poised for wider use.

VENETIA, VENITA, and **VENICE.** All three call to mind the radiance of that fabled Italian city. **VERONA,** a short drive west, provides another name with the same antique, Italianate charm.

VENUS. An awful lot to live up to, conjuring up as it does the supreme Roman goddess of beauty and love, the incarnation of female perfection. But tennis champion Venus Williams has put a more modern and accessible feminine spin on the name.

VERA. This name was the height of flapper chic in the 1920s, but now it's almost impossible to picture embroidered on a baby blanket or felt-tip-penned onto a child's lunchbox. Still common in several Slavic countries, its meaning is associated with the Latin for *truth*. Two other, more usable, names with the same root are **VERENA**, and the Puritan virtue name **VERITY**.

VERONICA. This name has a dual image: saintly (Veronica was the name of the compassionate woman who wiped Jesus's bleeding face when he was on his way to Calvary and whose cloth was miraculously imprinted with his image; she is now the patron saint of photographers) and sensuous (there was Veronica Lake, the peekaboo blonde of the 1940s, and the sultry, dark-haired rival of Betty in the Archie comics). If the sexy image is the one you want, you could clinch it by choosing the seductive French version, **VÉRONIQUE**.

VIANNE. This velvety French name was brought to these shores via the Juliette Binoche character in *Chocolat*.

VICTORIA. The epitome of gentility, cultivation, and refinement, the name Victoria derived this image from the queen who reigned over England from 1837 to 1901, and who lent her name to a controlled and corsetted era. In the United States it has been popular since the 1940s and is still in the Top 25. In the 1960s and seventies, its short form, **VICKY/VICKI/VIKKI**, became one of the energetic nickname names most often used on its own.

VIENNA. One of the most promising of the newly discovered European place-names, with a particularly pleasant sound.

VIOLET. A sweet but colorful flower name just on the brink of rediscovery. It was used as far back as the Middle Ages, so it far predated the flower-name vogue around 1900 (Lily, Daisy, etc.). We see it now as an attractive possibility: familiar but not faddish. **VIOLA** is the Italian and Scandinavian version, used both by Shakespeare in *Twelfth Night* and the writers of the soap opera *The Guiding Light*. **VIOLETTA** is the frillier, more operatic rendition.

VIRGINIA. For parents tiring of such trendy classics as Elizabeth and Katherine, Virginia is another traditional name worth considering, one that is beginning to sound new again after a forty-year nap. Its geographical association gives it a slightly Southern flavor and its Latin derivation adds a virginal quality. The state was given its name by Sir Walter Raleigh in honor of Elizabeth I, known as the Virgin Queen, and the first child to be born of English parents in the New World in 1597 was called Virginia Dare. One advantage if you do choose it: You'll really be able to say, "Yes, Virginia, there is a Santa Claus"—for a few years at least. One disadvantage: virgin jokes.

VITA, VIDA, VIVA. The Latin word for alive is *vivus,* and all three of these names share that meaning, although none of them is very much alive at this time. **VIVECA,** the Scandinavian version à la actress Lindfors, definitely sounds more contemporary.

VIVIAN. This name, which also means "life," actually shows signs of a revival—it was the name of Julia Roberts's character in *Pretty Woman* and was chosen for her daughter's name by trendy choreographer-performer Debbie Allen. Although in Arthurian legend it was the name of an enchantress who was the mistress of Merlin, for centuries it was used more for boys than girls. **VIVIEN, VIVIANNE, VIVIANA** are variants.

VRAI. This unique name possibility is an exotic translation of a key virtue— the French word for *true.* We think it's one that could just catch on.

W

WALLIS. This name represents the best of both worlds: it has the force of a masculine name, while its distinctive spelling sets it apart from the boys. History buffs will remember it as the name of the American woman, Wallis Warfield Simpson, for love of whom a British king was willing to sacrifice his throne in the 1930s. Anthony Edwards revived it for his daughter.

WANDA. Rarely heard these days, Wanda has a vaguely old-fashioned Slavic or German feel and for some reason has been used as a witch's name in several children's books. Not a good omen. And then there was a fish called . . .

WENDY. Wendy has the date-stamp of the 1950s imprinted all over it, as well as an unfortunate fast-food connection. A bouncy, peppy, perfect-baby-sitter name, it was invented by Sir James Barrie in 1904 for the big-sister character in his play *Peter Pan*. The story goes that he took it from the nickname Fwendy-Wendy used for him by a young girl acquaintance.

WHITNEY. Whitney took the path from place-name to last name to high-fal-lutin' male first name to popular girls' name in record time, thanks in part to the phenomenal popularity of singer Whitney Houston. At this point it has lost its efficient-executive edge and is more pretty than powerful.

WILHELMINA. It has not shaken off its heavy Dutch image of thick blond braids and clunky wooden clogs, despite the rising popularity of other *wil* names (William, Will, Willa, Willow) and the association with a major model agency.

WILLA. Willa combines the strength and tradition of a pioneer name (per-haps through its association with frontier novelist Willa Cather) with the coziness of a grandmotherly name and the slender beauty of the willow tree. Originally a pet form of Wilhelmina, it was chosen for their daughter by playwright David Mamet and actress Lindsay Crouse, and as a middle name for Meryl Streep's Mary, called Mamie.

WILLOW. This name has transcended its one-time hippie aura to move into the realm of reappraised and appreciated nature names. Among the most graceful of trees, the willow is believed by Gypsies to possess magical powers to heal the sick and revitalize the aged. Will Smith and Jada Pinkett as well as actress Gabrielle Anwar named their daughters Willow. Super-model Willow Bay has accentuated its willowiness.

WILMA. Yabba-dabba-doo, we're afraid Wilma is still fossilized in Bedrock.

WINIFRED. One of those once out-of-the-question nineteenth-century great-grandmother names that is decidedly ready to be reconsidered by the twenty-first-century parent. You might not guess it, but its roots are in Wales and it was in fact the name of a legendary Welsh saint. Its nickname **WINNIE** has a decidedly sassy charm of its own and on its own.

WINONA. No, this rhythmic, resonant name wasn't invented by Ms. Ryder's parents. She was named after the Minnesota town in which she was born and which in turn is a Sioux Indian word (often spelled, as it was by the mother of Hiawatha, **WENONAH**), meaning "firstborn daughter." Another of its many variant spellings is **WYNONNA,** as in Judd.

WINTER. Definitely the least popular of the season names, perhaps because of its chilly associations, Winter sounds like the most intriguing of the four choices right now. Montel Williams used the spelling **WYNTER** for his daughter.

WYLIE. Wylie is, like Carter and Carson, another surname occasionally used by namers of girls, one of whom is Richard Dean Anderson.

WYNN, WYNNE. Spelled with or without the final *e,* Wynn means "white" or "fair" and is, like Gwyn and Bryn, an attractive ambigender Welsh name. All three are especially worth considering if you are seeking an original one-syllable middle name.

X

XANTHE. As in most words starting with *x,* the first letter of this name has a *z* sound (ZAN-the), a concept most children's friends might have trouble with until they reach the point of being able to spell *xylophone*. It comes from the Greek, meaning "golden yellow," and conjures up the picture of an exotic, otherworldly being.

XENA and **XENIA.** Two more Greek-derived names with a *z* sound and that same sirenish allure. Xena is, of course, television's warrior princess. If you want to make your child's life easier, you can just spell these names Zena or Zenia.

XAVIERA. The female version of Xavier, this name came into prominence a while back when it was attached to the author of the best-seller *The Happy Hooker*.

Y

YADIRA. A name popular among Hispanic Americans, one source says this means "friend" in Hebrew.

YAEL. If you're looking for an unusual (in this country if not in Israel) and appealing Hebrew name, this might be it. Just ignore the fact that its derivations have to do with wild mountain goats and remember that it is pronounced with two distinct syllables.

YAFA, YAFFA. A modern Hebrew translation of Shayna, which means "beautiful."

YASMINE. A name whose sweet and delicate essence, like that of the jasmine flower it represents, is widespread across the Near Eastern world, in a wide variety of different spellings—in addition to the original, **YASMIN, YASMEEN, YAZMIN** and **YASMINA** are the most often used here. Actress Yasmine Bleeth has helped popularize this exotic name.

YESENIA, YESSENIA. An Hispanic favorite popularized by a character on a Spanish-language soap opera.

YETTA. Too close to *yenta* for our taste.

YOLANDA. This name conjures up the costume epics of the 1940s and fifties (e.g., *Yolanda and the Thief*), complete with gauzy veils, harem pants, and invisible navels. It is actually Greek, meaning "violet," the flower of the sign of Aquarius.

YVONNE and **YVETTE.** Two French names which bring to mind the kind of dark and sultry actresses who might have starred in the movie mentioned above. If you are seeking an *ette*-ending French name, a few preferable, fresher-sounding alternatives might be Arlette, Blanchette, Musette, Nicolette, or Violette.

Z

ZAHARA. Although it sounds desertlike, this is actually a Muslim and Swahili name meaning "flower." In Hebrew, it denotes brightness.

ZANDRA. When iconoclastic British fashion designer Zandra Rhodes changed the first initial of her name from *S* to *Z,* she legitimized what had formerly been a diminutive of Alexandra. And, indeed, Zandra is much more creative and fresh-sounding than the now dated Sandra.

ZARA. Princess Anne defied British royal convention by giving her daughter this exotic Arabic name in 1981, thus bestowing on it instant upper-class status. And unlike many other foreign-sounding names, it has the advantage of being completely accessible in terms of spelling and pronunciation. **ZAHRA** is the middle name of Iman and David Bowie's daughter Alexandria.

ZARIA. An Arabic name meaning "rose," this can also be considered a place-name: There's a city in Nigeria called Zaria. **ZARIAH** is a spelling variation; **ZARI** is a short form. The similar-in-feel **ZARYA** is a water priestess in Slavic mythology.

ZAZA. Along with **ZSA-ZSA, ZUZA,** and **ZUZU,** an Eastern European nickname for any one of the Susan variations.

ZELDA. Zelda is these days best known as the redheaded, elfin-eared hero (yes, male) of the popular Nintendo video game *The Legend of Zelda.* This name has been in label limbo for the past number of years but there are signs that it is due for a comeback. One of them is that the zany Robin Williams, who appears to like the letter *z,* named two of his children

Zachary and Zelda. Another strong associations with the name is that of F. Scott Fitzgerald's tortured wife.

ZELIA. An appealing name almost unknown in our culture but with roots in several others including Latin, French, and Hebrew. It might be considered a sultry variation on Celia.

ZENA, ZINA. Another multicultural name: In Persian it means "woman," in Ethiopia, "fame," and in Hebrew it signifies "stranger." These days, it's most likely to be mistaken for its homonym Xena, as in Warrior Princess. The similar-in-feeling **ZITA** was the name of a thirteenth-century Tuscan saint, who is the patron saint of housewives.

ZENOBIA. Clearly this is not a name for everyone, but, for the daring, it does have a rhythmic sound and some rich historic and literary associations. It was the name of a beautiful and intelligent third-century queen who for a time ruled the eastern Roman Empire, and it can be found in the novels of both Nathaniel Hawthorne (*A Blithedale Romance*) and Edith Wharton (*Ethan Frome*). Its roots are Greek, and derive from Zeus.

ZIA, ZEA. A nontraditional name with Latin roots that has a certain minimalist appeal. Zia also means "aunt" in Italian.

ZILLA, ZILLAH. Although this name is soft and delicate—an Old Testament name, it was used by the Puritans and again in the nineteenth century—it runs the risk of being associated with the monstrous Godzilla.

ZINNIA. An underused English flower name, yet another possibility for the parent who wants to move beyond Rose and Lily.

ZOE. Short but with a lot of creative character, Zoe is a member of that select group of names that are both inventive and interesting, yet acceptable and accessible. Now in the Top 100 and moving up, variations include **ZOEY** and **ZOIE**. Most cultures have a name signifying the life force (e.g., Chaim, Viva, Fayola, Vidal), and in Greek it is Zoe, the equivalent of Eve, the mother of all life. Henry Winkler, Lisa Bonet, and Lenny Kravitz are all parents of Zoes, and there are young Zoeys on such shows as *Once and Again* and *The West Wing*.

ZOLA. An occasionally used name which in Italian relates to the earth. When the Eddie Murphys gave it to their fourth child, we suspect they were more attracted to its pleasant, rhythmic sound than to any reference to the nineteenth-century French novelist Emile Zola.

ZORA, ZORAH. A biblical name, representing a place rather than a person. Zora Neale Thurston was an important African-American writer. It also signifies "dawn" in the Slavic vocabulary, and appeared as a character in the Gilbert and Sullivan operetta, *Ruddigore*.

ZULEIKA. A challenging name but not out of the question. Its most famous association is with the eponymous heroine of the satirical 1910 Max Beerbohm novel, *Zuleika Dobson,* who was so drop-dead gorgeous (its meaning in Persian is in fact "brilliant beauty") that all the young men at Oxford University killed themselves for love of her. African-born model Iman spelled her daughter's name **ZELEKHA.**

BOYS

A

AARON. Aaron has been one of the most popular biblical names of the last twenty years, still weighing in at number 41, the softness of its initial double vowel giving it an appealing gentleness. In the Old Testament, Aaron, older brother of Moses, appointed by God to be his brother's spokesman, was the first high priest of Israel. Robert DeNiro chose the name for one of his twins with Toukie Smith, and U2 drummer Larry Mullen Jr. named his son **ARON** Elvis, a reversal of the original Elvis's name (with the singer's original spelling). The Hebrew version is **AHARON**.

ABBOTT. Both a fairly common last name and a noun meaning the head of a monastery, this name can also be spelled **ABBOT**. One of the surname names that has retained its masculine feel, Abbott makes an attractive, offbeat possibility for a modern baby boy.

ABDUL, ABDULLAH. This name, which means "servant of Allah" in Arabic, has been widely used by American Black Muslims since the early 1980s.

ABEL. In case you can never keep the siblings straight, Abel was the good son of Adam and Eve, the second born who was slain by his brother Cain. The name (along with its word equivalent) connotes positive qualities: someone supremely capable and competent, ready and willing. One of the few classic biblical boys' names not plagued by overuse.

ABIAH. A highly unusual Old Testament name—it belonged to Samuel's second son—which also appears as **ABIJAH**. This makes a good choice for the parent who wants a traditional biblical name that isn't bizarre but also is not overly familiar.

ABNER. Finally, after some sixty years, it's beginning to throw off its L'il Abner country-bumpkin comic-strip stigma enough to be reevaluated on its own merits as a perfectly respectable Old Testament name, that of the commander of Saul's army. Yet another traditional-yet-distinctive biblical name ripe for revival, it is also associated with the founding father of base-ball, Abner Doubleday. The modern Hebrew form is **AVNER.**

ABRAHAM. Originally named **ABRAM** (the syllable *ah,* meaning father of many, was added after he accepted the idea of a single god, when it was the Jewish custom to mark a great occasion with a name change), Abraham was the first of the Old Testament patriarchs and is considered the found-ing father of the Hebrew people. In the nineteenth century, President Lin-coln hung a beard on the name which a young child still might find difficult to pull off. But with playgrounds now filled with children named Nathaniel and Moses and Isaiah, Abraham is once again a viable possibility for males under the age of 110. *Simpsons'* creator Matt Groening named his son Abraham, while his fictional family's grandpa is named **ABE,** an honest, homey nickname, sometimes used on its own. A more contemporary and hip short form is **BRAM.** The frequently used Arabic version is **IBRAHIM.**

ABSALOM. More common on the printed page (Absalom was the hand-some and favored son of King David in the Bible, and the name appears in the works of Dryden and Faulkner as well), it projects a serious, even solemn image.

ADAIR. A name with flair, the panache of Fred Astaire. Just don't think about the fact that it's the Scottish version of Edgar, though the best-known Adair these days is female San Francisco columnist Adair Lara. **ALAIR,** which means "cheerful" (it's a Hilary variation), is another unusual Gaelic choice.

ADAM. One of those names that galloped in with the posse of TV cowboy shows of the 1960s (Adam Cartwright being the eldest of the *Bonanza* boys), then went on to become a soap-opera staple. At this point in time, the name of the first man to be created by God in the Book of Genesis, while still in the Top 50, is feeling a little faded from overuse and might deserve a rest. A more modern-sounding (if less biblical) spin would be **ADDISON,** which actually means "son of Adam."

ADEON. An alternative to Adam or Aidan, this was the name of a legendary Welsh prince.

ADLAI. Grandparents will link this name with the unsuccessful 1952 and 1956 Democratic presidential candidate and later UN representative, Adlai Stevenson, but we see it as an interesting and distinctive Old Testament/personal hero name ripe for discovery.

ADOLPH. This was a fairly prevalent name among German-Americans prior to World War II (it was also the real first name of Harpo Marx), but the rise of Hitler made it absolutely verboten not only here but in most countries throughout the world: Several nations—France and Norway are two examples—literally outlaw its use. However, Hispanic Americans do use **ADOLFO**: several hundred babies born in the U.S. are given the name each year. A minimally more acceptable variation would be the Latinized **ADOLPHUS** or the short form **DOLPH,** now linked to action hero Dolph Lundgren.

ADRIAN. Very popular in England for at least fifty years, Adrian is beginning to catch on here, recently moving into the Top 100. One problem with the name is that it sounds exactly like the female version Adrienne. But if you're not bothered by the gender confusion, it can be an appealing choice, one you would share with Edie Brickell and Paul Simon, who picked it for their baby boys.

AHMAD/AHMED. One of the five hundred or more names used by Muhammad. It is currently a favorite Black Muslim name (among its best-known bearers are former football player/sports commentator Ahmad Rashad and jazz pianist Ahmad Jamal), perhaps due to the adage that angels pray in any house where an Ahmad or Muhammad resides. In Swahili it means "praiseworthy."

AIDAN. An appealing Irish name introduced into the American melting pot of nomenclature by actor Aidan Quinn, the original version has risen from obscurity to become one of the Top 200 baby names. Spelling variations **AIDEN** as well as **ADAN,** which may be pronounced AH-don, also enjoy significant use. Particularly recommended for families with Irish roots, Aidan was the name of a famous seventh-century Irish saint, and is related to the Irish word for *fire.*

ALAN, ALLEN, ALLAN. A name whose burst of popularity paralleled the rise of taciturn tough guy Alan Ladd in the 1940s, Alan and its many spelling variations is still given to several thousand baby boys a year—many of whom, we suspect, are named after their dads or other older relatives. The Welsh spelling, **ALUN,** while minimally more attractive, might seem contrived here.

ALARIC. The name of a fifth-century king of the Visigoths, Alaric could be "ruler of all" in your house as well.

ALBAN. The ancient name of Britain's first martyr who, for his trouble, got a cathedral town named after him, Alban means "white" and is a contender for modern use.

ALBERT. This name became extremely fashionable in both England and America after Queen Victoria married Prince Albert in 1840 and it managed to stay in style for eighty-odd years. But with its serious, studious image (think of Einstein, Schweitzer, and Gore), Albert and its short forms **AL** or **BERT** are far from the height of fashion these days. The Latinate form **ALBERTO** is used nearly as often here as the original.

ALDO. A spirited Germanic name very popular in Italy and occasionally used in this country, especially during the period when gravel-voiced Aldo Ray was making movies. In Italy it can be short for such names as Rinaldo.

ALEXANDER/ALEXIS/ALEX/ALEC. The whole constellation of Alexi-related names has become tremendously popular for both boys and girls in the past few years, to the point where **ALEXANDER** has entered the Top 20 list of boys' names and all versions of the name considered together are firmly in the Top 10. (It's currently number 3 in England.) As opposed to many here-today, gone-tomorrow trendy names, however, **ALEXANDER** has a solid historical base dating back to Alexander the Great, and has been borne by such legendary figures as the liberal Russian Czar Alexander II, Alexander Hamilton, and Alexander Graham Bell. **ALEXIS** was a strong Russian male alternative until the influence of the unscrupulous Alexis Carrington on *Dynasty* established it as a predominantly female name. **ALEC** (thanks to the eldest Baldwin brother, born Alexander) has recently come to be a viable alternative short form to **ALEX**—both are often used on their own. *Star Trek: Voyager* star Kate Mulgrew and *NYPD Blue* actress Andrea Thompson both have sons named Alec, while William Hurt, John Hurt, Melanie Griffith, Chris Evert, and Timothy Dalton all have Alexanders. Some possible foreign variants: **ALESSANDRO** (Italian), **ALEJANDRO** (Spanish), **ALEXEI** and **SASHA** (both Russian). Other nicknames include **LEX, XAN,** and **XANDER,** alternately spelled **ZAN** and **ZANDER.** The latter has really heated up, heard of late on the soap opera *General Hospital,* while Xander appears on *Buffy the Vampire Slayer.*

ALFRED. Although Alfred the Great was a wise, compassionate, and scholarly king of old England, these days you're more likely to hear the Latin version of the name, **ALFREDO.** Actor Gary Oldman has a son named **ALFIE**—a name that Americans may find it difficult to believe is stylish in London.

ALGERNON. Originally a nickname meaning "with whiskers," this just might take the prize as the jellyfish name of all time.

ALI. An Arabic name that really does mean "the greatest." A shortened form of Allah, it is used by Muslims in Turkey, Egypt, Iran, Jordan, India, Arabia—and now the United States. It is also associated with Ali ("Open sesame") Baba in the ancient Arabic tales *A Thousand and One Nights.*

ALISTAIR or **ALASTAIR.** That's the way the British spell it; the Scots prefer **ALASDAIR**—but they are all Gaelic versions of Alexander. To most Yanks, thanks primarily to the longtime host of *Masterpiece Theater,* it represents sophisticated Britishness at its most British. English impresario Andrew Lloyd Webber has a son named Alastair.

ALPHONSE, ALPHONSO, ALONZO. The Spanish form of this name, Alonzo, is by far the most popular of the three, probably thanks to star athletes Alonzo Stagg and Alonzo Mourning. Actor Morgan Freeman has a son named **ALFONSO.** But the name's most famous version is its nickname **FONZIE.**

ALVARO, ALVARRO. A Spanish name used for their sons by both Plácido Domingo and Lorenzo Lamas.

ALVIN. A Germanic name literally meaning "noble friend loved by all," Alvin has, alas, taken on quite a different meaning due to all the nerdy characters given that name in movies and television over the years. Not to mention the association with those screeching chipmunks. A more distinguished bearer was Alvin Ailey, founder of the Alvin Ailey American Dance Theater.

AMADEO. A euphonious Italian name, often associated with the painter Modigliani. It was chosen for his son by actor John Turturro. The Latinate version is **AMADEUS,** as in Mozart.

AMBROSE. An upper-class-British-sounding name, which carries with it an air of blooming well-being. It belonged to one of the four great Latin teachers of Christianity, who also developed the use of music in church services. Television fanatics might be interested to know that in 1961, Ambrose was designated the patron saint of educational TV by Pope John XXIII.

AMIAS, AMYAS. A name related to the Latin word for "love," some sources call Amias (it can be pronounced um-EYE-us or AIM-ee-us) a form of Amadeus. Others call it the male version of Amy, which, if true, would put it in a very elite category of boys' names that sprang from girls' rather than vice versa. Whatever its source or pronunciation, it's an obscure name with an attractive sound and feel.

AMIR. Boxer Mike Tyson used this name, which means "exalted one" in Arabic and is the general name for an elevated official, for his son.

AMORY. It comes from the Latin *amor,* suggesting a loving person, and is, like **AVERY** and **EMORY,** the kind of executive-sounding surname name that is so popular. Amory Blaine was the hero of F. Scott Fitzgerald's *This Side of Paradise.*

AMOS. A strong—literally: it means "strong" in Hebrew—biblical name that has been shunned since the 1930s due to its association with the racially stereotyped characters on the radio and TV show *Amos & Andy.* But some forward-thinking parents have moved beyond that outdated image and have begun to revive this appealing name. Italian singer Andrea Boccelli is one.

ANATOLE. This French name has a decided touch of the creative, the exotic, perhaps verging on the exaggerated, conjuring up an image of artist's beret, smock, and pencil-thin moustache.

ANDREW. Firmly in the Top 10 for two decades now, Andrew is that rare combination of being both classic and trendy, widely used yet still retaining a large measure of strength and character. Of all the leading boys' names, it was the one most favored by highly educated mothers, according to a Harvard research study. Most of the many little Andrews around these days are called by their full name, or sometimes **DREW,** less and less by the relaxed and friendly **ANDY,** exemplified by Raggedy Andy, Andy Hardy, Andy Rooney, Andy Griffith, and Andy Williams. It's also been connected to two of America's most famous artists, Wyeth and Warhol. Director Milos Foreman named his sons Andrew and James, after comedian Andy Kaufman and actor Jim Carrey, who played Kaufman in Foreman's film *Man in the Moon.* In the New Testament, Andrew was the first disciple to be called by Jesus and, although the origins of the name are Greek, Andrew is the patron saint of both Scotland and Russia. It also has several pleasant foreign manifestations that are sometimes used in this country, including **ANDRE** (French), **ANDREI** (Russian), **ANDRES** (Spanish), **ANDREA** (Italian),

ANDREAS (German, Dutch, and Greek), and **ANDERS** (Norwegian and Swedish). **ANDERSON** and **DEANDRE** are two other variations worth noting.

ANGEL. The saintly associations of this name make it difficult for a boy, in particular, to carry, except in Latino families, where it is quite commonly used. In *Buffy the Vampire Slayer,* Angel was a vampire who once dated Buffy and was sometimes good, sometimes evil. As such characters will, he moved to L.A. and got his own show. In a somewhat earlier reference, Angel Clare was the name of the decidedly nonangelic husband of Thomas Hardy's *Tess of the D'Urbervilles*. **ANGELO** is the Italian version, newly chic in the wake of Madonna's choice of the similar-in-mood Rocco for her son. **DEANGELO** and **DANGELO** are two other sometimes-used variations—and then there's **D'ANGELO,** the soul/hip-hop sensation.

ANGUS. The image of this name was, not that long ago, that of a fusty, fuddy-duddy old Scot dressed in kilts and playing the bagpipes. To us it has recently started to sound novel and new, with enough robust character to make it a plausible choice, particularly for parents with bloodlines that can be traced back to Glasgow or Edinburgh. In Gaelic it means "unique choice," one that was made by Amanda Pays and Corbin Bernsen for one of their twin sons. In Irish folklore, Angus Og is a chieftain-lord who used his magical powers and treasures for the pleasure and prosperity of mankind. And on top of all that, Angus is also a breed of fine cattle.

ANSEL, ANSELM, and **ANSON.** Three related names that are distinctive and might work well for a baby of today. Ansel is associated with the great Western photographer Ansel Adams, Saint Anselm was the archbishop of Canterbury in the twelfth century, and Anson Williams will go down in posterity as "Potsie" on *Happy Days*.

ANTHONY. This name's social setting ranges from da streetcorners of da Bronx to a debutante's ball and the same can be said for its pet form, **TONY.** The name of the patron saint of Italy and of the poor, Anthony (which means "priceless" in Latin), after being popular in this country since the 1920s, is still in the Top 25, a fact that can probably be attributed to its

Latinate charm. **ANTON** (the name of the twin son of Beverly D'Angelo and Al Pacino) is the version used in Russia and other Slavic countries, as well as in Germany, Sweden, and Norway; it is **ANTOINE** in France and **ANTONIO** in Italy, where the nickname name **TONIO** is also prevalent (Antonio is a Shakespearean favorite—he used it in no less than five of his plays), and in Spanish-speaking countries. And in England, whether it's spelled Anthony or **ANTONY**, it's often pronounced . . . à la Noël Coward, without the *h*— just as it is on some sidewalks of New York.

APOLLO. With mythological names as well as Latinate forms on the upswing, Apollo may be a viable possibility for the parent in search of something really different yet with a great deal of history. The name of the handsome son of Zeus, Apollo was the god of music, poetry, prophecy, and medicine.

ARA and **ARAM.** Two common Armenian names, the latter having become familiar in this country through the works of William Saroyan, the former via Notre Dame football coach Ara Parseghian.

ARCHER. A surname name that feels slightly more modern than its brethren because of its occupational associations: It can join the Sailors and Painters du jour, leaving behind the Parkers and Carters that are so five minutes ago. Archer Guest was a character in Edith Wharton's *The Age of Innocence*.

ARCHIBALD, ARCHIE. These are more apt to be attached to a beagle than a baby these days, but you might want to think about resurrecting them, especially if your last name is Campbell or Douglas, the families they have long been associated with in Scotland. Archie is actually very fashionably used in England, where all things Scottish carry an undying charm, but Americans would have to obliterate the image of *All in the Family*'s resident bigot, Archie Bunker, and the hapless hero of Archie comics.

ARIEL (and its energetic short form, **ARI**). Very popular in Israel, Ariel has several appealing associations: It is one of the Hebrew names for God, a symbolic name for Jerusalem, the name of a great Hebrew leader, and also the witty and clever spirit in Shakespeare's *The Tempest*. Ari was the heroic character Paul Newman played in *Exodus*. Major drawback: In America, Ariel is much more often used as a girl's name, and now relates very strongly to Disney's *Little Mermaid* character. Two related (to Ariel as well as to each other) names with a bit more masculine edge: **AURIEL,** the name of the archangel who overlooks those born under the sign of Taurus, and **AZRAEL,** the archangel of Scorpio as well as the angel who shepherds the soul from the body at death.

ARIES. The heavenly ram whose name is used for the first astrological sign, March 21 until April 19, and is also sometimes given to baby boys.

ARLO. Names ending in the letter *o* have a unique aura of friendliness and cheer, and Arlo is no exception. It came on the scene in the 1970s in the person of the shaggy singer Arlo Guthrie and is still infrequently enough used to remain distinctive.

ARMAND, ARMANDO. This French name has long been considered one of the world's most romantic, from the lover of Camille to such smoldering modern bearers as Armand Assante. These days in the United States, it's more recently found in its Spanish form Armando.

ARMANI. Better to use a real family name than to steal Giorgio's.

ARNOLD. Arnold started life as a powerful Teutonic tribal-chieftain name (it means "strong as an eagle" in German), but its strength has been sapped until it verges on the nerdy when seen as a name for a twenty-first-century child—Mr. Schwarzenegger to the contrary. But if you have a beloved Uncle Arnold you'd like to honor in your baby's name, you might consider the livelier **ARNO** or the Scandinavian **ARNE.**

ARTEMAS, ARTEMUS. Whatever the spelling, this name has a mythological, historical, Three Musketeer–ish ring, perhaps because Artemis was the Greek goddess of the hunt and wild animals. Artemas is also mentioned in the New Testament.

ARTHUR. It once shone as the legendary head of the Knights of the Round Table in Camelot. Now the name leaves a much quieter, more intellectual impression and is used only occasionally. Vintage television was full of Arthurs and Arts—from Godfrey to Linkletter to Arthur "Fonzie" Fonzarelli on *Happy Days*. More recently, tennis champion Arthur Ashe, the first African-American to win the U.S. Open, restored some dignity to the name. The Latinate **ARTURO** is heard nearly as often as the Anglo version.

ASA, AZA. The name of a biblical king of Judah who reigned for more than forty years, Asa means "physician" in Hebrew. Its soap-opera image is that of a strong patriarch (Asa Buchanan in *One Life to Live*), so using this name would require a bit of foresight.

ASHER, ASHTON, ASH. Asher is a wonderful choice if you're looking for an Old Testament name—Asher was a son of Jacob—that's not as overused as, say, Aaron or Adam. While Asher has moved out of obscurity, it's still a distinctive and accessible name. **ASHTON,** a surname name without Asher's biblical roots, is more popular: Ashton Kutcher is a hot young actor. The diminutive of both names, **ASH,** is the name of the Pokémon trainer Ash Ketchum—at the moment the dream name of every six-year-old in America. But fashions fade and children get older, and when they do they may want to shed the Pikachu connection. At least a more grown-up Ash can draw on the name's Rhett Butler–ish Southern charm.

ASHLEY. Even if the sensitive Ashley Wilkes was your favorite character in *Gone With the Wind,* bear in mind that Ashley was throughout the 1990s the number 1 most popular name given to girl babies in America, making it far from the most viable or virile choice for a boy. However, the name's masculine image has been buffed up recently by the very cute Ashley Angel, a member of the boy band O-Town, and hunky actor Ashley Hamilton.

ATTICUS. Hollywood's Baldwin brothers seem to be working hard to outdo each other in the unusualness of the names they pick for their children. Daniel Baldwin and Isabella Hofmann, both of TV's *Homicide,* chose this name for their son. Atticus (which means "of Athens") was an important

Roman literary figure. But more people associate the name with Atticus Finch, the heroic lawyer who defended a black man in *To Kill a Mockingbird*.

AUBREY. This is an upper-class British name rarely used on this side of the Atlantic. One handicap it might have would be its similarity to and possible confusion with the female name Audrey. Its most famous bearer was the nineteenth-century artist-illustrator Aubrey Beardsley. **AUBERON** was the writer son of Evelyn Waugh.

AUGUST, AUGUSTUS, AUGUSTINE. None of these have been heard very often in the last hundred years, but they are exactly the kind of names trendsetters are looking at with fresh eyes, considering whether they might be ripe for revival—Mick Jagger and Jerry Hall did use Augustine as the third name for their son. **GUS,** of course, is the more user-friendly nickname, one that picks up on the grandpa-ish Max and Sam trend so popular in recent years. The German form, August, was chosen by actress Lena Olin for her son in honor of Swedish playwright August Strindberg, and it belongs to another famed playwright, Pulitzer prizewinner August Wilson.

AUSTIN. This name is hot, hot, hot, poised to move into the Top 10. Its popularity is due to its combination of a number of desirable elements: It's got a sexy Southwestern feel, place-name panache, and the solid base of having long been an Anglo-Saxon surname. Austin Powers, however, adds a jokey element to the name that may undercut its runaway success. Celebrities with sons named Austin include Sela Ward, Paula Zahn, Michelle Phillips, and Tommy Lee Jones. The spelling **AUSTEN** may be used by fans of Jane; **AUSTYN** and **AUSTON** also make the Top 1,000.

AVERY. Growing in popularity as a last-name-first name, Avery got a giant boost from its use for Murphy Brown's baby (he was named after Murphy's mother; the creator of the show has a known penchant for giving her female characters strong male names). Still, the name is slightly more popular for girls than boys, always a negative for a name's future as a masculine entity.

AVI. This is the short form of several Hebrew names, including **AVIAV, AVIDOR, AVIDAN, AVIEL, AVIRAM,** and **AVITAL.**

AXEL. The Scandinavian form of the Hebrew Absalom has been brought out of obscurity and into the spotlight by two distinctive contemporary characters: rocker Ax'l Rose and Axel Foley, the policeman portrayed by Eddie Murphy in the *Beverly Hills Cop* series. It's a name with the strength of ten Ashleys.

AZARIAH. If you want an Old Testament name and you're ready to move beyond Adam and even beyond Abraham, Azariah is one idea you might consider.

B

BAILEY. An extremely amiable, open-sounding surname (it originally signified a bailiff) that hails from Britain, not—as it might sound—from Ireland. Throughout the 1990s, it moved up the popularity charts. Today, there are more than twice as many girl Baileys born each year as boys, though television's *Party of Five* featured a male Bailey and *ER*'s Anthony Edwards as well as actress Tracey Gold both named their sons Bailey. Other occupational surname names worth a moment's thought: **BAKER, BARKER** (it meant shepherd or tanner), **BREWSTER.**

BALTHASAR, BALTHAZAR. This is a choice recommended only for the intrepid baby namer—it has been used in the oil-rich Getty family, for example. Balthasar was one of the three Wise Men of the Orient who brought gifts to the infant Jesus, and it was also the name assumed by Portia in her disguise as a male lawyer in Shakespeare's *The Merchant of Venice.*

BARNABY. Barnaby fits into that golden triangle of names that are neither too common nor too bizarre, but strike the happiest of mediums. Its genial and exceptionally attractive image make it appealing for both a little boy and the man he'll grow up to be. Actress Isabelle Adjani has a son whose name carries the French spelling, **BARNABE**. **BARNABUS** is a weightier, more somber version, having been one of the first Christian converts and missionaries.

BARNEY. This name has gone through many incarnations, the latest of which is as a megapopular purple dinosaur, undoubtedly the first association of every kid in your child's nursery school class. Until the dinosaur craze dies down, it could be somewhat difficult for a child to live with this otherwise warm and friendly name.

BARRY, BARRETT. Barry pre-dates the Gary-Larry-Carrie-Shari 1950s and is showing no signs of a twenty-first-century rerun. And although its roots are Irish, its best-known bearer, Barry Manilow, is not. Barrett is a nineteenth-century surname name still occasionally used—and definitely the better choice of the two.

BARTHOLOMEW. This a pretty heavy moniker to hang on a child, but for the bold parent (actor Timothy Bottoms is one) this apostle's name may have some unorthodox appeal. But then there's the nickname **BART** to consider. Until *The Simpsons'* popularity subsides, especially among elementary-school kids, a child might feel the terrible obligation to live up to that little wise-guy character's reputation. **BARTON** is a decidedly unstylish relative.

BASIL. Although Greek in origin (in the fourth century, a bishop by that name established the principles of the Greek Orthodox Church), it has taken on the aura of aquiline-nosed upper-class Britishness ever since Basil Rathbone was cast as Sherlock Holmes. And in recent years, the Pesto Generation has added the fragrant aroma of the herb to its image. Trivia note: Saint Basil bore the distinction of having a grandmother, father, mother, older sister, and two younger brothers who were all saints as well.

BAYARD. An Old English red-haired name—one of the few that doesn't begin with the letter *r*. Its first syllable can be pronounced either as *bay* or *by.* For the parent in search of a surname name, this is one possibility that hasn't been overexposed. **BAY** would make a good nickname—or might stand on its own; Lucy Lawless used it as one of her son's middle names.

BEACH, BEECH. Surf's up, dude! If the tide is coming in on a new wave of word names, this one is sure to be a favorite especially among parents for whom sun and sand are the best things in life. Those who prefer the woods to the sand might spell the name Beech—or consider Ash, Birch, or the whole Forest.

BEAUREGARD. This name harks back to the old plantation and would not be easy for a child of today—Northern or Southern—to pull off. Its short form, **BEAU,** is another story, suggesting as it does someone devilishly handsome (it originally was a nickname meaning just that); and has been used for characters fitting that description in novels, TV westerns, and soap operas. Country singer Tanya Tucker has a son named Beau.

BECKETT. This might have remained just another obscure surname name—there are thousands of them—had Melissa Etheridge not chosen it for her son. Irish-born Pierce Brosnan made it his son Paris's middle name, perhaps in honor of the Irish playwright/novelist, Samuel Beckett. A "beck" is a small stream in Scotland; **BECK** might be a short form or can be used on its own, à la the one-named rock star, born **BEK** David Campbell.

BENEN. An ancient name that's been obscure for centuries but has a strong, spare feel perfect for today, Benen was an Irish follower of Saint Patrick revered for his musical talents.

BENEDICT has quite a different history. As the name of the saint who founded the Benedictine Order and of fifteen popes, it might be seen as a more distinctive alternative to Benjamin, except for its lasting link to Revolutionary War traitor Benedict Arnold.

BENICIO, BENECIO. This name—the two spellings are interchangeable—is a somewhat obscure Spanish member of a family of names related to the Latin Benedict, which means "good and kind," rather than the Hebrew Benjamin, which comes from the word for son. It's been made famous by the smolderingly handsome Puerto Rican actor Benicio (that's his spelling) Del Toro, and his magnetic appeal has been enough to inspire many parents to consider adopting this attractive name for their own sons.

BENJAMIN. This sensitive Old Testament name was for centuries used primarily by Jews. In modern times, it came into more general favor in the 1960s, partly through the influence of the character Dustin Hoffman played in *The Graduate,* and has been used through recent decades by many celebrities for their sons, among them Warren Beatty and Annette Bening, Carly Simon and James Taylor, Richard Dreyfuss, Harrison Ford, Raul Julia, and Jeff Daniels. In the Bible, Benjamin was the youngest of the twelve sons of Jacob, and there have been numerous other notable Benjamins in the past, from Benjamin Franklin to Benjamin Spock. Though the use of Benjamin has been widespread for thirty years—it's now number 26—it is still a strong and viable choice. **BEN** is the nice-guy nickname that can stand on its own. **BENNO** is another possibility, though **BENJI** is in the doghouse.

BENNETT, BENTLEY, BENTON, and **BENSON** are four last-name first names that list toward the pretentious. Of the group, Bennett is the most popular and the most appealing.

BERNARD. A name with a highly intellectual image quite in keeping with that of the saint bearing that name, who was a brilliant scholar, but not one that a twenty-first-century child would be likely to thank you for. Bernard, the patron saint of mountain climbers, is frequently found these days as **BERNARDO,** the head of the Puerto Rican Jets in *West Side Story* and a name with much of the strength the English version lacks.

BERT/BURT, BURTON. Two names hibernating in the Land of Nerd, especially since onetime macho men Burt(on) Lancaster and Burt(on) Reynolds no longer represent those images. Ditto for **BERTRAM.**

BEVAN. A Welsh surname meaning "son of Evan," this might be an alternative for that increasingly popular name, though the initial *bev* sound calls to mind a fifty-five-year-old woman named Beverly.

BEVIS. An unusual and interesting British name (pronounced with a soft *e*) that we could have recommended more highly before the arrival of the outrageous MTV animated twerps Beavis and Butt-Head a few years ago.

BIRCH. A rarely used nature name that calls to mind the attributes of the tall, strong but graceful tree. Its best-known bearer is Senator Birch Bayh. The parent taken with the notion of tree names might also consider **ASH,** of course, as well such offbeat ideas as **OAK** and **PINE,** even perhaps **HICKORY.** Not to mention **BRANCH.**

BIX. Like **DEX** and **JINX** and other names ending with *x,* Bix is distinctive and energetic. It might also be a hero name for jazz lovers who admire the great musician and composer, Bix Beiderbecke—whose birth certificate name was Leon.

BJORN. Although one of the most popular boys' names in Scandinavia, in this country Bjorn is connected to one particular individual, the Swedish tennis star and five-time Wimbledon winner Bjorn Borg. We hope it doesn't lose any of its agility when we tell you it's the Scandinavian form of Bernard.

BLAKE, BLAIR, BLAINE, BLAISE. Blake, an androgynous name popularized in the 1980s by the slick, silver-haired Blake Carrington character of *Dynasty,* is by far the most popular of this group, firmly in the Top 100. Rosie O'Donnell's adopted third child is named Blake Christopher, which couldn't have hurt either. But the *Blair Witch Project* is sure to undermine the much weaker Blair, used as often for girls as boys. Blaine has the feel of a name on the way up. Despite its of-the-moment sound, it's actually the name of a seventh-century Scottish saint. Blaise is also an ancient Christian name, one of an early martyr. Blaise comes from a Roman family name that means "stutterer." **BLAZE** would be another, more incendiary spelling.

BLUE. An evocative color that some hip parents have called into service as a middle name. Any favorite or appropriately symbolic color could work the same way: **GREEN, BLACK,** ad infinitum.

BOAZ. An unusual Old Testament name with a lot of contemporary pizzazz. It was used by the seventeenth-century Puritans, but at this point in time, yours would surely be the only Boaz on the block. Among Jews, it is associated with the holiday Shavuot (as that is when the Bible story of Ruth is read in the synagogue, and Boaz was Ruth's wealthy second husband) and so is sometimes given to boys born on that day. Added attraction: It has one of the all-time great nicknames, **BO,** which on its own has actually moved into the Top 1,000. A very popular name in Denmark, Bo is associated in this country with sports great Bo Jackson (born Vincent) and musician Bo Diddley (born Ellas).

BOONE. A long and lanky cowboy name, Boone can be traced back to the French, meaning "a blessing."

BORIS. This Russian-inflected name has been as dead as one of Mr. Karloff's mummy characters for a long time, and shows no signs of resuscitation, despite the fame of German-born tennis star Boris Becker. Boris Badenov is a *Rocky and Bullwinkle* villian: 'nuff said.

BOSTON. An attractive and distinctive place-name, used for their son by the equally uniquely named Season Hubley and then-mate Kurt Russell.

BOWIE. An Irish surname (although not the real one of David B., who was born with the considerably less marketable moniker David Hayward-Jones), Bowie successfully combines Gaelic charm with a Western drawl. **BOWEN** is another possibility, the kind of two-syllable surname name so fashionable for boys today.

BOYD. Only slightly more contemporary than Lloyd or Floyd, Boyd has a bit of a hayseed image. In Gaelic it means "blond one," and is a well-used Scottish clan name. If this is a family name for you, best use it in the middle.

BRADEN. There is a significant group of two-syllable names that have emerged over the past few years to zoom up the popularity charts, and Braden is one of its leading members. It has no history (unless you consider a decade on *All My Children* history), and that's the point: These names just sound cool and come unencumbered by baggage. (Though if it's meaning you want, *bradan* is the Gaelic word for *salmon*.) Braden, number 208 in the most recent year counted, has many spelling alternatives: **BRAYDEN, BRAYDON, BRAEDEN,** and **BRAEDON. BRAYAN** is a related selection, while **BRAISON** (which might also be spelled **BRAYSON**) is of note as the son of singer Billy Ray Cyrus.

BRADLEY, BRAD. Just now dropping out of the Top 100, this name is almost always used in full by contemporary parents. Maybe that's because Brad—despite the appeal of current heartthrob Brad (born William Bradley) Pitt—is still out on a surfin' safari with Todd and Scott.

BRADY, BRODY. Two high-energy Irish surnames that have become wildly popular over the past few years. Brady, the more widely used of the two, literally means "spirited one" in Irish Gaelic, while Brody is a well-known Scottish clan name.

BRAM. Bram has an unusual amount of character and charm for a one-syllable name. It started life as a hipper-than-Abe diminutive for Abraham, but is also an independent Irish and Dutch name, made familiar to American ears by the creator of Count Dracula, Bram Stoker.

BRANDON. Brandon is one of the most popular names today: It just misses the national Top 10—but is as high as number 4 in some states. Several soap-opera characters named Brandon have helped popularize the name, along with Jason Priestley's character on *Beverly Hills 90210.* Doomed actor Brandon Lee as well as Brandon Teena, the woman who lived as a man and whose life story was depicted in *Boys Don't Cry,* for which Hilary Swank won an Oscar, are two other notable bearers of the name. Celebrities who've named their sons Brandon include Pamela Anderson and Tommy Lee, Marie Osmond, and Babyface. **BRANDEN, BRANDAN,** and **BRANDYN** are spelling alternatives; all versions relate to the ancient Irish name Brendan.

BRAXTON, BRAWLEY. Two more two-syllable surname names beginning with *b,* this formula can't seem to fail to achieve popularity these days.

Both have Old English roots and were originally place-names: Braxton means "brock's (or badger's) settlement" and Brawley means "meadow at the slope of the hill." Nick Nolte's son is named Brawley King.

BRECKIN. One of the many new surname-sounding choices for boys that have two syllables, begin with *b* and end with *in, en, on,* or *an.* This one, however, has a nickname, **BRECK,** that's a bit sudsy.

BREEZE. One of the most laid-back, loose, and self-assured of the new word names. Has middle-name possibilities as well.

BRENDAN. Brendan is an Irish saint's name, currently attached to handsome star Brendan Fraser. But its literal meaning is anything but attractive: If you must know, it means "stinking hair." According to Irish legend, Saint Brendan the Voyager was the first European to reach American soil. **BRENDEN** and **BRENDON** are spelling alternatives that are frequently used; **BRENTON** is a hybrid relative.

BRENNAN. An attractive Brendan/Brandon alternative, Brennan is coming into its own along with its Irish-surname brethren such as Conor and Riley. Several hundred baby boys receive this name each year nowadays, sometimes with the spelling **BRENNEN** or **BRENNON.** Actor Alan Thicke has a son named Brennen. **BRANIGAN, BROGAN,** and **BRENNER** are other surname choices with the same feel.

BRENT, BRETT, BRET. These three names swept into the public consciousness in the wake of the smash-hit late 1950s to early 1960s TV western *Maverick* (in which the male family members were called Bret, Bart, Beau, and Brent). Of late, they've lost a bit of their masculine swagger, especially since Brett is also used for girls. Bret Harte, whose given first name was really Francis, was an important novelist of the early West; Bret Easton Ellis is the brat novelist who wrote *American Psycho,* and tennis great Jimmy Connors named his son Brett. **BRANT/BRANDT** is a related possibility.

BREVIN. If you're tired of Kevin and Devin, you might consider the newly coined Brevin.

BRIAN, BRYAN. Over the past quarter of a century Brian has fallen from its seat in the Top 10, but it's still among the fifty most popular boys' names and has managed to hang on to a large degree of its jaunty Gaelic charm. The names of the most famous of all Irish warrior-kings, Brian Boru, it was part of the second generation wave of Irish names to emigrate to this country, along with such compatriots as Kevin and Dennis. Bryan is an alternate spelling, as in singers Ferry and Adams, as is **BRYON.**

BRICE, BRYCE. The image here is sleek and sophisticated, elegant and efficient, to the degree that this name veers toward a soap-opera-ish cliché. **BRYSON/BRYCEN** is an increasingly popular alternative.

BRIDGER. An example of the two-syllable semi-surname semi-occupational name name so popular for boys today, Bridger has an attractive sound and an appealing spirit—this is a boy who can bridge any gaps in history or logic.

BROCK. Another name with a soap-opera gloss, this supermacho choice is derived from the Old English word for a badger. **BROOKS** has a similar sound and a Waspier, limper image.

BRODERICK, BRONSON. Two surname names that have become familiar through the use of a pair of single actors—Academy Award–winner Broderick Crawford and sitcom star Bronson Pinchot. Although it sounds somewhat formal and cold, Broderick actually means "brother" in Old Norse, while Bronson, a softer-sounding name, derives from the Old English for "son of the dark-skinned one." **BRANSON** is another surname-name possibility.

BROOKLYN. Despite two high-profile boy babies named Brooklyn—the son of Posh Spice and soccer star David Beckham and that of director Jonathan Demme—this remains predominantly a girls' name. In the most recent year tallied, there were about two thousand girls named Brooklyn (some of them Brooklynn, which gives you a clue to why the name is considered so feminine) and not enough boys to make the official records.

BROWN. This name is as rich and warm as the tone it denotes, and much more simpatico than its harsher Italo/German equivalent, **BRUNO,** which has traditionally been used to represent a bear in children's stories. Color names like Brown and Gray are highly evocative and, we think, unfairly neglected.

BRUCE. Its somewhat sissyish image was completely turned around when a batch of ultravirile Bruces suddenly hit the large and small screens a few years back—namely B. Lee, B. Willis, B. Springsteen, and B. Jenner, although this did nothing to resuscitate it as a baby name. An earlier attachment was to Robert "the Bruce," who ruled Scotland as King Robert I in the fourteenth century, and was said to have been inspired by the perseverance of a spider.

BRYANT. Bryan with attitude.

BUCK. A name that would have barely merited a footnote had comedienne Roseanne not chosen it for her son.

BURL. This name has a fragrant, woodsy feel. Its only well-known owner, folk singer Burl Ives, was born with the first name of Icle.

BYRON. For centuries this name had a long-haired, windswept image due to its strong connection to the poet Lord Byron, who inspired its use as a first name. These days it gives off a somewhat more serious, even intellectual message, one that might have appealed to actress Mel Harris, who chose it for her son. Golf legend Byron Nelson helped give it a touch of panache.

C

CADE, CADEN. Two of the new boys' names rising fast on the popularity charts, Cade and Caden—this version is the most widely used—have already spawned several offspring: **KADEN, KADE, CAYDEN,** and **KADIN** all make the Top 1,000. While Cade is related to the Old English word for *round* or *lump* the name's popularity is more closely tied to the style status of Braden and Jaden than to any historic significance of its own. Actor Keith Carradine has a son named Cade Richmond.

CADMUS. A prince in both Greek and Roman mythology who invented alphabetic writing. The *mus* ending may have unpleasant connotations, though.

CAESAR/CESAR. The name of the greatest Roman of them all is rarely used outside Latino families. In the early years of this country Caesar became a typical slave name, along with such other classical appellations as Cato and Octavius. The Latinate version Cesar, as in activist Chavez, is well used. Sonny Bono phoneticized it for his son as **CHESARE.**

CAIN. Seldom heard outside of soap operas, Cain carries the stigma of being associated with the world's first murderer, according to the Old Testament, who killed his own brother in a fit of jealousy. If it weren't for that—a very big if—Cain would be a strong, acceptable, and viable name. One way around the problem might be to sidestep the biblical connection and transform the name via spelling into the Irish surname **KANE.**

CALEB. A biblical name that could make a distinctive alternative to the less creative-sounding and increasingly common Jacob, now the most popular boy baby name in the country. The meaning of Caleb is faithful, intrepid, and victorious, an apt description of the Old Testament Caleb who was one of only two ancient Israelites (Joshua was the other) who set out with Moses from Egypt to finally enter the promised land. Actress Julianne Moore's young son is named Caleb. A contemporary-sounding variant is **CALE,** which has the drawback of being a homonym for a vegetable although it was used for the character voiced by Matt Damon in *Titan A.E.* **KALEB** and **KALEN** are newfangled variations that pick up on the trendy *k* initial.

CALUM, CALLUM. Think Caleb and Colin are too popular? Then Calum, the Scottish form of Colm, may be your man. Spelled with the double *l* it is currently in Great Britain's top 10.

CALVIN. Calvin is a slightly quirky but cozy name, which doesn't at all reflect the rigid precepts of Calvinism. There have been a number of notable Calvins past and present, including President Coolidge (born John), basketball star Calvin Murphy, baseball's Cal Ripken, and fashion's Calvin Klein, who once made the first name a synonym for jeans. It's also the real first name of rapper Snoop Doggy Dogg. **KALVIN** is a modern spelling variant; **CAL** is the unprepossessing short form.

CAMDEN. A place-name for those who love New Jersey. If you want to put a classier spin on it, there's an area of London called Camden Town. **KAMDEN** is a spelling variation that takes it out of the geographical arena.

CAMERON. Definitely one of the hottest names around, especially for boys, Cameron is edging toward the Top 25. Though also increasingly popular for girls, newborn male Camerons still outnumber females by about eight to one. Scottish by heritage, Cameron gives off a handsome, sensitive aura, one that's been utilized by the writers of several soap operas. Emma Samms, Jimmy Buffett, and Michael Douglas all have sons named Cameron. Director/writer Cameron Crowe based *Almost Famous* on his own life. Variations found among the Top 1,000 include, in order of popularity, **KAMERON, CAMRON, KAMRON,** and **CAMREN. CAM** or **KAM** is the usual nickname.

CANNON. TV personality Larry King chose this for one of his late-in-life sons. One of the more unusual surname names, it's consistent with the style for two-syllable boys' names. **KANNON** is a Buddhist deity who has both male and female aspects and is the patron of childbirth and children, as well as of dead souls.

CARL, KARL. This no-nonsense German form of Charles is strong but lacks much sensitivity or subtlety. Its most famous bearers include poet Carl Sandburg, scientist Carl Sagan, and track superstar Carl Lewis. The Latin forms **CARLO** and **CARLOS** have far more fire—and Carlos is in the Top 100.

CARLETON, CARLTON. An upscale name almost to the point of caricature, although baseball's Carlton Fisk has done his share to bring the name down to earth. The same description would fit **CHARLTON** and **CARLYLE,** which tend to sound more like hotels than people.

CARROLL. This name, which began life as a hundred-percent male name, has gradually invaded the female camp (dropping one of its *r*s and *l*s in the process), to the point where it has now lost virtually all remnants of its masculine punch.

CARSON. An androgynous-executive name of the type that is rapidly growing in popularity; this one becomes more and more viable as Johnny Carson fades from public view. Although writer Carson McCullers was of course female, the name retains all its original masculinity, and feminist mothers may appreciate the symbolism of naming a son after a notable female. **KARSON** is an alternative.

CARTER. Carter is another posh and trendy surname name, often used to signal a television character's upper-class status. Another fashionable element: the presidential association. TV personality Alan Thicke has a young son named Carter.

CARY. One of those names, like Oprah and Orson, whose popularity can be traced back to one celebrity—in this case Cary Grant (born with the name Archibald, he renamed himself after a character he was playing). But although his image was that of the quintessentially debonair man-about-town, this name, like its homophone **CAREY,** now sounds soft and feminine due to the preponderance of girls named Carrie and **KERRY**—the only spelling of the name that edges onto the boys' Top 1,000. We doubt that even the attractive star Cary Elwes can turn the gender image of this name around.

CASEY. A name with a big wide grin, Irish, friendly and open, Casey reflects its association with American folk heroes like Casey Jones, the engine driver of the Cannonball Express who gave his life to save his passengers, the legendary Casey at the Bat, and baseball's other Casey—Stengel. The name Casey is also notable because at the moment it occupies the exact same position on the popularity charts for boys and girls—number 176—

though parents should be aware that that represents an enormous rise on the female side. Just a handful of years ago, boy Caseys outnumbered girls three to one, and now the raw numbers of boys and girls given the name are nearly even. Beau Bridges has a son named Casey. As seems to be true of all *C* names, it is sometimes spelled **KASEY**. To update it with a surname spin, some parents have coined **CASEN**.

CASPER, CASPAR. After thirty years, this otherwise feasible name is still quite firmly linked to the white-sheeted image of the cartoon ghost. The Dutch form of Jasper, it also belonged to one of the Three Magi who brought gifts to the infant Jesus.

CASSIAN. Why hasn't anyone discovered this name yet? A Latin clan name, Saint Cassian, an early martyr, is the patron of stenographers. Cassian, still virtually unused, seems to be a prime candidate for name success—though the girls may grab it before boys get the chance.

CASSIDY. A lean and lanky Irish cowboy name that is in danger of being taken over by the females of the species (once Kathie Lee Gifford captures a name . . .). Evidence: While it's just made the female Top 100, it doesn't even appear in the male 1,000. The nickname **CASS,** as in Mama, is sometimes used independently and does nothing to bolster the name's masculine image. Of course, **KASSIDY** is also found.

CASSIEL. The name of the archangel who protects those born under the sign of Capricorn, this might make a distinctive choice for a boy with a January birthday.

CASTOR. Along with Pollux, one of the mythological twins that make up the constellation Gemini. Mythological names in general are on the cutting edge of fashion, a trend that Metallica's James Hetfield either helped set or was one of the first to discover when he named his baby son Castor Virgil.

CATO. It may once have conjured up images of ancient Roman statesmen or Southern antebellum retainers, but now the reference is more likely to be former O. J. Simpson houseguest **KATO** Kaelin.

CECIL, CEDRIC. A pair of stereotypically soft British names. Cecil, which had a lofty heritage as a famous Roman clan name and then as the surname of a prominent sixteenth-century English family, has gradually lost its color and potency over the years; it was the name of the prissy character played by Daniel Day-Lewis in the movie version of E. M. Forster's *A Room with a View* (and was also the first name of Day-Lewis's real-life father, the one-time poet laureate of England). With Cedric, a name invented by Sir Walter Scott for a character in *Ivanhoe*, this happened in one fell swoop, via the character of the long-haired, lace-collared Little Lord Fauntleroy in Frances Hodgson Burnett's 1886 novel, whose given name was, yes, Cedric, and who became an unwitting symbol of the pampered mama's boy. There are, of course, Cedrics and Cecils who have fought the stereotype and achieved success, including baseball player Cedric Maxwell, pioneer movie producer/director Cecil B. de Mille, photographer Cecil Beaton, and jazz pianist Cecil Taylor.

CHAD. Chad, like Brad and Tad, became popular in the late 1950s, and escalated even more in the era of hot TV doctor shows, when Chad Everett (born Raymond) starred on the long-running *Medical Center*. Rarely used now, it was also the name of a seventh-century saint and is a country in north-central Africa and it may take forever to overcome its hanging, dangling and pregnant associations via the 2000 Presidential election. **CHAD-WICK** is a tony-sounding surname name that is sometimes found.

CHAIM. Many cultures have attempted to bestow longevity on their children by giving them names that signify life—among them Viva, Zoe, Fayola, Vidal—and another prime example is Chaim, the Hebrew word for *life*, as in the toast *l' chaim*, to life. It is a name that barely survived the first wave of Jewish immigrants, being passed on to later generations in such watered-down forms as **HYMAN** and **HYMIE**. Today Chaim lives on in the stories of Isaac Babel and Isaac Bashevis Singer, in Israel and in more orthodox Jewish communities. It is also, improbably, the real first name of rocker Gene Simmons of KISS.

CHANCE. One of the most popular of the trendy new word names, Chance may be a statement on how a child came to be. The name has a dangerous swagger, a gambler's edge. Its most famous bearer is the Tennessee

Williams character Chance Wayne, portrayed by a young Paul Newman in the movie *Sweet Bird of Youth*. Talk-show host Larry King and actor Walt Willey both have young sons named Chance, and country singer Billy Ray Cyrus gave his son Braison the middle name Chance.

CHANDLER. This would be just another obscure surname name were it not for the Matthew Perry character on *Friends*. The popularity of the TV Chandler has helped propel the name to an impressive number 176.

CHARLES. The use of Charles has been so widespread in English- (and French-) speaking countries for so long that it is virtually faceless—it can conjure up anyone from Dickens to Chaplin to Bronson. Arising from a Germanic word meaning "free man," it owed its initial popularity to the emperor Charlemagne, which translates as "Charles the Great." It has been an elegant royal name—designating both Bonnie Prince Charlie, leader of a 1745 rebellion, and the present Prince of Wales, and also has one of the most buoyant and classless of nicknames: **CHARLIE,** also spelled **CHARLEY.** Actress Jodie Foster uses the nickname for her own little Charles, also the name of the sons of *Seinfeld*'s Julia Louis-Dreyfus and of onetime Charlie's Angel Kate Jackson. Some parents today are also considering the jazzier **CHAZ** (or **CHAZZ,** as in actor Palminteri) and should also be aware of such British spins as **CHAR** and **CHAS,** as well as the Scottish version, **CHAY. CHUCKIE** is a television Rugrat, and **CHUCK** is now only for dads, beef, or Public Enemy rapper Chuck D.

CHASE. Chase is an ultraprosperous-sounding name redolent of the worlds of high finance and international banking. A soap-opera favorite, parents seem to love it as well: It's moving toward the Top 50.

CHAUCER. One of the most distinguished names in literature could become a hero name in a family of poetry lovers. A few other such poetic possibilities: **DANTE, MARLOWE, POE, KEATS, BYRON, YEATS, TENNYSON, FROST, DICKINSON, LOWELL, LORCA, AUDEN, ELIOT**—but you can skip Milton and Shelley.

CHAUNCEY. A name halfway between its old Milquetoast image and a more jovial Irish-sounding contemporary one. But most modern parents interested in the name would probably rather opt for its onetime short form, Chance.

CHESTER. A comfortable, solid, teddy bear of a name that we would place in the so-far-out-they-could-be-on-their-way-back-in category, one that hasn't been used in so long it suddenly sounds both quirky and cuddly. Perhaps this was what impelled Tom Hanks and Rita Wilson to use it for their son. **CHET** is the usual, but still dated, nickname; one television Chester was called the more contemporary-sounding Chase.

CHEVY. This, like Cher and Madonna, falls into the category of who-needs-a-last-name? names. In fact, the Chevy Chase we all know and love entered the world as Cornelius and was probably nicknamed after the Washington suburb.

CHEYENNE. Once upon a time it was the name of the eponymous hero of a TV western; now it's a trendy Southwest-style name, very popular for girls and thus rarely used for boys.

CHRISTIAN. Christian has zoomed up the popularity charts in recent years, now in the Top 25 and still rising. Once a bit too pious for most people's taste, young stars Christian Slater and Christian Bale have helped put a human face on the name. It's also a fresher-sounding alternative to the ever-popular Christopher. In the Middle Ages, Christian was a female name, but turned male with the introduction of the hero of John Bunyan's *The Pilgrim's Progress*. In the more recent past, most Christians of note have had a French accent—the lover of Roxanne in *Cyrano de Bergerac*, for instance, and the designers Dior and Lacroix. Mel Gibson, Eddie Murphy, and singer Marc Anthony all have sons named Christian. Well-used spelling alternates include **CRISTIAN** and **KRISTIAN**. **CHRISTMAS** is also very occasionally used.

CHRISTOPHER. This fashionable classic was the second most popular boy's name of the 1990s and remains firmly in the Top 10. Parents seem to like its strong, sincere, straightforward image combined with its softer, more modern sound. It's one of the few traditional male names that escapes the outmoded masculine pipe-and-lawnmower feel that plagues such choices as Robert and John. A Greek name meaning "bearer of Christ," it is sometimes used to honor Saint Christopher, a third-century martyr who became the protective patron saint of travelers. The name appeals to a wide range of parents, evidenced by the diverse celebrities who've chosen Christopher for their sons: from Puff Daddy to Donny Osmond, Dean Cain to Arnold Schwarzenegger and Maria Shriver. The almost ubiquitous American nickname is **CHRIS,** but there are British variations that might add a more individual spin to the name—Kit, Kip, and **CHRISTY,** the last of which is more common in Ireland and may be too feminine for use here. Two Christophers known to every schoolchild: Christopher Robin and Christopher Columbus. Spelling variations and foreign versions abound, including **CRISTOPHER, KRISTOPHER, KRISTOFER, CRISTOBAL,** and **KRISTOF.**

CICERO. Another Roman statesman's name that was used here for slaves, when the names were chosen by slaveholders eager to show off their classical educations, and not much since. An intriguing possibility.

CLANCY. A lively, almost pugnacious Irish surname; full of moxie and more distinctive than Casey.

CLARENCE. This name pops up on TV every year around Christmastime, in the guise of Clarence Oddbody, Jimmy Stewart's sagacious guardian angel in the perennial classic *It's a Wonderful Life,* and is rarely if ever heard from the rest of the year. Nor do we expect it to be.

CLARK. In the heyday of Clark Gable, this name had a smooth, debonair charm, but it now sounds rather stiff and outdated—more like Clark Kent.

CLAUDE. A soft-spoken French name that conjures up the pastel colors of Monet and the harmonies of Debussy. Still used for women in France, it was ambisexual everywhere in its early history. The attractive Italian version, **CLAUDIO,** is also sometimes heard in this country.

CLAY. A rich one-syllable name that has been a soap-opera staple and has a Southern-inflected handsome-rogue image. Actress Annie Potts chose it for one of her young sons. Long form **CLAYTON** is used more often than the original, probably because it's similar in sound and feel to the wildly popular Jaden Braden Caden clan. **CLAYBORNE** is another, more pompous, possibility.

CLEMENT. If Clement has a papal ring, that could be because there have been fourteen heads of the Catholic church by that name, as well as several early saints. It also has a mild, pleasant, slightly antiquated feel, as in the phrase "clement weather." **CLEMENTS** is a variant. The short form, **CLEM,** is homey and humble, with a distinctive down-home charm.

CLEON. A rare and distinctive name with historic and literary overtones: Cleon was the leader of the Athenians during the Peloponnesian War and a character in Shakespeare's *Pericles.*

CLEVELAND. An old place-name not nearly as interesting as some of the more recently coined ones. The short form, **CLEVE,** used on its own, has a more individual, original sound.

CLIFFORD. Clifford is beginning to overcome a slightly stodgy, intellectual impression and is showing signs of a revival—Ken Olin and Patricia Wettig, for example, chose it for their son. **CLIFTON,** on the other hand, is showing no signs of life. **CLIFF** can be seen on reruns of *Cosby* and *Cheers.*

CLINTON. The fate of this old English family name probably will depend on the ultimate reputation of former president Bill, or on your political point of view. Its short form, **CLINT,** associated as it is with the legendary Mr. Eastwood (born Clinton), has a much steelier image.

CLIVE. We can't think of any name that could be more clipped or British than Clive—conjuring up as it does a terribly couth chap in high boots and khakis and a pencil-thin moustache. An old English family name, it was launched as a first name by the nineteenth-century novelist William Thackeray for a character in his novel *The Newcomes.*

CLOVIS. An aromatic, unconventional name, Clovis is of German descent, related to the later forms Ludwig and Lewis. Clovis I was the first Christian ruler of the Franks, and Clovis Ruffin was an inventive clothing designer.

CLYDE. A cross between a nerd and an outlaw, this name's reputation rested for years on the imprint of Clyde Barrow of Bonnie and Clyde fame. It's also the name of a river that runs through Glasgow. And in the "so far out it's in" spirit of Hollywood, indie actress Catherine Keener recently named her son Clyde.

COBY. See **JACOB.**

CODY. Lest you think that Kathie Lee Gifford single-handedly invented this name and spread it across the land, be reminded that before Cody Gifford there was Buffalo Bill, there was Cleveland Browns tackle Cody Risien (after whom baby Gifford was named), and there were the sons of other celebrities, including Kenny Loggins and Robin Williams. But it cannot be denied that Regis's former cohost's day-by-day reports on her son's accomplishments did ignite the name's meteoric success. Still in the Top 50, Cody shot at one point into the Top 10 in some states. The name's star is now waning, and parents attracted to Cody might want to consider something less trendy, like Brody or Clancy. Not surprisingly, variations abound: several hundred baby boys a year are named **KODY, COTY, CODEY,** and **CODIE,** including Yankee pitcher Roger Clemens's Kody.

COLBY. Kind of a cross between the ultratrendy Cody and Cole, and marginally more distinctive than either, is Colby, yet another vogueish two-syllable surname name. The hunky contestant on *Survivor* will surely only help Colby's popularity. While it is frequently found as a last name, it in fact derives from an Old English place-name meaning "dark farmstead." Well-used variations include **KOLBY, COBY,** and **KOBY**—the latter two of which may be nicknames for the highly popular Jacob.

COLE. A short name that manages to embody a lot of richness and depth, perhaps because of its association with the great, sophisticated song-writer Cole Porter. Now well into the Top 100, Cole was the name of the boy in the movie *The Sixth Sense* and is sometimes spelled **KOLE** or varied to **COLT**.

COLIN. Colin is a name on the way up, partly because of its dashing British image, somewhat because of its c-initialed two-syllable sound, and also thanks to General Colin Powell, the first African-American secretary of state. The name can be pronounced with a soft *o* as in *collar*, or (less appealingly we think) the way the general does, like *colon*, the end part of the intestine. Originally a short French form of Nicolas, Colin was a popular name for shepherds in English pastoral poetry (and retains some of that lyrical quality) and was a favorite of the MacKenzie and Campbell clans in Scotland. Spelling it **COLLIN** puts a surname spin on the name.

COLM, COLUM. Two highly unusual names in this country—but widely used in Ireland—that mean "dove," the symbol of peace. Colm Meaney is an Irish actor. **COLUMBA** and **COLUMBAN** were early Irish saints; **COLUMBUS** was, of course, the explorer who inspires a namesake here and there. **COLMAN/COLEMAN** is a surname form.

COLTON. A fast-rising surname name edging into the Top 100. Tennis great Chris Evert and Olympic skier Andy Mill have a son named Colton Jack. Originally an occupational name relating to horses, **COLT** and **COLTER** are also found.

CONAN. The memory of Schwarzenegger's Barbarian has faded and Conan's image has softened, partly due to the amiable persona of late-night host Conan O'Brien, and also because of the acceptance of lesser-known Irish names in general. Conan, which means "intelligence" or "wisdom" in Gaelic, was the name of an illustrious seventh-century Irish saint.

CONNOR, CONNER, CONOR. An appealing and wildly popular name—the three spellings considered together boost it into the Top 25—that derives from Irish mythology. In Ireland, it's particularly favored by the O'Brien and (of course) O'Connor families. Tom Cruise and Nicole Kidman's son is named Connor, the most popular version. A more unusual alternative with the same distinguished Irish pedigree might be **CONN,** as in the hero Conn of the Hundred Battles—though no parent wants to raise a future con man.

CONRAD. This is a somewhat neglected English version of the German **KONRAD** that some see as intellectual and manly, but others view as nerdy and old-fashioned. Your call.

CONSTANTINE. A rather bulky and unwieldy name for a modern child to bear, despite—or because of—its heavy historical associations. It was the name of the first Christian emperor of the Roman empire, as well as three Scottish kings. In Ireland, it's traditionally used by the Maguire clan.

CONWAY. Once upon a time this name belonged exclusively to country crooner Conway Twitty, but now it may join the Connor/Colton/Corbin contingent. **CONROY** is a similar possibility.

COOPER. An upscale, preppy yet genial surname that originated as an occupational name—it referred to a barrel maker—and was chosen both by uber Playboy Hugh Hefner and actor Tim Matheson for their young sons. A more modern related choice might be **COOK.**

CORBIN. Corbin Bernsen starred in a hit television series (*L.A. Law*) in the 1980s, but his first name is more popular today, capitalizing on the mania for two-syllable names that sound like surnames and start with c or k. **KORBIN** is a spelling variation. With its roots in the Latin for *dark,* a related and lesser-known choice is **CORBIT** or **CORBET,** either of which can be spelled with two t's. There was a French saint whose mother changed his name to **CORBINIAN** after originally naming him **WALDEGISO.**

CORD. A severe, soap-operaish name without much soul. **CORDELL** is used slightly more often.

CORENTIN. A Breton name that's totally unknown here but is very popular in France. Saint Corentin possessed a miraculous fish that regenerated itself each night, feeding Corentin and his lucky visitors in perpetuity.

COREY. A name with energy but not much muscle. There seemed to be an epidemic of Coreys (Haim, Feldman, Parker) in 1980s teen entertainment, but, along with other nickname-type names like Jamie and Jody, Corey's image has definitely dimmed. Alternative versions: **COREY, KORY, KOREY.**

CORIN. An unusual name used by Shakespeare in *As You Like It,* Corin might make a more distinctive alternative to Colin or Corey. Actor Corin Redgrave is the brother of Vanessa and Lynn.

CORMAC. This traditional Irish name was brought to the attention of the American reading public in recent years via best-selling author Cormac McCarthy. An Irish version of Charles, it's an evocative name that runs through Celtic mythology as the legendary king of Tara. British movie bad guy Tim Roth named his son Cormac.

CORNELIUS. As soon as the word *corny* came into the slanguage, this name was in trouble. Even before that, it had come to sound pompous and pretentious—perhaps through its association with financier Cornelius Vanderbilt. **CORNELL** and **CORNEL** are short forms.

CORTEZ, CRUZ. The craze for surname names has so far been limited to English and Irish selections, but the next wave includes more unusual and exotic family names from around the world. Cortez and Cruz are two Spanish possibilities that have edged into the Top 1,000 and seem poised to move much higher.

COSMO, COSMAS. A friendly, expansive Greek name that seems to embrace the whole world—or cosmos. The name of the Arabian-born patron saint of doctors, Cosmas or Cosmo (as *Seinfeld* afficionados know, Kramer's seldom-used first name) could make an exotic, creative choice.

CRAIG. A once-popular one-syllable baby-boomer name (frat brother of Kirk, Clark, Scott et al.), Craig has Scottish origins (it's still the third most common name in that country) and an overly smooth image. Modern parents would probably tend to prefer Kyle.

CRISPIN. Introduced into the mainstream by actor Crispin Glover, this name, which means "curly-haired" in Latin, has an image very much like its first syllable, crisp, autumnal, and colorful. Saint Crispin was the patron saint of shoemakers. **CRISPIAN** is an interesting, rarely used variation, as is **CRISPUS,** associated with African-American hero Crispus Atticus, the first colonist to die for independence in the Boston Massacre.

CROSBY. A laid-back Irish surname, reflecting the nonchalance of crooner Bing Crosby and David Crosby of Crosby Stills Nash & Young. A mellow musical choice made by fellow singer Kenny Loggins for his son.

CULLEN. An Irish Gaelic surname meaning "handsome one" that might make an appealing alternative to Colin—although it could also be confused with it. To avoid that, you might consider the related **CURRAN,** which means "champion" or "hero."

CURTIS. A rather elegant Old French name that actually does mean "courteous." One notable bearer of the name is music great Curtis Mayfield. The short form **CURT** is a lot more macho, and has been borne by several outstanding athletes, including Flood (baseball) and Strange (golf), as well as sportscaster Curt Gowdy.

CYPRIAN. Meaning "from Cyprus," Cyprian was a common name from the early Christian era through the eighteenth century, when it began to fade from view. Saint Cyprian was a lawyer and pioneer of Catholic literature. With its long and noble history, Cyprian might be an interesting option for the parent in search of a truly unusual choice.

CYRIL. A name with a monocle in one eye, wearing an ascot in place of a tie. Despite its Greek roots, Cyril definitely has a British accent, and an upper-class, intellectual one at that.

CYRUS. An old-fangled, sitting-on-the-porch, smoking-a-corncob-pipe kind of name that might just be funky enough to appeal to parents looking for a so-far-out-it's-in-possibility. Its origins were far more lofty—Cyrus the

Great was a sixty-century founder of the Persian empire. Cybill Shepherd named her twin son Cyrus Zachariah, in honor of two ancestors, but he is known to the world as Zack. **CY** is the very short form.

D

DAKOTA. This geographic and Native American tribal name has for quite some time been trendy for both boys (chosen by Melissa Gilbert) and girls (as used by Melanie Griffith and Don Johnson)—though the male Dakotas still outnumber the females by nearly five to one. In the Top 100 for boys, the name has lots of spirit and charisma, though you may decide you want your little cowboy to live in a less crowded name territory. **DAKOTAH** is sometimes found.

DALE. A pleasant-sounding nature name, evocative of shaded glens and valleys, the androgynous Dale tipped slightly toward the girls' side with the 1950s fame of cowgirl Dale Evans. Though *Twin Peaks'* FBI agent Dale Cooper (played by androgynously named Kyle MacLachlan) gave the name some modern masculine attention, it would still be a somewhat risky choice for a boy.

DALLAS. An attractive, attention-catching, cowboy place-name that's become more visible in recent years, partly due to the influence of baseball's Dallas Green and, to a lesser degree, newscaster Dallas Townsend. But none of these Western place-names—Dallas, Austin, Dakota—packs the same style power it did even a few years ago. **DALLIN** is a strange relative.

DALTON. A classic English surname with a roguish Western overlay—probably related to the legendary Dalton brothers, two of whom were killed while trying to rob two banks at once. Though blacklisted screenwriter Dalton Trumbo was for a long time the only known bearer of this name, this name has galloped on a dark horse onto the Top 100 list and has all the ingredients, for better and worse, to go even further. Actresses Linda Hamilton and Kathleen Quinlan as well as actor J. Eddie Peck all have sons named Dalton.

DAMIAN, DAMIEN. A Greek name with exotic, otherworldly overtones, mainly because of its links to the possessed child in *The Omen* movies and the priest, Father Damien Karras, in *The Exorcist*. Black magic notwithstanding, Damian has a flip side—Irish and antic, with considerable charm. It is the name of four saints, including the patrons of doctors, chemists, barbers, and the blind. **DAMION** is a spelling alternative.

DAMON. A name with a strong, pleasing sound and extremely positive ancient associations. In classical mythology, Damon and Pythias are the symbols of true friendship, as Damon risked his life to save his friend from execution. In Latin pastoral poetry, Damon is often used to denote a young lover. And Damon of Athens was the fifth-century philosopher who taught both Pericles and Socrates. Damon Runyon wrote *Guys and Dolls,* though the most famous Damon these days is Damon Wayans—or maybe Matt Damon.

DANA. It was the 1940s movie star Dana Andrews (born Carver) who made this name viable for boys. Then, as his influence faded and Dana became almost completely feminized, along came Dana Carvey to reinject the name with a little masculine punch. Still, not too long ago, a reporter wrote a whole feature story on the trials and tribulations of being a male Dana. **DANE** has both more male and more style edge.

DANGER. A word name with a frightening meaning chosen as the middle name for their second son, Jacob, by Green Day lead singer B. J. Armstrong and his wife Adrienne.

DANIEL. A perennial favorite—still in the Top 10—Daniel was popular in the days of Daniel Webster and Daniel Boone. And its appeal is international—not only is it found all over expected places like Israel and Ireland, but it is currently high on the popularity list in Germany as well. What is it that makes this name so attractive to so many different kinds of parents? A prime factor is that although it was the name of one of the greatest biblical heroes (what child has not thrilled to the story of the prophet whose faith protected him when he was thrown into a den of lions?), it does not seem at all solemn or pretentious compared, say, to Ezekiel or Abraham. Daniel is, in fact, one of the very few male names that's both traditional and modern-sounding, that has charm as well as weight. Liam Neeson and Natasha Richardson have a son named Daniel Jack, and one of TV's Patricia Heaton's four sons is named Daniel. And its nicknames—**DANNY** and **DAN**—make it sound even friendlier, although, as with other classics, more and more parents are opting to use the name in full.

DANTE. An Italian name strongly associated with the thirteenth-century poet (whose full name at birth was Durante), who described, in the epic poem *The Divine Comedy*, his journey through heaven and hell. Actors Chazz Palminteri and Jordan Knight both have sons named Dante. It's also a name that's spawned many alternates, among the most popular of which are **DONTE, DONTAE,** and **DEONTE.**

DARBY. A lighthearted, light-footed name that conjures up the whimsy of the 1950s Disney film *Darby O'Gill and the Little People*.

DARCY, D'ARCY. A handsome, roguish kind of appellation that combines elements of French flair, aristocratic savoir faire, and a soft Irish brogue. But Darcy's problem is a big one: It sounds more like a girls' name than one for boys.

DARIUS. Darius is a name that is increasing in popularity, among the overall 200 most popular names and in the Top 10 for African-American babies born in some states. The name of several Persian kings—including the one responsible for throwing Daniel to the lions—it now has a creative, artistic image, and would not look out of place on a concert program or art-gallery announcement. CNN's Christiane Amanpour and politico James Rubin named their son Darius. **DARIO** is another interesting possibility.

DARRELL, DARRYL, and **DARYL.** One of the beach-boy names that sounded so hep in the 1950s and 1960s, Darrell and his brothers Darryl and Daryl have pretty much ridden their last style wave—as males, anyway. There are still several hundred boy babies a year who are given the name, but it's only fashionable these days when used for a girl, as in Daryl Hannah. Its root meaning is attractive, however: It comes from the Old English for "darling."

DARREN. Darren is a member in good standing of the Karen-Sharon coalition of the 1950s—a club that is out of fashion favor. But its influence has been strong enough over the decades to spawn a battalion of variations. Spelling alternatives include **DARRIN, DARIN,** and **DARON.** A slight variation that has a bit more panache is **DARIEN** (as in the posh Connecticut suburb)—also spelled **DARIAN, DARION, DARRIAN, DARRION,** and **DARRIEN.** Spelled **DAREN,** it's a West African name meaning "born at night."

DARWIN. Parents with a scientific bent may want to use this name to honor the evolutionary theorist. It has a lovely meaning too: "dear friend."

DASHIELL. This name has a great deal of dash and panache, and although it's always been linked to a single personality—Dashiell Hammett (whose given first name was actually Samuel), creator of Sam Spade—it is now up for general grabs.

DAVID. David is the kind of name, like Michael and Stephen, that girls have been writing in the margins of their notebooks for generations, because David sounds so sweet, serious, and simpatico. David is still popular with parents too, firmly in the Top 20. The name has deep biblical roots, David being the Hebrew name (meaning "beloved") of the second king of Israel in the Old Testament, who, as a boy, slew the mighty warrior Goliath with his slingshot, then grew up to become a wise and highly cultivated leader who enjoyed music and was a poet, as well as becoming the inspiration of such great sculptors as Michelangelo and Donatello. The name has a special resonance for Jews, the Star of David being the symbol of Judaism. A sixth-century David became the patron saint of Wales—where there are several different pet forms, such as **DAI** and **TAFFY.** There have been countless Davids of note in history, entertainment, sport, and fiction, including Bowie, Copperfield, Crockett, Letterman, and Winfield. **DEVLIN** is an appealingly devilish Irish form of David, while **DEWEY,** an Anglicized version of the Welsh form, **DEWI,** is no more popular than Huey or Louie. **DAVIS** is an attractive surname linked with David, and also with old Southern traditions via Confederate president Jefferson Davis.

DAVIN. One of the popular new hybrid names that relates to Gavin, Darren, and David.

DAWSON is another David relative that's gained considerable standing of its own via the title character of television's *Dawson's Creek*. Since the show has been on, the name has gone from obscurity to number 168 and rising, and could make a strong modern choice to honor an ancestral David.

DAYTON. Of course Dayton is a place-name, though it's doubtful many people choose it in order to honor the Ohio city. Rather, it's got the kind of two-syllable surname feel so popular for boys' names today. Another possibility: **DAXTON.**

DEAN. Dean is a 1950s kind of name with something of a goody-goody image, associated with such period personalities as Dean (born Dino) Martin, Dean Stockwell, and Secretaries of State Acheson and Rusk. The Italian version, **DINO,** is sometimes used in this country as well, although we know one little Dino who was mercilessly teased about his connection to Dino the Dinosaur.

DEANDRE, DEMARCO, DEJUAN, DESHAWN et al. Many boys' names these days start with the popular *de* prefix. Particularly prevalent in the African-American community, this practice has its antecedents in the traditions of the Free Blacks of New Orleans, many of whom had children with white French settlers and used the *de* prefix to indicate paternity. This still can be a more interesting alternative to Junior.

DECLAN. Very popular in the Emerald Isle, but hardly known here, Declan (pronounced DECK-lan)—the name of an Irish saint and the real first name of Elvis Costello—might just be ripe to join such recent Irish imports as Connor and Kieran. Singer Cyndi Lauper named her son **DECLYN.** Nikki Sixx of Motley Crue's son is **DECKER.** There are characters named **DEACON** on both *the Bold and the Beautiful* and *The King of Queens.*

DELANEY and **DEMPSEY.** These are two good old Irish family names that would translate well into strong, singular given names.

DEMETRIUS, DIMITRI. The Greek Demetrius, the name of an early saint who ventured into North Africa, is the most popular form of this name these days, perhaps thanks to the Hall of Demetrius in the popular *Tomb Raider* video game. Demetrius is also the name of several athletes as well as two Shakespearean characters. The Russian version Dimitri (or **DMITRI** or **DHIMITRI**) is a name dressed in high boots and high collars, one that conjures up feverish czardas and ballet dancing and impassioned orchestra conducting. It is the name of one of the brothers Karamazov and also the choice of Ursula Andress and Harry Hamlin for their son.

DENNIS. Although it has come to sound so Irish, Dennis is actually of French derivation (Saint **DENIS** is the patron saint of France) and harks back even further to **DIONYSIS,** the Greek god of wine and debauchery. It was considered a pretty cool name for an adult through the 1950s and 1960s, but then Dennis the Menace took over. It would be more modern to put a surname spin on the name and call it **DENNISON.**

DENVER. A place-name that suggests high altitudes and clean air, becoming familiar via the versatile character actor Denver Pyle.

DENZEL, DENZIL. This old Cornish family name has taken on a whole new identity in the person of the dashing and talented actor Denzel Washington, who has inspired several thousand namesakes.

DEREK, DERRICK. This name, with its sophisticated, slightly British accent, had been growing in popularity over the last decades of the twentieth century but now is starting to fade. Yankee superstar Derek Jeter may be responsible for a whole new generation of namesakes, though. **DERICK** and **DERIK** are alternate spellings; **DIRK** is the Dutch form of the name, made infamous—and definitely unfit for a baby—by the Dirk Diggler character in *Boogie Nights*. **DERRY** is an Irish variant.

DERMOT. Actor Dermot Mulroney might do for this Irish name what Aidan Quinn and Liam Neeson did for theirs. Its Celtic meaning is "free from envy," an enviable quality to impart to any child.

DESMOND. A debonair British/Irish name now taking off in this country. It is most closely associated with Desmond Tutu, the black South African bishop who won the Nobel peace prize in 1983.

DEVIN, DEVON. A handsome, windswept place-name that is also given to girls—but is used ten times more often for boys. The Devin spelling, which relates the name more closely to the longtime favorite Kevin, is firmly in the Top 100. Devon, spelled like the beautiful seaside county in southwest England, is not far behind that. Other spellings and versions include: **DEVAN, DEVEN, DEVYN, DAVON, DAVIN, DAVION, DEVONTE, DEVANTE,** and **DAVONTE.** Vanessa Williams and comedian Denis Leary both have sons named Devin.

DEVLIN. See **DAVID.**

DEWEY. See **DAVID.**

DEX, DEXTER. Names with *x*s tend to have a lot of energy and sex appeal and we see this one as a retro name waiting to rehappen. Over the years, it's been attached to a varied assortment of public personae—C. K. Dexter Haven, the witty Cary Grant character in *The Philadelphia Story* (which gave the name a sparkling, sophisticated, upper-class twist), jazz tenor saxophonist Dexter Gordon, and gridiron star Dexter Manley. The short form, Dex, has even more pizzazz. It was the bold choice Dana Carvey made for his son's name, while Diane Keaton made the even bolder choice of Dexter for her daughter.

DIDIER. A French name—it's pronounced DID-ee-ay—that has possibilities here.

DIEGO. This name, which is a Spanish form of James, has a lot of verve when combined either with a Latin or an Anglo surname. It belonged to Diego Rivera, the Spanish leftist muralist who was the husband of Frida Kahlo.

DIETER. A classic German name (it rhymes with Peter) that parents in search of an exotic but traditional choice may want to consider. **DIETRICH** is a related possibility.

DION. Short for **DIONYSIS** (a name that would be too much for any child to handle), the Greek god of wine, Dion (usually pronounced DEE-on) would make a creative choice. Classic rock 'n' roll buffs might associate it with the 1960s group Dion and the Belmonts, responsible for such hits as "A Teenager in Love." **DEON** and **DEION** are often found.

DJANGO. The nickname of early twentieth-century Belgian jazz guitarist Django (silent *D*) Reinhardt, this was chosen by *Star Trek: Deep Space Nine* actors Nana Vistior and Alexander Siddig for their son.

DOLAN. Although it has never officially entered the main stockpot of first names in the way that, say, Nolan, has, Dolan (which means "black hair") is definitely another energetic Irish surname possibility.

DOMINIC, DOMINICK. Until the twentieth century, this was a name used almost exclusively by Roman Catholics, often for children born on Sunday, "The Lord's Day." Now teetering on the edge of the Top 100 in the United States, it is a name with high-fashion status in England. Basketball star **DOMINIQUE** Wilkins — "the human highlight reel" — prefers the French version. **DOMINIK** and **DOMENIC** are other possibilities.

DONALD. Used for centuries in Scotland, where the McDonald clan is one of the most ancient and there have been six kings by that name, Donald was a Top 20 name in the U.S. throughout most of the early twentieth century. But first there was Donald Duck to distort its image, and then there was The Donald Trump, until now there's not much potential for it as a modern baby name. More promising and more authentically Celtic-sounding is **DONAL,** which is quite commonly used in Ireland, or its more surnamey equivalent, **DONNELL.** Then there are the related surnames, **DONNELLY** and **DONOVAN.** Donovan (or **DONAVAN** or **DONAVON**), the version moving most quickly up the popularity charts, was one of the earliest Irish surnames to take off as a given name in this country, thanks largely to the 1960s folk-rock ("Mellow Yellow") singer, who dropped his last name of Leitch.

DORIAN. Since it means "child of the sea" in Greek (the Dorians were a division of early Greeks that included the Spartans), Dorian is often given to boys born under water signs—Pisces, Cancer, or Scorpio. It was introduced as a first name by Oscar Wilde in *The Picture of Dorian Gray,* the story of a dissolute character who retains his youthful good looks while his portrait in the attic ages hideously. Rhythmic and unusual, Dorian is a distinctive choice—made by Lindsay Wagner for her son—but one that to some may sound slightly feminine.

DOUGLAS. Douglas, and more particularly its nickname, **DOUG,** had a real romantic swagger in the 1950s and 1960s dating back to swashbuckling Douglas Fairbanks but is faded today. Originally a Celtic river name, it became attached to a powerful Scottish clan, renowned for their strength and courage. In its earliest incarnation Douglas was used equally for girls and boys. The variant **DOUGAL** is heard in the Scottish highlands.

DOV. A Hebrew name that means "bear," Dov is frequently heard in Israel.

DRAKE. A sleek surname name with roots that link it to dragons and ducks, Drake is fast moving from obscurity up the popularity ladder—there were over a thousand baby Drakes born in the most recent year counted. It was the name of the character Ronald Reagan played in the movie *King's Road*—his greatest (or perhaps second-greatest) role.

DREW. Drew gives off a polished, somewhat intellectual impression. It's used as a name in its own right and often, these days, as a nickname for the popular classic Andrew—Andy being deemed somewhat retrograde. Actress Drew Barrymore has feminized the name to some degree, while Drew Carey has dimmed some of its polish.

DUANE, DWAYNE. An Irish name meaning "swarthy," this name (Dwayne is the most popular spelling, and **DEWAYNE** is sometimes used) has become almost a stereotype, denoting an unsophisticated guy.

DUBLIN. A place-name possibility that seems to fall on the masculine side of the often ambiguous fence—though Kim Basinger and Alec Baldwin named their daughter Ireland.

DUDLEY. It's easy to love a name that rhymes with "cuddly" and has a nickname like **DUD**—not that you'd actually want to stick your kid with such a downbeat moniker. All this contradicts Dudley's origins as an aristocratic surname.

DUFF. A somewhat rough, rowdy, ragged Celtic name, at home in a noisy pub or out walking on the moors. In Scotland, it was originally a nickname for someone with dark hair or a swarthy complexion. Duff (born Michael) McKagen was a member of Guns N' Roses. **DUFFY** is another possibility.

DUNCAN. Jaunty, confident, and open, this name is brimming with friendly charm, and definitely makes it into our golden circle of ideal names that are neither too ordinary nor too far-out. Duncan was the name of two Scottish rulers, one of whom was the well-loved and beneficent king killed by Macbeth. Television personality Gordon Elliott has a son named Duncan.

DUNSTAN. It could sound like a confused cross between Duncan and Dustin, but Dunstan is very much a name of its own. Its best known bearer was the exceptional tenth-century English saint who was the Archbishop of Canterbury and principal advisor to the kings of Wessex. Also a skilled metalworker, calligrapher, and harpist, Dunstan is the patron saint of locksmiths, jewelers, and the blind. If there are too many Dustins in your neighborhood, you might consider this alternative.

DUSTIN. While the popularity of Dustin is beginning to sag a bit, there were still nearly three thousand of them born in the most recent year counted. The mass appeal of the name is, we think, more due to its similarity to Justin than to any idolization of actor Dustin Hoffman, himself named for silent-screen star Dustin Farnum. **DESTIN** is a variation climbing the popularity ladder rather than sliding down it, though we think it sounds a mite medicinal, and **DUSTY** is a not-very-fresh nickname.

DWIGHT. This Anglo-Saxon name that means "white" was big in the Eisenhower years, but hasn't been heard from much since. A sports hero who brought more recent fame to the name is New York Mets megastar pitcher, Dwight Gooden.

DYLAN, DILLON. One of the most poetic and romantic of boys' names, and one that is now ensconced in the Top 25, Dylan can no longer be considered a rebellious or iconoclastic choice. A Welsh name tied to the sea, Dylan was a legendary sea god for whom all the waters of Britain and Ireland wept when he died. It also belonged, of course, to the great Welsh poet Dylan Thomas, whose name Bob Dylan adopted in tribute. And it's been used in recent years by a veritable host of celebrities for their sons, including Michael Douglas and Catherine Zeta-Jones, Pamela Anderson and Tommy Lee, Pierce Brosnan, Joan Cusack, and Stephanie Seymour. Spelling alternatives include **DILLAN, DYLON, DYLLAN,** and **DILLION.**

E

EARL. It may have started out as a noble name—ranking right between a marquis and a viscount—but Earl has plunged from that lofty perch and has rarely been given to babies since the 1920s, when it made the Top 40.

EASTON. Did *American Psycho* author Bret Easton Ellis or the city of Easton, Pennsylvania, inspire the growing popularity of this name? More likely is the fact that it's got that two-syllable surname feel so popular for boys today. **EATON** is a similar possibility.

EBENEZER. Old Mr. Scrooge pretty much annihilated this biblical name (actually used for a stone in the Good Book rather than a person) for all time. On the other hand, the short form **EBEN** would make an unusual and creative choice.

EDGAR. As unlikely as it seems, there were more than two thousand baby Edgars born in the most recent year tallied, more than the number of trendy Caseys, Carters, or Bradys. There have been many notable Edgars in the past, including Edgar the Peaceful, the first recognized king of England;

Edgar Rice Burroughs, creator of Tarzan; writer Edgar Allan Poe; and FBI chief J. Edgar Hoover. Joan Rivers' daughter Melissa named her son Edgar after her father, but he is called by his middle name, Cooper. **EDGARDO** is found in the Latino community.

EDISON. A last-name-first name that invokes all the creativity and inventiveness of Thomas A., without whom we wouldn't have our DVD players or broadband Internet access.

EDMUND. "There is nobleness in the name of Edmund," says a Jane Austen character. We would have to agree, as would the unhappy poet John Keats, who once bemoaned, "Had my name been Edmund, I would have been more fortunate." Perhaps he knew that its literal meaning is "happy, fortunate, and rich." Edmund is a name that is heating up in England (where it's been the name of three kings); actor Ben Kingsley used it for his son. **EAMON** is its quintessentially Irish equivalent.

EDWARD. EDDIE and **ED** are out, Edward is in. This Anglo-Saxon classic, one of the most frequently used names for British kings (there were eight of them), is definitely back in vogue, either used in full or, possibly, with the nostalgic Nancy Drew nickname **NED,** or the further afield **WARD.** Hot young actor Edwards Norton, Furlong, and Burns only help the name's image. Even **EDWIN** and **EDUARDO** are on the rise.

EFRAIN, EPHRAIM. Efrain, the Spanish version of this neglected biblical name (Ephraim was the second son of Joseph) is the only one making a significant appearance these days. The name's most famous bearers were **EFREM** Zimbalist Sr. (violinist) and Jr. (star of *The FBI* TV series and father of Stephanie), who preferred the phonetic spelling.

EGAN. The sound of this Irish surname, related to the word *eager,* gives it a ready-to-please, effervescent energy.

ELDON, ELTON, ELVIN. None of them is very popular, but they're all famous anyway: Eldon (also spelled **ELDIN**) as the name of Murphy Brown's house-painter cum nanny, Elton as singer John, and Elvin as basketball's Elvin Hayes and pianist Elvin Jones.

ELDRIDGE. An old German name (it means "wise, mature counselor") still viable because of its association with African-American activist Eldridge Cleaver, author of *Soul on Ice.*

ELEAZER. Four-syllable names (that's a pronunciation clue) are not the easiest for a child to handle, but this rarely used Old Testament name (Eleazer was a son of Aaron), has distinct possibilities, as long as some fourth-grade wise guy doesn't dissect it to get at some devastating nickname. **ELIEZER** is another spelling used more frequently than the original; **ELISEO** is the Latin version.

ELI, ELY. This solid but not heavy biblical name (Eli was the high priest and last judge of Israel, who trained the prophet Samuel), is making a strong comeback along with its Old Testament brethren, perhaps influenced by the kid character, often called E, on TV's *Once and Again.*

ELIAN. A Spanish name from the ancient Roman clan Aelia, Elian was catapulted before the American public in the person of little Elian Gonzalez, the Cuban boy rescued at sea over whom an international custody battle raged. The boy's winning personality and smile are sure to inspire many namesakes.

ELIJAH. Another venerable Old Testament prophet name—he was the one who went to heaven in a chariot of fire—as well as the name of Elijah Muhammad (born Robert), founder of the Nation of Islam, Elijah was suddenly rejuvenated when Cher and Greg Allman bestowed it on their son Elijah Blue in 1976. Elijah is now number 54 on the hit parade. James Spader, Tiffany, and Wynonna Judd have more recently named their sons Elijah, and U2's Bono named his Elijah Bob Patricius Guggi Q—called Eli. **ELIAS,** the German and Dutch version and Bo Diddley's real name, is an equally attractive and strong possibility for a modern boy. Other forms include the Greek **ELIHU,** the Greek and Italian **ELIA—ELIO** is another Italian form—and the French **ELIE.** An Anglicized, somewhat adulterated version is **ELLIS,** the name Emily Brontë took as a male pen name and that of the father of the musical Marsalis brothers.

ELISHA. This creative name belongs to yet another Hebrew prophet, the successor to and disciple of Elijah. Its limitation is that it might sound too much like a girls' name, i.e., Alicia or Elissa.

ELLERY. This is one of those interesting names that we would like to liberate once and for all from its limited single-note identity. In this case, of course, it's that of mystery writer Ellery Queen, who never even existed—it was the pen name of two cousins called Frederic Dannay and Manfred B. Lee. The rhythmic, three-syllable sound of the name corresponds to such popular female names as Mallory, Brittany, and Stephanie—not easy to find in a boy's name. But alas, that very association might limit its success.

ELLIOT, ELLIOTT. With two main spellings both used just about equally as often—that is to say, not very—the Elliots got their last style boost in the early 1980s when the name was used for the young hero of the movie *E.T.* But actor Robert DeNiro bucked the fashion trend and named one of his young sons Elliot. A feminist parent today might want to vary it to **ELIOT,** in honor of (female) writer George.

ELMER. Thanks to Elmer Fudd, Elmer the Cow, and maybe even Elmer's glue, this name has become something of a joke, the quintessential so-far-out-it-will-never-be-in nerd name that we don't see ever coming back into favor. It is actually a variant of the Old English name, **AYLMER.**

ELMO. This name calls to mind the image of Saint Elmo's fire—the light show sometimes visible around ships' masts during storms at sea—quite appropriate since Saint Elmo (another name for **ERASMUS**) is the patron saint of sailors. Toddlers of today will link the name with the most popular Muppet to hit Sesame Street since Cookie Monster—not the most auspicious association with which to saddle your preschooler.

ELVIS. Once seemingly the ultimate one-person name, Elvis seems to have by dint of sheer energy shaken off the vise grip of the King and emerged as a real possibility for consideration. Partly, that's thanks to other famous Elvises who've come to share the spotlight in recent years: singer Elvis Costello, who changed his name from Declan in tribute to Presley, and Olympic skater Elvis Stojko. Actor Anthony Perkins and director Roman Polanski both used the name for their sons—something 375 other parents also did in the most recent year counted. The name has roots beyond Memphis—there was a sixth-century Irish Saint Elvis—who was also known as **ELWYN, ELWIN,** Elian, and Allan.

EMANUEL, EMMANUEL. In the Bible, this is the name given to the promised Messiah, in the prophecy of Isaiah. Commonly used by Jewish families from the 1920s to the 1940s, it was somewhat devalued by its reduction to the nickname **MANNY.** But it is now beginning to be reevaluated in its complete form and has in fact been chosen by such high-profile parents as Debra Winger and Timothy Hutton, who named their son Emanuel Noah.

EMERSON, EMERY, EMORY. Three sturdy, rather serious surnames sometimes used as first names.

EMIL, EMILE, EMILIO. Emilio, the Spanish form, is the winner of this trio, partly thanks to actor Emilio Estevez. Despite the charm of the children's classic, Emil and Emile are just too close to the megapopular girls' name Emily as well as to other current female favorites such as Emma and Amelia. **EMILIANO** is another Latin version.

EMLYN is a common Welsh name that holds the danger of being perceived as feminine in this country. The renowned Welsh actor and playwright Emlyn Williams was actually christened George, which he used as the title of his autobiography.

EMMETT, EMMET. This name—which comes from the Hebrew meaning "truth"—has an honest, sincere, long-legged, laid-back, creative quality. Its most famous bearer was America's best-loved clown, Emmett Kelly, and it definitely makes a stylish choice today.

ENOCH and **ENOS** are two unconventional names from the Book of Genesis. Enoch, which has a sound that is not very appealing to the modern ear, was the eldest son of Cain, born after he killed his brother Abel. Enos was another direct descendant of Adam and Eve.

ENZO. Originally a nickname for Vincenzo, Enzo is very popular in Italy right now and beginning to be used in this country as well. And not only by Italian-Americans—actress Patricia Arquette chose it for her son.

ERIC, ERIK. This is the most popular Scandinavian boys' name ever in the United States, among the Top 50 for several decades, and though its star is beginning to dim, some parents are still attracted to its Norse strength, reminiscent of Viking hero Erik the Red. Erik is the version used in recent years by swimsuit model Kathy Ireland for her son. The spelling **ERICH** adds a more Germanic spin.

ERNEST. This is probably the only name a whole play was based on— Oscar Wilde's *The Importance of Being Earnest*—in which one character says, "There is something in that name that seems to inspire absolute confidence. I pity any poor woman whose husband is not called Ernest." Well, not many women in the year 2030 will have husbands named Ernest, because it is rarely given to babies of today, despite the fact that it does conjure up positive associations—Hemingway, Ernie of the Bert and Ernie team, and Ernie Kovacs. But perhaps earnestness is a dated virtue.

ERROL. Unknown in this country until Errol Flynn made his smashing, swashbuckling debut in *Captain Blood* in 1935, this Scottish place-name has been used quietly since then, perhaps to honor jazz great Errol Garner.

ESAU. This falls into the category of rarely used Old Testament names, possibly because of its hirsute connotations ("for Esau was an hairy man"), Esau being the twin of Jacob, son of Isaac and Rebecca. That aside (and the fact that a child might have to put up with the jingle "he saw Esau on the seesaw" a few hundred times), it's a perfectly usable name.

ETHAN. Ethan is a biblical name that's been slowly climbing the popularity lists over the past several years, edging now toward the Top 25. Its history includes ties to such real and literary heroes as Ethan Allen and Ethan Frome, Ethan Hawke and *Mission Impossible*'s Ethan Hunt. **ETAN** and **EITAN** are modern Hebrew spellings; in that language the name is pronounced Ay-tahn, with both syllables given equal stress, and means "firm and strong."

EUGENE. This Greek-based name, which belonged to no less than four popes, had a long run of popularity—from about 1875 to the 1940s—but it's definitely in limbo now. As Jim Carrey said in an interview, "My middle name is Eugene. I always figured my parents named me that to keep me humble. You can never get too cool with a name like Eugene." If you like the *eu* sound, though, some more modern alternatives might be the British **EUAN,** or **EWAN** or **EWEN**—as in hot young actor Ewan McGregor—which are Scottish and Welsh forms of John.

EUSTACE. As sedate and stuffy as the monocled Eustace Tilley of *New Yorker* magazine fame, Eustace is a Greek name that belonged to a saint who was said to have been converted to Christianity by the vision of a crucifix between the antlers of a stag as he was hunting. Its twentieth-century claim to fame is that it gave birth to Stacy, once an androgynous nickname name but now purely a girl's choice.

EVAN. This Welsh version of John has a mellow nice-guy image, one that's propelling it toward the Top 50. Bruce Springsteen's son is named Evan James. The longer form **EVANDER** was a name prominent in Greek and Roman mythology; in classical lore he was an Arcadian hero who founded the city in Italy that preceded Rome. And of course the legendary Evander of today is boxing champ Holyfield.

EVERARD. Hardly ever used here, Everard is a decidedly upper-class name in England. Decidedly. **EVERETT** is a somewhat formal and stately surname name spin-off, chosen by writer John Irving for his youngest son.

EWAN. See **EUGENE.**

EZEKIEL. The name of this visionary Old Testament prophet—actor Beau Bridges has a son named Ezekiel—is most often reduced to the nickname **ZEKE** when used by modern parents.

EZRA. A Hebrew name that is both heroic and somewhat quirky. According to the Bible, Ezra led a group of fifteen hundred Israelites out of slavery in Babylon and back to Jerusalem. A more familiar Ezra is poet Pound. Comedian Paul Reiser named his son Ezra Samuel.

F

FABIAN. Fabian still has a 1960s teen-idol aura, reminiscent of beach-blanket movies—even though the singer was never in one—and songs like "Hound Dog Man." Before that it was the name of a third-century pope, and a socialist society associated with George Bernard Shaw. **FABIO,** on the other hand, has long leonine hair, a seductive Italian accent, and glistening biceps, just like the model of that name.

FARRELL. Farrell is a strong Irish surname—it means "man of courage" in Gaelic—that would be far preferable to the outdated Darryl at this point.

FELIX. A very adult yet feline name, from the Latin meaning "happy and fortunate," Felix is definitely on the upswing: It's already made inroads with the swank Sloane Rangers of London. In the past, it belonged to no fewer than four popes and sixty-seven saints, and for a while suffered from its affiliation with the overly fussy Felix Unger character in *The Odd Couple*.

FERNANDO, FERDINAND. The sexier Spanish Fernando is the version that makes the hit parade here. For years, the name was associated with the quintessential Latin lover, Fernando Lamas, as well as with baseball hero Fernando Valenzuela. Bulkier and less graceful, maybe because of the bull, Ferdinand was a handsome young prince shipwrecked on Prospero's island in Shakespeare's *The Tempest*. British actor Ben Kingsley has a son named Ferdinand.

FERGUS. A traditional name in both Scotland and Ireland, Fergus sounds much better when spoken with an Irish brogue. In Celtic lore, Fergus was the ideal of manly courage, and it was also the name of ten Celtic saints.

FIDEL. The name Fidel, undoubtedly in honor of Castro, squeaks onto the Top 1,000 in this country. Not surprisingly, it means "loyal."

FIFE, FYFE. A Scottish place-name occasionally used there as a first and a possible import to our shores.

FINIAN. As Irish as Irish can be, this lilting saint's name shone in neon lights on Broadway, via the classic musical *Finian's Rainbow,* later made into a film staring Fred Astaire as Finian McLonergan. Finian O'Toole was a character on *General Hospital.* **FINNIAN** is another spelling; **FINNEGAN** is a related surname; **FINTAN** and **FINBAR** are native names well used in Ireland that could easily be adopted here. Any of these may be abbreviated to the even more appealing Finn, the name of one of the greatest heroes of Irish mythology (with one of the coolest names ever), Finn McCool.

FINLAY. This Scottish royal name (it belonged to the father of Macbeth), which sounds a tad fusty, is rarely heard on these shores but may be considered along with other surname names. Corbin Bernsen and Amanda Pays have a Finlay, as does actress Sadie Frost.

FINN. A name with enormous energy and charm, Finn has a rich and vivid heritage, having belonged to the greatest of all mythological Celtic heroes, Finn MacCool, an intrepid warrior with mystical, supernatural powers, noted as well for his wisdom and generosity. The name, which means "fair-haired" in Irish Gaelic, is now also used in Norway and Denmark. Actor Zen Gesner, no slouch in the name department himself, has a son named Finn.

FISHER. If Cook and Sailor can be used as first names, why not Fisher? Or, taking the name in a different direction, why not **PIKE, TROUT,** or **PERCH**? And going yet another way, **FISK** means "fish" and has a brisk surname appeal.

FITZ+. Any number of Fitz names—**FITZROY, FITZGERALD, FITZPATRICK, FITZWILLIAM**—have been used as Christian names, but be warned that there used to be a tradition that Fitz names were given to the illegitimate sons of royalty. Fitzwilliam was the Christian name of the dashing Mr. Darcy in *Pride and Prejudice*.

FLANN. A friendly, freckle-faced Irish name that started life as a nickname meaning "red-haired." Flann O'Brien (born Brian O'Nolan) was a well-known Irish columnist and novelist. Potential problem: Too reminiscent of the Spanish custard? **FLANNERY,** also a girls' name via writer O'Connor, is another, non-food-related possibility.

FLETCHER. A straitlaced surname with a touch of quirkiness—mainly because of the nickname **FLETCH,** used for the protagonist of a couple of clever Chevy Chase movies based on novels by Gregory McDonald. Fletcher originated as an occupational name meaning "arrow-maker."

FLINT. You can't find a much tougher, steelier sounding name than this; macho to the max. Unfortunately, it also has over-the-top soap-operaish overtones.

FLORIAN. Its first syllable gives this name a blooming, flowery, almost feminine feeling. Florian is the patron saint of those in danger from water, be it from floods or drowning. It's a popular name in Germany.

FLOYD. Somewhere along the line, Floyd has developed an almost comical hayseed persona—quite a contrast to its origins as an Anglicization of Lloyd, said to have come from the inability of the English to pronounce the double *l* of the Welsh name.

FLYNN. An Irish family name, Flynn has an easygoing, casual, cowboy kind of feel. It was chosen by James Earl Jones as the first name of his son. It's also the middle name of two other starbabies: Gary Oldman's Gulliver Flynn and Elle Macpherson's Arpad Flynn.

FORBES, FORD. Two surname that convey that rich family feeling, Forbes thanks to publisher Malcolm Forbes and Ford to car magnate Henry Ford. Or you can get straight to the point and name the child **FORTUNE.** Ford Madox Ford was a writer.

FORREST, FOREST. A sylvan name made famous by the redoubtable Forrest Gump, Forest's strong but sensitive, down-to-earth yet distinctive image is furthered by newsman Sawyer, actor Whitaker, and ex-Green Bay Packer Gregg. Three other virile surname names with the same touch of gentility: **FOSTER,** which like Forrest was originally an occupational name meaning "woodsman"; **FERRIS,** used in France and Ireland to indicate an iron worker; and **FAULKNER** (originally **FALKNER**), which means "falconer" and is perfect for fans of writer William.

FOX. A nature name with real possibilities. The only caveat: Your adolescent Fox better be attractive.

FRANCIS. This name, which was in the Top 10 at the turn of the last century, has been pretty much confined to Irish and Italian Roman Catholics in the past decades (e.g., Francis Albert Sinatra, F. [Francis] Scott Fitzgerald, Francis Ford Coppola), and still has something faintly sacrosanct about it. The fact that it means "Frenchman" in Latin accounts for the name change of Saint Francis of Assisi, who was born Giovanni, then nicknamed Francis because his wealthy businessman father had taught him to speak French. A deeply spiritual man, he devoted himself to caring for the poor and infirm, established the Franciscan order, was said to have been able to communicate with animals, and was made the patron saint of ecology. Another Francis, Saint Francis de Sales, is the patron saint of writers and editors. Today, the name is more often found as a middle name than as a first—it's the middle name of such disparate characters as Regis Philbin, Jon Bon Jovi, and the young son of rocker Liam Gallagher—and takes a back seat to the Latin form **FRANCISCO** or **FRANCESCO.** But Francis may receive some support via the appealing oldest brother in *Malcolm in the Middle.*

FRANK, FRANKLIN. Frank, a diminutive of Francis and Franklin, has been standing on its own since the seventeenth century. On the Top 20 list in this country from 1875 through the 1930s, it is now a warm and friendly grandpa name, a conceivable style heir to Max and Sam. Franklin, the name of two Presidents, is much less approachable (and usable), more the name of a distant ancestor, though Roosevelt admirers may find it an honorable choice.

FRASIER. Dr. Frasier Crane made this name popular—maybe too popular, as it hasn't achieved the success of other surname names. Other spelling possibilities: **FRASER, FRAZER, FRAZIER.**

FREDERICK, FREDERIC. When that somewhat pretentious but voguish couple, the above-mentioned Frasier and Lilith Crane, tagged their telebaby Frederick, a lot of people sat up and took notice, and a name that had hardly been used for half a century suddenly started to sound kind of spiffy again. Before that it had taken on a rather forbidding, foreign, uptight, military air, reminiscent of Frederick the Great, the enlightened King of Prussia who laid the foundations of the powerful Prussian empire. For African-Americans, it can be seen as a hero name, honoring Frederick Douglass, who rose from slavery to power as a political activist. But most Fredericks inevitably wound up as **FRED**s, a far more genial, neighborly moniker, as in Flintstone, MacMurray, Mr. Rogers, and even Astaire. The German diminutive, **FRITZ,** is also occasionally used, usually in families of German or Swedish origin. **FREDRICK** and **FREDRIC** are other acceptable spellings.

FRISCO. A swaggering, frisky, roguish place-name, but perhaps not sturdy enough for a real live human.

FROST. We're warming to this name, which has a surname appeal akin to Forest, but without the Gump connection, a connection with the venerable poet Robert, as well as a nature association.

G

GABRIEL. Gabriel is one of the newest entrants to the boys' Top 50. A hearty, upbeat name with multiple religious overtones: Gabriel is an archangel who appears in Christian, Jewish, and Muslim texts, the angel of mercy, life, joy, judgment, truth, and dreams, who presides over Paradise. In addition to all the above responsibilities, Gabriel is the patron saint of broadcasters and diplomats, and governs Mondays and the month of January. An appealing alternative to the ubiquitous Michael as well as to some of the more common biblical boys' names, such as David and Daniel, it has been chosen for their sons by a range of celebrities, including Mick Jagger and Jerry Hall, Daniel Day-Lewis and Isabelle Adjani, Jason Alexander, Amy Irving, Meredith Vieira, and Mia Farrow.

GAGE. A name that owes its popularity and in fact its very life to the current craze for surname names, Gage has risen from obscurity to its current standing among the Top 200 boys' names.

GALEN. Galen was the great second-century physician who formed the basis of early European medicine—and the name still projects a scholarly image, though perhaps is too close in sound to the female Gail for comfort.

GAMAL. An Arabic name meaning "camel."

GANNON. A surname used as a first name after an Irish leader, Gannon has a solid, yet spirited, feel.

GARDENER, GARDNER. Whichever way you spell it, this is one of the most pleasant and evocative occupation names going. Another surname spelling is **GARDINER.**

GARFIELD. This name is probably too tightly tied to the fat cartoon cat right now to be realistically considered for a human child.

GARRETT. An Irish-inflected name that's enjoying a new burst of popularity, solidly among the Top 100 boys' names. Chosen for their sons by football player Bo Jackson as well as actor Jason Gedrick, Garrett derives from **GARETH,** which is the Welsh for *gentle.* Gareth was a knight—and Lancelot's long-lost son—who sat around King Arthur's Round Table in Camelot. The related **GARTH** has taken on a pronounced country twang since becoming attached to Nashville megastar Garth (born Troyal) Brooks. Alternate Garrett spellings include **GARRET** and **GARETT; GARRICK** is a similar choice. And violà!, it becomes an Irish surname when you spin it to **GARRITY**.

GARRISON, GARSON. Two related surname names notable for their famous bearers, radioman/writer Garrison Keillor and director/writer Garson Kanin.

GARY, GARRY. In 1950, the top nine names for boy babies were Robert, Michael, James, John, David, William, Thomas, Richard—and Gary, making it probably the first nonclassic name ever to crack the Top 10. The rise in popularity of the name can be traced directly to the rise in popularity of Gary Cooper who, ironically, was born Frank. His agent, who hailed from Gary, Indiana, suggested he adopt the name of her hometown. Now, forty years later, Gary/Garry has lost its glitter, although it is still borne by two of our most prominent cartoonists, Trudeau (born **GARRETSON**) and Larsen.

GASTON. A gallant Gallic name chosen by Jaclyn Smith for her son but, less attractively, also used for the vain antihero of Disney's *Beauty and the Beast*.

GAVIN. A Scottish-Welsh name that's less overused and fresher-sounding than the Irish Kevin, Gavin has been moving up the popularity charts over the past several years and is now poised to break into the Top 100. **GALVIN** and **GARVIN** are also found.

GEHRIG. This hero name is suggested only for the baseball fanatic family, especially since it is also tied to a disease. A few more baseball names to consider: **GRIFFEY, CLEMENTE, MARIS, SABO, KOUFAX, ROBINSON,** and **DIMAGGIO.** But make your child's life easier and use them as middle names.

GENE. A nickname name sometimes used in the past on its own, although strangely enough many of the most famous Genes were not originally called Eugene: G. Tunney was James, G. Autry was Orvan, and G. Wilder was Jerome. The Latin form, **GINO,** appears more often than the Anglo one.

GEOFFREY. This is the classic British spelling of what we almost universally condense to Jeffrey, except when we're writing a paper on Chaucer.

GEORGE. George was a name that, until recently, seemed eternally fifty-eight years old, with thinning gray hair and a Republican Party membership card. But a new feeling about such traditional names, especially for boys, has breathed some life back into George. It's got a good chance of joining such classics as Henry and Jack, John and Paul—and, not incidentally, Georgia—on the comeback trail. George (which is Greek for "tiller of the soil," or "farmer") was among the five most popular names in America from 1830 to 1900, and retained its position in the Top 10 until about 1950. It belonged to the king of Great Britain for 116 straight years, as well as to the patron saint of England, Saint George, who, by slaying the dragon, became the symbol of good conquering evil. America's most famous George, of course, is Washington. The attractive Italian version is **GIORGIO,** as in Armani. Celebrities with young sons named George include *CBS This Morning*'s Jane Robelot, Lesley-Anne Down, and Oliver Platt. Boxer George Foreman named all five of his sons George.

GERALD, GERARD. We've all known a dozen **JERRY**s, most of whom are in their fifties at this point, and although they are perfectly nice, we probably won't be naming our babies after them. If by some remote chance you do, you could make the name fresher by using the English pet form, **GED. GERALDO** and **GERARDO** have a bit more zest than the originals.

GERSHOM, GERSHON, GERSON. These are three versions of a biblical Hebrew name that was favored by the Puritans and, more recently, by Orthodox Jews.

GERVASE. This unusual saint's name was rarely heard outside Roman Catholic rectories until laid-back *Survivor* contestant Gervase made it famous, at least for fifteen minutes. The original Gervase was martyred in

Milan as a child, while the twenty-first-century one was voted off the island after refusing to eat a grub.

GIOVANNI, GIANNI, GIANCARLO, GIACOMO. We don't mean to lump all these names together by ethnicity, though that's exactly what we're doing. This is a group of Italian boys' names that is beginning to be adopted by American parents, sometimes because of their family heritage and sometimes because they are simply in love with Italy and its culture. Giovanni, which you may be surprised to hear is edging toward the Top 200 boys' names, is Italian for John, and is represented by up-and-coming star Giovanni (born Antonio) Ribisi. Its short form is Gianni, pronounced like Johnny, and Giancarlo is a double name, tantamount to John Charles. Giacomo, which Sting and Trudie Styler used for one of their sons, equals James.

GIDEON. An unjustly neglected Old Testament name—Gideon was both a judge and military leader of the Israelites—possibly because of all the jokes made about Gideon Bibles in hotel rooms. But it's an excellent choice for parents looking to move beyond the overused Benjamins and Zacharys, one you'd share with actor Mandy Patinkin.

GILBERT. A name with a sober middle-aged to elderly image, Gilbert once was attached to one of the dashing members of Robin Hood's band, and was considered ultradebonair in the days of silent movies. Its British nicknames, **GIB** and **GIBBY,** are spunky alternatives to the American **GIL.** Actress Connie Selleca, whose husband is named Gil, has a son called Gib. **GILBERTO** is sometimes found.

GILES. Pronounced jiles, this is one of those names that most Americans find too teddibly British to consider. Because its literal meaning is "young goat," it is sometimes used for Capricorn boys. And since it was at one time a Scottish girls' name, that might be a more dramatic way to look at it.

GLENN. Glenn appealed to a lot of post–World War II parents for its cool, leafy image, calling up the sweet sounds of Glenn Miller and the calm, composed impression of Glenn Ford, whose name at birth was the Welsh

GWYLLYM (those were the days before ethnic names were in). Now Glenn is no longer fresh, yet not old enough to sound new again—except maybe for a girl. **GLYN** is a Welsh name with the same meaning and a less familiar, but more conventionally feminine sound.

GODFREY. The downside of this name, which was very popular in the Middle Ages, is that it might be difficult for a boy to handle a name with God as the first syllable. And the upside? We're still thinking.

GOMER. It may surprise fans of Jim Nabors, Gomer Pyle, and the old *Andy Griffith Show* to learn that in the New Testament, Gomer was a grandson of Noah, and that he was never once quoted in the Bible as saying, "Aw-shucks."

GORDON. Gordon is an upstanding Scottish clan name, more substantial than the trendy Jordan, and would make a good conservative but not stodgy choice.

GOWAN, GOWER. A pair of Welsh names that, depending on which source you believe, relate to the occupation of blacksmithing or mean "pure."

GRADY. Another energetic, friendly Irish family name eminently usable as a first.

GRAHAM. Although this jaunty Scottish clan name has been very popular in England since the 1950s, it is just beginning to catch on here. The Scots sometimes spell it **GRAEME,** and the Brits use **GRAM** as its nickname. Warning: A child with this name might have to endure a couple of years of graham-cracker jokes.

GRANT. This onetime beach-boy name, compadre of Glenn, Greg, and Gary, is inching back up the popularity ladder along with seemingly every other surname name in existence.

GRAY, GRAYSON. Original form Grayson is by far the more popular of this pair, surprising to us until you consider that it's got that all-important surname feel. And while Gray is, to our thinking, a choice made all the more attractive by its simplicity, some parents may feel it's a bit somber. Gray Davis, governor of California, certainly conveys the name's dullness with none of its dash. **GREY** and **GREYSON** are the alternate spellings.

GREGORY. This Greek name that was the second most common papal name (no fewer than sixteen popes, not to mention at least fifteen saints, were called Gregory), has been big in this country since the emergence of Gregory Peck (born Eldred) in the late 1940s, and is only now beginning to slip in the popularity polls. These days, though, kids with this name are more likely to be called Gregory than the Brady-Bunchish **GREG.** Television's Ray Romano has a son named Gregory. **GREGOR** is a version rising in popularity in the British Isles.

GRIFFIN, GRIFFITH. Griffin, an Irish last-name-first name, is on the upswing. Griffith, the Welsh version, is still much quieter, probably because that lispy ending is just more difficult to say and to live with.

GROVER. Forget the furry little blue Muppet by this name. Forget corpulent President Cleveland (who was born Stephen anyway), and consider this name anew. We think it's spunky and a little funky and well worth a second look.

GULLIVER. Gulliver was the traveler and only the traveler until actor Gary Oldman chose this unusual name for his son.

GUNNAR, GUNNER, GUNTHER. Gunnar/Gunner is a name on the way up, but we doubt it's because parents have discovered en masse the appeal of this traditional Scandinavian favorite. Rather, we think Gunnar/Gunner is being favored—Motley Crue's Nikki Sixx chose it for his son—for its surnamey and perhaps (though we shudder to think so) occupational image. No doubt about it, it's a macho name. Evidence: The original form Gunther is enjoying nowhere near the success of offshoot Gunnar or its Americanized spelling.

GUS. Gus is a homey, slightly grizzled grandpa nickname name that's knocking at the gates of style heaven, hoping to take the place of Max and Sam.

Most fashionably used on its own these days, Gus can also be short for an unusual number of different names, including **GUSTAVE/GUSTAV** (a royal name in Sweden), **GUSTAVO** (the only one of this bunch actually to crack the Top 1,000), Augustus, Augustine, Angus, and, in the case of Gus the Theatre Cat in T. S. Eliot's *Old Possum' s Book of Practical Cats*—Asparagus!

GUTHRIE. This attractive Irish name has a particularly romantic windswept aura, with a touch of the buckaroo thrown in.

GUY. Sesame Street and Guy Lombardo to the contrary, this name still feels upper-crust English to most Americans (think of Madonna's British husband, director Guy Ritchie), or else a bit too everyman to be used for their own little guy. Guy is, however, the patron saint of comedians and dancers. Latinate form **GUIDO** may be used here as an epithet denoting a guy who might be one of Tony Soprano's lieutenants, but throughout Europe, believe it or not, it's a chic choice.

H

HABIB. Habib is a North African name, particularly popular in Tunisia and Syria, meaning "beloved." This Swahili and Muslim name belonged to the first president of Tunisia, Habib Ben Ali Bourguiba.

HADRIAN. Most parents would find this old Roman name pretentious when compared with the more accessible Adrian, but some history buffs might just want to commemorate the enlightened emperor, who was also a scholar, poet, and musician, most famous for building a wall across northern England.

HAKEEM. Increasingly used in America, this Muslim name is also popular in Ethiopia and the Sudan. In Arabic it signifies "wise, all-knowing ruler," one of the ninety-nine qualities of Allah listed in the Koran.

HALE. The name Hale projects a sense of well-being (it does come from the Old English meaning "healthy"), but is also a bit cold. Possibly better as a middle name choice.

HALIFAX. Do you want to honor your grandfather Hal but can't rev up too much enthusiasm for his full name of Harold? Consider the more stylish Halifax, a place-name (the capital of Nova Scotia) that has an abundance of energy and class, if a bit of pretentiousness.

HALVARD. Halvard was the patron saint of the Norwegian capital, Oslo. He was famous for his compassion, and the name has a certain stalwart strength.

HAMILTON. Unless it runs in your family, or Alexander Hamilton is a particular hero of yours, you might want to consider something not quite so imposing, and with a less teasable nickname than **HAM.**

HAMISH. This warm, fuzzy Scottish name, pronounced with a long *a*, is a form of the Gaelic Seamus, which in turn is a form of James. While a bit too foreign for most tastes in this country, it does also mean "homey, comfortable, and unpretentious" in Yiddish.

HANS. Although this German, Dutch, and Scandinavian form of John (via **JOHANNES**) is familiar to all of us because of such childhood icons as Hans Brinker, Hans(el) and Gretel, and Hans Christian Andersen, few Americans have chosen it as a name for their children because of its intractably Old Country image. **HAN,** as in Star Wars adventurer Solo, may be a more contemporary choice.

HARDY. A spirited and durable surname that has been used as a first name abroad since the 1840s, Hardy is starting to be discovered in this country, fitting in with other names in this trendy category, like Harper and Brady.

HARLAN and **HARLEY.** Two once highly respectable, Waspy surnames, the latter has now become considerably more renegade because of its association with the motorcycle of the same name—which inspired nearly five hundred sets of parents to bestow it on their son in one recent year. Writer/director Kevin Smith named his daughter Harley Quinn (harlequin: get it?) after a *Batman* character.

HAROLD. This name belongs more to the turn of the last century than this one, having taken on a rather prim, pipe-smoking, bespectacled image. Its sole asset is the relaxed and newly stylish nickname **HAL**—a compatriot of such fashionable earthy guy names as Sam and Max, Jack and Harry.

HARPER. Harper has a sweet, gentle sound, with Southern overtones, and might be as likely a choice for boys as for girls. Harper Lee, author of *To Kill a Mockingbird,* was a female. Paul Simon chose it for his older son: it was the surname of the boy's mother.

HARRIS, HARRISON. Harrison Ford, aka Indiana Jones and Han Solo, is almost certainly the reason for the name Harrison's popularity—it is by far the more popular of these two choices, and also beats out its progenitor Harry.

HARRY. After years of being an all-purpose, regular guy, good-neighbor name, Harry has joined the contingent of fashionable names along with its parent name, Henry. Classic but not pretentious, Harry combines the accessibility of a grandpa with a princely history with the popular élan of Harry Potter. Young Potter, in fact, has made the name appealing to children in this country; they're less likely to snicker at its similarity to "hairy." In England, Harry is more firmly established—it has jumped to number 6—having been the nickname for all eight King Henrys. Actor Billy Bob Thorton's two sons have, improbably, the same names as those of the Princes of Wales: William and Harry.

HART. A soap-operaish name—what could better signal the presence of a romantic hero?—despite the poetic heritage of Hart Crane, who was born a Harold anyway.

HARVEY. At one time, there were so many dweebs on TV with this name that a league of Harveys (we're not kidding) was formed in protest or maybe self-defense. It's a name that is definitely in baby-name purgatory.

HASKEL, HASKELL. This intellectual-sounding name, not often used now, is, in fact, the Yiddish form of Ezekiel.

HASSAN. This Arabic name that translates to "handsome" is used by one Nigerian tribe for the first born of a pair of male twins.

HAYDEN. Moving up the popularity ladder arm in arm with brethren Braden, Caden, and Jaden, Hayden (or **HADEN**) is actually quite a common name in Wales. Originally a place or occupational name referring to hedges, related choices include **HAWES, HAWLEY, HAYES, HAYWARD,** and **HAYWOOD/HEYWOOD.** Musical parents may prefer to give it a different twist with **HAYDN** (pronounced Hi-den) as in the composer.

HEATH. This romantic-sounding surname name is near certain to rise in popularity over the next several years in tandem with that of hot young Australian star Heath Ledger. The related but over-the-top **HEATHCLIFF** is, of course, the hero of *Wuthering Heights,* as well as a very fat comics cat.

HECTOR. This heroic ancient Greek name is used primarily by Latino families in this country. Hector was the most noble of all the Trojans in Homer's *Iliad,* incorporating such laudable virtues as compassion, loyalty, and physical strength.

HELLER. If Harley and Gunner are on the rise, can Heller be far behind? While the surname name is German for "brilliant," we fear the future of any child named Heller would be anything but.

HENRY. If you haven't hung out at a playground lately, or checked the "Passages" section of *People,* you may not be aware that Henry is among the hottest names around, chosen for their boy babies by such high-profile parents as Meryl Streep, Julia Louis-Dreyfus and Brad Hall, Viggo Mortensen, Patricia Richardson, Dennis Hopper, and Daniel Stern. Henry is also the middle name of the sons of Meg Ryan and Dennis Quaid and of Michelle Pfeiffer and David E. Kelley, plus it was the real first name of Indiana Jones. It's one of the few illustrious, classic male names not overused to the point of cliché in recent years, sounding both more distinctive and more interesting to the contemporary ear than Richard or Robert or John or James. And maybe more fussy, to some: Henry is coming off a long decline that followed its status as sixth most popular boys' name in 1930. It was sixth most popular in 1830 too, and has a distinguished royal (eight British kings, plus the current prince) as well as literary (Longfellow, James, Thoreau, to name a few) tradition. Although most modern parents prefer to use the full and formal version of the name, another of Henry's charms is its range of attractive nicknames: from Harry and Hal to **HANK,** in honor of baseball great Henry Aaron or music great Hank (born Hiram) Williams.

HERBERT. With the exception of Robert, all names ending in *bert,* from Norbert to **EGBERT** to **DILBERT** are now in terminal exile.

HERMAN. This old German name, which became associated with certain enemy leaders during World War II, fell into definitive disfavor at that time, and has by no means recovered, not having been helped by the Frankenstein-looking Herman Munster. If you're really thinking about Herman for some personal reason, you might want to consider the French version, **ARMAND,** or the Spanish **ARMANDO.**

HERMES. With the rising fashion status of names from mythology, the name of the Greek messenger god—he was the one with wings on his feet—may be worthy of consideration. Style bonus: It's also the name of an upscale designer label, and should be pronounced air-MEHZ.

HERSCHEL. The Hebrew word for "deer," this name takes many forms, including **HERZL, HESHEL,** and the shortened **HERSCH, HIRSCH, HIRSH,** and **HERSH.** Its most prominent bearer is football great Herschel Walker, who may have been among the few tough enough to withstand the inevitable Hershey bar nicknames.

HILARY. With the advent of Mrs. Clinton, Hilary has lost whatever masculine potency it possessed, despite the fact that the name was 100 percent male until the 1890s. Coming from the Latin, meaning "cheerful," it was the name of one of the most esteemed theologians of his time, Saint Hilary of Poitiers.

HILLEL. This popular Israeli name derives from the Hebrew word for "praised"—Hillel the Great was a famous Talmudic scholar of the first century A.D., who fostered a systematic, liberal interpretation of Hebrew Scripture and was the spiritual and ethical leader of his generation.

HILTON, HYATT. Two surname names to use only if you wish to imply a family connection to the hotel chains.

HIRAM. This is the kind of biblical name that adventurous parents who wish to move beyond David and Daniel are beginning to consider for their sons, even though Hiram still has large pieces of its old repressed, stiff-collared image clinging to it. Coming from the Hebrew meaning "noble brother," the name belonged to an Old Testament king who helped Solomon plan and build the temple in Jerusalem, and was a favorite in the eighteenth and nineteenth centuries.

HOGAN. A vibrant Irish surname, sometimes associated with the 1960s TV show *Hogan's Heroes* or wrestler Hulk Hogan.

HOLDEN. Closely tied to the character of Holden Caulfield in *Catcher in the Rye,* with whom almost every adolescent in America has probably identified at some time, Holden has a correspondingly complex image—preppy, angst-ridden, and rebellious. Edging up in the popularity polls and sure to go higher, Holden was chosen for their sons by actor Rick Schroder and comedian Dennis Miller.

HOMER. This name has traveled an odyssey from ancient Greece, where it was the name of the composer of the greatest classical epics, to becoming a proper Victorian name given to future politicians and captains of industry, to the name of Bart Simpson's doltish dad. But Simpson's creator Matt Groening chose the name Homer for his son—as did Richard Gere and Carey Lowell (after Gere's father) and actor Bill Murray for theirs.

HOPPER. A surname name (as in painter Edward and actor Dennis) chosen by Sean Penn and Robin Wright for their son.

HORACE. Horace is hopelessly mired in its bespectacled, feeble, elderly image, made even worse by its similarity to "horrors." Its most famous bearer was newspaper publisher Horace Greeley, famous for saying, "Go West, young man."

HORATIO. Last heard of as the middle name of former Vice President Hubert Humphrey, Horatio actually has an exotic past, and just could be considered for a comeback. It was the given name of Lord Nelson, one of the most dashing of British heroes, the naval commander who led the British fleet to destroy the French at Trafalgar, and also belonged to Hamlet's loyal friend. **HORACIO** is the Spanish version (pronounced or-AH-see-o).

HOSEA. There are many Hebrew prophet names, including Joel, Amos, Daniel, Jonah, Nathan, and Samuel, and Hosea is one of the least used, so this might fit the bill if you feel adventurous and are looking for a distinctive biblical option.

HOUSTON. This lanky, roguish place-name is right in style, with its Texas accent and hip cowboy boots. A more distinctive alternative to Austin or Dallas.

HOWARD. This is a real dad-granddad kind of name. It started life as an aristocratic family name, gradually metamorphosing into a first name in the nineteenth century. It was in the Top 50 list in this country from the 1870s to the early 1950s, but the thought of naming a baby Howard right now seems less likely than using Horatio. Weird trivia item: Vampire novelist Anne Rice's given name is Howard Allen—and yes, she's always been female. **HOWIE** is the dweeby nickname.

HUBERT. This name may mean "brilliant mind or spirit" in Old German, but it comes as close to being spiritless as any modern name we can think of, and probably did nothing for Hubert Humphrey's image. Variants **HOBART** and **HUBBELL** have a bit more style due to their surname sounds.

HUDSON. It's a last name—that of one of the hottest young actresses around, Goldie Hawn's daughter Kate Hudson. And it's a river, one that runs down the west side of Manhattan, hotbed of trendy naming. So how can it miss as a baby name? It can't. Short form **HUD**, the name of the macho title character of an early Paul Newman movie, was used by rocker John Mellencamp and supermodel Elaine Irwin for their son.

HUGH. This name is patrician to the core—you can almost see its hair swept back, its nostrils flaring, wallet bulging: an image personified by the British leading man Hugh Grant—and is definitely fashionable with upscale Americans. The name, which means "intelligent," has always been particularly prevalent among the Irish—there have been twenty Irish saints by the name, and it's traditionally associated with the O'Donnell clan there. Hugh was an early emigrant to the New World: There were two of them in the first English-speaking settlement in America. Hugh's biggest drawback is its very sound, barely more than an exhaled breath. **HEW** and **HUW,** are the distinctively (probably too distinctively) spelled Welsh forms.

HUGO. The Latin form of Hugh, Hugo has more heft than the original and considerable energy; it's definitely an up-and-comer among those with high-fashion tastes—it was chosen by onetime First Daughter Amy Carter. It may be the most stylish boy baby name in London today and also holds appeal for Franco- and bibliophiles in its relation to writer Victor Hugo.

HUMPHREY. This name may still have a life beyond Bogart, the icon who was given the maiden name of his successful magazine illustrator mother, Maude Humphrey Bogart (who used baby Bogie as a model for baby-food ads). The name, which has a deep resonance, is a royal name in Britain, where it is used far more frequently than here. Relative **HUMBERT** is too close to *Lolita* antihero Humbert Humbert, though the Latin form **HUM-BERTO** is given to several hundred American-born babies a year.

HUNTER. Hunter is a front-runner in the family-name pack, nearing the Top 25. It has a semibold, semiconservative, indoor-outdoor image, and is sometimes connected to gonzo journalist Hunter Thompson. Supermodel Niki Taylor as well as soap-opera star Jerry Douglas and E! correspondent Kymberly Douglas have sons named Hunter. While boy Hunters outnumber girls by about twelve to one, actress Hunter Tylo popularizes the name's feminine side. **HUNT** is the more active, less trendy, version.

HYATT. See Hilton.

HYMAN. Hyman means "life" in Hebrew, as does Chaim. Along with the pet form **HYMIE,** it was commonly used by first-generation Jewish immigrants in New York's Lower East Side and other ghettos, but it is not a name that appeals to the modern ear, too redolent, in any case, of terms like "heinie" and "hymen."

I

IAGO. This Spanish and Welsh form of James was tied in Shakespeare's play *Othello* to a villain so treacherous that it's never been heard of again.

IAN. This most attractive Scottish form of John was rather late making inroads on our shores—it was already the seventh most popular boys' name in England in 1965. After the emergence of Ian Fleming, creator of James Bond, Americans gradually began warming to the jaunty charm of the name; now it is finally gaining a foothold on some popularity lists, although at number 71 is not yet overused. **IAIN** is an alternate, authentic, but needlessly fussy spelling.

ICHABOD. An eccentric Old Testament name that took on a kind of goofy image thanks to the Disney animation of the innocent and shy schoolmaster Ichabod Crane in Washington Irving's *The Legend of Sleepy Hollow.* We can't imagine a parent of today naming a child "icky bod."

IGNATIUS. This was the name of several saints, including the early Christian martyr who was the first to use the word *"Catholic,"* a Greek churchman who was the patriarch of Constantinople, and also Saint Ignatius of Loyola, founder of the Jesuit order in the sixteenth century. As sanctified as it is, therefore, it is more apt to be borne by churches and schools than babies, though very religious parents might disagree and may even enliven the name by shortening it to **IGGY,** à la Pop. **IGNACIO** is somewhat more secular.

IGOR. A Russian name with unfortunate Frankenstein-assistant associations, but also some musical ones as well, such as composer Igor Stravinsky and the opera *Prince Igor*.

IKE. Freckle-faced and friendly, Ike is rarely used on its own; General/President Dwight Eisenhower and Mr. Tina not withstanding, it's most often a nickname for Isaac.

ILYA. This Russian form of Elias is occasionally heard in this country in families of Slavic heritage.

INDIANA. One of the new breed of popular place-names, its image is wedded to that of the dashingly adventurous Raider of the Lost Ark, Indiana Jones. **INDIO** is the unusual and exotic appellation chosen for their son by Deborah Falconer and Robert Downey Jr.

INIGO. Almost unknown in the United States, this name, with its strong beat and creative, evocative sound, is used primarily in England, Spain, and Russia. The only famous Inigo we know of is Inigo Jones, one of England's first great architects and stage designers. It's pronounced with short i's: IN-i-go.

INNIS, INNES. This Scottish place-name turned surname is now, occasionally used as a first name, though it is not one of the most attractive.

IRA. These days Ira is considered more an acronym than a proper name—be it as a retirement account or group of Northern Irish insurgents. Even when it was most widely used as a name, its image was somewhat on the soft side—though it is macho star Russell Crowe's middle name.

IRVING. Surprisingly enough, this name originated as a Scottish place and surname name (as in Washington Irving). It was a popular name for first- and sometimes second-generation Jewish-American boys, such as best-selling writers Irving Stone and Irving Wallace, although Irving Berlin changed his name from Israel. The sons and nephews of these gentlemen might have been called **IRWIN,** though their grandsons most definitely would not. **IRVIN** is a variation from the Gaelic meaning "handsome," and **EARVIN** is a basketball immortal. But if you think Irving is terminally uncool, consider that it's the full name of ultrahip actor Ving Rhames, whose imaginative shortening transforms and energizes it.

ISAAC. Isaac is one of the Old Testament names being dusted off by parents bored with Benjamin and Joshua, who've now catapulted it to number 53 on the hit parade. A favorite of the Puritans, Isaac went on to assume something of a bearded, rabbinical image. The biblical Isaac was the long-awaited son of the elderly Sarah and the even more elderly (he was one hundred) Abraham. The name means "laughter," since that was what it provoked when Sarah was told she would conceive at her advanced age. Baby Isaac lived on to marry Rebecca and to father Esau and Jacob. Celebrity baby Isaacs today include the sons of Mandy Patinkin and Annie Potts. Other distinguished bearers of the name include Isaacs (and **IZAAK**S) Newton, Walton, Bashevis Singer, Asimov, Stern, and Hayes, and it even appears on a daytime drama— *As the World Turns.* **IZZY** is the adorable nickname.

ISAIAH. Another biblical name being restored to its former glory—it's just broken into the Top 50—Isaiah was one of the greatest prophets of the Old Testament. Mia Farrow, one of the most creative baby namers in the annals of modern parenthood, has called one of her adopted sons Isaiah. Other parents may be inspired by longtime Detroit basketball superstar star **ISIAH** Thomas. Other forms include **ISAIAS, IZAIAH,** and **ISAI.**

ISHMAEL. The first line of the great novel *Moby Dick* is "Call me Ishmael," spoken by the book's young narrator. Although it is a perfectly respectable biblical and literary name, think about some of the more unfortunate nicknames it might invoke if you call your son Ishmael. Ishmael Reed is a noted African-American novelist and poet, Ishmael Merchant is a noted filmmaker. **ISMAEL** is also used.

ISIDORE. This name has one of the more surprising origins—how many people would be able to identify it as Greek? But it was, indeed, a common ancient Greek name belonging to several saints, including Saint Isidore the

Ploughman, patron saint of Madrid. It was adopted by Spanish Jews to the point where it became their almost exclusive property—**ISIDRO** is the now more common form.

ISRAEL. With the establishment of the state of Israel in 1948, this name was transformed from a traditional Jewish favorite into an icon of Judaism—one that was given, surprisingly enough, to more than 1,200 baby boys in the U.S. in the last year counted. In the Bible, Israel was the name bestowed upon Jacob after he wrestled with an angel.

IVAN. Whether pronounced with the accent on the first or second syllable, this Russian and Czech (as in tennis star Ivan Lendl) form of John is a bit harsh and heavy-booted. It is, however, number 151 on the boys' pop list: not too shabby. The pet name **VANYA** does a lot to soften it.

IVO. An interesting, unusual name with the energetic impact of all names ending in *o*. Hardly heard in this country, it is used a bit more frequently in England, as is the related **IVOR,** a favorite of such novelists as P. G. Wodehouse and Evelyn Waugh. A variant spelling is **IVAR** (A Norse god, popular in Sweden), and if you're looking for a really singular version, you might consider the Welsh **IFOR.** Yet another variant is **IVES,** sometimes suggested by astrologers for boys born under the sign of Sagittarius, as the name means "little archer."

J

JABARI. An Arabic name enjoying quiet use, with a few noted athletes to help promote it. **JABAR** and **JABIR** are related Arab choices.

JABEZ. A biblical name popular with the Puritans, the rarely used Jabez now has a distinct Southern accent and a sensual, anything but puritanical image. **JABOT,** in addition to being a lace frill, is a character on *the Young and the Restless.*

JACE, JAYCE. This name may have started out as initials—J. C.—that got transformed into something that blended the popular Jason and Macy.

Cute, but it's probably worth the effort to look for something with a bit more spine.

JACK. Jack is back, poised to enter the Top 50. This new old name is so durable, dependable, unaffected, and cheery it's being chosen for their sons by trendsetters in Hollywood and beyond, including Meg Ryan and Dennis Quaid, Susan Sarandon and Tim Robbins, Ozzie Osbourne, Ellen Barkin and Gabriel Byrne. Not to mention Luke Perry, Kirk Cameron, John Heard, Bill Pullman, Val Kilmer and Joanne Whalley, Tim Roth, Kim Delaney, Antonio Sabato Jr., and Christie Brinkley. Familiar to all of us from earliest childhood, via Jack and Jill, Jack Sprat, Little Jack Horner, Jack Be Nimble, Jack and the Beanstalk, Jack Frost, jack-o'-lantern, and jack-in-the-box, the name Jack was so common in the Middle Ages that it became a generic term for a man. Jack was originally a nickname for John, the name most of the leading Jacks of our time—Kennedy, Lemmon, Nicholson— were christened. Today's parents might go that conventional route, might choose to use Jack on its own, or might use the name as a nickname for another proper form. The French **JACQUES** is sometimes used—but that *q* adds something that fancifies the name's image in a way that's unappealing to most Americans. **JAQUAN** is another variation; **JOCK** is a Scottish form.

JACKSON. This stylish presidential name has moved up to the Top 75 and has also been the choice of several celebrities for their children, among them rocker Patti Smith, director Spike Lee, and Dixie Chick Natalie Maines. Some parents insist on inserting an *x* and making it **JAXON** or **JAXSON,** with the nickname **JAX,** now appearing on a soap opera.

JACOB, JAKE. It's official: Jacob is now the number 1 boys' name, a position it seized from Michael, which had held the crown for four decades. One of the most venerable of the Old Testament names, it's easy to see what makes Jacob so appealing: It conveys an image of honesty and warmth, and nickname Jake shares a certain unpretentious earthy feeling with equally stylish cousins Max, Sam, and, yes, Jack. Jacobs and Jakes abound among the junior celebrity set: Sting, Sinead O'Connor, Green Day's Billy Joe Armstrong, Dustin Hoffman, James Caan, Rhea Perlman and Danny

DeVito, and Nora Ephron and Carl Bernstein, have all chosen it for their off-spring. For you, this means that although Jacob/Jake is a fine name, it's also a very widely used one. In the Bible, Jacob, the youngest son of Isaac and Rebecca, husband of both Leah and Rachel, was one of the central patriarchs in the Book of Genesis, the twelve tribes of Israel evolving from his twelve sons. Name change: Jacob's name was changed to Israel after a wrestling match with an angel. **JAKOB** is the spelling used by the Dutch, Scandinavians, Germans, and the sons of Bob Dylan and Roseanne Cash; **JACOBY** is also found here. An interesting alternative nickname is **KOBY/COBY**. **JAGO** is the intriguing Cornish form.

JADEN. We never heard of this name before Jada Pinkett and Will Smith chose it for their son, and so assumed they'd invented it as a variation on Jada. Since then, two other celebrities have used it for their sons—Christian Slater (spelling it **JADON**) and Cheryl Tiegs—and the name has been zooming up the popularity lists. Its similarity to other trendy choices such as Braden and Caden, as well as to yesterday's oh-so-popular Jason, seem to predestine it for success. Variations—this is the kind of nontraditional name that spawns a lot—include **JAYDEN, JAYDON, JAIDEN,** and **JADRIEN.**

JAEL. This ambisexual Israeli name (pronounced yah-ehl), comes from the Hebrew for "mountain goat" and hence is sometimes used for children born under the sign of Capricorn. It is also spelled Yael.

JAGGER. Yes, this really was an authentic English name before Mick and before Pamela Anderson and Tommy Lee adopted it as the middle name of their son. It swaggers.

JALEN. Basketball star Jalen Rose is single-handedly responsible for the considerable popularity of this name, which basically didn't exist before he came along and is now number 108. That means there were more than three thousand little Jalens born in the last year tallied, as well as a few thousand more named **JAYLEN, JAYLON, JAYLIN, JAYLAN,** and **JALON.** The related **JELANI** was chosen for his son by actor Wesley Snipes.

JALIL, JALEEL. An Arabic name that reflects majesty, an attribute not particularly identified with Jaleel White in his portrayal of the nerdy Steven Urkel on *Family Matters*.

JAMAL, JAMAAL. Almost as popular in America as it is in the Sudan, this Muslim name means "handsome" in Arabic. It might have been given a push by the popularity of Malcolm Jamal-Warner on the old *Cosby Show*. **JAMAAL, JAMIL,** and **JAMEEL** are variations. The *ja* prefix is also used in such related choices as **JAMAR, JAMARI,** and **JAMARCUS.**

JAMES. James is one of the classic Anglo-Saxon names. Through the ages it's been biblical (the name of two apostles in the New Testament), royal (kings of both England and Scotland), presidential (there have been more United States presidents named James—six—than any other name), and menial (in the nineteenth century it was used as a generic term for a manservant, as in "Home, James!"). Right now it's upmarket and very popular—James is at the very top of the British list and among the Top 20 in this country. Mick Jagger and Jerry Hall have a little James, as does singer Liz Phair, actress Annie Potts, and Wonderwoman Lynda Carter. Rapidly disappearing are the nicknames **JIM, JIMMY, JIMBO,** and even **JAMIE**—baby Jameses tend to be called James. Actually an English form of Jacob, James has some interesting foreign variations: **DIEGO** and **JAIME** (Spanish), **JAAKO** (Finnish), **JACQUES** (French), **GIACOMO** (Italian), **SEAMUS** (Irish), **HAMISH** (Scottish), and **JAAP** (Dutch). The British have been using the catchy Cornish form, **JAGO.**

JAMISON and **JAMESON.** Literally "the son of James," these offshoots are making inroads in their own right. *Star Trek* star Jonathan Frakes and *General Hospital* star Genie Francis have a son named Jameson Ivor. James Belushi and William Baldwin both have *girls* named Jamison/Jameson—presumably since this is not Iceland and Jamesdotter would not be acceptable.

JAPHETH. This is the name of the youngest son of Noah, whose descendants were supposed to have populated Europe. It was well used by the seventeenth-century Puritans, but pronunciation difficulties would surely hinder its popularity in our day.

JARED. A name that's been hovering around the Top 50 for the past few decades, Jared is a sturdy, attractive, current, but not unduly trendy name that could be an inspiration to late-blooming parents. In the Bible, Jared was a descendant of Adam who became the father of Enoch at the age of 162. But lest you feel sorry for poor little Enoch, his father lived on for another eight hundred years. Paula Zahn chose the name for her son. There are several variations on the name: **JARROD, JARRED, JAROD, JARRETT, JARET, JAREN,** and even the surname **JARVIS.**

JASON. It was one of the buzz names of the 1970s, riding in with the posse of sensitive, new-manly monikers that resurfaced in the westerns of the period, following a century-long siesta. But Jason's long run of popularity eventually outran itself and the name came to be seen as a cliché of trendiness, as in the title of one of our other baby-naming books, *Beyond Jennifer & Jason*. Though still hanging on at number 40, it's more fashionable today as the name of gen x actors such as Jason Priestly, Jason London, Jason Lee, and Jason Biggs than as a newborn baby. This is one of the first names to inspire several spelling variations, including **JAYSON, JAYSEN,** and **JACEN.**

JASPER, JASPAR. Jasper has long been a hip and charming name in England and is beginning to be one here as well. Although it doesn't appear in the Bible, Jasper is the usual English form for one of the three Wise Men who brought gifts to the infant Christ according to medieval tradition, and it is also the name of a reddish semiprecious stone, one of the few such names for boys. One celebrated bearer of the name is artist Jasper Johns; jazzman Wynton Marsalis has a son named Jasper Armstrong.

JAVIER. The Spanish version of Xavier made double Oscar headlines when actor Javier Bardem was nominated for *Before Night Falls* and Benicio Del Toro won his award for the role of Javier in *Traffic*. Javier is widely used in Latino families—last year there were more than 5,700 Javier/Xaviers born in this country.

JAVON, JAVONTE. Two up-and-coming names. Javon, the more popular of the two, is made more attractive by its association with young jazz saxophonist Javon Jackson.

JAX, JAXON. See **JACKSON.**

JAY. At one time a few decades ago, Jay sounded more dapper than James, but certainly does no longer. Besides, most of the most notable Jays (Gatsby, Leno) started life as James anyway.

JEAN. The French for John sounds attractive when pronounced the correct way, zhan, but not when it sounds like Gene.

JEB, JED, JEDIDIAH. Jeb and Jed, shortened forms of such mouthfuls as Jedidiah, were used almost interchangeably in early TV westerns. Today, Jed's television exposure has gone upscale as the nickname of the president (his real name is Josiah) on *The West Wing*. And Jeb is best known as the name of the Florida Governor Bush, ex-President George Bush's son and President George W.'s brother. Jedediah was the name given by the prophet Nathan to Solomon in the Old Testament.

JEFFERSON. Presidential names—Tyler, Taylor, Madison, Carter, even Clinton, whose middle name is Jefferson—are decidedly in these days and Jefferson counts as a charter member of this stylish club. Used as a first name long before our surname-crazed era, Jefferson was most famously the name of President of the Confederacy Jefferson Davis. Even if you have no wish to honor these nineteenth-century political Jeffersons, the name may be of interest as a much fresher alternative to the outmoded Jeffrey. Actor Tony Randall named his late-in-life son Jefferson Salvini.

JEFFREY. Jeffrey just dropped out of the Top 100 and is heading for the Land of Daddom, as in "Jeffrey and Jennifer are proud to announce the birth of Jaden."

JEREMIAH, JEREMY. Jeremiah, the name of one of the chief prophets of the Old Testament, is moving up to the Top 100 after a long hiatus between the pages of a dusty Bible, taking the place of the overused Jeremy, which is falling in favor. Another interesting possibility is **EREMIAS.** The big drawback of all these names is the lack of viable nicknames, the British **JEM** sounding too feminine and **JERRY** being the name of the family dentist.

JERMAINE. Jermaine is as much a Jackson Family name as Tito and LaToya. A spelling twist on Germain, which originally indicated someone who came from Germany, the female version is the identical-sounding Germaine. Jermaine Jackson, by the way, topped his brother Michael's boy Prince on the royalty scale by calling his **JERMAJESTY.**

JEROME. This name has a bespectacled, serious, studious image, as well it might, since Saint Jerome was the brilliant scholar who translated the Bible from Greek and Hebrew into Latin and is now the patron saint of students, librarians, and archeologists. But, despite such varied namesakes as Kern, Robbins, Salinger, Seinfeld, and even "Chef" on *South Park,* and the Jude Law character in *Gattaca,* Jerome is definitely unstylish right now. Adventurous parents might want to consider the variants **JERONIMO/GERONIMO** or the Dutch **JEROEN.**

JERRICK. A product of the contemporary Scrabble approach to baby-naming, Jerrick replaces the *d* in Derrick/Derek with the more modern-sounding first initial *j*. Your response to this name will reflect your attitude toward this practice in general.

JERSEY. Like Brooklyn, Jersey is a northeastern place-name that started out playing baseball with the boys but is now more often found in the girls' locker room.

JESSE. The laid-back, easygoing cowboyish image of this name somewhat belies its biblical roots—Jesse was in fact the father of King David in the Old Testament. It came to the fore in the 1970s, as one of the fashionable ambigender, back-to-basics band, peaking in 1988, when it reached number 8 on the hit parade. These days, especially because of the long-running popularity of the female Jessica and Jessie, the name's energy has flagged and we feel it deserves a respite. The shortened form **JESS** is sometimes used independently, but feels a little flimsy.

JESUS. Widely used in Hispanic families (and pronounced hay-ZOOSE), but rarely in others, this name is currently in the Top 25 names in the state of Texas.

JETHRO. Jethro may mean "kindly and wise," "wealth and abundance," and may be the Old Testament father-in-law of Moses, but the name's popular image is pure rube, thanks partly to *Beverly Hillbillies* son Jethro, partly to country-music combo Homer and Jethro. The 1970s English rock group Jethro Tull was named after an eighteenth-century agricultural reformer. Some really adventurous parents might consider updating and urbanizing Jethro's image.

JETT. Perhaps because this was the name of the character James Dean played in his final move, *Giant,* Jett has a dark and dashing persona. John Travolta used it as his son's name in tribute to his aeronautical interests.

JEVIN, JEVAN. A newly created variation on the theme of Kevin, this name has a pleasant sound but no real history or meaning.

JEX. A decidedly offbeat name—we've run into only one of them—that combines jauntiness with sex appeal and would certainly set your son up for life outside the mainstream.

JINAN. This unisex Arabic name meaning "garden" or "paradise" is occasionally used by African-American parents.

JIRO. This is a Japanese name that is often given to the second son in a family.

JOACHIM. The name of a king of Judah, Joachim, pronounced Jo-A-chim, was in medieval Christian tradition the father of the Virgin Mary. Most modern baby namers would probably prefer the Spanish version, Joaquin, pronounced wha-KEEN (see below).

JOAH. An attractive, rarely heard biblical name made accessible via its familiar *jo* first syllable and kinship with the popular name Noah.

JOAQUIN. With the emergence of Joaquin Phoenix, the actor formerly known as Leaf, this Spanish version of Joachim has taken on a certain panache. Jimmy Smits chose it for his son.

JOB. With the rise of seemingly all the male Old Testament names, even Job has to be considered as a possibility, although it's hard to imagine many parents being able to ignore its heavy associations.

JODY. A quintessentially sweet and wide-eyed unisex name of the 1960s and 1970s Jody has none of the strength today's parents demand of a name. For many people it's still associated with the wistful young boy in the novel and movie *The Yearling*.

JOEL. Parents of the 1940s and 1950s who were trying to jazz up or formalize the old standby Joe revived the biblical name Joel, borne by one of the minor Old Testament prophets and the angel who suggested to Adam that he name all things. It was last heard from as a first name on *Northern Exposure* (Dr. Joel Fleischman) and, more recently, as the middle name of young *The Sixth Sense* star Haley Joel Osment.

JOHN. Without doubt the most timeless, perennially popular of all Christian names, John led the pack for four hundred years, from the time the first Crusaders carried it back to Britain until the 1950s. At that point, American baby namers finally seemed to be tiring of this most straight-arrow, almost anonymous John Doe, John Q. Public of names and started to replace it with fancier forms—Jonathan, Jon, the imported Sean and Ian. But now the pendulum appears to be swinging back, with John firmly ensconced once again in the Top 20, ahead of such trendoids as Jordan and Justin, and being embraced by such high-profile parents as Michelle Pfeiffer and David E. Kelly, Denzel Washington, Rob Lowe, and Jane Seymour. Once the name of one fourth to one half of all baptized boys in the English-speaking world, John was, of course, a key name in early Christianity, borne by John the Baptist, John the Apostle, John the Evangelist, plus eighty-four saints and twenty-three popes. Forms of John are often among the top choices in other counties as well and have sometimes been imported here—**IAN** or **IAIN** in Scotland, **EVAN** in Wales, **SEAN** in Ireland, Jean in France, **JUAN** in Spain, **JOHANN, JOHANNES,** and Hans in Germany, **JENS** in Scandinavia, **IVAN** in Russia, **JAN** in Holland, **JAÕA** in Portugal, **JANNIS** in Greece. That hottest of hot names, Jack, is sometimes used as a nickname for John, replacing the previously ubiquitous **JOHNNY**, which probably means the end of a whole genre of Johnny movies: *Johnny Allegro, Johnny Angel, Johnny Apollo, Johnny Cool, Johnny Dark, Johnny Dangerously, Johnny Guitar* et al.

JONAH. This would be an excellent choice for parents who are seeking a biblical name that is neither too popular (like Jacob or Joshua) nor too obscure (say Ozni or Uzi). In the familiar Old Testament story, Jonah was the prophet who disobeyed God, precipitating a storm at sea during which he was thrown overboard, swallowed by a whale, and then disgorged, unharmed, three days later. At the very least, the modern Jonah would be assured of a ready-made room-decorating motif. Jonah was the name of Tom Hanks's character's appealing young son in *Sleepless in Seattle.*

JONAS. Jonas, the Greek form of Jonah, has long been associated with Dr. Jonas Salk, developer of the antipolio vaccine. The first name of the skipper on *Gilligan's Island,* it has a more grandfatherly image than the English version does, but could be rejuvenated.

JONATHAN. This is the name that started to replace the stalwart John in the late fifties, sounding at once more suave, sensitive, and playful, as well as being both biblical and modern—and it's still going strong. At last count, Jonathan stood as the twenty-first most popular name in the country. In the Old Testament, Jonathan was the valiant eldest son of King Saul, and it was his loyal friendship with brother-in-law David that gave rise to the expression "Jonathan and David" to describe devoted, steadfast friends. It has been misspelled so often—both mistakenly and creatively—that **JONATHON** and **JOHNATHAN** have both come to be accepted forms. A far more unusual first cousin is **JONIGAN.**

JORDAN. Jordan is one of the few names now shared almost equally between boys and girls, although when this happens it's an almost sure bet that eventually it will be taken over by the female camp. Jordan has in fact always been a unisex name, originally given to a child of either sex baptized in holy water brought back from the river Jordan, the only river in Palestine. Its statistics are all over the board: It was the most popular name for African-American boys born in Texas last year, number 36 for all boy babies in the United States and 51 for girls. But whatever the numbers, it's had a trendy, ephemeral-sounding quality from the get-go and our advice is to seek something a little less faddish. An attractive Italian variant is **GIORDANO**.

JORGEN. See **GEORGE**.

JORN, JOREN. See **GEORGE**.

JOSÉ. With the rapidly growing Latino population, José is fast becoming one of the most popular boys' names in the United States. Last year it was in top place in both Texas and California. The Spanish version of Joseph, with many famous bearers ranging from baseball's José Conseco to opera's José Carreras, it has a couple of peppy nicknames: **PEPE** and **PEPITO**.

JOSEPH. One of the classic names in American nomenclature, Joseph continues uninterrupted in the favor of parents from many ethnic backgrounds. Through the 1940s and beginning again recently, Joseph has had some style power, but even when its fashion status was at its lowest ebb, it was a name with dual-religious appeal. In the Old Testament, Joseph is the twelfth and favorite son of Jacob and Rachel, in the New Testament it is the name of the upright carpenter husband of Mary, mother of Christ, and there is also Saint Joseph, the protector of working men. The nickname **JOE** is the all-time regular-guy name (as in regular Joe, Cowboy Joe, G. I. Joe, Joe Blow, etc.) and several celebrities, including Kevin Costner, Sting, Christine Lahti, and Patricia Heaton, have chosen it as a full name for their sons, while Kristin Scott Thomas, Patricia Richardson, Ray Romano, and Marilu Henner have opted for the complete version. Some foreign variations of interest: **JOSEF** (Scandinavian and German), **GIUSEPPE** (Italian), José (see above), **PEPE** and **CHE** (Spanish-speaking countries), **YUSUF** (Arabic), **JOOP** (Dutch), and **JOZIO** (Polish).

JOSHUA. After being one of the Top 10 boy baby names since 1983, Joshua is still the fourth most popular name in the country (reaching number 1 in Hawaii, and number 2 in Louisiana), indicating that there are masses of Joshuas and Joshes answering to that name. Why do parents like it so much? Because Joshua manages to retain a relaxed, attractive image, with a bit of the old West mixed in with its biblical persona. In the Old Testament, Joshua was the successor to Moses who finally led the Israelites, after many battles, into the promised land, thus inspiring the rousing hymn "Joshua Fit the Battle of Jericho."

JOSIAH. A biblical name with a quaint, old-fashioned charm, Josiah may well become more popular as parents seek worthy substitutes for such long-running favorites as Joshua and Joseph. It can be agreeably abbreviated to Joe— although on TV's *The West Wing*, President Josiah Bartlet (Martin Sheen) is nicknamed Jed. Josiah was the son of Jedediah, who succeeded his father as king of Judah when he was only eight years old. **JOSIAS** is the Greek version.

JOSS. Joss sounds like a hipper version of Josh, but it actually originated as a pet name for Jordan or Judah. Associated of late with the creator of *Buffy the Vampire Slayer*, Joss Wheden, it could make for an unconventional middle name.

JUAN. Juan is second only to José in popularity among Hispanic names and is familiar to all ethnicities through such references as Don Juan and San Juan. The Spanish form of John, it was bestowed on 1,880 babies born last year in the state of Texas alone.

JUBAL. A possible name for musical families: Jubal was the descendant of Cain who is credited in Genesis with the invention of the lyre, harp, organ, and other musical instruments. It's also associated with the joyful word "jubilee."

JUD, JUDD. Jud was originally a pet form of Jordan or Judah, but asserted its independence early on. The seminal Rogers and Hammerstein musical *Oklahoma!* celebrated the demise of its villain with the song "Poor Jud Is Dead." The name has been before the public eye via such actors as Judds Hirsch and Nelson for several decades now, and doesn't seem to have retained much dynamism.

JUDAH. This strong, resonant Old Testament name belonged to the fourth son of Jacob and Leah, founder of the twelve tribes of Israel. Though Judah is getting some attention along with the emerging wave of less common Bible names, it may be too reminiscent of the unpleasant **JUDAS** to become widely popular. In Hebrew, the name is **YEHUDA,** source of the words *Judaism, Jew,* and *Jewish.*

JUDE. Jude is a name that had been shunned in the past, partly because of its connection to the traitorous Judas Iscariot, then later to Jude Fawley, the tragic hero of Thomas Hardy's *Jude the Obscure.* Of late, though, a couple of things have happened to refresh its image. First there was the poignant Lennon–McCartney song, "Hey, Jude," and even more recently the emergence of the compelling British actor Jude Law, who has been quoted as saying his parents named him after the Hardy character. Saint Jude was the apostle who interceded for people with problems and became the patron saint of lost causes.

JUDSON. Most surname names—such as Parker and Carter, for example— don't have the kind of friendly, ready-made short form that this one does. And Judson could also be thought of as a less widespread alternative to Justin.

JULES. The French form (as in the classic Truffaut film *Jules et Jim*) of the name Julius, Jules is rarely given to contemporary babies, although it boasts such notable bearers as Jules Verne and Jules Feiffer. These days, it's more apt to be heard as a nickname for the female Julia or Julie.

JULIAN. Twin names Julia and Julian are very fashionable these days, Julian having successfully overcome the somewhat pale, almost effete image it projected in the past—not too surprising as it does, indeed, come from the Greek word meaning "soft and fair-complexioned," and for many centuries was used for women as well as men. Saint Julian the Hospitaler is the patron saint of travelers; other links to recognition include singer Julian Lennon, African-American activist/politician Julian Bond, the great jazz saxophonist Julian "Cannonball" Adderly, and the hero of Stendhal's *The Red and the Black.* Celebrities who have chosen the name for their sons include Robert De Niro and Lisa Kudrow. An unusual variation very occasionally used in England is **JOLYON,** the name of a character in the *Forsyte Saga* series.

JULIO. What with the popularity of the Paul Simon lyric about Julio down by the schoolyard, and the renown of Argentinean writer Julio Cortazar and singer Julio Iglesias, this much livelier Spanish version of Julius has become familiar to the non-Hispanic community and would make a great choice for a bicultural family.

JULIUS. Even if New Zealand-born, powerful female role-model Lucy (*Xena: Warrior Princess*) Lawless did choose this name for her son, most parents of today are opting for its softer, more modern-sounding derivative, Julian. Julius was the name of a Roman clan to which Caius Julius Caesar belonged, the given name of Groucho Marx and also basketball great Dr. J, Julius Winfield Erving II.

JUPITER. Though it has a hippyish feel, Jupiter has a legitimate history as a first name, used in this country as far back as the eighteenth century—in fact, Jupiter Hammon was the first African-American poet published here, in 1771. Jupiter reigned as the supreme deity of Roman mythology, god of thunder and lightning, who acted as conscience, protector, and guardian of his followers, and it is also the name of the largest planet of the solar system.

JUSTICE, JUSTUS. Parents' current search for names implying virtue— much easier to find for girls than for boys—has led to a minirevival of this long-neglected name in both its forms. Justus is actually a German offshoot of Justin, and has been borne by several noted scholars and scientists. Justice was the name chosen for his son by Steven Seagal.

JUSTIN. This crisp, British-inflected name has been fully embraced in this country, to the point where it is now high on popularity lists and consequently no longer sounds like such a fresh choice. For the last few years Justin has been favored by parents looking for a less conventional *J* name than older favorites like Joshua, Jason, Jeremy, and Jonathan. It stems from the Latin word meaning "upright," "righteous," and "true"—in other words, just. Saint Justin was the first great Christian philosopher, thereby becoming the patron saint of philosophers. A modern rep is heart throb Justin Timberlake of the group NSYNC. **JUSTINO** is the Spanish form.

K

KADEEM. An African-American name made familiar by the actor Kadeem Hardison, who first became known as Dwayne Wayne in the sitcom *A Different World*. It offers a fresher alternative to the better known Kareem.

KADIN, KADEN. This is the kind of newly coined boys' name parents are using in increasing numbers—others of the same contemporary-sounding ilk are Braden/Braeden and Jaden/Jayden. Also spelled **CADEN, KAIDEN,** or any other way you want to spin it.

KADIR. Kadir derives from the Arabic Qadir (many of the Arabic *k* names are phonetic versions of *q*-starting names), which means "capable" and reflects one of the ninety-nine attributes of Allah.

KAHIL. Meaning "young and naïve" in Turkish, and "friend" in Arabic, this is one of a group of similar names beginning with *k* that are being chosen by growing numbers of African-American parents.

KAI. This exotic name (which rhymes with "pie") is found in several languages: In Hawaiian it means "ocean" and in Welsh "keeper of the keys." But Kai is perhaps most famous as the name of the boy enchanted by the Snow Queen in the fairy tale. Kai's problem: It has a somewhat feminine sound, especially if mispronounced (as it well might be) as Kay.

KALE. Kale can be thought of as a nature name (that of the kind of healthy green vegetable we all optimistically hope our children will love) or a soap-style name—it belongs not to a character but to an actor on *Another World*.

KALEN. Another nouveau name reflecting the recent practice of adding an *n* or *en* to traditional boys' names, as in Bricen and Chasen.

KALIL, KAHIM, KHALIL, KAHLIL, KALEEL. In their sundry spellings, these names, first brought into the American consciousness by the popular inspirational Lebanese poet Kahlil Gibran in the 1920s and 1930s have various meanings (all of them pleasant) in various cultures: in Arabic it is "good friend," in Hebrew "complete, perfect," and in Greek, Kalil means "beautiful."

KALMAN. See **KARL.**

KAMAL, KAMIL. Both these names mean "perfect," one of the ninety-nine qualities of God listed in the Koran. They are also associated with the evocative lotus flower.

KANE. This soap-operaish single-syllable name is connected to both the Celtic (meaning "beautiful") surname and the name of the world's first murderer, the biblical Cain. When found in Japan and Hawaii, it expands to KA-neh. Another phonetic spelling would be **KEYNE** and it becomes a French place-name when spelled Caen.

KAREEM, KARIM. A favorite in Muslim countries, particularly in the Sudan, this Arabic name means "generous, noble, exalted," generosity being another one of the ninety-nine qualities of God listed in the Koran. Seven-foot-three-inch basketball star Kareem Abdul-Jabbar was born Lewis Ferdinand Alcindor, but changed his name to Kareem when he converted from the Catholic religion to the African-American orthodox Hanati sect. And now there is a second Kareem Abdul-Jabbar, the football pass receiver who adopted the name of his hero.

KARL. The somewhat severe German and Scandinavian form of Charles, Karl, quite appropriately, means "strong and manly." Translating it into other languages can have a softening (sometimes feminizing) effect: **KAREL** in Czech, **KALMAN** in Hungarian, **KALLE** in some parts of Scandinavia, **KAROL** in Poland. A contemporary sports hero is basketball star Karl Malone; Karl Lagerfeld is its fashion rep.

KEAN, KEANE, KEENE. In the Golden Age of radio, there was a series called *Mr. Keen, Tracer of Lost Persons,* and this surname name does have a sharp, investigative quality, not a bad one to impart to a child.

KEANU. This evocative Hawaiian name was brought to the mainland by actor Keanu Reeves. Born in Beirut to a part-Hawaiian, part-Chinese father, his name means "cool breeze over the mountains" in Hawaiian.

KEATON. Keaton has several notable surname associations, from Buster to Diane to the family on *Family Ties,* which affords it a certain warmth and sense of humor.

KEEFE. An energetic Irish surname (as in O'Keefe) occasionally used as a first. Possible problem: Will people think your little Keefe is a Keith with an enunciation problem?

KEEGAN. One of several similar Irish surnames, this one means "little fiery one," and it does have an animated, spirited feel. Spelling variations include **KEEGEN** and **KEAGAN**.

KEENAN, KEENEN. This upbeat Gaelic name (the Irish spell it **CIANAN**), which was the name of three Irish saints, is a very feasible choice. The grandparent generation may remember actor Keenan Wynn (born Francis), while younger folks will associate it with Keenen Ivory Wayans, one of the talented family of Wayans brothers and sisters.

KEIR, KEIRAN. See **KIERAN.**

KEITH. Strong but gentle, Keith is one of the Scottish surnames that, along with Douglas and Bruce, were considered the epitome of cool in the 1960s and early 1970s, just when teen heartthrob David Cassidy was playing a Partridge named Keith. Since then Rolling Stone Keith Richards and baseball great Hernandez have kept the name alive, but it's rarely used for babies these days.

KELBY. This British last-name-first name might appeal to the parent seeking a more masculine alternative to Shelby.

KELLAM. Kellam came into the spotlight as the character Kellam Chandler on the soap opera *Days of Our Lives* in the 1980s, but definitely has twenty-first-century possibilities, with its stylish *k* opening, its strong first syllable and softer second. Similarly, **KELLEN,** associated primarily with NFL star Kellen Winslow, could make a distinctive choice.

KELLY. When Bill Cosby's costar Robert Culp's character was given this Irish surname name in the 1960s series *I Spy,* it was a perfectly acceptable—and virile—male name. By the time of *Charlie's Angels,* a decade later, it had become almost exclusively female, and so it remains. Today's parents seeking a name with an Irish brogue would probably prefer an authentic first name, like Cormac or Declan, or a more substantial surname, such as Brannigan or Maguire.

KELSEY. If it weren't for Kelsey (Dr. Frasier Crane) Grammer, this name would be considered a completely feminine name. And although it isn't as widely used for girls now as it was in the Chelsea/Kelsey era of the early 1990s, we suggest that it best be left in the girls' camp.

KELVIN. An unfortunate cross between Kevin and Melvin.

KEMUEL. This infrequently heard biblical name belonged to a nephew of Abraham in the Old Testament, and might appeal to the parent seeking a name somewhat similar to the megapopular Samuel but far more distinctive.

KENDALL. This nature name—it's a river in western England—is one that today would have more power for a girl than a boy, especially since Ken is not a very au courant nickname. It was the kind of name often given to the stuffy butler in 1930s movies.

KENELM. This is one of the least known of the Ken names, making it the freshest sounding. The name of a venerated ninth-century saint, it has the somewhat meaningless—in our day anyway—literal meaning "brave helmet."

KENNEDY. Kennedy is currently a trendy name for both boys and girls, one of the leaders of the parade of Irish surname names, and now distanced to some degree from its relationship to the thirty-fifth president and his family. Kennedy has long been used as a first name in Ireland—King Kennedy of Munster was the father of the famous medieval high king, Brian Boru. Unfortunately, Kennedy translates from the Gaelic as "ugly head," a meaning certainly in contradiction to its once-shining image as the name of America's Camelot clan.

KENNETH. It may sound lackluster now, but in ancient Scotland Kenneth, which comes from the Gaelic meaning "handsome," was as dashing as a name could be. The first king of Scotland was Kenneth, and Sir Kenneth, a Christian Crusader, was the hero of the Sir Walter Scott novel *The Talisman*. Kenneth had its moment of glory in this country as well—it was among the Top 20 boys' names in 1925, and was still there in 1950, lasting even longer for nonwhite boys. And for many girls growing up, **KEN** was the name of Barbie's eternal boyfriend and ultimate dream date. **KENN** is an occult name for babies born under water signs—Pisces, Cancer, and Scorpio.

KENT. One of several no-nonsense, brief, brisk, one-syllable *k* names, Kent has both a noble old image (via the devoted earl who risked his life to save King Lear) and a more modern daytime-drama one (there have been Kents on both *All My Children* and *As the World Turns*). It can also be considered a place-name, when one thinks of the lush English county of that name.

KENYON. Kenyon is one of the more appealing British surname names, the middle *y* giving it a kind of a Southwestern, canyonesque undertone.

KERMIT. The question here is, can anyone forget the frog? This otherwise very appealing variation on the Irish name Dermot would, except for the powerful Muppet connection, be an ideal choice. It isn't easy being green.

KERRY. An Irish county but, more important, now a well-established girls' name that is occasionally used for boys, but shouldn't be. **KERRIGAN** is a much more modern and masculine choice.

KEVIN. Not too long ago, Kevin seemed to be the name assigned to every cute preteen boy in almost every sitcom and large-screen movie. Flash-forward to the present, and Kevin has grown into a young man, with his name reflecting an adult image, which explains why Kevin is being used as a baby name less and less frequently, replaced by a new batch of Irish names. Irish Gaelic for "handsome," it was first popularized by the seventh-century Saint Kevin, who founded a monastery near Dublin, distinguished by its scholarship, and who was rewarded by being made one of that city's patron saints. In contemporary America, Kevin has had a long run of popularity—well over thirty years, and we are still reminded of its charm via such leading men as Kevins Costner, Bacon, and Spacey.

KIERAN. This Anglicized form of the Irish name **CIARAN,** although widely used in both England and Australia (it's currently in the British Top 30), is just beginning to make inroads onto our shores. Meaning "dark-haired, dark complexioned one," it was the name of twenty-six Irish saints, including the Kieran considered Ireland's firstborn saint. A name with a strong, attractive, fashionably Irish sound, Kieran's one drawback is its possible confusion with such feminine choices as Karen and Kyra. **KIER** is an attractive short form, and some other similar Celtic surnames are **KIERNAN, KIERNEN, KEIRAN,** and **KEIREN.** We've also heard the variation **KIERCE.**

KILLIAN. A sprightly yet resonant Gaelic surname that was borne by several Irish saints and could make a distinctive replacement for the now feminine Kelly. Yes, Killian's Red is a trendy beer, and no, we don't think the first syllable would be a problem.

KIMBALL, KIM. If this old Welsh surname has never been heard very much as a first name, its short form surely has, albeit more for girls than for boys. It gained prominence through Rudyard Kipling's 1901 novel *Kim,* the story of a clever, orphaned Irish boy named Kimball O'Hara growing up in India. These days the full name Kimball would be preferable for a boy to the outmoded, feminized Kim.

KING. While some people might think of King as more of a canine choice, others see it as a strong name with lots of offbeat style and a full court of rich associations, from Elvis to Sky King to jazz great King Oliver to Martin Luther King Jr. Originally a last name evolving from the nickname for someone employed in a royal household, King later began to be used as a given name by plantation owners for their slaves. Today, King might be used on its own or as a short form of the geographical **KINGSTON** or the literary **KINGSLEY**, as in Amis.

KIP, KIT. These are two nickname names, usually short for Christopher, that are more prevalent in England and rarely used on their own even there.

KIRBY. An attractive English place-name with a sense of humor. Kirby Yorke is the name of the character John Wayne played in John Ford's 1950 epic western, *Fort Apache* (he also happened to play four other characters with the last name of Kirby), and Kirby Puckett is a retired baseball superstar.

KIRK. For more than half a century, this name was associated with one person: Kirk Douglas (whose given name was Issur), all through that period being used fairly sparsely as a baby name. It's definitely far more friendly and open than such similar one-syllable names as Kent and Kurt. A British surname (as in *Star Trek*'s Captain James Kirk) meaning "church," Kirk appeared in several soap operas and sitcoms of the 1980s, which didn't give it the impetus many other soap names had.

KLAUS. This German pet form of Nicolaus has some unpleasant associations—the Nazi Gestapo chief Klaus Barbie, for example. And while Santa Claus certainly projects a much more jolly persona, we don't think a modern American child would appreciate the inevitable teasing.

KNUT, KNUTE. The *K* is silent in this rarely used Scandinavian name that is, in this country, linked with a single figure—the iconic Notre Dame football coach Knute Rockne, further immortalized in the film *Knute Rockne, All American,* in which Ronald Reagan costarred as the Gipper. Long before that, the mighty Danish King Knute II, also called Canute, ruled over England, Norway, and Denmark.

KOBE. Young NBA sensation Kobe Bryant (who was actually named after a steak house in Pennsylvania) has brought a new name into the mix, a name

with all the star forward's high energy and appeal. Kobe is also a geographical name, that of a Japanese city near Osaka and Kyoto.

KOREN. An unusual and gently attractive Hebrew name that means "shining or beaming."

KRISHNA. Krishna is the name of the greatest of all Hindu gods, but is considered secular enough to be used for mortal children and is often found in
Indian families. J. Krishnamurti was a renowned Hindu spiritual teacher.

KRISTOFER, KRISTOFFER. This Scandinavian spin on Christopher gives
that enduring classic a lighter, more individual twist, but may ultimately
make it seem too airy. Despite singer Kris Kristofferson, **KRIS** is almost
always a girls' spelling.

KURT. It's difficult to separate this German name from the meaning of the
adjective, although some celebrity bearers, including Kurt Vonnegut and
Kurt Russell, have done their share to humanize it. Kurt is actually a German diminutive not of Curtis but of **KONRAD,** a name we prefer.

KWAME, KWAMI. This is a popular name among the Akan of Ghana for
boys born on Saturday. Kwame Nkrumah was the first president of independent Ghana in 1960, placing it in the category of hero names.

KYLE. Kyle was in the Top 20 through most of the 1990s and, although it is
just now beginning to slip slightly, this Scottish name is still appreciated by
large numbers of parents for its combination of simplicity, strength, and
style. It is, however, increasingly being used for girls as well, and whether
this will cause the name to fade completely among boys remains to be
seen. Deborah Norville chose it for her son, and Kyle Broslofski is probably
the least obnoxious kid character on *South Park*.

KYLER. For centuries, boys' names were considered sancrosanct, not to be
embellished or tampered with. All that seems to be changing in today's
more fluid baby-naming climate, and the addition of an *r* to Kyle, to make it

more "distinctive," relating it to the popular Tyler and Skyler, is an example of a practice that is becoming more and more prevalent. But in this case, we would vote for keeping Kyle Kyle.

L

LABAN. Less well known than his female biblical relations—sister Rebecca, daughters Rachel and Leah—and certainly less frequently used as a name, Laban, which means "white," and its diminutive **LAEB,** are occasionally found in Jewish families. **LABAAN** is a Somali boys' name.

LACHLAN. A name as Scottish as haggis and tartan plaid kilts, Lachlan has hardly been heard in this country in the past, but could blend in well with such Irish classmates as Liam and Lorcan—and the more closely related **LAUGHLIN.** A hot name in other English-speaking countries (currently top of the pops in Melbourne), it's also been heard on the soap opera *Days of Our Lives*. And since it derives from the Gaelic word referring to a "migrant from Norway," it would be perfect for a family that combines both Scottish and Scandinavian roots.

LADO. This singular African name is traditionally given to the second-born son in a family.

LAEL. Although this is an ancient Old Testament name meaning "belonging to Jehovah," it has a pleasant contemporary feel that might appeal to today's parents.

LAIRD. A Scottish name for wealthy landowners—lairds of the manor—this name projects an aristocratic image, with a pleasant Highland burr.

LAMAR, LAMONT. Two once-toney surnames that have lost their upperclass edge. Lamars Hoyt, Odim, and Griggs are acclaimed athletes, and Lamont Cranston will be remembered as the affluent young alter ego of *The Shadow* on the vintage radio series and later movie.

LANCE. Lance, like Thorne and Ridge, can be seen as one of the quintessential, over-the-top soap-opera names whether it actually is one or not, despite the heroic achievements of Lance Armstrong.

LANCELOT. Lancelot is one of those probably-too-loaded names to impose on a baby, in spite of—or because of—its rich legacy. In Arthurian legend, Sir Lancelot was one of the most dashing and romantic of the Knights of the Round Table, who eventually betrayed King Arthur's trust by having an affair with Queen Guinevere, which led to war.

LAND. Pioneer aviator Charles Lindbergh and his writer wife, Anne Morrow Lindbergh, had a son named Land, an attractive choice with more universal appeal than most of the place names. And as a word name, it has an appealing meaning whether you spend most of your time in the air or on solid ground.

LANE. This is a unisex name that is still perfectly viable for the males of the species, a surname that projects the pleasant picture of narrow, tree-lined country roads.

LANFORD, LANDON, LANDAN, LANGDON, LANGFORD, LANGLEY, LANGSTON. A group of names reserved for those with a legitimate ancestral connection, or who want to honor playwright Lanford Wilson or poet Langston (born James) Hughes, the latter chosen by Laurence Fishburne for his son. Of the assemblage, Landon is the one that seems to be getting the most attention from baby namers.

LARAMIE, LAREDO. Two swaggering Western place-names with a lot of cowboy bravado and panache, not yet trendy enough to be considered touristy.

LARS. Lars is a perfect candidate for a cross-cultural passport. The Scandinavian version of Laurence, it has been heard often enough in this country (particularly associated with Metallica's Lars Ulrich) to sound familiar and friendly, yet retains the charisma of a charming foreigner.

LATEEF, LATIF. A Muslim male name that is popular in North Africa and whose meaning in Arabic—"pleasant, gentle" (one of the ninety-nine attributes of Allah)—is reflected in its sound.

LAUGHLIN. See **LACHLIN.**

LAWRENCE, LAURENCE. A solid, sturdy name poised in that netherworld between stodginess and style, Lawrence had a long run of popularity, covering the first seventy years of the twentieth century, a fact to which the large number of balding, forty-five-year-old Larrys will attest. Going back further in history, it was a favorite in the Middle Ages, largely resulting from the fame of a third-century saint, and was revived in the Tudor period after Shakespeare bestowed it on the benevolent friar who married the young lovers in *Romeo and Juliet.* Lawrence of Arabia (Lawrence was his surname) added further dash, but of late the only fashionable young Laurence we've heard of was a girl (it's used as a female name in France). **LAURENT** is another French version, additional translations are Lars and Lorenzo (see separate listings), **LORENZ** (German), **LAURENS** (Dutch), and **LAURITZ** (Danish). **LOWRY** is a possible last name variation and there's a Scottish nickname with more life than Larry: **LAURO.**

LAZARUS. This is one name that most people would agree has too much heavy biblical baggage to be considered feasible for a modern baby. A Greek form of Eleazar, it belonged to two New Testament figures: the brother of Mary and Martha, who was raised from the dead by Jesus, and a beggar who appears in the parables. And to add to its problems, in the Middle Ages the name was used as a generic term for lepers.

LEANDER. This is an almost unknown name that we think is worthy of consideration, perhaps as a substitute for the overused Alexander. In Greek legend, Leander was the powerful figure who swam across the Hellespont every night to visit his beloved Hero, a priestess of Venus, but who was eventually drowned in a violent storm. **LEANDRO** is the Spanish form.

LEE. A name with a feeble shouldn't-I-be-a-middle-name? image, despite its long-term attachment to such macho men as Lee Marvin and Lee Majors (who was born Harvey Lee). Another famous Lee, Iacocca, was christened **LIDO**. All in all, new millennium parents would probably prefer a more substantial name, such as Liam or Leo.

LEIB. This Hebrew name has the literal meaning of "my roaring lion," but also sounds like the word for *dear*.

LEIF, LEAF. Two names with the same pronunciation but very different job descriptions. Leif, the name of the Norse navigator credited with discovering the New World, has an exotic Scandinavian feel, while Leaf, the former name of the actor now billed as Joaquin Phoenix, has a distinctly New Age, nature-boy aspect.

LEITH. An unusual Scottish surname with a substantial sense of weight, Leith could make an interesting alternative to the aging Keith.

LEMUEL. This unjustly neglected biblical name is much more strongly associated with the hero of Jonathan Swift's satirical *Gulliver's Travels,* than with the obscure Old Testament king of that name. If you're tired of the ubiquitous Samuel/Sam combo, you might want to consider the fresher Lemuel/**LEM**.

LENNON. When cool couple Patsy Kensit and Liam Gallagher gave their son this Beatle-inspired name, they joined the growing band of high-profile parents choosing to honor their musical heroes, including Mingus, Bechet, Presley, and Jagger.

LENNOX. This aristocratic Scottish surname and place-name has a lot of brute power, probably due to world heavyweight boxing champion Lennox Lewis. A more fine-china-shop image results when you spell it **LENOX**.

LEO. Consider it the Leonardo fallout factor if you will, but Leo has become one of the trendiest boys' names going right now, for babies and for movie characters as well (Robert Downey Jr., Dylan McDermott, and Richard Dreyfuss have all played Leos in recent films). Besides being the well-publicized nickname of di Caprio, Leo has a lot of other elements going for it. Its leo-nine associations suggest strength of character and physique. Its zodiacal reference appeals to New Agers and its *o* ending gives it added energy. It is a name that looms large in religious history, having belonged to a number of early Christian saints, including Pope Leo the Great, and, going to another extreme, it's even appeared on a couple of soap operas. Famous Leos of the past have ranged from Tolstoy to Leo "the Lip" Durocher, the irascible manager of the Brooklyn Dodgers. It was given the ultimate British seal of approval when Prime Minister Tony Blair chose it for his youngest son, after his paternal grandfather. The Portuguese spelling is **LEÃO,** pronounced LAY-o, which is also the French pronunciation.

LEON. Just goes to show what the addition of one letter can do. Leon, the Greek form of Leo, shows no sign of a similar rejuvenation, not having been really popular here since the 1890s. It last made the headlines when Leon Spinks defeated Muhammad Ali in 1978.

LEONARD. Leonard is a real limbo name—it's not so far out it will always be out, like an Elmer or a Bertram, but neither has it been in style for the past several decades. Another lion-related name, Leonard comes from the German, meaning "lionhearted," and one Saint Leonard is the patron saint of childbirth. Popular from 1900 to 1930, it is perhaps more famous for those who dropped the name when they entered show business than for those who kept it: Former Leonards include Roy Rogers, Tony Randall, and Buddy Hackett.

LEONARDO. If Leonard is out, the Italian version of the name is quite the opposite, all due to one celebrity bearer, young Mr. di Caprio. He was sup-posedly given the name because his pregnant mother felt a kick while she was looking at a Leonardo da Vinci painting in the Ufizzi Gallery in Florence.

LEOPOLD. This Germanic name often used by the Austrian aristocracy and also for one of Queen Victoria's sons is not likely to hold much appeal for the modern American parent, except perhaps for those who are ardent admirers of the hero of James Joyce's epic *Ulysses,* Leopold Bloom.

LEROY. From a French nickname meaning "the king," originally bestowed on servants in a royal household, LeRoy/Leroy came to be considered a typical African-American male name of the last generation or two. The given name of baseball great Satchel Paige, its image wasn't helped by the song "Bad, Bad Leroy Brown." It is sometimes switched to its anagram, **ELROY.**

LESLEY, LESLIE. This ancient Scottish clan name, the birth name of Bob Hope, is almost exclusively female at this point, except in Britain where it is still occasionally used for boys.

LESTER. A British place-name (it's the phonetic form of **LEICESTER**) and surname, Lester has gone the way of Hester, Esther, and Sylvester, all sharing a sound that is not pleasing to the modern ear. It did come into the spotlight recently as the complex character that won Kevin Spacey his Oscar for *American Beauty*.

LEV. The Russian form of Leo, which means "heart" in Hebrew, Lev was chosen by actress Candace Cameron for her son.

LEVI. Lighter and more energetic than most biblical names, the ending vowel giving it an extra shot of spunk, Levi could be tomorrow's Jacob. Already, more and more parents—Dave "The Edge" Evans of the group U2 is one—are appreciating its unique combination of Old Testament profundity (Levi was the name given by Jacob's wife Leah to her third son, and also the given name of Saint Matthew the apostle), with the casual flair associated with Levi Strauss jeans.

LEWIS, LOUIS. Lewis is the common English form of the French Louis and yes, the latter can be pronounced either like the former or as **LOUIE.** Both versions have been in the Top 25 in this country at various times—Louis (the name of sixteen French kings) peaked around 1900, and Lewis was most popular around 1930. Modern parents in search of interesting names from their family trees have been holding Lewis/Louis up to the light to see if it has any life left. The verdict? Maybe: If you've got an adventurous sense of style, if you're confident your child will have other entrées to the mainstream, if you can picture Lou/Lew becoming the next Max/Sam/Jake. Princess Stephanie of Monaco, Mel Gibson, and Bill Pullman have already rediscovered it for their sons and it's in England's Top 20. For a completely different spin, you might consider the other French form, **CLOVIS,** the Spanish **LUIS** (see separate listing), the Italian **LUIGI,** the Irish **LEWY** (more formally known as **LUGHAIDH**)—but probably *not* the Latinized form, **ALOYSIUS.**

LEX. It started as a short form of Alexander (the birth name of its most famous bearer, onetime Tarzan Lex Barker), but is now sometimes used on its own, just as Lexie is used for girls. And like all the other names that rhyme with *sex,* it does have a seductive edge. One bad-guy Lex is *Superman* villain Lex Luthor.

LIAM. Liam is one of the Irish names parents are increasingly choosing to replace the fading Sean, Ryan, Kevin, and Brian. Originally a pet Gaelic form of William (or Uilliam) in the Emerald Isle, it is currently among the Top 20 in England as well. It is both jaunty and richly textured, and continues to be well represented by Irish-born actor Liam Neeson. Rachel Hunter and Rod Stewart chose it for their son, Liam McAllister, as did Calista Flockhart.

LIGHT. This name was one of the sunny, moony names of the 1960s and 1970s and has begin to twinkle again for parents who seek what they frankly call a "hippie" name. Others might prefer a substitute with light embedded in its meaning, such as Lucius.

LINCOLN. Lincoln is a fresher-sounding presidential candidate than the excessively used Taylor, Tyler, Jefferson, Jackson, and Madison. Reflecting its namesake, it has a tall, rangy, honest image. And **LINC** is a cool nickname, as reflected in several TV characters of the past.

LINDSAY. The girls have definitely filched this one from the male box.

LINUS. If you can separate the name from the little boy clinging to his security blanket in *Peanuts*—not an easy task—you could discover a name with a great deal of charm and other kinds of associations. In Greek mythology Linus is both a musician and poet, the inventor of rhythm and melody who taught music to Hercules. In the Christian era, Linus was the name of the second pope, Saint Peter's successor. More recently, Linus Pauling won two Nobel prizes, for chemistry and peace. And though it may be hard to picture, Humphrey Bogart, James Stewart, Matt Damon, and Harrison Ford have all played characters named Linus.

LIONEL. This French diminutive of Leon has been fairly well used over the years (there were Lionels Barrymore, Trilling, Hampton, and Richie, a knight of King Arthur's Round Table, and characters on *The Jeffersons* and *Santa Barbara,* to name a few), but has never become trendy or dated. We think it would make an interesting, multidimensional choice.

LLEWELYN. One of the commonest first names in Wales would make a distinctively offbeat American alternative for a child with Welsh roots. Llewelyn has some appealing, if quirky, short forms as well—**LLEW** and **LLEU,** and **LLELO.**

LLOYD. Originally a nickname for a gray-haired man, Lloyd, at this point in time, still possesses a gray-haired image. A Welsh name that had some degree of popularity here in the 1940s, it's rarely used today, maybe because that *oy* sound in the middle, as in Boyd and Floyd, is so hard to transcend.

LOGAN. Logan has found favor with a lot of parents looking for this kind of bright and genial Scottish surname name—there were more than nine thousand Logans born in this country last year. It was chosen for his son by Led Zeppelin's Robert Plant, and a character named Logan Stafford has been featured on the soap opera *The Guiding Light.*

LORCAN. A name rich in Irish history, just waiting for its entry visa into this country, Lorcan was the name of several Irish kings, including the grandfather of the most famous high king of Ireland, Brian Boru. Lorcan O'Toole (known in English as Laurence O'Toole) is the patron saint of Dublin, so it's not too surprising that Irish-born actor Peter O'Toole named his son Lorcan.

LOREN, LORNE. With the steady popularity of Lauren as a girls' name, Loren has lost whatever potency it once had for a boy. Lorne, on the other hand, still has masculine feasibility, especially in Canada, where it has always seen greater use (the name's two most well-known bearers, *Bonanza*'s Lorne Greene and *Saturday Night Live*'s Lorne Michaels were both born there).

LORENZO. Like Leonardo, this attractive Latin version of Lawrence has been somewhat integrated into the American stockpot of names, thanks in large part to the fame of actor Lorenzo Lamas. Other associations are with Lorenzo de'Medici, the Florentine Renaissance merchant prince and art patron, and the upstanding young man who married Shylock's daughter Jessica in Shakespeare's *The Merchant of Venice*. **RENZO** is an appealing nickname, sometimes used on its own.

LOUIS. See **LEWIS.**

LOYAL. One of the few virtue names for boys, this is an honorable and principled appellation with a long history that could send a worthy message to your son without putting undue pressure on him.

LOWELL. Upstanding and somewhat conservative, Lowell calls to mind the genteel, patrician families of nineteenth-century New England, like the one poet Robert Lowell was born into. Lowell Bergman is a journalist played by Al Pacino in *The Insider*. An interesting British upper-class spelling is **LOEL.**

LUCA. An Italian version of Lucius (others are **LUCIANO** and **LUCIO**) that, while appealing, has the possibility of being misread as a girl's name—in fact former *Beverly Hills 90210* resident Jennie Garth did bestow it on her daughter, while former *Melrose Place* bad boy Thomas Calabro used it for his son. There has been a character on *ER* named **LUKA.**

LUCAS. An amplified, Latinate version of Luke, Lucas has proved to be a favorite of scriptwriters, from the early TV days of *The Rifleman* (Chuck Connors as Lucas McCain) to the schoolteacher series *Lucas Tanner,* to the 1980s teen flick *Lucas,* to appearances on several soaps. Parents who find

Luke too casual might want to upgrade to Lucas, which is sometimes spelled **LUKAS.**

LUCIAN. Lucian is a sleeker, more sophisticated version of Lucius which, when spelled **LUCIEN,** has a distinctive French accent. Actor Steve Buscemi named his son Lucian.

LUCIUS. This exotic old Roman clan name has lots of religious and other resonances. It was the name of three popes, appears in several Shakespeare plays, and in Ireland is sometimes associated with the O'Brien family. All the names beginning with the *luc* syllable relate to the Latin word for light.

LUDWIG. This Germanic name is as heavy as a marble bust of Ludwig von Beethoven.

LUIS. With the Hispanic population of America both growing and developing an increased sense of ethnic pride, which is reflected in their baby-naming practices, names like Luis, Juan, José, and Miguel are making their way onto the general popularity lists. Luis, the Spanish version of Louis, is currently in the Top 50, and it is the most frequently given boy's name in the commonwealth of Puerto Rico.

LUIGI. See **LEWIS.**

LUKE. One of the quintessential kicked-back cowboy names of the 1970s and 1980s, Luke still has many supporters among parents seeking a relaxed name that comes with New Testament references as well. It's a hot name in Great Britain right now, currently ranking number 11 for boys. The most famous bearer of the name is the first-century Greek physician, evangelist, friend, and convert of Saint Paul, and author of the third Gospel, who became the patron saint of doctors, artists, and butchers. Other Lukes of lesser note have been Luke Skywalker of *Star Wars* fame, Luke Duke, one of *The Dukes of Hazard,* Cool Hand Luke, and half of that classic soap-opera couple, Luke and Laura of *General Hospital.* Historically, it was a name that craftsmen often gave to their sons; more recently, Bill Murray, Rick

Schroder, and Lance Armstrong all named their sons Luke. The French version is **LUC**.

LUNDY. A particularly lively and engaging Scottish surname particularly appropriate for a boy born on Monday, as it's related to the word for that day in the Romance languages.

LUTHER. In the past this German surname was pretty much restricted to evangelical Protestants honoring the ecclesiastical reformer and theologian Martin Luther, leader of the Protestant revolution. In more recent times, it has been heavily used by African-Americans to honor civil rights hero Martin Luther King Jr. A current bearer of the name is singer Luther Vandross, and rapper Coolio played a Luther in *Independence Day,* as did Ving Rhames in *Mission Impossible.* **LOTHAR** is another German form.

LYLE. This English and Scottish surname—originally it indicated someone who lived on an island—is a perfectly respectable, straightforward single-syllable name, but be warned that by the time he's four, any child bearing it will be sick of hearing the chant "Lyle, Lyle, crocodile," from the popular children's book.

LYNDON. The fact that this was the name of the thirty-sixth president of the United States did not engender any great epidemic of baby boys named Lyndon, even though it has the pleasant meaning of "hill with lime trees." Its feminine first syllable doesn't help it much either.

LYSANDER. This distinctive Greek name belonged to one of the four young lovers in Shakespeare's comedy *A Midsummer Night's Dream.* Like Leander, it could be thought of as a more creative cousin of Alexander.

M

MAC, MACK. In Ireland and Scotland Mac is the part of a name that means "son of," but here, with or without the final *k,* it's sometimes used on its own and makes an engagingly congenial choice. It is also suggestive of Mack the Knife and a whole family of computers. Then there is an extended clan of appealing Mac last-name-first names, including **MACALLISTER, MACARTHUR, MACAULEY, MACDONALD** (beware the fast-food connection), **MACINTOSH** (the computer company), **MACDOUGAL, MACGEORGE, MACKENZIE** (now often used for girls), **MACKINLAY, MACLEAN, McADAM, McCABE, McCALLUM, McCLENNON, McCOY, McCREA, McDERMOT, McPHEE, McQUILLAN, McSORLEY,** and **McTAVISH.**

MACON. An attractive place-name, with a thick Georgia accent, Macon means "to make, perform, create," which might give it some additional appeal to parents interested in the arts. Macon Leary was the protagonist of Anne Tyler's novel *The Accidental Tourist.*

MAGEE. Although Magee has the literal meaning "son of Hugh," we see it having a broad and bouncy appeal for the sons of anyone from Adam to Zachary.

MAGNUS. A name with a somewhat weighty, magisterial quality, Magnus comes from the Latin meaning "great one." It belonged to several important early Norwegian kings, but its spread was due almost entirely to Emperor Charlemagne, who was called Carolus Magnus, meaning Charles the Great. Some unknowing followers of his picked up on the Magnus part and started using it as a first name. During the Middle Ages, the name traveled from Scandinavia to Ireland and Scotland, where it became very popular and remains well used to this day. **MANUS** is a related name.

MAGUIRE. Another popular Irish surname with a lot of verve. But no matter how big a baseball fan you are, we'd advise you not to spell it **McGWIRE.**

MALACHI, MALACHY. This Old Testament name, which is a great favorite in Ireland, has an expansive, boisterous image. In the Bible, Malachi (pronounced with the final syllable as *eye*) was the last of the twelve Hebrew prophets, who prophesied the coming of Christ. Malachy (which ends with an *ee* sound) was the name of two famous high kings of Ireland, one of whom defeated the Norse invaders in an important battle. In Eire, it has been associated with the O'Kelly, O'Morgan, O'Flanagan, and MacCann clans, and would be especially appropriate for anyone with one of those surnames. It came to the attention of the readers of the best-selling *Angela's Ashes* as the name of author Frank McCourt's father and brother, the latter of whom wrote a best-seller of his own.

MALCOLM. Malcolm's in the middle—of a definite revival. It's a name that's heard on TV and in movies (Bruce Willis's character in *The Sixth Sense,* for one) and, increasingly, on birth announcements. A warm and friendly Scottish appellation (it was originally Mael-Colum) that fits into our golden circle of names that are distinctive without verging on the bizarre, Malcolm was the name of four Scottish kings—including the son of Duncan who succeeded to the throne after Macbeth murdered his father—and has always been one of the most popular names in that country. An admired hero for many in the U.S. is the radical civil rights activist Malcolm X; the star of his Spike Lee film biography, Denzel Washington, named one of his sons Malcolm, as did Harrison Ford.

MALIK. This name has ranked very high with African-American parents for several years now, and is also often heard in Senegal and other parts of Africa. It's an Arabic name meaning "king" or "master."

MALONE. A classic Irish surname with a lot of character, originally Mael Eoin, which means "descendant of the devotee of Saint John." Malone was the title character of a Samuel Beckett novel.

MANDELA. An African surname ripe for adoption as a hero name honoring Nelson Rolihlahla Mandela, South African lawyer, organizer of the African National Congress, and president of South Africa, who was imprisoned from 1962 to 1990 for his antiapartheid activities.

MANFRED. A rather dated Old German name meaning "man of peace" that got some twentieth-century attention via the pop singer Manfred ("Doo Wah Diddy Diddy") Mann—who was actually born Michael Liebowitz. Parents seeking a "Fred" name would be better advised to stick to the classic Frederick.

MANUEL. See **EMANUEL.**

MAOZ. Pronounced MAH-ohz, it means "strength" or "force" in Hebrew and is a symbolic name given to boys born at Chanukah, because of the song "Maoz Tzur" ("Rock of Ages") sung at that time.

MARCEL. This French diminutive form of Marcus, despite having such distinguished namesakes as author Proust and artist Duchamp, suffers from a stereotypical headwaiter image in this country. It was chosen for his son by gangsta rapper Dr. Dre (real name André).

MARCH. The girls have adopted April, May, and June (and, more recently, September), making March, along with August, among the few month names available to boys. A single-syllable name with a brisk beat, as well as being a surname (as in *Little Women*), March might be worth considering as a first or middle name.

MARCO, MARCELLO, MARINO. Three Italian names with distinct cultural-crossover possibilities. Marino has pleasant seaside undertones.

MARCUS. This is the original Latin form of Mark, and has a bit more verbal substance. It was commonplace in classical Rome—not surprising as it was one of only about a dozen given names in general use then—and a renowned bearer was the emperor and stoic philosopher Marcus Aurelius. African-American parents might find it appealing as a hero name honoring Marcus Moziah Garvey, the Jamaican political leader who led the Back to Africa movement in this country. On TV, we've seen Marcus Welby, the kindly physician on the popular 1970s medical show, and Marcuses have appeared on several soap operas since then. Michael Jordan has a son named Marcus. Some foreign spellings are **MARCOS** (Spanish), **MARKOS** (Greek), and **MARKUS** (German).

MARIO. Like Emilio and Carlo, Mario is a Latin name that has become integregrated into the North American mainstream (initially because of singer Mario Lanza), adding a lot of punch to any compatable Anglo surname.

Marios in the public eye have included former New York Governor Mario Cuomo, auto racer Mario Andretti, *Godfather*-author Mario Puzo, and actor-director Mario van Peebles. **MARIUS** is the more formal Latin version.

MARK, MARC. After a long history of lagging behind many of the other apostolic names, Mark leaped into massive popularity around 1950, suddenly sounding a good deal fresher and more modern than Peter or Paul. By 1960, Mark had become the sixth most popular boy's name in America. Deriving from the Latin name Marcus, which in turn derived from Mars, the Roman god of war, it was borne by numerous Roman luminaries, including Mark Antony, and by Saint Mark the Evangelist, author of the second Gospel of the New Testament and the patron saint of secretaries, notaries, and the city of Venice. The most notable American Mark was the great humorous writer Mark Twain, born Samuel Clemens, a Mississippi River steamboat pilot who took his pen name from the nautical term meaning "mark two fathoms." But although Mark made its mark on baby naming in time to impress itself on many baby boomers, it has very little life left for their offspring—no matter how many headlines baseball superstar Mark McGwire makes with his record-breaking feats.

MARLON. For half a century, this name has been identified with Marlon Brando, who inherited the French-inflected name from his father. More recently there have been Jackson and Wayans family Marlons and a press secretary named **MARLIN** Fitzwater. Your own little Marlon? Iconoclasts Dennis Miller and Keith Richards each have one, but most modern parents would consider it beyond the pale.

MARQUIS. We have Princes and Earls, so why not this rank of nobility as well? Some parents might see it as a variation on Marcus.

MARSH. A soft, and mellifluous nature-surname name, Marsh is sometimes used as a nickname for Marshall, but can also be used on its own.

MARSHALL. This rarely used name has subliminal ties to the military (martial, field marshal), and the old West (Marshals Matt Dillon et al.). It had some play during the heyday of communications maven Marshall McLuhan, but would probably be seen as outdated and slightly pretentious today. The first "em" in controversial rapper Eminem's name stands for Marshall.

MARTIN. An "in" name in upper-class England, Martin still has a long and winding road to travel before it arrives back in style here, though the current cool of such former musties as Homer and Henry leads us to believe Martin's revival could conceivably be just around the corner. It has definite potential as a hero name, honoring the Reverend Martin Luther King Jr. (trivia note: Both Martins Sr. and Jr. were originally named Michael Luther King, which was changed in honor of religious leader Martin Luther). There have been many other notable Martins as well, including Saint Martin of Tours, patron saint of France, Charles Dickens's *Martin Chuzzlewit* and Jack London's *Martin Eden* in literature, director Martin Scorcese, writer Martin Amis, performers Martin Sheen and Martin Short, and the Mel Gibson character in *Lethal Weapon*. **MARTINO** is the Italian version, **MAIRTIN** the Irish.

MARVIN. Talk about unexpected origins! Would you believe that this now (let's face it) schleppy name hails from Wales? The real first name of playwright Neil Simon and of the singer known as Meatloaf, it did take on a little of the charisma of Marvin Gaye in the 1960s and 1970s. But not much.

MASON. An occupational surname that has suddenly become very hot— it's been chosen for their sons by Cuba Gooding Jr., Laura San Giocamo, Josie Bissett, and Rob Estes, among others. One reason might be that it's a fresher sounding successor to the now-passé Jason.

MATTHEW. Currently the third most popular boys' name in America, Matthew is the epitome of the fashionable classic, having been in the Top 25 for more than a quarter of a century now. Why? Because it's safe and sturdy, yet has a more engaging personality than, say, John or James, which can be perceived as being common to the point of anonymity. The biblical Matthew was the apostle who wrote the first Gospel of the New Testament, and media **MATT**s have included *Gunsmoke*'s Marshal Matt Dillon, and such other video heroes as Matt Helm and Matt Houston, not to mention such real-life leading men as Matthews Broderick, Modine, and

McConaughey, and Matts Lauer, Damon, and Dillon. Among the celebs who have made this semiconservative choice for their sons are Christopher Reeve, Rob Lowe, Alex Trebeck, Ray Romero, Marie Osmond, and Eddie Money. Some variations from other cultures: **MATTEO, MATEO,** and **MATH-IEU. MATTHIAS,** the Ecclesiastic Greek name borne in the New Testament by the apostle chosen to replace Judas Iscariot, was the form used by the Puritans and would make an interesting alternative today.

MAURICE. See **MORRIS.**

MAX. Only a generation ago, Max was an unthinkably fusty, cigar-smelling old grandpa name, completely out of the question as a baby-naming choice. But then, sometime in the 1980s, perhaps partially influenced by Mel Gibson's Mad Max character, Max—along with his pinochle-playing partners Sam and Jake—suddenly became hip, one of the starbaby names of the decade, chosen by any number of high-profile parents and also making it onto soap operas. At this point its popularity has faded among the avant-garde, replaced by less ethnic classics such as Jack and Henry. But there's one arena where it's still on top—according to the ASPCA, Max is the number 1 name for American pets.

MAXEN. Parents looking for a fresh Max alternative might consider this Welsh version of Magnus.

MAXIMILIAN. From the Latin meaning "greatest, biggest, best," Maximilian seems a bit grand for the American baby boy, but some parents might want to consider it as a route to the nickname Max. Maximilian I, emperor of the Holy Roman Empire, patronized the arts and was considered the first knight of his age. **MAXIMUS** is the name of the Russell Crowe character in *Gladiator*.

MAXWELL. Maxwell lies somewhere between the formality of Maximilian and the laid-back unpretentiousness of Max. A Scottish Gaelic surname, it was for a long time associated with playwright Maxwell Anderson, and was chosen for his son by Andrew Dice Clay.

MAYNARD. An offbeat German name still somewhat attached to beatnik Maynard G. Krebs on the old *The Many Lives of Dobie Gillis* TV show or with Canadian jazz trumpeter Maynard Ferguson.

MELCHIOR. This name of one of the three kings who attended the birth of Christ is rarely used in modern times, but it is a slightly better Mel choice than Melvin.

MELVIN. This once perfectly respectable Scottish surname has been demeaned over the past several decades, not least of all by Jerry Lewis turning it into a demented, spastic character in the 1950s. **MELVILLE** is equally out of the question, as are all other names ending in *ville*. **MEL** is sometimes used on its own, more in other countries than here, as superstar Mel Gibson protests to people who assume his given name must be Melvin. Mel is, in fact, the full name of an Irish saint.

MENACHEM. This fairly obscure biblical name, long associated with one-time Israeli Prime Minister Begin, is a symbolic appellation used for boys born on the Jewish holiday of Tishah-b'Av, a day of fasting and mourning for the destruction of the temple. The Yiddish version is **MENDEL.**

MERCER, MERCE. Two names with likable, artistic images, thanks to their associations with the late bandleader-musician Mercer Ellington and dancer-choreographer Merce Cunningham.

MERCURY. Adventurous parents of the new millennium have begun to look back to names from the first millennium before Christ, those of the ancient pagan gods and goddesses. Mercury was the Roman messenger of the gods, as well as the god of commerce, eloquence, cleverness, travel, and—uh-oh—thievery. It is also the name of the planet closest to the sun, as well as the silvery element used in thermometers. A challenging name for a child, it does have the more user-friendly nickname **MERC.**

MERLE, MERRILL. Both Merle, which means "blackbird" in Latin and was originally given as a nickname to someone who loved to sing or whistle, and Merrill have lost virtually all of their masculine punch.

MERLIN, MERTON, MERVYN. A trio of completely antiquated names almost unheard of for decades. Of the three, Merlin has the most interesting history, being the name of the famous fifth-century sorcerer and mentor of King Arthur, who helped him rise to power.

MESHACH. This Old Testament name of the companion of Daniel, Shadrach, and Abednego has a rousing, gospel feel. It was rescued from complete obscurity a few years back by the genial actor Meshach Taylor, who made his mark in *Designing Women*.

MEYER. An obsolete German name that was favored by first-generation Jewish families, including the affluent Guggenheims and Lehmans, but is now pretty much relegated to poolside gin games in Miami and Boca Raton. **MEIR** is an alternative spelling.

MICAH. Growing numbers of parents are looking at Micah as a more unusual alternative to Michael, projecting a shinier, more lively image. Micah is the name of a biblical prophet and was used fairly frequently by the seventeenth-century Puritans. It also made an appearance on the soap opera *Santa Barbara* in the 1990s, and was used by Neil Diamond for his son.

MICHAEL. Michael has just ended its reign as king of boys' names, a position it held for close to half a century. One reason for this phenomenal record is that Michael has been embraced by parents from an exceptional range of religious and ethnic groups and so continues to enjoy an unmatched usefulness as a compromise name. If one of you is Catholic, for example, and the other Jewish, or you're trying to meld wildly disparate ethnic considerations; if you want a name with music and your mate's looking for one with muscle, then Michael is sure to be on the shortlist of names that satisfies everyone's tastes and requirements. The biblical Michael is one of only two archangels (the other is Gabriel) recognized by Jews, Christians, and Muslims alike, while Saint Michael is the patron of bankers, radiologists, and policemen. An image that diverse, however, can hardly help becoming somewhat enervated and diluted, even though Michael still projects a genuine sweetness and honesty. Several of its foreign versions are sometimes used in this country, including the French **MICHEL** (which has the disadvantage of sounding just like the female form), the Spanish **MIGUEL**, the Irish **MICHEAL** (the form used by Liam Neeson and Natasha Richardson for their son), and the Scandinavian **MIKAEL**.

MICKEY. Once upon a time it seemed that every other big-city cab driver, cop, and boxer was called Mickey—at least if Hollywood was to be believed. Its pugnacious and spunky image was embodied in the young Mickey Rooney, the animated Mickey Mouse, and later Mickey Mantle (who credited his catchy name with contributing to his fame). Now, with as many Michaels being called Michael as Mike, Mickey is rarely heard. **MICK,** most often associated with Rolling Stone Jagger, is also used as a generic, often derogatory, term for an Irishman.

MILES, MYLES. Miles has had a sharp rise in popularity with the movers and shakers, largely due to its polished, cool, confident image, inspired in large measure by jazz great Miles Davis. Celebrities who have chosen the name for their offspring have been split between the two spellings: Susan Sarandon and Tim Robbins, Lionel Richie, and Elisabeth Shue have used the Miles Standish version, while the Eddie Murphys and Sherilynn Fenn and Toulouse Hardy have spelled it with a *y*.

MILO. With its German, Greek, and jaunty British input, Milo is, in our opinion, a real winner. Its image combines the strength of the great ancient Greek wrestler of that name—a six-time winner of the Olympic games—with the debonair charm of a World War II RAF pilot. Ricki Lake and Mel Gibson have both chosen this name for their sons. **MILOS** (pronounced MEE-losh) is a European variant.

MILTON. Long before the outrageous antics of Uncle Miltie (born Uncle Mendel) invaded videoland, Milton was an upper-class British surname, conjuring up etched impressions of rustic mills and placid streams or the epic poetry of John Milton. Nowadays, Milton is about as far out of step as a name can be, and we don't see it coming back in any of our lifetimes.

MINGUS. When supermodel Helena Christensen gave this name to her son, she did so in honor of jazz great Charles Mingus, just as Woody Allen honored the earlier musician Sidney Bechet. If you are a jazz buff, other possibilities you might consider: **ARMSTRONG, BASIE, BLAKEY, BAKER, BRUBECK, KENTON, CALLOWAY, COLE, DAVIS, ELLINGTON, GILLESPIE, JACQUET, JOPLIN, MULLIGAN, TATUM,** or **TRISTANO**—not to mention **THELONIUS.**

MITCHELL. A name that had quite a bit of panache in the 1940s and 1950s, seen as a sharper alternative to Michael, Mitchell then went into a steep decline, though it seems to be making a bit of a comeback. Maybe it's because the nickname **MITCH** retains some of the old flair, having been heavily used by scriptwriters of such shows as *Baywatch* and *General Hospital*.

MOE. The Max of tomorrow? Could be, but perhaps not as long as *The Three Stooges* are in reruns. Moe was originally a diminutive of Moses and might still make a friendly nickname for that somewhat weighty appellation.

MOHAMMED, MUHAMMED, MUHAMMAD. These are only three versions of the over five hundred names for the Arab prophet who founded the Muslim religion. Others include **MAHMUD, MEHMET, AHMAD,** and **HAMMAD.** In fact there is a Muslim saying, "If you have a hundred sons, name them all Muhammed," and as a consequence it is generally considered to be the most common boys' name in the world. The most famous bearer on this continent is Muhammad Ali, who changed his name when he joined the Nation of Islam in 1964, dropping his "slave name" of Cassius Clay.

MONTANA. A relaxed Western place-name that has so far not been completely usurped by the girls, Montana is the name chosen for their sons by Richard Thomas and Laurence Fishburne. But be warned: This whole posse of similarly trendy names, including Sierra and Dakota, definitely has a so-far-in-they're-out feel.

MONTEL. Is this strictly a one-person name or will enough people admire the shiny-domed talk-show host to bring it into the mainstream of names?

We'd vote for the former, although the name is receiving some appreciative attention from African-American baby namers.

MONROE, MUNRO. Unlike Jackson, Jefferson, Tyler, and Taylor, Monroe is one presidential name we don't see zooming to popularity. It's slightly more appealing as **MUNRO,** a Scottish clan name.

MONTGOMERY. This is not the kind of surname name that is in favor right now, feeling far too fussy and formal.

MORDECAI. Although it has a noble heritage, Mordecai has never caught on in this country and we see virtually no possibility of it ever doing so. It is a symbolic name for boys born on the holiday of Purim, because this cousin of Queen Esther helped her save the Jews from destruction at the hands of Haman.

MORGAN. For a while Morgan was split pretty evenly between boys and girls, but at this point it is far more prevalent on the girls' list, currently in the Top 25. An attractive Welsh name that means "born in the sea," and has in the past been used for boys born under water signs—Pisces, Cancer, and Scorpio, Morgan is still a very common male name in its native Wales and is represented here by the distinguished actor Morgan Freeman.

MORLEY. This soft, pleasant English surname has long been primarily associated in this country with Canadian-born 60-Minuteman Morley Safer.

MORRIS, MAURICE. These names, which have identical pronunciations in England, have very different images in this country, Morris being much more quiet, as comfortable as a Morris chair, while Maurice, often Frenchified in the United States to mor-EES—is far more flamboyant. They both spring from the Latin meaning "moor," and spread as a result of the fame of Saint Maurice, a third-century Swiss martyr. Children at a young age are sure to become familiar with the engaging tales and illustrations of Maurice Sendak. Common pet names are **MOREY, MAURY,** and **MORRIE** (as in

Travels With . . .). Two contemporary surname variations are **MORRISSEY** (see below) and **MORRISON.**

MORRISSEY. When British rocker Steven Patrick Morrissey decided to perform under his last name alone, it suggested the possibility of using Morrissey to other people as well. Sounds a lot more contemporary than the dusty Morris or Maurice.

MORTIMER, MORTON. Two English family names used a few generations ago as Anglicizations of Moses, but of late better known as posh restaurants than as baby-name possibilities. Mortimer was Walt Disney's original choice for the name of his mouse, until his wife talked him out of it.

MOSES. Some people may find this name just too overwhelmingly biblical—conjuring up images of white beards and the sacred Ten Commandments—but we see it as a definite candidate for rejuvenation in the modern world. In the Old Testament, of course, Moses, the brother of Aaron and Miriam, led the Israelites out of Egyptian bondage and into the Promised Land, and brought down God's commandments from Mount Sinai. In contemporary life, Moses Malone is a basketball superstar. **MOSHE** is the Hebrew version, **MOISE** is French, **MOZES** Dutch, and **MOE** and **MOSE** frequently used nicknames.

MOSS. An evocative combination nature-surname, Moss has long been associated with the playwright Moss Hart.

MUIR. This rarely heard Scottish last-name-first name means "moor," which gives it a fragrant, heathery feel.

MUNGO, MONGO. Mungo is a Scottish name meaning "beloved," and was originally used as a term of endearment, while Mongo means "famous" in Yoruba. And although these names may be widely used in those disparate cultures, we're afraid they might be too close to the word "mongrel" ever to have much success in this country.

MURPHY. A jaunty Celtic surname so widespread in Ireland—it's the most common last name there—that it became the slang word for that country's staple food, the potato, and also has the negative association with Murphy's law ("If anything can go wrong, it will."). Murphy has something else going against it as a boy's name: the lingering image of the female Murphy Brown. So it might be better to think about Maguire or Magee.

MURRAY. This venerable Scottish surname name meaning "sea warrior," has become a Hollywood joke name, as used, for example, as the moniker of the dog in *Mad About You*. On the other hand, *Friends'* Lisa Kudrow was adventurous enough to use it as the middle name of her son Julian.

MYRON. This name has not retained much of its original essence—Myron means "sweet and fragrant" in Greek. It belonged to the famous ancient Greek sculptor best known for *The Discus Thrower*. The given name of newsman Mike Wallace, it was one of many *m* names (among them Murray, Marvin, Morton, Milton, and Melvin) given to first-generation Jewish immigrant boys in place of Moses. Today, if you want to honor Grandpa Myron, the best choice might be the original Moses.

N

NAIRN. Although it's short, this Scottish nature name, linked with rivers and alder trees, might prove a bit of a confusing tongue twister for the younger set.

NANDO. See **FERDINAND.**

NAOR. This Hebrew name, pronounced nah-ohr, has the estimable meaning of "cultured and enlightened," attributes that are universally desired for our sons.

NASH. This dashing surname name, which is associated with the ash tree, came to mass public attention via the eponymous hero of the long-running series *Nash Bridges,* starring Don Johnson. It's also the name of the cofounder of the American Civil Liberties Union—Nash Baldwin—as well as a defunct car marque. Other car brands of the past worthy of consideration: **REO, ESSEX.**

NATHAN. A somewhat serious, reserved name, Nathan is an Old Testament option that one wouldn't think of as trendy in the sense that, say, Joshua is trendy, yet in its own quiet way Nathan has been steadily climbing the popularity charts, and is now among the Top 40, exactly where it happened to be at the start of the twentieth century. It has appeared on the daytime drama *The Young and the Restless* (funny, you don't sound like a soap-opera name), was the name of the characters played by Kevin Kline in *Sophie's Choice* and Jack Nicholson in *A Few Good Men,* and has been chosen for their sons by John Lithgow, Mark Hamill, and Leeza Gibbons. And every schoolchild knows the name through Nathan Hale, the Revolutionary War spy. **NAT** and **NATE** are just the kind of old-fashioned nicknames that are coming back into style.

NATHANIEL. Nathaniel, sometimes spelled **NATHANAEL,** has a slight edge on big brother Nathan in terms of style, though its popularity is rising so rapidly that, much as we essentially like the name, it would not be a great choice for parents in search of something that will really stand apart. In the New Testament, Nathaniel was the apostle who was also called Bartholomew. And no matter what its fashion standing, Nathaniel does have some other worthy namesakes: writer Nathaniel Hawthorne, rebel slave Nat Turner, and singer Nat "King" Cole. Another singer, Barbara Mandrell, chose it for her son, and it was the name of Denzel Washington's character in *Courage Under Fire.*

NAVARONE. Navarone has a pronounced cowboy swagger, even though the classic film *The Guns of Navarone* was not a western but a World War II action flick. Priscilla Presley added the name to the baby mix when she gave it to her son.

NAVARRO. A Spanish geographical surname—it's related to the area of northeastern Spain called the Navarre—with a lot of brio. One thing for sure—any child with this name is bound to be the only Navarro in his class.

NED. This Nancy Drew/Bobbsey Twins–era nickname for Edward has been neglected all through the long epoch of Eddies, Eds, and Teds, during which, if Ned existed at all, it was as a kind of nerdy country bumpkin. Now, however, Ned is showing signs of a comeback, not only as a short form for Edward (which is generally used in full these days), but also as a nostalgic, clean-cut name on its own, making appearances on such TV shows as *Party of Five* and *General Hospital*.

NEHEMIAH. A bearded, Old Testament/Puritan name that's lain near extinction for several hundred years, but conceivably could (admittedly, it's a stretch) be revived, à la Jeremiah, in the new wave of interest in more uncommon biblical names. Nehemiah was the Jewish leader given a mandate to rebuild Jerusalem, which might make it an apt possibility for the child of an architect or a building contractor.

NEIL, NEAL, NIALL. Neil is an affable, neutral, somewhat dated, but safe kind of name that has moved a long way from its Irish roots, being now more associated with people like Neil Simon and Neil Sedaka than the dauntless Niall of the Nine Hostages, one of Ireland's most famous kings, and ancestor of all the O'Neills and Mac Neils that followed. Popular, particularly in Scotland, since the Middle Ages, Neil or Neal, which means "champion," was a favorite in the United States in the 1940s, but hasn't been heard from much in the intervening decades. Today's parents of Irish descent might want to return to the original Gaelic spelling of Niall, which can also be pronounced NYE-al, or a surname name such as **O'NEAL. NILO** is the Russian and Finnish version, **NEEL** is an unrelated Hindu name meaning "sapphire blue."

NELSON. This name, which literally means Neil's son, is miles away from the father name in image. There is a bit of formality still clinging to it from old associations with Lord Nelson, New York Governor Nelson Rockefeller, and that stiffest of singers, Nelson Eddy. It was also the given name of "Rabbit" Angstrom, protagonist of John Updike's series of novels and the character played by Keanu Reeves in *Sweet November*. On the other hand, it could be a heroic choice for parents who admire South African activist Nelson Mandela.

NEMO. You've probably never known anyone called Nemo, and yet this Greek name has a familiar, friendly, and likable ring. It may recall Captain Nemo, the dominant figure in Jules Verne's *20,000 Leagues Under the Sea* or Winsor McCay's beautifully drawn early comic strip *Little Nemo's Adventures in Slumberland*, which was made into a film in 1992.

NESTOR. This is not a name that is likely to appeal to the modern parent, simply on the basis of its Lester-Hester sort of sound, despite the fact that Nestor was a perfectly admirable Greek mythological figure, a leading general in the Trojan War known for his wisdom and eloquence.

NEVADA. Nevada is a Western place-name that has been around for decades—first Alan Ladd then Steve McQueen played a character named Nevada Smith in the 1960s—yet it falls into the trendy map-name category of the 1990s that already feels dated.

NEVILLE. Most names ending in *ville* fall into the unthinkable class, but this one, perhaps because of its more laid-back associations with singer Aaron Neville and the Neville Brothers, moves up into the almost-rethinkable category.

NEVIN. A Gaelic name that's fresher than Kevin and friendlier than Neville. It can also be spelled **NEVAN.**

NIALL. See **NEIL.**

NICHOLAS. Nicholas has an unusually genial and robust image for a classic first name—could it be because of our collective warm childhood connection to jolly Saint Nick? Unfortunately, or fortunately, depending on your feeling toward trendy names, this sentiment has been shared by so many parents of all backgrounds that Nicholas is now the sixth most popular boys' name in the country. A Greek name stemming from Nike, the goddess of victory, it is a New Testament name also well used in literature, as in Dickens's *Nicholas Nickleby*. And Saint Nicholas has a lot more to do than take a sleigh ride through the sky once a year—he is also the patron of schoolchildren, merchants, sailors, scholars, brides, bakers, travelers, and

Russia, where the name was a star of the czarist dynasty. **NICHOLSON,** a surname name brought to wider attention by best-selling author Nicholson Baker, may be a fresher, if less classic and user-friendly alternative, that still gets you to nicknames **NICK** and **NICKY.** Nick, like Tony, has long been a favorite of novelists and screenwriters, for rich boys, Romeos, thugs, and detectives. The British form **NICOL** may remind Americans too much of the female Nicole. Nicholas has many international variants and offshoots, including **NIKOLAS, NIKOLAI, NIKITA,** and **KOLYA** (Russian), **NICOLO** (the Italian version used by actor Stanley Tucci for his son), **NIKOLAUS, NIKLAS, KLAUS,** and **CLAUS** (German and Scandinavian), **NIKOLAI** (Norwegian), **NELS** and **NILS** (Scandinavian), **NICOLAS** (the spelling used by Mr. Cage, as well as the populations of France and Spain), **NIKOS** (Greek), **NIILO** and **LASSE** (Finnish), plus **NICO, COLE,** and **COLIN.** Singer Brian McKnight named his son **NIKKO.**

NICODEMUS. There must be an easier way to get to the nickname Nico.

NIGEL. For most Americans, Nigel is probably just too steeped in tea and crumpets to be considered, but, combined with the right last name, it does have a measure of Sherlock Holmes–era dash that could appeal to devout Anglophiles. Nigel Wick is a character on *The Drew Carey Show*.

NILES. The perfect name for Frasier's persnickety brother, Niles is megamiles away from the trendy Miles. But drop the final letter, and you have the hipper geographical name **NILE.** Or replace the *e* with an *o*, and you have **NILO,** a unique spin on Milo.

NINIAN. This Scottish-Irish name, still widely used in Scotland, has rarely been heard in the United States. Although it has the attractive *ian* ending (as in Julian), its first syllable, and possible Ninny nickname, could lead to dire playground problems.

NIR. Pronounced like the world *near,* this is a Hebrew name traditionally used for boys born on the holiday of Tu b'Shavat, the New Year of the Trees, or Arbor Day. Extended forms are **NIRAN, NIRAM, NIREL, NIRIEL,** and **NIRYA.**

NOAH. Noah could make an ideal choice for parents seeking a traditional Old Testament name that is not quite as pandemically popular as Jacob or Joshua but is still widely accepted enough to have edged near the top 25 list. As every Sunday school alumnus knows, Noah was deemed the only righteous man of his time, singled out by God to survive the great flood sent to punish an evil world. The name was helped on its current rise up the ladder by the celebrity of longtime *ER* star Noah Wyle, and perhaps even by the hunky character named Noah on *All My Children*. Among the starbabies bearing this name are the sons of Kim Alexis, Jason Alexander, and Scott (Stone Temple Pilots) Weiland. Foreign translations included the Russian **NOY,** the Polish **NOE,** the French **NOÉ** and the Swedish **NOAK.**

NOAM. This is a modern Jewish name that doesn't have the traditional weight of Noah, but could make an attractive alternative. It has any number of positive attributes in its meaning—delight, grace, charm, tenderness—and was made famous by the noted linguist Noam Chomsky. **NOAZ** is an even more unusual Hebrew name.

NOBLE. A name that has rarely been heard since the nineteenth century, but conceivably could come back in the current favorable climate for names reflecting admirable attributes. And what could be more admirable than nobility in terms of having strength of character, dignity, and high moral ideals?

NOEL. British, fey, slender, and sophisticated—à la playwright Nöel Coward—this is not for you if you're seeking an assertive kind of masculine name. On the other hand, it also connotes wit and creativity. It was once reserved for children of both sexes born at Christmastime, but that exclusivity no longer holds.

NOLAN. A spirited Irish surname, related to the word "noble," that has been used as a first name since the end of the nineteenth century, but has really only come to the fore since the recent renown of star pitcher Nolan (born Lynn) Ryan and designer Nolan Miller.

NORBERT. Even a hipster in search of a boy's name so clunky it's cool—like Richard Gere's Homer or Jack Nicholson's Raymond—would bypass

Norbert—or so we hope. The same is true of **NORVILLE,** whose one claim to fame is being the real name of Oliver Hardy.

NORMAN. Maybe it's because it sounds so much like the word "normal," but the name Norman has a serious image problem, conjuring up the picture of a normal-looking guy, with a normal kind of job, living in a Norman Rockwell kind of town—unless of course he's Norman Mailer or a twisted mama's boy like Norman Bates. Either way, not the kind of image you would want for your son.

NORRIS. Seen as a contemporary last-name-first name, Norris has a certain offbeat appeal, never having been as well used as Morris and so not saddled with that name's scruffed-up baggage.

NORTH. A fresh-sounding word-name option evoking images of snowy landscapes and bracingly cold breezes.

NYE. This nickname for the rarely heard Welsh name Aneurin, and sometimes for Nigel as well, would make a highly unusual middle name for the parent looking for a singular single-syllable *n* name.

O

OAK. In the past parents might have opted for such elaborations as **OAKLEY,** or **OAKES,** but today's baby namer is more likely to prefer the sturdy original, the very symbol of strength and longevity. Good, solid middle-name material.

OBADIAH. Only for the seriously audacious name seeker, this near-extinct Old Testament name (he was one of the twelve minor prophets) has, like Jedediah and Zebedy, its own measure of old-fangled charm. Moderately well used from the seventeenth to the nineteenth century, it was bestowed by Anthony Trollope on the character of a hypocritical chaplain, Obadiah Slope, in his novel *Barchester Towers.* **OBIE** is a Mayberry-type nickname.

OBERON. The Shakespearean character Oberon in *A Midsummer Night's Dream* is King of the Fairies, and the name does have a bit of a fey quality. The alternative spelling, **AUBERON,** gives it a somewhat more virile image.

O'BRIEN et al. The Connors and the Dylans have been around for several years now, leading contemporary parents to the next set of Irish descendant names, all of which make an innovative way of honoring a relative with a less desirable name such as, for example Donald. A few prime examples (many of which have spelling variations): **O'DONNELL, O'DONOVAN, O'KEEFE, O'HARA, O'NEILL/O'NEAL, O'SHEA.**

OCEAN. Last heard in the hippy-dippy 1960s and 1970s, names like Ocean and River are flowing back into favor, especially with nature lovers and environmentally minded parents. Actor Forest Whitaker, an inspired baby namer (his other children are called Sonnet and True) has a son named Ocean Alexander.

OCTAVIUS. In the age of huge Victorian families, parents sometimes ran out of ordinary names and turned to those denoting the child's place in the birth order, and so, for example, might give Septimus to the seventh child or Octavius to the eighth. Few families these days have eight children, but the name remains a possibility for the intrepid name seeker. It's sometimes spelled **OCTAVUS,** and foreign variations include **OTTAVIO** and **OCTAVIO,** as in the distinguished Mexican poet Octavio Paz.

ODIN. An unusual Scandinavian name (pronounced OH-din) with a lot of strength and power, in keeping with the fact that it belonged to the supreme Norse god, who oversaw poetry and magic—as well as the underworld. This is definitely a name with assimilation potential.

ODION. This is a strong Nigerian name that is used in Africa for the firstborn of twins.

ODYSSEUS. See ULYSSES.

OLAF. Olaf is one of those ethnic names that's become completely familiar without ever being assimilated—the German Hans and Franz are two others—so that a child named Olaf will still be perceived as somehow out of the American mainstream. Also note that if you remove just one letter, Olaf becomes Oaf.

OLIVER. Oliver has been a fashionable favorite since the 1960s and 1970s, when new productions of Dickens's *Oliver Twist* and a general taste for things British brought the name to wide attention. Perhaps its biggest boost came from the hit book and then movie *Love Story,* which also catapulted the name Jennifer to stardom. Since then there have been several high-profile Olivers on the scene, from Oliver North to Oliver Stone (hint to parents: this is a three-syllable name that works particularly well with single-syllable surnames), and it's been chosen by such high-profile parents as Goldie Hawn and Martin Short. Where does it stand today? It is still an attractive and stylish name that doesn't quite tip over the edge into trendiness, retaining the flavor of Britain without seeming at all twee. For some foreign flair: **OLIVIER** (French), **OLIVERO** (Spanish), **OLIVIERO** (Italian).

OMAR. An Arabic and Muslin name poised for appeal to a wider audience, Omar's got the perfect mix of exoticism and familiarity, plus that strong, open initial *o*. Deriving from the Arabic meaning "long life," the name has been tied for centuries to the Persian mathematician and poet Omar Khayyám (author of the *Rubáiyát:* "A loaf of bread, a jug of wine, and thou . . ."), and later to General Omar Bradley, actor Omar Sharif (who was born Michael), and current leading man Omar Epps.

ONYX. Most gem names are distinctively feminine—Pearl, Ruby, Diamond—but here is one for the boys. The name of a variety of layered agate often used in making cameos, Onyx sounds strong and virile, an impression reinforced by its final *x*.

OREN, ORAN, ORRIN. These rather soft, sensitive names have almost as many different ethnic origins as they have spelling variations. Oren is a Hebrew name, symbolizing the pine tree, that is quite popular in Israel. Oran is both Hebrew (meaning "light") and a Celtic saint's name, as well as an Algerian place-name. It also appeared as the name of a character in the novels of Raymond Chandler, while Orin was used by Eugene O'Neill, and Orrin has been made known nationally by Senator Hatch.

ORION. This rarely heard name belonged to the legendary Greek hunter who pursued the seven daughters of Atlas, was slain by the goddess Artemis, and then was placed as a constellation in the sky by Zeus. You could also conceivably modernize it by transforming it into its homophone **O'RYAN.**

ORLANDO. An ornate Italianate twist on the name Roland, Orlando has an impressive literary résumé, including Shakespeare's *As You Like It* and Virginia Woolf's enigmatic eponymous novel. We like Orlando's bookended *o*s and exotic feel—although since the widespread acceptance of names like Leonardo, it doesn't seem prohibitively daunting anymore. A champion athlete bearing the name is basketball star power forward Orlando Woolridge.

ORNETTE. This name, the meaning of which relates to the cedar tree, has long been associated with jazz great Ornette Colman. Its one problem is that almost all other names ending in *ette*—from Annette to Claudette to Georgette to Jeanette—are unequivocally female.

ORSON. A Norman French nickname meaning "bear cub," Orson does have a round, teddy-bear image, one that was reinforced by Orson Welles (who early on dropped his more ordinary given name of George in favor of his more distinctive middle one), for many years the most prominent possessor of the name. But now that the creator of *Citizen Kane* is gone and Orson no longer seems like a single-person signature, it becomes an interesting possibility for any parent seeking a nearly unique yet solid name.

ORVILLE. We consider this a middle-name-only choice that should be confined to the babies of parents either deeply interested in aviation or seriously addicted to popcorn.

OSBERT, OSMOND, OSWALD, OSGOOD, OSBORNE. Names that begin with the Anglo-Saxon *Os* may have been a minor rage a century ago, but they rate less than zero today. Poor Osbert suffers from the double whammy of the soft *os* beginning and the wimpy *bert* ending. Osmond is too tightly tied to the aging musical clan featuring Donny and Marie, and Oswald (despite Oswald the Lucky Rabbit, Walt Disney's first successful cartoon character), is one of the biggest joke names around. Osgood has a small measure of surname-name charm, but only Osborne—or Osborn or Osbourne—possesses any real style or masculine punch, perhaps because rock star Ozzy Osbourne lent it some rock 'n' roll pizzazz. See **OZ** for some other ideas.

OSCAR. Rotund and jovial, Oscar is a good-natured grandpa name, which, with the current fashionability of others like Jake and Harry and Chester, finds itself sticking a toe into the limelight again. True, most parents will still consider it far too fuddy-duddy for a baby, but some style-conscious souls who understand that Max isn't Max anymore may be open to this alternative. In Irish legend, Oscar was one of the mightiest warriors of his generation, the grandson of Finn MacCool. In addition to being a Swedish royal name, Oscar has also been especially popular with Latino families. Famous Oscars include Wilde (whose given name was the Irish Fingal), Madison, Hammerstein, de la Renta, the Academy Award, and the Grouch.

OTIS. Otis has had something of a split-screen image over the years. On the one hand it's been associated with the seductive, bluesy tones of Otis Redding (coincidentally, its Greek meaning implies someone with a good ear for music), on the other hand with the upscale activities of such society figures as Otis Chandler, onetime publisher of the *Los Angeles Times*. The two images seem to be merging now as Otis becomes more and more upwardly mobile and fashionable, with parents attracted to its catchy *O* initial and combination of strength and spunk.

OTTO. Truly cutting-edge parents may consider the old German name Otto outlandish enough to be cool. Our advice: Unless you're a rock star, a major movie personality or a billionaire (it does literally mean "prosperous"), let Otto lie. Trivia tidbit: How many people remember (or care) that Don Rickles's first name on the old *CPO Sharkey* series was Otto?

OWEN. Owen is the wonderfully resonant Celtic name that is picking up where the overfashionable Ian left off. Kevin Kline and Phoebe Cates have a son named Owen, so does Christopher Reeve, and so, truth be told, does one of us. Owen (or Eoghan or Eoin in its impossible Irish Gaelic spellings—Owen is the phonetic Welsh version) was an ancient and legendary saint who was kidnapped and sold into slavery, but released after the slave master found him reading while an angel did his chores. Smart boy. Through the years, Owens have appeared in Shakespeare plays (*Henry IV, Part I*), Irish drama (*Deirdre of the Sorrows*) and on TV (*Owen Marshall, Counselor at Law,* and, more recently, as the youngest Salinger sibling on *Party of Five*). Another Welsh version is **OWAIN.**

OZ. It may be a Hebrew name meaning strength, power, and courage, but to the average American child, it's sure to evoke illustrations of wizards and yellow brick roads. Like the mid-century sitcom name **OZZIE,** it's also a nickname for Oswald, **OZNI** (a grandson of Jacob in the Old Testament), and the Greek **OZIAS.** Australians often refer to their homeland as Oz. Caveat: Some people may now associate Oz with the HBO prison series.

P

PABLO. This Spanish version of Paul has aesthetic associations to all the fine arts—there's Picasso the protean painter, Casals the master cellist, and Neruda the acclaimed Chilean poet.

PACEY. This name, which seemed to come out of nowhere to become the name of an attractive character on *Dawson's Creek,* has begun to attract the attention of parents seeking a relaxed and unusual, modern-sounding name. **PACE** is a more serious surname spin.

PACO. see **FRANCIS.**

PAINTER. One of the newer notions in baby naming is the consideration of occupational names (e.g., Sailor, Scout, Archer, Mason), and this is one with both a pleasant sound and creative associations.

PALMER, PARKER. Two Waspy surname names that would tend to put an instant upper-class gloss on a boy, and have a certain snob appeal. Palmer Cortlandt is a patriarchal character on *All My Children,* while Parker is the name of Rosie O'Donnell's much-discussed oldest child. Others of this ilk: **PAXTON, PARRISH, PARNELL.**

PARIS. The romantic capital city of France has become a hot unisex baby name—Pierce Brosnan gave it to his son, Michael Jackson to his daughter. In ancient times, it was the Trojan prince Paris who abducted the beautiful Helen, bringing about the long siege of Troy, as chronicled in Homer's *Iliad.*

PARRY. Unheard of in this country, the energetic Parry means "son of Harry" in Wales, where it is quite commonly used.

PASCAL. The French-accented Pascal is associated with Easter, and might be an interesting choice for a boy with Gallic roots born around that holiday. **PASQUALE** is the Italian version, **PASCUAL** the Spanish, **PASQUAL** the Greek. **PASCOE** is a last-name-first variation.

PATRICK. For decades Patrick had a difficult time transcending its hyper-Irish image in the United States, but now it seems finally on the verge of doing so, beginning to achieve the mainstream acceptability and style cachet it has long held in England, where it is one of the most fashionable names for young gentlemen. One problem with Patrick's American image may have been our tendency to abbreviate names: Where the formal Patrick seems masculine and distinguished, the almost inevitable **PAT** feels weak and prohibitively androgynous, as does the now rarely heard **PATSY.** Another Patrick nickname, **PADDY,** was chosen by Mare Winningham as the full name of her son. Some parents attracted to Patrick's strong nationalistic flavor—Saint Patrick is, after all, the patron saint of Ireland—may want to look at the name's native version, **PÁDRAIG** (pronounced PAH-rig), which was used for his son by Patrick Ewing. Some European versions include **PATRICE** (French) and **PATRIZIO** (Italian).

PAUL. To the thousands of girls who screamed the name of their favorite Beatle in the 1960s, Paul had a thrillingly unique image, but to the rest of the world, then and now, it's a name that's so simple and yet so widely diffuse that it could belong to almost anyone. One of the traditional male names, Paul has been out of favor for so long that it's starting to sound fresher than, say, John or William to the current generation of parents, who are beginning to reappraise its classic strength. It also has a rich religious background: Saint Paul (originally called Saul but baptized Paul after his conversion) was a cofounder with Peter of the Christian church, and there have been six Pope Pauls. There are scores of famous Pauls whose individual personae have colored the name, from Paul Bunyan to Paul Revere, Paul Newman to painters Cézanne and Gauguin. Some creative foreign versions, in addition to Pablo (see above): **PAOLO** (Italian), **PAVEL** (Russian), and **PAAVO** (Finnish).

PAX, PAZ. The Latin and Spanish words for "peace" could make meaningful middle names; Paz is also a Hebrew name meaning "golden" or "sparkling." **PAXTON** is a related surname.

PERCIVAL. Percival, a name coined by a twelfth-century poet for King Arthur's most perfectly pure and innocent knight, the first to glimpse the Holy Grail, has been stigmatized by a persnickety, Milquetoasty image, one from which we don't see it ever recovering.

PERCY. Despite what it seems, Percy is not a short form of Percival, but a Norman place-name long used as both a first and last name. But whatever its origins, Percy is viewed as one of the ultimate sissy names, in contrast to the poet Percy Bysshe Shelley's dashing persona.

PEREGRINE. Most people will skip right by this entry, and we really wouldn't blame them. But if there is anyone out there looking for an outrageously eccentric British name to set a child apart from all others, this one's for you. In England it is a name heard at hunting parties (a peregrine is, after all, a kind of falcon that can be trained to hunt birds) and borne by trainees at Sotheby's, and it has literary and historical points as well: Peregrine was the name of the first child of British parentage born on the *Mayflower;* it was the name of Smollett's swashbuckling scoundrel, Peregrine Pickle; and **PEREGRIN** was a lively Hobbit in *The Lord of the Rings.*

PERRY. Perry, which came into being as a pet form of Peregrine, has recently acquired a measure of style for girls, but for boys, it's a pipe-smoking, cardigan-sweatered remnant of the Perry Como/Perry Mason/Perry White era that we don't expect to see rising out of its easy chair any time soon.

PERU. A unique geographical name, evocative of gleaming silver and the snowcapped Andes, with a pleasant and catchy sound.

PETER. For generations, there have been pleasant childhood associations with this name—what with Peter Rabbit; Peter Piper; Peter, Peter, Pumpkin Eater; and, especially, Peter Pan. But as user-friendly as this makes the name, it has a solid, traditional side as well. One of the most important figures in the Christian hagiography is Saint Peter, keeper of the Gates of Heaven. Born Simon bar Jonah, he was given the nickname Peter (which means "rock") by Jesus, to signify that he would be the rock on which Christ would build Christianity. Centuries later, there was Peter the Great, the czar who developed Russia as a major European power. Never as widely used as some of the more traditional Anglo-Saxon stalwarts, Peter has an enduring appeal to parents seeking a name that is outside questions of style and trendiness, familiar but not faddish. Peter also has some interesting derivatives: The Brits like **PIERS,** the Irish **PEARSE** and **PIERCE** (as in Irish-born Pierce Brosnan), all of which were introduced to England by the Normans. Other versions around the world include **PIERO** and **PIETRO** (Italian), **PEDRO** (Spanish)—the name Frances McDormand and Joel Coen gave their son—**PIETER** and **PIET** (Dutch), and **PIERRE** (French).

PHELAN. Pronounced FAY-lan, this Irish surname meaning "wolf" was used as a first name in a short story by O. Henry.

PHILIP, PHILLIP. Philip, which means "lover of horses," has a certain built-in reserve, as straight and staid as the public image of the Duke of Edinburgh, qualities that gained a measure of favor during the upwardly mobile 1980s. Saint Philip was one of the twelve Apostles, King Philip the Great was the father of Alexander the Great, and there have been numerous other French and Spanish rulers bearing the name. Nicknames include **PHIL, FLIP,** and **PIP,** and the French version is **PHILIPPE.**

PHILO. A dynamic and distinctive Greek name (it means "friendly"), Philo has been used in literature—as a minor figure in Shakespeare's *Antony and Cleopatra,* the S. S. Van Dine detective, Philo Vance, and Clint Eastwood's character in both *Any Which Way You Can* and *Every Which Way But Loose,* but rarely in real life. Possible drawbacks: *(a)* people might think it was an abbreviation for Filofax, and *(b)* it could sound like a dog's name.

PHINEAS. Only an adventurous parent with a sense of humor would dare choose this Old Testament name for his or her child. It is associated with Phineas T. Barnum, who started the Greatest Show on Earth, and was also the name of the hero of Trollope's novel about a young Irish lawyer, *Phineas Finn.* In early movies, characters named Phineas had last names like Whipsnake, Prune, and Whoopee. The guy who went around the world in eighty days was actually **PHILEAS** Fogg.

PHOENIX. A place-name with mythological overtones, Phoenix is both the capital of Arizona and, in Egyptian myth, the beautiful bird that lives in the Arabian desert for five centuries, sets itself on fire, and then rises from the ashes, thus symbolizing immortality.

PIERCE. See **PETER.**

PIERS. See **PETER.**

PLÁCIDO. A Latin name with calm (because of its meaning), yet operatic (Plácido Domingo) associations, Plácido is also a saint's name.

PLATO. The name of one of the greatest Western philosophers is often used as a first name in its land of origin, Greece. It is remembered here as the character played by Sal Mineo in *Rebel Without a Cause.*

PO and **POE** are the Bo and Beau of the new millennium—relaxed and sexy. Both are literary—Poe relates to Edgar Allan, while Po is the first name of the chronicler of the technological age, Po Bronson. Po also has a geographical association: It's a river in northern Italy. But parents drawn to the name's minimalist cool should also be aware that one of the Teletubbies is named Po.

PRESLEY. Unabashed Elvis fans have turned his surname into a viable baby name. First Tanya Tucker chose it for her daughter, then Cindy Crawford, somewhat more logically, gave it to her son.

PRESTON, PORTER, POWELL, PRENTICE, PRESCOTT. This is just a sampling of the many *P* surnames that have been occasionally used as solid, serious, verging-on-pretentious first names (see also Palmer et al.) over the years. The most commonly heard Preston, was invested with appeal by the great screwball comedy director Preston Sturges. Powell and others have made daytime drama appearances.

PRIMO. Among the Latin birth-order names—Octavius et al.—Primo, which means "first," is the one most likely to be used in these days of smaller families. Primo's jaunty *o* ending and Italianate flavor are appealing, though some may see its image as offensively egotistic. Author Primo Levi was a famous bearer.

PRINCE. The performer formerly and then again known by this name was actually born with it, and it was also regally bestowed on his son by Michael Jackson. It's your call as to whether this crown would weigh too heavy on your child's head.

Q

QUARRY. A word name that has the offbeat quality and the macho feel—think Rock, think Stone—that appeals to increasing numbers of today's parents.

QUEBEC. This geographic name has a longer history than you might imagine—Charles Dickens used it for a character in his novel *Bleak House*.

QUENTIN. An offbeat name with a lot of character, Quentin relates to the Latin for the number 5 and is by far the most usable of the birth-order names, masculine as well as stylish and distinctive. Sir Walter Scott wrote the novel *Quentin Durward* in 1823, about a young, upper-class Scotsman; Quentin Crisp was a British eccentric and author of *The Naked Civil Servant*; Quentin Tarantino is a cutting-edge movie director, and the name has also appeared on soap operas, sitcoms, and in such works as *Wonder Boys*.

QUINCY. *Q* names are quirky, and Quincy is quirky with some measure of wimpiness, despite the fact that the talented and cool musician Quincy Jones has done a good deal to counter that stereotype, and that it has been used for stronger characters, such as the one played by Omar Epps in *Love and Basketball*.

QUINLIN, QUINLAN. This Irish surname meaning "fit, shapely, and strong" is one that could make a child feel unique, while still having the regular-guy nickname of Quinn.

QUINN. Quinn, which means "wise" in Celtic, is an engaging Irish surname that has some history as a unisex first name. Actress Sean Young chose it for her son, as did writers Anna Quindlen and Sally Quinn—both for obvious reasons.

QUINTEN, QUINTIN, QUINTON. These variations of the more prevalent Quentin have been gaining in currency of late. Quinton has been a character on *Moesha,* and is also the name of the son of Loni Anderson and Burt Reynolds, no doubt referring back to the character Reynolds played in *Gunsmoke* back in 1962—**QUINT** Asper. Two further out possibilities: **QUINTAS** and **QUINTO**.

R

RAFFERTY. A raffish Irish surname with lots of congenial charm, Rafferty, which means "rich" in Gaelic, was chosen for their son by British acting pair Sadie Frost and Jude Law.

RAFIKI, RAFIQ. Rafiki is a Kiswahili word meaning "good will" and a name children might relate to as the wise guru character in *The Lion King*. Rafiq is the appealing Muslim version, for which **RAFI** is a nickname.

RAINER. A German name that suddenly sounds like a good possibility here, though the related **REINER** is still too Teutonic.

RALPH. Ralph is one of the few names on which the two of us adamantly disagree, probably because it can be looked at in two diametrically different ways. At its most positive, Ralph is an upper-crust British favorite— think of actors Sir Ralph Richardson and Ralph Fiennes—sometimes pronounced as **RAFE,** and charmingly quirky when imported with that pronunciation to our shores. On the other hand, Ralph is also (and to most Americans) Jackie Gleason's Ralph Kramden, the eternal blue-collar bus driver, bowler, and blowhard. Love it or hate it, Ralph is a name that's been around for a thousand years, was in the Top 30 from the 1870s to the 1920s, and just could make a comeback somewhere down the line.

RAMSAY, RAMSEY. A place-name on the Isle of Man, this has long been used occasionally as a first name.

RANDOLPH. Randolph is a name that had its last hurrah in the days of the black-and-white westerns starring Randolph Scott. Nickname **RANDY,** which offered some aw-shucks appeal to baby namers of yesteryear, including those of country singer Randy Travis, has gone the way of the parent name. The Matt Damon character in *Legend of Bagger Vance* is **RANNUPH,** but don't try that at home. The medieval form **RANDALL** has the slightly more stylish ring of a surname name.

RAOUL, RAUL. These French and Spanish forms of Randolph have a lot more élan than the original.

RAPHAEL, RAFAEL. An excellent cross-cultural possibility, Raphael is a Hebrew name that is also well used in Latin countries. Raphael was one of the seven archangels who attended the throne of God and, as the angel of healing, is the patron of doctors, as well as of travelers, science, and knowledge. Another worthy namesake is the great Renaissance painter Raphael (born Raffaello), and it is the name chosen for their sons by Robert DeNiro and Juliette Binoche. **RAFI** is the familiar Hebrew nickname, and **RAFE** is sometimes used as well.

RAVI. This alternate name for the Hindu sun god Surya has become known in this country via the legendary sitar player Ravi Shankar.

RAYMOND. Does everybody love Raymond? Another split decision between the authors on this one. To one of us, Raymond is the coolest of the cool, an opinion undoubtedly shared by Jack Nicholson, who used it for his son. To the other, Raymond is as dull and dismal as a name could possibly be, stuck back in 1925, when it was in the Top 20. The nickname **RAY** has long been a Southern ambigender middle-name favorite (Billy Joel and Christie Brinkley named their daughter Alexa Ray after Ray Charles), and a memorable fictional Raymond/Ray is the autistic character played by Dustin Hoffman in *Rain Man*. Other Raymond relatives you might find more palatable: the sultry Latin **RAMON** and **RAIMONDO**, the Irish **REAMONN** (and nickname **REA**) and the surname **REDMOND**.

REAGAN. This Irish surname meaning "descended from the little king" can be pronounced either as the former president did (RAY-gan) or REE-gan, which can also be spelled **REGAN**. To complicate the matter, Regan was a female in Shakespeare's *King Lear*.

REECE, REESE. See **RHYS**.

REED. A slim, elegant, silvery surname name, Reed combines a brisk masculinity with an artistic air: Reed might be an executive in the family firm, or an equally successful painter. Originally meaning "redhead," it can also be spelled **REID**, but **READ** might be too ambiguous in terms of pronunciation.

REGINALD. Reginald sounds like the name of the chap in the smoking jacket in a 1930s English comedy, though **REGGIE** manages a more modern, macho image thanks to sports greats Reggie Jackson and Reggie White. Several show-biz personalities wisely dropped their given name of Reginald in favor of Rex (Harrison), Ray (Milland), and Elton (John). **REYNOLD** or **REYNOLDS,** medieval variations on Reginald, might be slightly better choices today, if a bit stiff.

REGIS. A venerable old saint's name, quite common in France with an accent over the *e,* meaning "regal," Regis might have gone down in history as the name of a New York hotel, or one found on alumni lists of long-gone Catholic-school students, had it not been for Mr. Philbin, who has just about succeeded in making it a one-person name. And yes, that's our final answer.

REILLY. See **RILEY.**

REMBRANDT. There are heroes in the arts as well as in history, politics, sports, and entertainment, and the Dutch painter Rembrandt van Rijn is probably the most renowned of the Old Masters, making his name a potential, if somewhat problematic, option for families who put an emphasis on the creative. The attractive nickname Remy would make it less conspicuous.

REMINGTON. Pierce Brosnan, the suave and debonair future James Bond, lent his savoir faire to this name via his eponymous character in the TV series *Remington Steele.* Since the 1980s, then, the name has been in the public consciousness, sounding like the ultimate corporate title. Actress Tracy Nelson turned Remington around by giving it to her little girl.

REMY. Remy (also spelled **REMI**) is a relaxed Gallic offshoot of **REMUS** (permanently terminated by the image of Uncle Remus), with a lot of charm, and is sometimes associated with the Cajun cadences of New Orleans, although it actually means someone from the French city of Rheims. Remus was one of the legendary twins who founded Rome.

RENÉ. Almost exclusively a girls' name here, though Celine Dion's little René-Charles has brought the name's masculine origins before the public eye.

RENO. This geographic name has a lively and swaggering sound, but also a few unfortunate associations—gambling, and marriages that didn't make it.

REO, RIO. A pair of seductive ranchero place-names with an attractive Tex-Mex lilt. Rio was Marlon Brando's name as a young desperado in the 1961 *One-Eyed Jacks,* has been a character on the soap opera *Loving,* and was chosen for her son by Sean Young.

REUBEN. Reuben has several ingredients for success: an Old Testament pedigree—Reuben was Jacob's only son by Leah and the founder of one of the tribes of Israel—plus the distinction of not ever having been heavily used, and boasting a friendly, down-home image. So it's not hard to envision the current crowd of Jacobs growing up and following the lead of the biblical Jacob by naming their own sons Reuben. Panama-born salsa singer **RUBEN** Blades represents the Latin version (with the accent on the second syllable); **REUVEN** is the name in Hebrew.

REX. Rex Harrison (born Reginald) prompted the epithet "Sexy Rexy," which has managed to stick to the name like Super Glue, and in a cartoony, glossy-haired way. (It does in fact belong to a comics character, Rex Morgan, M.D., who's been practicing since 1948.) That said, there is still the charm of Rex's final *x* and an offbeat simplicity that you might find more than make up for its slickness. Caveat: Rex has long been a popular name for canines.

RHAIN. Sort of the opposite of Ryan—it's pronounced RAY-in—this Welsh name might make a distinctive alternative to that overused favorite.

RHETT. In addition to being a powerful storyteller, Margaret Mitchell, the author of *Gone With the Wind,* was a great character namer as well—think of Scarlett, Melanie, Ashley, Bonnie Belle, and even the mansion, Tara. Rhett was among them, emerging from the story as one of the ultimate dashing, romantic names. These days, however, Rhett, like the name of his rival Ashley, sounds more girlish than gallant.

RHYS. A common Welsh name meaning "ardor" in Celtic, Rhys is seldom heard in this country in its original spelling—it's more likely to be Anglicized with the phonetic spellings **REECE** or **REESE**. Reese has been somewhat feminized by the emergence of actress Reese Witherspoon, although it was also the name of the character played by Ice-T in *Judgment Day,* a male doctor on *The Young and the Restless,* and one of the brothers in *Malcolm in the Middle.* Rhys, which could make an interesting middle-name choice, belonged to two twelfth-century Welsh warrior heroes. **ROYCE** is a variant, as is Rhett (see above).

RICHARD. A classic male name popular for a thousand years and favored for kings (Richard Nixon was named after Richard the Lionhearted), as well as the hoi polloi (every Tom, Dick, and Harry), Richard was the sixth most popular boys' name in 1925, and was still number 8 in 1950, but has been considered unfashionable in recent decades, despite a revival in Britain. We predict that if parents do readopt the name Richard, it will be in its full and formal version: The nicknames **DICK** and **DICKY** are too tricky and too subject to punning, **RICKY** too *I Love Lucy,* **RICHIE** too *Happy Days.* The Latin **RICARDO** and **RICO** may offer more colorful variations.

RIDER, RYDER. A word name with the little cowboy appeal American parents seem to love—Hey, Jesse! Wha'sup, Austin and Cody!—this can be spelled either the obvious way or Ryanified as actor John Leguizamo did when he named his son Ryder.

RIDGE. This quintessential daytime drama name is too close to the word "rigid" to be recommended.

RIO. This rakish name, Spanish for "river," has been used for heroes of cartoons and video games. It's a name your child would probably thank you for—until he grew up and wanted to be, say, an accountant.

RIORDAN. This Irish surname has a legitimate history as a first name in its native land and an appealing meaning—"royal poet, or bard." The only obstacle: Its pronunciation—REER-den—is far from obvious from its spelling.

RILEY, REILLY. One of the jauntiest and least pretentious of the Irish surname names, Riley (the more common spelling) has been used as a first name for over a century. Appropriate for children of both sexes, Riley is the name of the sons of director David Lynch and actress Mare Winningham, and the daughter of comedian Howie Mandel; it is also the given name of blues singer B. B. King.

RINGO. Better stick to John, Paul, or George.

RIVER. A tranquil nature name, somewhat unsettled by the unfortunate fate of bearer River Phoenix.

ROBERT. This classic was among the American male Top 25 for an entire century, now having slipped just outside that magic circle to twenty-ninth place, a significant drop when you consider that the name was number 1 in both 1925 and 1950. Now, Robert relies on its place in history rather than any sense of style; a good percentage of baby Roberts these days are juniors or thirds. Parents in search of a distinctive twist on the name might consider using the surnames **ROBINSON** or **ROBERTSON** (which mean "son of Robert"), the Latin **ROBERTO** or the German form **RUPERT**. Nicknames **BOB** and **BOBBY** are stuck in the past, **ROB, ROBB,** and **ROBBY/ROBBIE** have an ever-so-slightly more modern appeal. Perhaps it's time to go back and dig up some of Robert's old-time long-forgotten nicknames: **DOB, HOB,** and **NOB.** Perhaps not.

ROBIN. Still as well used for boys in England today as it was from the time of legendary outlaw Robin Hood to childhood favorite Christopher Robin, this name is almost exclusively female in America. Even the popularity of Robin Williams hasn't been enough to inspire a generation of little boy Robins here.

ROCCO. Until Madonna bestowed it on her baby boy, Rocco seemed like one of those quintessential immigrant names that no modern parent long off the boat would consider, but now that she's given it her stamp of approval, it points out Rocco's embodiment of the quirky appeal of some other so-far-out-they're-in names, like Bruno and Hugo.

ROCK, STONE, BRICK. The Rocks and **ROCKY**s—as in Hudson and Balboa—have long since sunk as naming inspirations (if they ever were), but for parents who favor this sort of tough elemental name we offer two tough elemental substitutes: Stone and Brick, which represent the new trend toward word names. Brick was the hero of Tennessee Williams's *Cat on a Hot Tin Roof,* and Stone Phillips has gained recognition as a TV newsman.

RODERICK. A rather haughty, highfalutin' name that has lots of literary allusions (including the novels *Roderick Random* by Smollett and *Roderick Hudson* by Henry James), but very little history of real-life usage in this country. **ROD** is the soap-operaish short form, **RODDY** the boyish one. **RODERIC** is an alternate spelling, but the only way to squeeze any real pizzazz from this name is by using the Latin version, **RODRIGO,** or the Irish **RORY.**

RODNEY. A British place-name that was once considered the height of elegance and refinement by some parents—but then again, so was Seymour.

ROGER. In the World War II era, Roger had nothing but the most positive associations, actually used by military personnel to mean "A-OK"—and before that there was the Jolly Roger (which wasn't so jolly—a pirate's black flag with skull and crossbones). But despite several distinguished bearers—Rogers Maris, Moore, Daltry, Ebert, and Rabbit—the name is totally out to pasture for babies of this generation.

ROLAND. Roland is a chivalrous-sounding name made famous by the supposedly eight-foot-tall romantic hero and nephew of Charlemagne, celebrated in medieval poetry and song. After a long nap, it's a name that could conceivably, in time, sound possible again, as itself or, even better, in its more graceful Italian form, **ORLANDO,** or perhaps in its genial *o*-ending version, **ROLLO,** which is currently quite fashionable in England. **ROLLIN** is another variant; baseball fans might like the association with the great relief pitcher **ROLLIE** (born Roland) Fingers.

ROLE. See **RUDOLPH.**

ROMAN. This is a name with heft and a touch of the exotic, as reflected in the images of quarterback Roman Gabriel and the character on the soap *Days of Our Lives,* and obviously means a resident of the Italian capital.

RONALD. As popular as President Reagan was in his day, he did nothing for the style status of the name Ronald, a mid-century favorite (it was number 8 in 1940, number 11 a decade later) that's a dud today, made even more dated by nicknames **RON** and **RONNIE.** First used extensively in Scotland, Ronald is a traditional favorite of the McDonald clan, making the name of the Golden Arches spokesman all the more appropriate.

RONAN. This Irish name of ten saints means "little seal" and could make a less barbaric choice than Conan.

ROONEY, ROONE. Rooney is one of many attractive Irish surname names, but we think it's Roone (as in TV executive Roone Arledge) that's the possible winner here—lively, distinctive, and strong—if you can get past its similarity to the word *ruin.*

RORY. This spirited Gaelic classic, which became popular in Ireland via the illustrious twelfth-century king Rory O'Connor and legendary chieftain Rory O'More, is still fashionable there today, as well as in England and Scotland. In this country it is equally appealing as a girls' name—it is borne by Robert Kennedy's youngest daughter. In Ireland the name has been associated with several surnames in particular (including McCann, McKinley,

Mulloy, O'Doherty, and O'Donnell), so if you happen to share one of those, Rory would be particularly apt. And although Gates isn't on that list, Mr. Microsoft chose the name for his son. Rory Culkin, younger brother of Macauley, is an appealing child actor: He was the little boy in *You Can Count on Me*.

ROSS. A quiet, understated Celtic surname name, Ross came into millions of American living rooms in the person of the character played by David Schwimmer on *Friends*. Its other associations are quite varied: tycoon and maverick presidential candidate H. (for Henry) Ross Perot, mystery writer Ross (born Kenneth) Macdonald, and one of the twin sons of Jane Pauley and Garry Trudeau. Ross originated as a nickname for a redhead and was the surname of a famous Scottish clan, as well as a place-name in that country.

ROWAN. Another Irish redheaded name, Rowan is the name of a red-berried tree as well. Its image is not enhanced by its association with Rowan Atkinson, better known as the goofy "Mr. Bean." **ROHAN** and **ROGAN** are two more carrot-top cousins, **ROAN** is the spelling Sharon Stone chose for her son.

ROY. Roy is a down-to-earth, denim kind of name that's been consigned a country/cowboy image by such figures as Roys Rogers (born Leonard), Acuff, and Clark. Another in the list of *r* names related to the word *red* (the famous Rob Roy, for example, was a Robert nicknamed Roy because of his red hair), as well as to the French for *king*. Roy hasn't been seen as a baby name for several generations, and isn't likely to make a speedy return. **ROYCE** means "son of Roy."

RUDOLPH, RUDOLF. Rudolphs have many distinguished accomplishments: they've helped guide Santa's sleigh on a foggy Christmas Eve, portrayed the Sheik of Araby on the silent screen, been one of the greatest male ballet dancers of the twentieth century, and have even become mayor of New York City, but we don't consider this stiff, Germanic name a very good bet as a baby name. And as for **RUDY**, it's hardly been heard from since the days of the crooner Rudy Vallee (born Hubert), at least until the nation went *Survivor* crazy. **ROLF** is a more interesting Scandinavian version.

RUFUS. A rumpled redheaded name, originally associated with Britain's King William who had hair of that color, that some would consider more suited to a pet than a person. Rufus Thomas is a well-known soul singer.

RUPERT. The increased visibility of attractive actor Rupert Everett has given this name a more youthful spin than when it was attached to figures like middle-aged media mogul Rupert Murdoch. Though it sounds quintessentially British, Rupert is actually a German form of Robert, and was the name of the hero of D. H. Lawrence's *Women in Love,* as well as a beloved British cartoon bear.

RUSH. If you think of this as a word name, it implies speed, excitement, even danger—not quite the qualities conjured when you connect it with conservative radio personality Rush Limbaugh.

RUSSELL. Russell is one of the many *R* boys' names that began as nicknames for redheads. It had some popularity from the early twentieth century through the 1950s—one of the earliest heartthrob crooners was **RUSS** Columbo—but now sounds like one of the palest of the many surname names available except when you consider the macho sudden superstar, Russell Crowe. *Make Room for Daddy*–period nickname **RUSTY** is definitely just that.

RYAN. The energetic Ryan—which means "little king"—is currently the twelfth most popular boys' name in the country, and as high as number 4 in the state of Connecticut, which is kind of surprising since it's been around for so long. Ryan (born Patrick) O'Neal brought it to light in the mid-1960s, when parents responded to the Irish surname aspect of Ryan, seeing it as a fresher alternative to names like Brian and Kevin. Now, however, namers looking for something more distinctive than Ryan have many other attractive Irish first and surname names to consider, from Conor to Cormac to Kieran to Rory, from Brady to Sullivan to Quinn. **RÍÁN** is the spelling of the Irish saint. **RION** is another variation.

RYLAN, RYKER. Parents who like the name Ryan but consider it overly popular have begun casting about for substitutes, and these two have been suggested. Unfortunately, they lack the jaunty Irish charm of the original. Ryker might have some unfortunate associations with New York's Riker's Island prison.

S

SACHA, SASHA, SASCHA. This Russian pet form of Alexander and Alexandra is now being used more and more on its own, and for both sexes, chosen for its energy and ethnic flair. The Steven Spielberg–Kate Capshaw family, Jerry Seinfield, and Vanessa Williams and Rick Fox all have daughters named Sasha, while one of Mia Farrow's sons is Sascha.

SAGE. Voted "herb name most likely to succeed," Sage has intimations of wisdom as well as fragrant flavoring properties. It's been chosen for their sons by both Sylvester Stallone and Tracey Gold.

SALEM. Salem was a Phoenician god whose name means "evening star." Salem was also, of course, the town in Massachusetts where all that witch stuff went on, as well as the name of the talking cat on TV's *Sabrina*.

SALVATORE, SALVADOR. Salvatore, whose meaning relates to the word *savior,* has long been used in Italian-American families (isn't there a Sal in almost every movie with an Italian setting?), but has never crossed over to more general use, and is not likely to be pulled along in the Leonardo wake. The Spanish version is associated with the Surrealist painter Salvador Dalí.

SAMSON. With the widespread popularity of Samuel, some parents are considering this more (literally) powerful biblical name, which shares the nickname of Sam. Samson was, of course, the superhumanly strong champion of the Israelites against the Philistines who was betrayed by Delilah— the stuff of Cinemascope classics—but the more it is used, the more the name is able to disassociate from that image. **SAMZUN** is the interesting Celtic spelling, **SANSONE** the Italian version.

SAMUEL, SAM. When most of us were growing up, Sam was, like Jake and Max, a cigar-chomping movie mogul name, totally unthinkable as a possibility for an innocent, apple-cheeked baby boy, just as Uncle Sam was the white-bearded symbol of our country. Then some adventurous parents started to recognize the earthy attributes of these names, and before you could say Samuel F. B. Morse, Samuel and Sam were among the most stylish names around, as laid-back and enegmatic as Sam Shepard, as upfront and funny as Sam Malone, as upstanding and righteous as Sam McCloud. These days, Sam has lost a good deal of its style edge, at least among trendsetters—and it's almost as well used as a short form of Samantha as Samuel—but Samuel is still appreciated enough to be among the Top 30 boys' names in the country. **SAMO** is the Czech version, **ZAMIEL** the German.

SANTIAGO. Santiago is a spirited Spanish name with lots of crossover potential. Favorable elements include its being a geographical name, and a surname, as well as the patron saint of Spain (it was formed by the combination of Sant (saint) and Iago (a form of James). Catchy pet names are **CHAGO, CHANO,** and **VEGO.**

SAUL. Jewish parents in particular may be attracted to this name of the first king of Israel, for its symbolic power above any questions of style or trendiness. A name that is both quiet and composed, Saul was also what Saint Paul was called before his conversion, and is associated today with the novelist Saul Bellow.

SAWYER. Sawyer is beginning to be appreciated by parents seeking a less usual surname name that has a more relaxed, down-home feel than others in this upwardly mobile group. Originally an occupational name for a woodworker, it still would make an apt choice for someone in that profession. Kate Capshaw and Steven Spielberg are the parents of a son named Sawyer. **SAYER** is a similar possibility.

SCHUYLER. Schuyler is a name that was brought to this continent by the early Dutch colonists, and has always had a somewhat upscale image. It means "scholar," and boasts the winning nickname **SKY.** Many parents are now opting for such phonetic spellings as **SKYLER, SKYLAR,** and **SKYLOR** (see **SKYLER**).

SCORPIO. A zodiacal name with an almost overbearingly potent presence that might prove to be a burden to a young boy—that and its resemblance to the word *scorpion.* In the soap opera *General Hospital,* Scorpio is the character's last name.

SCOTT. In 1965, Scott was the hippest name on the beach—the muscular, windswept, surfer-lifeguard attracting all the girls. Even earlier it had an attractive image, attached as it was to the handsome, doomed writer F. Scott Fitzgerald; later it seemed like the perfect astronaut name, as in Scott (born Malcolm) Carpenter. It originated, not surprisingly, as a surname for someone of Scottish descent. Although the occasional diehard's license-plate frame still reads BEAM ME UP SCOTTY, the name is now definitely treading water.

SCOUT. Scout surfaced as a girl's name when Demi Moore and Bruce Willis chose it for their middle daughter, taking a leaf from the book of Harper Lee, who used it as the nickname for the young girl character in *To Kill a Mockingbird.* Then skating champ Tai Babilonia chose it for her son, establishing it as a unisex possibility. Its image combines the upstanding qualities of a Boy (or Girl) Scout, with the perspicacity of someone scouting in nature or for talent.

SEAMUS. The Irish form of James, Seamus (pronounced SHAY-mus) once symbolized a fresh-off-the-boat Irish greenhorn, and later (at a time when most cops were Irish), spelled phonetically as *shamus,* became the generic term for a detective. But as such stereotypical ethnic epithets have faded away, the perfectly fine names behind them—from Seamus to Jake to Jemima—have come to light and back into use. Seamus Heaney is the acclaimed Irish poet, and Seamus was the villain's name in the movie *Ronan.*

SEAN. This Irish form of John, always common in the Emerald Isle (it's currently number 2 on their list), has been au courant here for thirty years now, helped along by the popularity of Sean Connery, Shaun Cassidy, and Sean Penn. It has slipped in usage in recent years, superseded first by such names as Ryan, and now by other authentic Irish names. Alternate forms **SHAUN** and **SHAWN** have been almost as widely used, though those spellings are seen more frequently for girls.

SEBASTIAN. Parents considering this name often dismiss it as being just too flamboyant and ornate, and, indeed, it is a lot more dramatic than other British-inflected choices like Trevor or Ian. But Sebastian is also a name with a substantial history, first as the third-century martyr whose sufferings were a favorite subject of medieval artists, then as the name of colorful characters in such varied works as *Twelfth Night* and *Brideshead Revisited,* not to mention the invisible Sebastian Caine in *Hollow Man.* Meaning "majestic" in Greek, it is also associated with British Olympic runner Sebastian Coe, superstar Spanish golfer Sebastian Balesteros, and was chosen for his son by actor James Spader. And although it may seem like a name with no possible nickname (a plus for some parents), in Europe **SEB, SEBBIE, BAS,** and even **BASTIAN** are used.

SELBY. A rarely heard British last name related to the willow tree that, although rather gentle, still has more masculine drive than the Southern-inflected **SHELBY.**

SEPTIMUS, SEXTUS. In the days of large Victorian families, the imposing Latin Septimus was a name saved for a seventh son. Virginia Woolf gave the name to one of the principal characters in her novel *Mrs. Dalloway.* Daunting as it might be for a modern boy, it's still preferable to sixth-son name Sextus, ruled out on the basis of its first syllable alone.

SERGE. In Russia, Serge, which comes from **SERGEI,** is a common name, often used to honor one of that country's most beloved saints, known for his kindness, gentleness, and Saint Francis–like relationship to nature. The name traveled to France in the 1920s, with White Russian exiles and the Ballet Russe, and still retains an artistic, almost effete, air. It is also the name of the hero in the hit video game Chrono Cross.

SETH. Not as well remembered as brothers Cain and Abel, Seth was the third, postfratricide son of Adam and Eve. (As a consequence, this gentle, muted name was often used by the Puritans for children born after an older sibling's death.) It was widely heard in the American old West, as reflected in such vintage TV oaters as *Wagon Train,* whose hero was Major Seth Adams, and more recently has had leading roles on *As the World Turns* and in such films as *The Fly* (Jeff Goldblum), *City of Angels* (Nicolas Cage), and *Absolute Power* (Ed Harris).

SEVEN. Is this a trend? There have been characters named Six and Seven on TV sitcoms, and Seven is what singer Erykah Badu named her son. Does this mean we're going to start numbering our children rather than naming them? We sure hope not.

SEYMOUR. Sorry, Seymour is busy playing shuffleboard out by the pool at his condo in Sun City and won't be available for several generations.

SHAMUS. See **SEAMUS.**

SHANE. In this country, Shane ambled into the picture via the 1953 movie of the same name, adding a cowboy twist to its Irish essence. Its history goes back to an Elizabethan-era Irish prince, Shane the Proud, who was the head of the O'Neil clan. Today, however, although it's still number 11 in the Old Sod, here Shane now sounds as tired as Shaun and Shawn.

SHAQUILLE. Although this seemed destined to be a one-person name, the charisma of the primary bearer, L.A. Laker star Shaquille O'Neal, has inspired hundreds of parents to adopt it for their own future athletes. We hope they all have as perfect a last name to go with it as he does.

SHARIF. An exotic surname long associated with Egyptian-born actor and bridge expert Omar, it is now within the realm of possibility for those exploring this territory.

SHEA. A common surname in Ireland, Shea projects a complex image for a short, one-syllable name, combining spirit and substance, which may have prompted best-selling author John Grisham to use it for his son. Also spelled **SHAY,** it can be used as a pet form of Seamus.

SHELDON. In a class with Melvin and Marvin, Sheldon is about as far outside the realm of possibility as a baby name can get, even though there are very pretty towns in Devon and Derbyshire that inspired the name. **SHELBY** is a possible variation (Reba McEntire used it for her son), but is employed far more often for girls. Director Spike Lee's given name is **SHELTON.**

SHEPHERD, SHEPARD. An occupational surname with a pleasant pastoral feel, and the friendly nickname **SHEP.**

SHERIDAN. This Irish surname came to public recognition with the charismatic character of Sheridan Whiteside in the play and movie *The Man Who Came to Dinner.* Drawback: the feminine nickname Sherry.

SHERMAN. Not quite as over-the-hill as Herman, but not far behind either. Just picture Sherman Klump.

SHILOH. A biblical place-name, like Jordan, Zion, Bethany, and Sharon, Shiloh is also a town associated with a Civil War battle. It means "God's gift" and is occasionally used as a boy's name.

SIDNEY. With Sydney continuing to grow in popularity as a name for girls, the male version has lost virtually all the testosterone it ever had. A contraction name (it comes from Saint Denis and is related to Dionysius, the Greek god of fertility and wine), Sidney is an aristocratic British surname (as in the Elizabethen poet Sir Philip Sidney), and attained a considerable measure of dignity through its association with the self-sacrificing hero of *A Tale of Two Cities,* Sidney Carton, and with Oscar-winning actor Sidney Poitier.

SIEGFRIED, SIGMUND. Not recommended unless you're looking for a circuitous route to the nickname Ziggy, or are a devout Freudian.

SILAS. Until recently a folksy-sounding, farmerish, old-fogey name, killed off for many of us by having read *Silas Marner* when we were too young to appreciate it, Silas just might be up for reevaluation in this era of George Eliot enthusiasm. Like the similar-flavored Caleb and Abner, it has a funky feel that might appeal to parents who long to return to their grass roots. In the New Testament, **SILUS** was one of Saint Paul's companions.

SILVER. This shimmery 1960s and 1970s unisex flower child name is making a comeback with free-spirited parents of the New Millennium, along with strictly female gem names like Diamond, Emerald, Jade, and Ruby.

SIMEON. For parents looking for a less simple version of Simon, we recommend considering the possibility of Simeon, the original Hebrew (and modern French) form. Musician Wynton Marsalis chose it for his son. Caveat: We must point out (before someone else does) its similarity to the word meaning "apelike."

SIMON. There is an appealing genuineness about this name, perhaps due to phrases like "simon-pure" and "Simple Simon." An Old and New Testament name (Simon was the second son of Jacob and Leah and the original name of Saint Peter) that gained an English accent around the time Roger Moore was playing Simon Templar on *The Saint*, Simon was one of the more appealing characters in *Lord of the Flies*, then became part of the British invasion of names that hit our shores along with the Beatles and Mary Quant. Simon never reached saturation point here and can still make a stylish and interesting choice.

SINBAD. Sinbad has always had an exotic air, having appeared in innumerable *Arabian Nights*–type costume dramas, complete with flowing veils and harem pants. When comedian David Adkins took it on as his stage name, it became somewhat feasible as a modern first name, but any child bearing it would be subject to some tough times in the playground.

SINCLAIR. Sinclair might well be just another of the scores of surname names clamoring to be heard today were it not for its connection to the writer Sinclair (born Harry) Lewis. A contraction of the Normandy place-name St. Clair, Sinclair could be a novel way to honor an ancestral Clare or Claire in a boy's name.

SKYLER, SKY. Skyler is by far the more popular of these two as a boys' name, partly because of its similarity to the megapopular Tyler. It's also spelled **SKYLAR**, and both are based on the Dutch surname **SCHUYLER**, though the original spelling is now seldom used. At this point, the name relates more directly to **SKY**, which was legitimized as a name on the Broadway stage by the *Guys and Dolls* character Sky Masterson and later was a hippie nature name—but now, strangely enough, has largely become a girls' name.

SLADE. Meaning "child of the valley," this British surname does evoke the image of a shady glen, and could make a distinctive middle name.

SLATE, SLATER. In the current crop of strong, single-syllable boys' names, Slate is one of the more unusual, evoking the images of both old-fashioned blackboards and modern stepping stones. Slater is an extended occupational last-name-first version.

SLOAN, SLOANE. A few decades ago, this name—which scarcely betrays its Irish roots—called to mind Britain's socially conscious Sloane Rangers, typified by the late Princess Diana. Nowadays, though still slim and sleek, it is almost exclusively used for girls.

SOLOMON. A wise old name that, along with other patriarchal classics, is finally beginning to shed its long white beard and step from the pages of the Old Testament into modern nurseries. From the Hebrew word *shalom,* meaning "peace," it was a favorite of Dickens, who used it for characters in three of his novels. The Arabic version is **SELIM** or **SULAIMAN,** in France it's **SALAUN,** in Spain **SALAMON,** in Yiddish, **ZALMAN**.

SOREN. Soren is a gentle Danish name, soft and sensitive but with a bit more masculine punch than Loren.

SORLEY. A rarely heard Celtic surname name with an unfortunate association to the word *sore.*

SPENCER. One of those names that has everything, Spencer is both distinguished sounding and perfectly accessible, dignified but friendly. It took on a noble air as Winston Churchill's widely known middle name and Princess Diana's family name, and a more down-to-earth and genial one in the persona of Spencer Tracy. Johnny Depp's name in *The Astronaut's Wife* was Spencer, and Robert Ulrich was the single-named private eye in the old TV series *Spenser for Hire*. Celebrities who have picked up on the name for their sons include Cuba Gooding Jr. and Gena Lee Nolan.

SQUALL. A video-game name: Squall is the main character in *Final Fantasy VIII*. Neither the meaning of the name nor the character who inspired it are very appealing, but may provide another alternative for parents considering such born-to-be-bad choices as Gunner or Storm.

STANLEY. Stanley is typical of the aristocratic English surnames (as in explorer Sir Henry Stanley, utterer of the famous greeting "Mr. Livingston, I presume?"), taken over by immigrant parents in the early years of the twentieth century, in an attempt to give their first-generation sons an instant Anglo gloss. Although *A Streetcar Named Desire*'s Stanley Kowalski personifies brute force, most Stanleys have been portrayed as mild and meek, and the name, along with confrères Seymour and Sheldon, is receiving its Social Security check each month.

STEEL. Hard and shiny, this surname name (it can also be spelled **STEELE**) projects a perhaps too daunting image.

STEPHEN, STEVEN. Sometimes a name's likability is tied to its nickname, which may account for the fact that Stephen, with its great-guy short form **STEVE** is still a favorite while Richard/Dick, say, or Robert/Bob have faded away. Already common in ancient Greece (it means "crown" or "wreath" in Greek), Stephen was the name of the first Christian martyr, one of the seven men chosen to help the apostles spread the gospel of Christianity, and a British king. In this country, it was in the Top 25 from the 1940s until just a couple of years ago. But although its glory days as a fashionable name may be over for now, Stephen (especially in its older spelling, although Steven is now more commonly used) remains a name with a good measure of strength and dignity and appeal. There have been innumerable pop-culture role models among its bearers—from Stephen Sondheim and

Stephen King to Steven Spielberg to Steve Jobs and Steve Martin. Foreign versions include **STEFAN, STEFANO, STEFFEN, ESTÉBAN, ETIENNE, STEPHANO,** and **STEPHANOS.**

STERLING. A name with some sterling qualities but a slightly pretentious air, it has been fading since the 1950s fame of actor Sterling Hayden and British racing driver Stirling Moss, despite the more animated image of ex-Green Bay Packer and sports announcer Sterling Sharpe.

ST. JOHN. The only American St. John we know finally became so frustrated in trying to explain the pronunciation of his name that he simply changed it to the phonetic spelling **SINJIN.** A British literary name (there's one in *Jane Eyre*), we think this would probably be too cumbersome for most American kids.

STONE. See **ROCK.**

STORM. A dramatic, windswept name that epitomizes the character list in such soap operas as *The Bold and the Beautiful.* TV weatherman Frank Fields bestowed it on his son, who became, quite appropriately—a weatherman.

STUART, STEWART. An ancient name tied to the royal family of Scotland, Stuart/Stewart had, in both spellings, a brief vogue in this country in the 1940s and 1950s. Although not quite as mired in that old-fashioned, upwardly striving Britishy group as the terminally dated Stanley, Seymour, and Sheldon, neither is Stuart/Stewart what anyone would consider a fresh choice for a baby boy of the twenty-first century.

SULLIVAN. A jaunty Irish surname name, immortalized in the 1930s movie classic *Sullivan's Travels* and more recently as the Richard Gere character in *Dr. T. and the Women.* An equally jaunty but slightly muddied offshoot is **SULLY.**

SVEN. Especially for parents of Scandinavian descent, Sven is an accessible and attractive name. It means "youth," and comes from the ancient

Swedish tribe, the Sviars, who gave their name to Svealand, which later morphed into Sweden.

SWEENEY. The double *e* gives this Celtic surname a genial sound, and also has an admirable meaning—"little hero." Only drawback is the association with Sweeney Todd, the bloodthirsty butcher of stage-musical fame.

SYLVESTER. Thufferin' thuccatash! Sylvester might have forever remained a cocky cartoon cat's name, had it not been for first Sly (Sylvester Stuewart) Stone and then Italian stallion Sylvester (born Michael) Stallone. But although it was also the name of three popes, we don't see it being picked up on by many modern parents.

T

TAJ. Taj, as in Taj Mahal, is a Sanskrit name meaning "crown," and was chosen by rocker Steven Tyler of Aerosmith for his son.

TANE. Tane was the Polynesian forest god who set the sun and moon in their places and studded the heavens with stars, a majestic legacy for a simple yet unusual name—which just might prove an unbeatable combination.

TANGIER. An exotic, unexplored place-name, Tangier (also spelled Tangiers) conjures up images of camels and palm trees and domed minarets. The city itself is a Moroccan port on the Straits of Gibraltar.

TANGUY. A popular French name—it sounds like *tangy*—that has not made the long journey across the ocean.

TANNER. Tanner is an occupational surname name that's been rapidly gaining favor for boys (there were almost 4,500 new baby Tanners born in this country last year), joining several other two-syllable *T* names—Taylor, Tyler, Travis, Trevor, Tristan, Trenton—enjoying increasing popularity. It's interesting to note the way stylish names seem to cluster around a few letters, and right now, for boys, the strong starting consonants are *T* and *K*—replacing the softer *J*, *S* and *M* beginnings. In the case of Tanner, it was also given a big boost via the soap-opera character Tanner Scofield on *Days of Our Lives*.

TARQUIN. This rarely heard name—only slightly more prevalent in England, where the late Sir Laurence Olivier chose it for his first child—has a decided creative, even dramatic flair and might appeal to parents whose taste runs in that direction. As Tarquinius, it was borne by two early kings of Rome.

TATE. A strong one-syllable British surname name that means "happy and cheerful," this could make an effective middle name. **TAIT** is the Scandinavian spelling, **TAYTE** is a variation. Cultural association: The Tate is one of the great London museums. **TATON** is a newly coined variation.

TAVIS, TAVISH. This Scottish form of Thomas evokes images of spirited bagpipe music and men in plaid kilts. The surname version—**MCTAVISH**—is another modern possibility.

TAYE. Although it could be thought of as a nickname for Taylor, Taye began to stand on its own with the emergence of appealing actor Taye (born Scott) Diggs. It also has definite middle-name possibilities.

TAYLOR. The fact that Taylor was the ninth most popular girl's name over the entire decade of the 1990s might give parents considering it for their sons ample reason to rethink, for once a name has been accepted in such great numbers for females, its masculine potency, not surprisingly, shrinks in proportion. Tyler rose to popularity around the same time, and now is more accepted for boys.

TEAGUE. A Scottish surname meaning "poet," Teague might fit the bill if you are seeking an utterly unique single-syllable first or middle *T* name for your son.

TEEL. Its homonym Teal, the name of both a grayish-greenish-blue color and a kind of wild duck, has long seen occasional use as a girl's name; now Teel, which is related to the sesame seed, has entered the boys' playing field.

TENNESSEE. When playwright Thomas Lanier Williams (who was born in Mississippi) took on the pen name of Tennessee, he brought a new possibility into the American lexicon of unisex place-names. A bit bulky in size, it could be made more user-friendly with the nickname **TENNY**.

TENNYSON. A literary hero-name possibility for admirers of the poetry of Alfred, Lord Tennyson, or for a child whose dad is named Dennis, as that is the meaning of the name, or even for parents who are tennis fanatics. At the same time, its three-syllable rhythm has a bouncy, modern feel.

TERENCE, TERRENCE. A name that seems to hail from the old Irish neighborhoods of Boston, Chicago, and New York, Terence actually dates back a lot further, to the time of a famous second-century poet, who started life as a North African slave in the house of a Roman senator. Today, the original forms retain little life, having given way to a battery of offshoots—**TERRANCE, TERRELL, TERRILL, TERRYL**—that are all popular among African-Americans. The nickname **TERRY** has been used as an independent name—one of the first breakaway ambigender names—since the days of *Terry and the Pirates*, but has become almost exclusively female. Marlon Brando won an Oscar for his performance as the sensitive Terry Malloy in *On the Waterfront*. **THIERRY** is a related French name.

TEVIN. Singer Tevin Campbell introduced this novel twist on the name Kevin.

THADDEUS. A distinguished, long-neglected name, Thaddeus (also spelled with one *d*) has an appealing three-syllable sound, plus a solid New Testament legacy—it was another name for the Apostle Jude, patron saint of lost causes. We're not too crazy about the nickname **THAD**—a little too reminiscent of Chad and Brad. On the soap opera *All My Children*, the character Thadeus Martin is called **TAD**, but we much prefer the Italian **TADDEO** or Spanish **TADEO**.

THANE. This early Scottish title for a clan chief who held the king's land, known to us from Shakespeare's *Macbeth*, has suddenly surfaced on the radar screen as a modern baby-name possibility, familiar sounding through its similarity to names like Zane, Wayne and Kane, with the substitution of the currently popular *T* beginning.

THATCHER. In Great Britain this name would automatically be associated with former Prime Minister Margaret Thatcher, but in this country it would be classed as one of many appealing "T" surnames, such as Tucker, Tupper and Tanner. It's an occupational surname dating back to the days of thatched roofs.

THEODORE. Although nowhere near as hot as its twin, Theodora, this Greek name has succeeded in shedding some of its old dorky stereo-types—the nerdy Chipmunk, the real name of Beaver Cleaver. Its route toward cool has been through its hip nickname **THEO,** via such TV shows as *Kojak* and *The Cosby Show* and was used on its own for one of their children by Kate Capshaw and Steven Spielberg and by Cheryl Tiegs for one of her twins. This pretty much leaves old standbys **TED** and **TEDDY** just that— old standbys. Some foreign versions are **FEODOR, FYODOR,** and **TEODORO.**

THOMAS. Thomas came into being because there were too many apostles named Judas; Jesus renamed one Thomas (meaning "twin") to distinguish him from Judas Iscariot and Jude. At first used only for priests, in modern times Thomas became one of the classic male names, prevalent for men both highborn and low. Like many traditional names, Thomas has a revived fashionability—currently the second most popular boy's name in England, and rising here as well. It is simple, straightforward, and strong, with more definition than names like James and John—in other words, everything the parent with a taste for the classics could want in a name. **TOM** (occasion-ally spelled **THOM**) is a similarly appealing nickname, as American as apple pie or Tom Sawyer—if we discount the negative stereotype of "Uncle Tom"—but **TOMMY** could sound like the son on a 1950s sitcom. Thomas has some noteworthy foreign versions: the multicultural **TOMAS,** the Ital-ian **TOMASSO,** the Spanish **TOMÁS,** the Portuguese **TOMAZ,** plus the Scot-tish nickname, **TAM.**

THOR, TOR. These powerful Scandinavian names, brought into the Ameri-can experience by explorer Thor Heyerdahl, are tied to one of the key figures in Norse mythology, the god of thunder, strength, rain, and agriculture. A cross-cultural connection: In Hebrew, Tor is the name of a bird that symbolizes the arrival of spring.

THORNE. Call your daughter Rose, but don't call your son Thorne. Even though it may, for better or worse, have the imprimatur of being a soap-opera name (one of the original characters on *The Bold and the Beautiful*), Thorne has nothing but unpleasant associations (e.g., "a thorn in my side").

TIERNAN, TIERNEY. Two Irish surname names that mean "lord" and have an attractive edge.

TIMOTHY. While Timothy has teetered on the edge of stylishness for several decades now, it's never tipped over into full-fledged trendiness (à la Christopher or Zachary) and remains a classic name with a modern-feeling twist. A New Testament name—Saint Timothy, born of a Jewish mother and a Greek father, was Saint Paul's companion, which might make the two appropriate and compatible twin names—Timothy was well used among early Christians but not popular in the English-speaking world until the eighteenth century. Its only real problem is that it somehow—maybe because of its *y* ending—sounds youthful to the point of childishness. **TIMMY** is certainly a babyish nickname, and even **TIM,** as in Dickens's small hero, Tiny Tim, does nothing to give the name a more mature image.

TIMON. For kids, this name (as pronounced tee-MONE) will be associated with the zany meercat character in Disney's modern classic, *The Lion King,* while English majors will tie it to the protagonist of Shakespeare's *Timon of Athens,* who is an amiable and benevolent man of considerable wealth. The name is so rarely heard in the real world that it could cause playground problems.

TITO. This nickname-sounding name has some widely diverse associations: the long-term Communist president of Yugoslavia, one of Michael Jackson's older brothers, and a character in Disney's *Oliver & Co.,* voiced by Cheech Marin—none of which we consider a very strong recommendation.

TITUS. A rather forbidding old Roman name from Shakespeare's gory tragedy *Titus Andronicus,* brought back to contemporary life in the TV comedy series *Titus 2000,* in which it is a surname. Names ending with the Roman *us* ending, such as Titus and Brutus—with the possible exception of Darius and Marcus—do not hold much modern appeal.

TOBIAS, TOBIAH. Tobias has the feel of a name on the way up, poised to join those other Old Testament/Dickensian–feeling boys' names like Caleb, Jonah, Elijah, Gabriel, Noah and Nathaniel that have already begun their ascent. It's a name with a distinguished pedigree—Tobias Smollett, for instance, was a major eighteenth-century English novelist—that also has a contemporary feel. And if you'd like an update of that Jody–Cody kind of thing, you have the option of jaunty androgynous nickname **TOBY,** the name of a character on *West Wing.* Actor Tobey Maguire adds an *e* to make the name his own. And then there is also the rarely used but still viable daddy of them all, **TOBIAH,** the name of a rebel Hebrew king.

TODD. Todd is a beach-boy name of the 1960s and 1970s, a surfing buddy of Scott, Brad, Dean, and Duane, only heard today in the names of dozens of twenty- to thirty-something movie characters, such as the Todd played by Ethan Hawke in *Dead Poets Society.*

TOLLIVER. If you like the sound of Oliver, but think it's gotten a tad too trendy, and you also respond to the new trend toward energetic, three-syllable surnames, you might consider Tolliver.

TOR. See **THOR.**

TOREN, TORIN. These names may have a Scandinavian ring, but they actually possess quite disparate ethnic roots. Toren is a Hebrew name related to ships, while Torin is an out-of the-ordinary Irish family name meaning "chief." Their one disadvantage is a softness verging on femininity, as in names like Loren.

TORQUIL. This rarely heard name, used mainly in Scotland, is actually an old Norse appellation related to Thor, the god of thunder. Pronounced TOR-quill, its middle *q* sound gives it a quirky appeal.

TRACY. Tracy and Stacy both began life as male names, but started to be taken over by the female camp in the 1950s, to the point where neither has much testosterone anymore. Tracy Tupman was a male character in Dickens's novel *The Pickwick Papers*.

TRENT, TRENTON. These are two prime instances of the kinds of names beginning to find favor with parents—the strong, single-syllable boy's name, and the same name with a syllable such as *on* appended. Both these examples have geographical references—the Trent is a river in England and Trenton is, of course, a city in New Jersey. Noted bearers of the former are rocker Trent Reznor and footballer Trent Dilfer.

TREVOR. Trevor is one of those quintessentially British flyboy names that has gradually lost its English accent, to the point where, along with others like Derek and Ian, it has started to climb up American popularity lists. Often a working-class name across the Atlantic these days, to most Yanks it still retains a touch of Anglo class. Trevor is the English form of the Welsh **TREFOR.**

TRISTAN, TRISTRAM. This interesting pair of interchangeable names has long been known largely through the tragic medieval romance called both *Tristan and Isolde* and *Tristram and Iseult*. The dual name gained further fame from the Wagnerian opera the tale inspired, and from the eighteenth-century comic novel *Tristram Shandy*. Both versions take on a slightly melancholy tone because of their relation to the French word for *sad*. Still, they can be thought of as a more original alternative to Christian, with **TRIS** a more unusual short form than Chris. In the past few years, the name has gained impetus from the character played by Brad Pitt in *Legends of the*

Fall, to the point where it recently entered the Top 100 list. It was chosen for their sons by Natasha Henstridge, Travis Tritt, and Wayne Gretzky.

TROUT. Don't laugh. Parents are beginning to expand the frontiers of baby naming to include all kinds of nature names, and a few ardent anglers are considering such choices as Pike and Trout. Our advice: Consider carefully before you cast your line into these tease-infested waters.

TROY. As a personal name and not an ancient city, Troy came to the attention of the American public via Troy Donahue (born Merle) in the 1960s and has managed to hold onto its blond-surfer image all these years. Along with other place-names such as Paris, Troy was a name used fairly commonly for slaves in the seventeenth century. More positive and modern associations include star quarterback Troy Aikman, a character on *One Life to Live,* and Ethan Hawke's character in *Reality Bites.*

TRUE. Many parents of the new millennium are seeking a return to more basic values and to a simpler lifestyle. This is reflected in the increasing appeal of such girls' names as Grace and Faith and Hope, and the emergence of such boys' names as True, often used as a middle name.

TRUMAN. A presidential name that was for years identified with writer Truman Capote, Truman radiates an aura of integrity and moral truth, taken to an absurdist extreme in the ingenuous character of Truman Burbank played by Jim Carrey in *The Truman Show.* Tom Hanks and Rita Wilson chose it for their son.

TUCKER. Tucker has more spunk than most last-name-first names, and also a positive, comforting (could it have to do with being tucked into bed at night?) feel. It's been heard on two soap operas — *All My Children* and *As the World Turns* — and, as a surname, in the Beau Bridges–starring biopic *Tucker: The Man and His Dream.*

TUDOR. We first came across this name on the cover of a book for which a man named Tudor was the illustrator. Certainly, this has possibilities in this era of two-syllable names that aren't really names. The Tudors were, of course, a British royal family as well as a style of architecture.

TULLY. This relaxed, rarely used Irish surname, an Anglicization of the original Tuathal, was chosen for her son by soap star Deidre Hall.

TYLER. Tyler is the tenth most popular boys' name in the country, and ranks number 9 for the whole decade of the 1990s, so if you're looking for something fresh and different for your son, this isn't the name for you. Along with Taylor, it rapidly became almost pandemic across the land and, to make matters even more confusing, both (especially Taylor) are used for girls as well. And although Tyler also has a presidential association, that isn't the reason most people have picked it. Travis Tritt has a son named Tyler. In an attempt to give it a more original spin, some parents have varied it to Skyler or **ZYLER.**

TYRONE. The name of a county in Ireland, Tyrone emigrated into American popular culture in the person of World War II–era star Tyrone Power, who inherited it from his father; it is now favored primarily by African-American parents. Nickname **TY** has been used on its own for their sons by such celebs as Pam Dawber and Mark Harmon, and hockey immortal Wayne Gretzky. **TYRUS,** the full name of baseball legend Ty Cobb, sounds too much like *virus*.

TYSON. Tyson, a surname meaning "firebrand," is beginning to be used by parents tiring of the ubiquitous Tyler. Drawback or advantage depending on your point of view: the associations with Mike Tyson and Tyson chicken.

U

ULRIC. An Old English name related to the word for *wolf,* Ulric also has German ties (via Ulrich) and a first syllable that is not appealing to the American ear. Better *ic*-ending choices: Eric, Dominic, Frederic.

ULYSSES. A name far too weighty for a modern child to carry, Ulysses still might make a distinguished literary middle name. There are only two Ulysses most people have ever heard of—one is the novel by James Joyce in which there is no character by that name but which is based on the Homeric epic of Odysseus, the Greek form of the name Ulysses. Then there was General/President Ulysses S. Grant, who in fact was christened Hiram Ulysses Grant. (The story that he changed his name around at West Point because he found his initials embarrassing is one prospective parents should definitely bear in mind.) On the other hand, the name has surfaced as the leading character in two recent movies—Peter Fonda's in *Ulee's Gold* and George Clooney's in *Oh Brother, Where Art Thou*—which could conceivably inspire some parents to revive it.

URIAH. This perfectly respectable Old Testament name seems to have been ruined forever as a result of its association with the odious character Uriah Heep—even people who haven't read *David Copperfield* tend to shudder when they hear the name. The biblical bearer fared badly as well—Uriah was the cuckolded husband of Bathsheba, disposed of by King David.

URIEL. This rarely used but evocative Hebrew name, which means "light," represents one of the four angels surrounding God's throne, and the one responsible for the inspiration of writers and teachers. It is a symbolic name given to boys born on Chanukah, and its nickname Uri (pronounced OO-ree), is often heard in modern Israel. But despite these attractive references, we do worry a little about the unsavory nickname possibilities.

V

VALENTINE, VAL. Valentine is an appealing name, not only because of its romantic associations, but because, among other things, it has an agreeable literary connection as well—Valentine, in Shakespeare's *Two Gentlemen of Verona*, was a devoted and generous friend. Val Kilmer has added some masculine resonance to that nickname; **VALENTIN** is the French version. Still, we'd hesitate before bestowing the name on a son because of both its tease potential and its feminine feel.

VALOR, VALOUR. Recently, we've seen this word taken up as a name, which in this case just may work. Valor—honor, bravery—is certainly a quality any parent would want to pass on to his child, and the word itself is obscure enough that it manages to sound like a real name.

VAN, VANCE. Van is not really a name. If you're wondering how the well-known Vans of the recent past got to be called that, there are a variety of explanations. One of them—Van Heflin—used it as a short form of Evan; Van Morrison was born George Ivan; Van Cliburn was named Harry Lavan; and Van Johnson was born Charles Van Johnson. So unless you are looking for a nonname, and especially if you drive one, forget Van. Vance is a proper name, which actually means "son of Van," but this book is full of far more attractive surnames. **VANNON** is an attempt to make the name stylish.

VAUGHN, VAUGHAN. This Welsh last name had a brief period, in the 1940s and 1950s, when it was used more in the United States than it was in Wales, but it's been pretty much forgotten by now.

VERNON. Originally an Old French place-name and aristocratic British sur-name, Vernon is now redolent of gas stations, tractors, and hot blacktop, as is its media-maligned nickname, **VERN,** although Vernon Jordan, the for-mer executive director of the Urban League, upgraded it somewhat.

VICTOR. One of the earliest of Christian names, Victor (in its Italian form, **VITTORIO**) was borne by several saints and popes, but only made it big in the English-speaking world during the reign of Queen Victoria. Seeing it as one of the very few male names popularized by its female version, instead of the other way around, lends Victor some slight feminist élan, but we're afraid it would take more than that to lighten the stodgy macho image it has been saddled with for the past half-century. The Italian version, on the other hand, has considerable charm, as does the French **VICTOIRE.**

VIGGO. This vigorous Scandinavian name was brought to the attention of the American public via the actor Viggo Mortensen, and has some potential for the seeker of a truly singular name.

VINCENT. Vincent's decidedly tarnished image over the past several decades—a time when if you committed the further sin of calling the baby **VINCE** or **VINNIE** it was tantamount to dressing him in a little black nylon shirt with a plastic comb sticking out of the breast pocket—has begun to reclaim some of its former sheen, thanks to such attractive emerging actors as Vincent D'Onofrio, Vincent Perez, and Vince Vaughn. Very popular among the early Christians, it was borne by several saints, one of whom, Saint Vincent de Paul, was famous for organizing laymen to care for the needy, and the name remained especially prevalent among Roman Catholic families. **VICENTE** is the Spanish form, **VINCENZO** the Italian.

VIRGIL. The name of the greatest of Roman poets, as well as an early Irish saint, Virgil (originally spelled **VERGIL**) is rarely heard nowadays but retains a certain likable Southern twang. Virgil Tibbs was the noble character played by Sidney Poitier in two movies, and is the given name of astronaut "Gus" Grissom.

VLADIMIR. A musical prodigy kind of name, Vladimir might be difficult to uphold for a boy whose interests lie in a different direction. A Russian name meaning "prince of the world," it was borne by the first Christian ruler of Russia, and is associated in this country with piano virtuoso Vladimir Horowitz and the author of *Lolita*, Vladimir Nabokov.

W

WADE. The grandpa of such more modern-sounding names as Cade and Slade, Wade has the disadvantage of being heard as Wayne with a stuffed nose.

WALDO. A German pet name that seems somewhat jokey to the American ear but also possesses a certain charm thanks to its final, jaunty *o*. The weighty reputation of Ralph Waldo Emerson adds a measure of backbone to the name, but, even though the craze is over, giggles might still ensue every time someone asks, "Where's Waldo?"

WALKER. Walker was one of the big Waspy surname names of the late 1980s and 1990s, along with relatives like Carter and Parker, but its popularity has faded in favor of names with more personal meaning. It does have some distinguished associations, though, to writer Walker Percy and photographer Walker Evans. Walker was originally an occupational surname that referred to someone who walked on fabric to clean it. Really.

WALLACE. Wallace and its *Leave It to Beaver*'s-big-brother short-form **WALLY** are names that have become so square they could almost be ripe for a turnaround, especially with the degree of cool imparted by the British claymation series *Wallace and Gromit*. The name was first associated with the thirteenth-century Scottish patriot Sir William Wallace, and later with the distinguished poet Wallace Stevens.

WALTER. Thanks to Sir Walter Raleigh and Sir Walter Scott, Walter was once seen as a name with nobility, and a few independent-minded, iconoclastic parents are again taking it into consideration, seeing it as classic, yet nowhere near as common as Robert, James, or William. A favorite Norman name, Walter was extremely popular in this country from the 1870s through the 1940s. And there are all those great Walters and **WALT**s from the past to consider—from Whitman to Disney to Cronkite to Matthau to the ultimate fantasizer, Walter Mitty. The early British pronunciation of the name—*water*—led to such surnames as **WATSON,** a possible Holmesian consideration if you want to name your son after an ancestral Walter but dislike the original form; another is **WALTON,** George Lucas's middle name. Two French versions are **GAULTIER** and **GAUTIER.**

WARD. Like Wally, still a Cleaver name.

WARNER, WERNER. Two Germanic names that lack any sparkle or sheen.

WARREN. Even back when Warren Beatty was America's number one Lothario, his name did not sound very romantic. (Maybe he should have stuck with his original Henry.) Warren is a sober onetime surname still stuck in the stiff-collared image of President Warren Gamaliel Harding, and we can't imagine many contemporary parents considering it for their babies.

WASHINGTON. In the current search for names with meaning, parents are looking to honor heroes and heroines, including United States presidents. And with surname names in vogue, choices such as Taylor, Tyler, Lincoln, and Kennedy have a fashionable sheen as well as historical backbone. Washington would not be as easy to handle as some of the shorter ones, and also is somewhat tainted by having been a common slave name, but it is certainly one of the most distinctive.

WAYNE. It's 1966. A fourteen-year-old boy is walking down the street wearing tight black pants and thick white socks. His name is Wayne. Or maybe Glenn, but the point is that Wayne is a name that was last in style back when Mick Jagger was a new face on the music scene, and is associated more with Wayne Newton than Wayne Gretzky.

WEBB. A cutting-edge surname name due to the rise of the Internet, Webb is really an old English occupational last name meaning "weaver." It is also a short form of **WEBSTER,** a name that was severely degraded by the 1980s sitcom.

WENDELL. A name that came to the forefront in the 1940s when Wendell Wilkie was a presidential candidate and is also associated with Oliver Wendell Holmes, Wendell does not seem like a very inspired choice for a new millennium baby, unless there is a family connection.

WESLEY, WESTON. Many boys given this English place-name in the past were done so to honor the founder of Methodism, John Wesley, and the name has far from disappeared: there were 2,240 little Wesleys born in this country last year. Its most prominent modern representative is actor Wesley Snipes. **WESTON,** another British place-name sharing the nickname **WES,** was given to his son by Nicolas Cage.

WILEY, WYLIE. This friendly, nonchalant cowboyish name has an almost irresistible charm, and could make a more relaxed stand-in for the more self-consciously stylish Wyatt.

WILLIAM. There has always been a constituency for a solid, established boys' name like William, but when the British prince was born in 1982, and even more so since he has reached attractive maturity, his name rose from the ranks of stalwart classics to confirmed regal fashion—it is now number 11 on the U.S. popularity list and number 1 in five Southern states—North and South Carolina, Alabama, Georgia, and Mississippi. William has become the ideal name for many American parents: conservative yet contemporary, traditional yet trendy, with the distinction of having been, for four hundred years, second only to John as the most popular name in the English-speaking world. The tendency these days is to call children by their full names, so that William is more and more frequently known as William. When nicknames are used, **BILL** and **BILLY,** the favored forms of our own youth, are decidedly out, while **WILL** (as in Will Smith, *Will and Grace,* and *Good Will Hunting*) and even **WILLIE,** are in, though the British **WILLS** seems a bit too precious for an American boy. Riding on the William bandwagon are the Irish spin-off Liam and the Dutch **WILLEM,** the latter chosen for his son by rocker Billy Idol, while other *Wil* names—**WILFRED, WILBUR, WILBERT, WILLARD,** and **WILLIS**— are gone and best forgotten. A few other foreign forms of note: **WIM** (Dutch and pronounced vim), **GUILLAUME** (French), **WILHELM** (German), and **GWILYM** (Welsh).

WILLOUGHBY. An energetic surname route to the short-form Will, the meaning of which relates to the willow tree.

WILSON. Another presidential surname with considerable substance, and far less prevalent than the trendy Taylors, Tylers, and Madisons, it too has the added asset of the likable nickname Will.

WINSTON. There's a good reason why this name has been so tightly identified with the Churchill family: The original Winston Churchill, who was given his mother's maiden name, was born in 1620. Over the years, it has been adopted more freely in Britain (it was John Lennon's middle name) and, more particularly, in the West Indies, but is rarely heard in this country, except among West Indian families—Winston was the name of a character in the best-selling book and film (played by Taye Diggs) *How Stella Got Her Groove Back*. With the current trend toward using hero names, we hope to see this upstanding Anglo-Saxon example considered more often. Minor irritant: the connection to the cigarette brand. The nickname **WINNIE** came into the public consciousness with the *Winnie-the-Pooh* books, but is now almost exclusively feminine. **WINTHROP** is a haughtier cousin.

WOLFGANG, WOLF. Wolfgang has become a sort of joke name, even though Valerie Bertinelli and Eddie Van Halen did choose it for their son, disputing our dictum that it was "so far out it will always be out." With that celebrity stamp of approval—plus the high visibility of ubiquitous restaurateur Wolfgang Puck—the name seems to be back in the realm of possibility again. Some parents might be attracted to its pedigree as Mozart's first name, though in the past most who wished to honor the composer have opted for a variation of Amadeus. The nickname **WOLF** (represented by CNN newscaster Wolf Bitzer) is sometimes used on its own, and may have a certain lupine appeal. **ULF** is the Scandinavian version.

WOODROW. To get to the good-natured nickname **WOODY,** you have to deal with its parent name, Woodrow, which sounds so formal and, well, wooden, that if you're considering using it to honor the president (whose given first name was actually Thomas), it might be wiser to opt for Wilson. Woody Herman, Woody Guthrie, and Woody Harrelson were all born Woodrows, but Woody Allen's name at birth was Allen.

WYATT. The name of the legendary gunfighter Wyatt Earp has been hot, which is to say cool, for several years now, given its first push when Peter Fonda played a Wyatt in the seminal film *Easy Rider*. Relaxed but still respectable, it has been used for their son by Goldie Hawn and Kurt Russell, and been visible in the soap opera *All My Children*.

WYLIE. See **WILEY.**

WYNN, WYNNE. This Welsh name meaning "fair" or "pure," has been used very sporadically since the 1930s. Its sound suggests success, but it also seems a bit feminine because of its similarity to the girl's names Gwynne and Winnie.

X

XAN, XANDER. See **ALEXANDER.**

XAVIER. Xavier carries two divergent images: There's the old stereotypical Latin bandleader type, à la Xavier Cugat, who sports a pencil moustache and a shiny cummerbund, and then there's the ultra-Catholic name that invariably lies behind the *x* in all those Francis *Xes.* That initial *x* does have a distinct appeal, but bear in mind that the correct pronunciation has it beginning with a *z* sound. The Spanish form is **JAVIER** (see listing) and other related possibilities are **XAVION, XAYVION,** and **SAVION.**

XENOS. This Greek name meaning "hospitality" poses definite pronunciation problems. Unless your roots are Greek and this is a family name, we suggest you consider the more kid-friendly Zeno instead.

XERXES. Even more of a challenge than Xenos, Xerxes (pronounced ZERKS-eez) was the name of several Persian emperors, but its comic-book aura, combined with the spelling and speaking issues, push it over the too-much-to-handle line.

Y

YAEL. Yael (pronounced with two syllables) is a Hebrew name that is popular in Israel, and also travels well across cultures. Spelling (and pronouncing) it **YALE** might seem to point to Ivy League rather than Hebrew roots.

YANCY. *Yancy Derringer* was an early TV western series, but the name of its hero, unlike others of the period such as Matt, Bret, Luke, Jason, Jeremy, and Joshua, never caught on with the baby-naming public. Maybe Yancy's too fancy.

YEHUDI. The Hebrew form of Jude, Judah, or Judas, Yehudi's fame was spread mainly through violinist Menuhin, but we don't think it's a name that would translate easily to American schoolrooms.

YURI. We don't see much chance of this Russian version of George, known in this country via the cosmonaut Yuri Gagorin and a character in *Dr. Zhivago,* getting the green card necessary to make it a permanent U.S. resident.

YVES. On paper, Yves, the French form of the Welsh Evan, with its ties to fashion legend Yves Saint Laurent (who was actually born Henri) and singer Yves Montand (born Ivo), looks good. The problem lies with its pronunciation, eeve, which makes gender confusion a prohibitive possibility.

Z

ZACHARIAH, ZACHARIAS. Zachariah is a biblical name occurring in both the Old and New Testaments, as a king of Israel and the father of John the Baptist, while Zacharias is the Latin/Greek form. Yet another of these somewhat white-bearded *Zac* names, all of which have an eccentric, daguerreotype charm, is **ZACCHAEUS.**

ZACHARY. Zachary has a lot more zip and style than most other Old Testament–inspired names, which is probably one reason why it has become so fashionable over the past few decades, now sitting quite comfortably at number 15 on the Top 20 list. Robin Williams and Cheryl Tiegs both have sons named Zachary. But while it, along with short forms **ZACK** and **ZAK,** does retain some measure of strength and distinction despite its trendiness, these are gradually fading due to the name's widespread popularity. A much more unusual name in this family is **ZAKAI,** found in the Book of Ezra.

ZADEN. A "Z" version of the highly trendy Caden-Haden-Jaden family.

ZALE. A somewhat obscure name of Greek origin, Zale could have some appeal to the modern parent seeking something short but spicy, unusual but easily spelled and pronounced.

ZALMAN. See **SOLOMON.**

ZAN, ZANDER. See **ALEXANDER.**

ZANDY. Zandy, like Gandy, is a rarely heard name (there was a 1970s movie called *Zandy's Bride*) that has a lot more energy and charm than more common cousins Andy, Sandy, and Randy.

ZANE. What, we wonder, would have happened if famed western writer Zane Grey had written under his real first name of Pearl? We certainly wouldn't be looking at Zane as a viable name right now, since the author was pretty much solely responsible for its cool cowboy image. Zane is, in fact, one of those names that may be too cool, if you believe that's possible, for any Zane would certainly have to grapple with people's expectations that he be sharp, sexy, and sophisticated in a way that a John or a George would not.

ZARED. If there are too many Jareds in your neighborhood, you might want to consider this more exotic Hebrew alternative.

ZEBEDIAH, ZEDEKIAH. Yes, these both are mouthfuls, and might well be too much for a small child to maneuver (let alone spell), but we're still not sure these venerable old biblical monikers should be dismissed out of hand, especially considering their appealing short forms, **ZEB** and **ZED.** Zebediah is the original Hebrew form of Zebedee (see below); Zedekiah was the last king of Judah.

ZEBEDY, ZEBEDEE. Unlike some of the longer biblical *Z* names, Zebedy/Zebedee has a more lighthearted usability. In the New Testament, he was the fisherman who was the father of two of the twelve disciples, James and John. Zeb is the attractive nickname it shares with Zebediah and Zebulon.

ZEBULON. Another route to Zeb is Zebulon, the biblical name of a son of Jacob and Leah. If it sounds at all familiar in the modern world, it's due to Zebulon Pike, namesake of Pike's Peak.

ZEKE. This pleasingly innocent nickname for Ezekiel could make a willing substitute for the overused Zack. It's also an African name derived from the name meaning "to laugh," and, in quite another realm, was the non-Oz name of the Cowardly Lion.

ZELIG. An alternate form of the Jewish Selig, Zelig became known to a wider audience through the Woody Allen film of that name—even though Zelig happened to be the character's last name. Unfortunately, the one Zelig we know changed his name to Alan as soon as he was old enough.

ZENO. A Greek name thought to be an offshoot of Zeus, this hardly heard name has a muscular dynamism lightened up by its cheerful final vowel, resulting in a kind of offbeat sci-fi/comic-book image. It was borne by several ancient Greek philosophers, one of whom founded the school of Stoicism. The spiritual **ZEN** is the name of a soap star.

ZEUS. The name of the supreme god of the Hellenic pantheon would make a daunting choice and we recommend it only to the most intrepid of baby namers.

ZHIVAGO. Many people were greatly moved by the novel and film *Dr. Zhivago*. Actress Nia Long went so far as to make it her son's middle name.

ZION. This geographical place-name applied to the city of Jerusalem and also used as a poetic name for Israel has been growing in popularity—there were more than a thousand Zions born in this country last year, among them the son of singers Lauryn Hill and Rohan Marley. It is quite user-friendly, with its familiar Ryan-Brian rhyming sound, and yet has the gravitas of religious significance.

ZIV. In Hebrew, this name, pronounced zeev, means "brilliance, glory." It is also a synonym for the second month of the Jewish calendar, in which Israeli Independence Day is celebrated. **ZIVI** is another form.

ZURI. The Kiswahili word for "good" and "beautiful," Zuri (pronounced ZOO-ree) is singular, strong, and exotic.

ABOUT THE AUTHORS

LINDA ROSENKRANTZ is the author of six other books in addition to the baby-naming series, ranging from *Gone Hollywood,* a social history of the film colony, to a childhood memoir, *My Life as a List: 207 Things About My (Bronx) Childhood.* A resident of Los Angeles, she also writes a syndicated weekly column on collectibles.

PAMELA REDMOND SATRAN is a contributing editor for *Parenting* magazine and a columnist for *Baby Talk* and *TV Guide.* The former fashion features editor of *Glamour,* her articles have appeared in publications ranging from *Self* to *Good Housekeeping* to the *Wall Street Journal,* as well as online at parenting.com and women.com. She lives outside New York City with her husband and three children.

As authorities on baby names, they have written a column for *Baby Talk* magazine, and have been quoted in *People, The Wall Street Journal,* and *The New York Times Magazine.* They have also made appearances on nationally syndicated shows such as *Oprah,* and the *CNN Morning News.* Their baby-name books have sold more than 750,000 copies.

BIBLIOGRAPHY

We have been engaged in onomastics, the study of names, for so long that a complete bibliography of references would be impossible. But the following are works that have been particularly helpful in formulating this book.

Amende, Coral, *Legends in Their Own Time: A Popular Biographical Dictionary,* Prentice-Hall General Reference, New York, 1994.

Arce, Rose Marie, and Maite Junco, *Bebes Preciosos: 5001 Hispanic Baby Names,* Avon New York, 1995.

Asante, Molrfi Kete, *The Book of African Names,* Africa World Press, Trenton, NJ, 1999.

Beaucarnot, Jean-Louis, *Les Prenoms et Leurs Secrets,* Editions Denoel, Paris, 1990.

Benaglia, Elena, *Il Nouovo Libro dei Nomi,* Giovanni De Vecchi Editore, Milano, 1992.

Butler, The Reverend Alvin, *Lives of the Saints,* Studio Editions, London, 1990.

Coghlan, Ronan, *Pocket Guide to Irish First Names,* The Appletree Press, Belfast, 1985.

———, Ida Grehan, and O. W. Joyce, *Book of Irish Names: First, Family & Place Names,* Sterling, New York, 1989.

Cottle, Basil, *The Penguin Dictionary of Surnames,* Penguin Books, Aylesbury, 1979.

Cowan, Tom, *The Way of the Saints,* Perigee, New York, 1999.

Delaney, John J., *Pocket Dictionary of Saints,* Doubleday Image, New York, 1983.

Diamant, Anita, *Bible Baby Names,* Jewish Lights Publishing, Woodstock, VT, 1996.

——, *What to Name Your Jewish Baby,* Summit Books, New York, 1989.

Dinwiddie-Boyd, Elza, *Proud Heritage,* Avon Books, New York, 1994.

Drabble, Margaret, and Jeremy Stringer, *The Concise Oxford Companion to English Literature,* Oxford University Press, Oxford, 1990.

Dunkling, Leslie, *The Guinness Book of Names,* Guinness Publishing Ltd., Enfield, UK, 1993.

——, and William Gosling, *The New American Dictionary of First Names,* Signet Books, New York, 1985.

Ellefson, Connie Lockhart, *The Melting Pot Book of Baby Names,* Betterway Publications, White Hall, VA, 1990.

Goring, Rosemary, Editor, *Larousse Dictionary of Literary Characters,* Larousse, Edinburgh, 1994.

Goulart, Ron, Editor, *The Encyclopedia of American Comics,* Facts on File, New York, 1990.

Hanks, Patricia, and Flavia Hodges, *A Dictionary of First Names,* Oxford University Press, Oxford, 1992.

Ingraham, Holly, *People's Names,* McFarland & Company, Jefferson, NY, 1997.

Kamath, M. V., *Jaico Book of Baby Names,* Jaico Publishing, Mumbai, India, 1988.

Kaplan, Justin, and Anne Bernays, *The Language of Names: What We Call Ourselves and Why It Matters,* Simon & Schuster, 1997.

Keister, Linda Wolfe, *The Complete Guide to African-American Baby Names,* Signet, New York, 1998.

Lieberson, Stanley, and Eleanor O. Bell, "Children's First Names: An Empirical Study of Social Taste," *American Journal of Sociology,* Vol. 98, No. 3, November 1992.

Lip, Evelyn, *Choosing Auspicious Chinese Names,* Heian International Publishers, Torrance, CA, 1997.

McFarland, Phoenix, *The Complete Book of Magical Names,* Llewellyn Publications, St. Paul, MN, 1999.

McNeil, Alex, *Total Television,* Penguin Books, New York, 1991.

Nicholson, Louise, *The Best Baby Name Book,* Thorsons Publishers, Ltd., London, 1990.

Norman, Teresa, *Names Through the Ages,* Berkley Books, New York, 1999.

——, *The African-American Baby Name Book,* Berkley Books, New York, 1998.

——, *A World of Baby Names,* Berkley Books, New York, 1996.

Ousby, Ian, Editor, *The Cambridge Guide to Literature in English,* Cambridge University Press, Cambridge, 1991.

Rosenkrantz, Linda, and Pamela Redmond Satran, *Beyond Charles & Diana: An Anglophile's Guide to Baby Naming,* St. Martin's Press, New York, 1992.

——, *Beyond Jennifer & Jason: An Enlightened Guide to Naming Your Baby,* St. Martin's Press, New York, 1988, 1994.

——, *Beyond Jennifer & Jason, Madison & Montana: What to Name Your Baby Now,* St. Martin's Press, New York, 1999.

——, *Beyond Sarah & Sam: An Enlightened Guide to Jewish Baby Naming,* St. Martin's Press, New York, 1992.

——, *Beyond Shannon & Sam: An Enlightened Guide to Irish Baby Naming,* St. Martin's Press, New York, 1992.

Salazar, Salvador G., *Los Nombres del Bebe,* Javier Vergara Editor, Buenos Aires, 1988.

Sidi, Smadar Shir, *The Complete Book of Hebrew Baby Names,* Harper & Row, New York, 1989.

Sierra, Judy, *Celtic Baby Names,* Folkprint, Eugene, OR, 1997.

Sleigh, Linwood, and Charles Johnson, *The Book of Girls Names,* Thomas Y. Crowell Company, New York, 1962.

——, *The Book of Boys Names,* Thomas Y. Crowell Company, New York, 1962.

Stetler, Susan, *Actors, Artists, Authors & Attempted Assassins: The Almanac of Famous & Infamous People,* Visible Ink, Detroit, 1991.

Stewart, Julia, *African Names,* Citadel Press, New York, 1993.

Todd, Loreto, *Celtic Names for Children,* The O'Brien Press, Dublin, 1998.

Trantino, Charlee, *Beautiful Baby Names from Your Favorite Soap Operas,* Pinnacle Books, 1996.

Tuan, Laura, *Il Grande Libro dei Nomi,* Giovanni De Vecchi Editore, Milano, 1987.

Walker, John, Editor, *Halliwell's Filmgoer's and Video Viewer's Companion, 12th Edition,* HarperCollins, New York, 1997.

Wallace, Carol McD., *The Greatest Baby Name Book Ever,* Avon, New York, 1998.

Woulfe, Patrick, *Irish Names for Children,* Gill and Macmillan Ltd., Dublin, revised edition 1974.

ONLINE RESOURCES

Celebrity Baby Names at www.celebnames.com

The Internet Movie Database at www.imdb.com

Social Security Administration at www.sss.gov/OACT

Aida
Aliza
Bella
Chaya
Danica

Ansel
Asher
Fidel